THE EVOLUTION OF BRITISH SOCIAL POLICY AND THE WELFARE STATE

Dedicated to my mother,
Catherine Laybourn (1925–1994),
who spent many years dependent upon the help
and resources of the National Health Service

The Evolution of British Social Policy and the Welfare State

c. 1800–1993

Keith Laybourn

RYBURN PUBLISHING
KEELE UNIVERSITY PRESS

First published in 1995
Keele University Press
Keele, Staffordshire

Composed by KUP
Printed by Hartnolls
Bodmin, Cornwall, England

ISBN 1 85331 076 X

Contents

List of tables and graphs

Abbreviations

COS	Charity Organisation Society
ILP	Independent Labour Party
LRC	Local Representative Committee
NAGH	National Association of the Guild of Help
PAC	Public Assistance Committee
SSFA	Soldiers' and Sailors' Association
SSHS	Soldiers and Sailors' Help Society
UAB	Unemployment Assistance Board

Acknowledgements

It is impossible to pay too fulsome a tribute to the many individuals and institutions who have helped me in the writing of this book. I have received enormous help from Peter Wood, a former Principal Lecturer and Subject Leader in History at Huddersfield Polytechnic (now University), who not only developed my knowledge of the history of British social policy but also read through the chapter on the Poor Law. I also owe a great debt to Dr David Taylor, currently the Section Leader in History at the University of Huddersfield, for reading through the chapter on policing and giving me valuable advice. I also received extensive help in gathering material from the University of Huddersfield Library from David James, the Bradford Archivist, Patrick Shorten and the Bolton Guild of Help (Incorporated) and many other people too numerous to mention. I might add, however, that the help and advice of Derek Heathcote, of the University of Huddersfield, in operating my Apple Mac was most invaluable.

Permission to quote from Crown Copyright materials was given by the Director of Publications of Her Majesty's Stationary Office. Patrick Shorten gave me permission to quote from the records of the Bolton Guild of Help. Mr S. Dey, Director of the Plymouth Guild of Community Service for South and West Devon, provided me with photocopies of some of the annual reports of the Plymouth Guild. John Knightly, Director of Croydon Voluntary Action gave me permission to quote from the records of the Croydon Guild. The British Library of Political and Economic Science gave me permission to quote selected extracts from the Beveridge Papers and the Violet Markham Papers. Every effort has been made to obtain copyright permission where it has seemed appropriate and where substantial sections of recent documents (in excess of 150 words) have been produced, but I do apologize for any inadvertent breach that has occurred.

CHAPTER ONE

INTRODUCTION

The classic Welfare State, in its modern sense, began in July 1948 when the Labour government put in place both its National Insurance and its National Health Service provisions. Since then, its form has changed as the Conservative governments of the 1980s and early 1990s have attempted to 'role back the state'. Yet one should remember that what occurred in 1948 was the end product of several centuries of development and the best part of 150 years of intensive activity and debate pressed forward by the rapid industrial growth of the late eighteenth and nineteenth centuries, with its consequent population growth. In that sense, the so-called Industrial Revolution appears to have provided the stimulus to actions which have helped to produce the modern Welfare State, even though there was Poor Law provision and government intervention in social policy well before the late eighteenth century.

The term 'Welfare State' is not easily defined beyond an acknowledgement that it involves, for its citizens, the protection of the state from the consequences of want, sickness or ignorance. The term does not appear to have been used widely until the 1940s and has been open to various interpretations, for it has no clear and obvious philosophy. However, there tend to be basic characteristics that would feature in any definition. As recent Conservative governments would admit, the British Welfare State interrupts the free market by protecting certain groups, such as children and the aged, by offering services, such as education, policing, medical provision and personal services, and by protecting the population against the exigencies of working life, such as sickness and unemployment. Within that range of activities, there is room for discussion as to whether or not the British Welfare State should be universal or selective – a debate which is currently of immense political importance. Equally, it has been questioned whether or not Britain is a Welfare State if one compares it with the more comprehensive and generous Swedish state. Indeed, it has been suggested that Britain is much more of a 'social security state'.[1]

The origins of the comprehensive and uniform policy of social provision that emerged in modern form by 1948 are almost as elusive as the definition of the term 'Welfare State'. There are several perspectives on, or explanations of, the evolution of welfare policy in Britain and it is quite conceivable that, from time to time, they may all have contributed to the development of Britain's social policy. Indeed, the argument of this book is that one should not expect the evolution of British welfare policy to follow a particular trajectory. Many factors contributed to its evolution and the balance of these has constantly changed in what has become an increasingly pluralistic society, even though pragmatism and ideology have often played a part, the latter being particularly evident since the late 1970s.

There are at least eight approaches to the study of the development of the British Welfare State, some of which overlap. The first seven, the Whig, pragmatic, bureaucratic, ideological, conspiratorial, capitalistic, and democratic approaches, have been discussed previously in some detail by Derek Fraser. The eighth – pluralism – is, in a sense, a development of the democratic approach and argues that political behaviour occurs in groups – political parties, pressure groups, trade unions and pressure groups – which compete for influence. These eight approaches give some sense of direction to our thinking, but are so general that it is unlikely that an integrated theory of the development of the British Welfare State could ever emerge. Indeed, each approach/perspective may vary in importance from one period to another, from one area of social policy to another, and from one political or social group to another.

The *Whig* approach to the Welfare State, which stresses the humanitarian concern of reformers to push forward from darkness to enlightenment, found much support in the early writings on the British Welfare State but ignores the slow rate of reform that often occurred. As a result, the *pragmatic* approach, by which social policy is an immediate response to a pressing problem, was developed as an alternative explanation.[2] Incrementalists, such as Dr Lubenow, who see the gradual accretion of responsibilities as a response to social problems as they arise, offer a development of this pragmatic approach.[3] Incrementalism also helps to explain the conflict between the demands of central government and the tendency towards a variety of local responses noted in the Poor Law, health, policing and other areas of social policy.

A third approach, which assumes more structure than the pragmatic and incrementalist one, is the *bureaucratic* one developed by historians such as Oliver MacDonagh. This assumes that the state perceives problems, attempts to deal with them, fails to do so effectively and creates a class of civil servants who ensure that the process of reform becomes self-perpetuating.[4] These views conflict with those of S. E. Finer, Henry Parris, Jenifer Hart and others, who have argued that the ideas of Jeremy Bentham and his supporters, committed to the ideal of efficiency, were far more pervasive than is often suggested.[5] These are not exactly Whig historians reacting to MacDonagh's Tory line, but they believe that Bentham's ideas – and *ideology* in general – have exerted a potent influence upon British social policy. In any case, the administrative approach of MacDonagh, as Pat Thane suggests, does not allow for the setbacks in administration that occurred in the 1840s and 1850s with health and the Poor Law.[6] The power of ideology and intellectual thought has also been pressed forward by José Harris with an eye to the late nineteenth and early twentieth centuries.[7]

There have been *conspiratorial* explanations, from Marxists in particular, which have stressed how the whole framework of the Welfare State has been one of control which delays but does not prevent the capitalist crisis. This has been most evident in the writings of R. D. Storch on policing, which stressed the structural approach in examining how the central authority created a structure and institutions to impose social control upon the working classes.[8] Some historians have taken this further to suggest that capitalism can only survive through social welfare. This *capitalistic* perspective has found support through the work of P. Thoenes but is also evident in some recent work which has stressed the role of employers in promoting their own form of welfare policies and provision.[9] Indeed, John Saville has denied that the concept of a Welfare State should be assumed to be a stage on the road to socialism, for 'both in Western Europe and the United States social security schemes are placed firmly within the framework of a free enterprise economy and no-one suggests that what is a natural development within a mature capitalist society should be given new names.'[10]

Ranged against such explanations is the *democratic* perspective, which suggests that the extension of the parliamentary and local franchises in the nineteenth and twentieth centuries did much to translate the demands of the working classes into political form and acted as a stimulus for reform. The 1870 Education Act and the Liberal reforms of the early twentieth century have often been explained in these terms. The demand for citizenship, both social and economic, was part of this development. Yet this cannot explain many developments in policy, for as Pat Thane has recently revealed, there was tremendous opposition to the National Insurance Act, as well as to some other Liberal reforms of the 1906–14 period, from the working class and their institutions.[11] At the same time, social policy has often been affected by strong extra-parliamentary agitation, as in the case of the Factory Acts and the Ten Hours Act of 1847 and various pieces of educational legislation.

Pluralism is an elaboration of the democratic perspective which suggests that political outcomes are the product of a competition between groups, such as political parties and trade unions. Some forms of pluralistic ideas recognize that the balance between these may be uneven and critics have also noted that the state is not necessarily a passive body when dealing with outside pressure groups.[12]

All these perspectives and approaches have their value, although the general approach of this book will be to examine the twists and turns of social policy rather than to examine theory. If there is a dominant perspective in this study, it is that pragmatism, incrementalism, pluralism, and ideology or values are the factors that have been mainly important in shaping British social policy, although that is not to discount other influences. Obviously, it is quite possible that many different forces were working in different spheres, and in contradiction to each other, at one and the same time.

Recently, José Harris has captured this spirit of competing interests in a most evocative book which deals with the late nineteenth and early twentieth centuries.[13] She stresses the interaction between the ideology of Victorian values and their need to meet the requirements of a society which was urbanizing and becoming more massed and national in focus. The values of the working class became universalized but were in conflict with Victorian values that belonged to a previous artisan age. She argues that this Victorian society was extremely pluralistic and that social policy often developed along contradictory lines at one and the same time. Clearly, this approach is worthy of application to a wider time-scale, and is obviously relevant to the inter-war years and to the conflicts that have gone on in British social policy since 1951.

In examining the evolution of British social policy, this book is divided into two types of study. Chapters Two to Six deal with a variety of social issues, most of which cover the years between the late eighteenth century and the 1860s or 1870s, although the chapter on education does extend to 1944. The next six chapters deal with periods of political development and the issues that shaped them. There is also a document section which offers a number of well-known and central documents alongside material that is almost unknown to the general reader and the undergraduate. It is hoped that this book will provide a clear pathway through the forest of social policy, an area which, using Harris's metaphor of Penelope's web, was 'a garment endlessly woven by day and unpicked again by night'. There is certainly a large amount of unpicking going on under the present Conservative government.

Notes

1.   G. Esping-Anderson, *Three Worlds of Welfare Capitalism* (Cambridge, 1990); F. Castles and R. D. McKinley, 'Does Politics Matter? An Analysis of the Public Welfare Commitment in Advanced Democratic States', *European Journal of Political Research* 7, 2 (1979).

2.   D. Fraser, *The Evolution of the British Welfare State* (1983), uses a variety of perspectives to explain the growth of the British Welfare State, although it moves more towards the pragmatic approach as an explanation.

3.   W. C. Lubenow, *The Politics of Government Growth: Early Victorian Attitudes towards State Intervention 1833–1848* (Newton Abbot, 1971).

4.   O. MacDonagh, 'The Nineteenth-Century Revolution in Government: A Reappraisal', *Historical Journal* 1 (1958); O. MacDonagh, *Early Victorian Government* (1977); O. MacDonagh, *The Passenger Acts: A Pattern of Government Growth* (1961).

5.   S. E. Finer, *The Life and Times of Sir Edwin Chadwick* (1952); J. Hart, 'Nineteenth-Century Social Reform: A Tory Interpretation of History', *Past and Present* 31 (1965), pp. 39–61; H. Parris, 'The Nineteenth-Century Revolution in Government: A Reappraisal Reappraised', *Historical Journal* (1958); V. Cromwell, 'Interpretations in Nineteenth-Century Administration: An Analysis', *Victorian Studies*, March 1966, pp. 245–55.

6.   P. Thane, 'Government and Society in England and Wales, 1750–1914', in F. M. L. Thompson (ed.), *The Cambridge Social History of Britain 1750–1950, vol. 3, Social Agencies and Institutions* (Cambridge, 1990), p. 21.

7.   J. Harris, 'Political Thought and the Welfare State 1870–1914: An Intellectual Framework for British Social Policy', *Past and Present* 135 (May 1992).

8.   R. D. Storch, ' "The Plague of Blue Locusts": Police Reform and Popular Resistance in Northern England 1840–1857', *International Review of Social History* 20 (1975), pp. 61–90; R. D. Storch, 'The Policeman as Domestic Missionary: Urban Discipline and Popular Culture in Northern England, 1850–1880', *Journal of Social History* 9 (1976), pp. 481–509.

9.   P. Thoenes, *Elites in the Welfare State* (1966), p. 143; R. Hay, 'Employers and Social Policy in Britain: The Evolution of Welfare Legislation, 1905–14', *Social History* 2 (1977), pp. 435–55; R. Hay, 'Employers' Attitudes to Social Policy and the Concept of "Social Control", 1900–1920', in P. Thane (ed.), *The Origins of British Social Policy* (1978), pp. 107–25; J. Melling, 'Welfare Capitalism and the Origins of Welfare States: British Industry, Workplace, Welfare and Social Reform, 1870–1914', *Social History* 17, 3 (1992), pp. 453–78.

10. J. Saville, 'The Welfare State: An Historical Approach', *New Reasoner* (1957), quoted in Fraser, *Evolution*, p. xxviii.

11. P. Thane, 'The Working Class and State "Welfare" in Britain 1880–1914', *Historical Journal* 27, 4 (1984), pp. 877–900.

12. E. A. Nordlinger, *On the Autonomy of the Democratic State* (Cambridge, Mass., 1981).

13. J. Harris, *Private Lives, Public Spirit: A Social History of Britain 1870–1914* (Oxford, 1993).

CHAPTER TWO

THE POOR LAW
c.1780–1870s

The history of the Poor Law in England and Wales has been one of the most controversial issues in the study of British social policy.[1] Reorganized and codified between 1597 to 1601, the Elizabethan Poor Law formed the basis of the poor relief until 1834, when the Poor Law Amendment Act was introduced. This in turn operated until it went out of formal existence in 1929. What was distinctive about the history of Poor Law relief was the fact that, whilst the basic system and obligations were laid down by central authority, there was always room for compromise and local variation. Not surprisingly, historians have been deeply divided in their attempt to explain the growth and development of the Poor Law and to explain why its enduring feature was the conflict between central and local administration.

Five main debates have divided historians. First, they have sought to explain why the Old Poor Law was replaced by the New Poor Law in 1834 and have focused particularly upon the misrepresentation of the allowance or outdoor relief system in the Poor Law *Report*. Secondly, they have examined the extent to which the landed élite accepted the 1834 legislation with open arms. Did landowners accept the principles of 1834 because they had no choice, because they offered another form of social control, or because they were committed to the new political economy that was emerging? Thirdly, there have been arguments about the severity of the New Poor Law. Was it a cruel system or rather more humanitarian than it is often presented as being? Fourthly, there has been some major questioning of the extent to which central authority was able to dictate the actual pattern of relief regulation. Anne Digby, Felix Driver and Michael Rose argue that the industrial North was able to negotiate its own version of Poor Law practice.[2] In fact, it would appear that there was persistent variety and continuity of practice before and after 1834.[3] Peter Wood also accepts this, although he suggests that the influence of central authority was very largely dependent upon the sensitivity of the inspectors to the needs of a particular area.[4] At the other extreme, Karel Williams suggests that central authority carried more influence, especially in promoting the building of new workhouses, than is often suggested, a view which is partly endorsed by Driver.[5] Fifthly, there has been much informal discussion, rather than debate, about the way in which the Poor Law developed in the second half of the nineteenth century. For instance, Peter Wood has argued that in the 1860s there was a much increased level of Poor Law spending which led the Poor Law Board to produce the Goschen Minute in 1869 to tighten up on the provision of outdoor relief. This is certainly a view accepted by Michael Rose, who feels that the 1870s saw the effective implementation of the principles of the 1834 Poor Law.[6] Yet it has been noted that the Poor Law adopted a more humanitarian attitude towards children, the aged and the infirm as the century progressed.

Some of these debates remain unresolved. Nonetheless, it will be argued that the pressures to control rising expenditure and the threat of social instability were the driving forces behind the reform of the Old Poor Law and the creation of the New Poor Law. Yet, despite the central intent of creating a more rigorous and controlled provision of relief, it is clear that the variety of responses under the Old Poor Law was mimicked by the New Poor Law unions, which continued to adopt their old practices in accordance to their relations with the Poor Law assistant commissioners/inspectors and local opinion. It would also appear that there was considerable support for the Poor Law amongst all political parties and particularly the southern landlords, who were anxious to reduce their rates. Even in the urban and industrial centres of the North, the centre of the anti-Poor Law movement's agitation, there was, by the 1840s, a recognition that the local union could get its own way by gradual attrition rather than open opposition to central authority. The New Poor Law, for whatever reason, did keep relief expenditure at a low point for about thirty years until it rose sharply in the 1860s, partly because of the change in the financing arrangements. By the 1870s, however, this enormous rise in expenditure had brought an increased tightening-up of provision under the newly formed Local Government Board (1871), which presided over the effective introduction of the 'principles of 1834'. But faced with changing political and social conditions in the late nineteenth century, the Poor Law authorities also began to adopt a more humanitarian attitude towards children and the old, as opposed to the able-bodied pauper. The history of the Poor Law follows no straight line and one must remember Derek Fraser's premise that 'the story of poor relief is but dimly (and often not at all) told through the pages of national legislation'.[7] Equally, the story of 15,000 parishes or 600 unions is not likely to produce a clear picture of events in the pluralistic society of the nineteenth and twentieth centuries.

The old Poor Law: its rise and fall

The Elizabethan Poor Law had its origins in the fourteenth century in legislation that was directed at the restriction of vagrancy in England

and Wales. This was strengthened in 1536 by the authorizing of parishes to collect money to support the impotent poor. The Elizabethan code was further developed in 1576 with the introduction of the idea of 'setting the poor to work'. The 1576 Poor Relief Act also required JPs to provide materials on which beggars could work in return for their relief. It was these and other requirements, though they had not spread widely, that were codified at the end of the century and appeared in the Poor Law Act of 1601, the 43rd of Elizabeth. This Act abandoned the idea of repression aimed at the beggars and paupers and decided that paupers should be classified in three different groups, to be dealt with in different, but appropriate, ways. First, there were the impotent poor (the aged, sick, blind and lunatic), who were to be provided with institutional relief and accommodated in the 'poor-houses' or almshouses. Secondly, there were the able-bodied, who were to be made to work and dealt with in a 'house of correction' or workhouse, which might be residential or non-residential. Children who were in need would be apprenticed to some trade. Thirdly, those who absconded or became persistent idlers and refused work were to be punished in a 'house of correction'. Although neatly divided, it is clear that the tripartite division of poorhouse, workhouse and house of correction never really caught on but rather gave way, particularly in the nineteenth century, to the single-institution mixed-pauper workhouse.

The whole system was to be operated by the local JPs, who would administer their own poor relief in a parish through the overseers. These overseers were allowed to levy rates on property to pay for the poor. Central control of some type was to be maintained through the Privy Council. Yet there were almost 15,000 parishes and each one seemed to operate by its own rules within a general nationally approved framework. Effectively, this meant that uniformity of approach was not going to be a feature of the Poor Law. This became apparent in the failure of the numerous attempts to make the system more uniform in the nineteenth century.

Each parish was supposed to look after its own poor, which raised the question of 'who were its poor?'. The Elizabethan formula that emerged was that the parish would be responsible for those born there, those who had resided there for a year and those who had previously passed through without punishment. Overseers, very conscious of the need to keep rates down, were thus tempted to remove paupers from their parish as quickly as possible, a situation which often led to litigation between parishes. The Act of Settlement of 1662 (an Act for the Better Relief of the Poor) was designed to clarify this situation and proclaimed that settlement was gained by birth, marriage, apprenticeship and, later in practice, by inheritance. A stranger to the parish could be removed within forty days of his arrival there unless he occupied freehold land, but was usually left alone as long as he did not need relief. The 1662 measure proved difficult to translate into effective action and was made more sensible in 1795, when it was decided that removal could only occur after poor relief had been claimed.

The Settlement Laws provided the basis for much criticism and fuelled frenzied arguments. Not only were they unwieldy but they were also prone to abuse. In parishes controlled by one or two landowners, the 'close' parishes, it was possible to draw labour from other parishes and to pass back the burden of poor relief to their 'open' neighbours when the situation required. The landowners could discourage people from settling in their parishes by pulling down cottages and refusing to build new ones.[8]

Other problems emerged in respect of the large number and disparate array of small workhouses that were built. The famous Corporation of the Poor formed at Bristol in 1696 provided the example for many. Its principle, that the poor should work to create self-sufficiency in a 'pauper manufactory', was encouraged by Sir Edward Knatchbull's General Workhouse Act in 1722. But such hopes were limited by the fact that many workhouses were merely small rented buildings and that there were actually few large workhouses where the 'pauper manu-factory' principle was possible. There was certainly a proliferation of small-scale accommodation, with about 2,000 workhouses in 1776 and 3,765, spread amongst 14,611 parishes, in 1802–3, most with between 20 and 50 inmates.[9] The problem with this type of institutional provi-sion was that it was costing almost a quarter of Poor Law expenditure at the beginning of the nineteenth century whilst only dealing with one pauper in twelve.

There were attempts to rationalize the system. Thomas Gilbert's Act of 1782 made the union of parishes possible without specific legislation if supported by two-thirds of the ratepayers, and over 900 parishes had joined to form 67 unions under that Act by 1834.[10] Yet, given the cost of developing workhouses, it is quite clear that many parishes and unions developed an infinite variety of payments – pensions, dole, bread allowances, payments in kind and other devices which came under the general term of outdoor relief. There was the 'roundsman system', whereby local farmers employed the parish poor on a rota system. In some parishes paupers were directly employed on the roads and paid from the highway rate. In the late eighteenth century the onset of serious economic conditions produced by bad harvests and the dislo-cation of the French and the Napoleonic wars increased food prices and shortage of work led to fresh expedients being developed. Thus, from the 1780s onwards parishes had often provided 'allowances in aid of wages' and the scheme developed at the Pelican Inn at Speenhamland in 1795, which also offered allowances for children, was just one of these attempts to deal with the poverty created by the acute economic situation. In 1797 this system was made famous by the Poor Law reformer Sir Frederick Eden, who gave the impression that the Speenhamland system was widespread over the southern rural counties.[11] In fact, it operated in only a few parishes from time to time and was often abandoned. The whole campaign against Speenhamland should also be seen within the context of the 1795 Act which released parishes from having to implement the workhouse test and allowed for the further development of outdoor relief, which had, in any case, been a common feature of poverty relief for more than two centuries. To those advocating the development of free market conditions, the allowance or outdoor relief, just as much as the Settlement Laws, appeared to interfere with the free operation of the market.

Up to the late eighteenth century, then, a chaotic system of poor relief had emerged to cater for the pressing social needs of the pauper. It was one which seemed acceptable within the context of a rural society conditioned by the seasonal nature of work and employment. Yet the developing industrialization and growing urbanization of the eighteenth century, combined with the social and economic impact of the French wars, created a new climate of opinion which encouraged the view that the Old, or Elizabethan, Poor Law was in need of reform.

The origins of the New Poor Law

From the late eighteenth century onwards, numerous schemes and ideas were put forward on how to reform or abandon the Old Poor Law. A very strong abolitionist case developed, which reached its zenith with the *Report of the Select Committee on the Poor Laws* in 1817. After 1820, however, there were moves towards a compromise which would get rid of the defects of the Old Poor Law, and the 1834 Poor Law Amendment Act was the final outcome of this arrangement.

The Revd. T. R. Malthus and the Revd. Joseph Townsend demanded the abolition of the Old Poor Law, Townsend arguing that 'These laws, so beautiful in theory, promote the evils they mean to remedy and aggravate the distress.'[12] Malthus's *Essay on the Principle of Population* (1798) also raised the prospect of geometrical rises in population against the slower arithmetic rise in food supplies. He argued for the need to delay marriage, the end of the Settlement Laws, which distorted the free market, and the end of the child allowance system of the Poor Law, which he felt encouraged the married poor to have children they could not afford. David Ricardo's *Principles of Political Economy* (1817) also postulated the wage–fund theory whereby the proportion of the national wealth available for wages was fixed at any given moment.

The more that was paid out for poor relief, the less there was for wages. The gist of the abolitionist arguments was that poor relief was counter-productive, self-defeating and should be abolished.

Yet there was great confusion about what should replace it. Should there be increased government expenditure, the repeal of the Corn Laws, more protection, fewer workhouses or more workhouses? Great emphasis was placed upon self-help and, as a result, savings banks, friendly societies, education and other measures were encouraged. Yet nothing dominated; Poor Law expenditure trebled during the French and Napoleonic wars and reached almost £8 million by 1817, amounting to 12–13s. (60–65p) per head of population. It was at this moment that the *Report of the Select Committee on the Poor Laws* supported the abolitionist case. Written by Frankland Lewis, who subsequently became the first chairman of the Poor Law Commission, and chaired by William Sturges Bourne, it condemned the existing system. But in a period of high post-war depression this was not a realistic possibility and reformers looked towards other solutions.

What emerged was rising pressure for a deterrent Poor Law, based upon indoor relief in a workhouse. George Nicholls, noting how this system operated in Southwall and Bingam in Nottinghamshire, stressed that the cutting-back of relief and the imposition of the labour test and workhouse test would be advantageous for all. It would reduce costs to the ratepayers and encourage the poor to seek honest work. The Revd. J. T. Becher wrote *The Anti-Pauper System* (1828), referring to the Nottingham developments, the improved schooling, the deterrent workhouse acting as 'a place of refuge as well as restraint', and the need to unite parishes into unions.[13] These ideas and schemes found favour with the Royal Commission on the Poor Law in 1832, not least because Nicholls was a member of that commission. Yet there was quite a strong groundswell in this direction and, as J. R. Poynter has written: 'If the workhouse test became a dogma, it did so because thirty years of debate and doubt created the need for one.'[14]

This Poor Law Commission had been set up because of the worening financial situation of the 1820s. Poor relief had fallen to £7 million in 1820 and to less than £6 million in 1822 but had begun to rise again in the late 1820s, reaching over £7 million in 1831 (just over 10s. per head) and £8.3 million by 1831–2 and 1832–3. Whether this was an oppressive rates burden is open to question and there is certainly evidence that the change and rises in the rates burden varied enormously. In Halifax, for instance, although there were fluctuations of up to about 50 per cent from year to year, the cost of the poor rate in 1804 was £4,235 3s. 8½d. In 1826 it was only £3,916 5s. 4¾d. and £4,304 15s. 3d. in 1830.[15] Nevertheless, the overall national burden increased rapidly and, according to Anne Digby, it is certainly possible that the tenant farmers were attempting to pass on some of the costs of increased rates to the landowners by negotiating lower rentals; there may also have been some loss of a moral commitment to the poor in the early nineteenth century, leading to increased pressure to do something about the higher poor rate levels.[16] In addition, the continued social instability, concern for which was revived by the 'Swing' Riots of 1830–1 in the rural counties, prompted immediate action, with the execution of nine rioters and the transportation of 900 others. One might add that the poorhouses had been attacked in thirteen parishes and that the Selborne and Healey workhouses had been destroyed and the overseers intimidated.[17] In the wake of these riots, there was a short period when more generous relief and wages were given but both were quickly scaled down. Subsequently, it was felt that the operation of the Poor Laws needed to be examined further and the new Whig government set up a Royal Commission in February 1832. The Swing riots of 1830–1 may well have been the final blow to the Old Poor Law and the final push for its reform.

The Poor Law *Report* of 1834, produced by the Royal Commission, was very largely the work of Nassau Senior, the *laissez-faire* economist, and Edwin Chadwick, and formed the basis of the Poor Law Amendment Act of 1834.[18] It has been the subject of considerable debate, largely because of the false image it appears to have given about the nature of the Old Poor Law. Nevertheless, it was a reflection of public concern and thinking at the time and a vital document in shaping the new social ethos of the New Poor Law.

The Royal Commission appointed twenty-six assistant commissioners who toured the country and submitted reports on the provinces. These assistant commissioners also elicited replies from the *Town Queries* and *Rural Queries* surveys sent out in August 1832. It is argued that they gave, for whatever reason, a misleading and selective picture of what was occurring and fuelled the concerns of Nassau Senior and Edwin Chadwick that the allowance system was demoralizing and pauperizing the rural labourer. In other words, the evidence of the assistant commissioners appears to have been designed, consciously or unconsciously, to pander to the preconceived notions of the leading commissioners.

Not surprisingly, there has been much questioning of the accuracy of the Poor Law *Report*. In the 1960s the main critic was Mark Blaug, who argued that many parishes had already dropped the provision of allowances which were the result, not the cause, of low wages. He also felt that both the *Rural* and *Town Queries*, which contradicted some of the *Report's* findings, were ignored. Another critic, D. A. Baugh, questioned whether the Speenhamland system was ever really important, because poverty itself determined the responses of the parishes and unions between 1790 and 1834. D. McCloskey has also supported Blaug's argument by distinguishing between the 'income supplement' character of most allowances and the 'wage subsidy' nature of the less common work-sharing devices of the roundsman system. J. P. Huzel has also attacked Malthus's link between generous allowances and increased population, for he argues that allowances may have been the response to, and not the cause of, population growth.[19] More recently, G. R. Boyer has argued much the same line, noting that farmers used the allowance system from the 1760s onwards as a form of unemployment benefit to ensure that they had an adequate labour force in periods of peak economic activity.[20] The balance of this research suggests that relief under the Old Poor Law was primarily a response to population growth, low wages and underemployment and not the cause of such conditions, as the *Report* and Benthamite attitudes suggested. It was underemployment, not allowances, that demoralized rural workers and reduced wages.

Notwithstanding its misrepresentation of the Old Poor Law, the *Report* laid down the three main principles of the new system: those of 'less eligibility', the workhouse test and the bureaucratic demand of administrative centralization and uniformity. Although the workhouse test became the focus of much contemporary criticism, it is clear that it only served to act as a mechanism to establish less eligibility, the central principle of 1834. Senior and Chadwick believed that the allowance system removed the fear of hunger, which made men industrious, and paved the way to idleness. In good Benthamite fashion it suggested that if the allowance system were removed, the idle pauper would be forced to seek comfort through work. Therefore, the standard of relief offered by the Poor Law had to be below, not above, the wages of the industrious worker. That would encourage self-help and social improvement. Those applying for poor relief had to be less eligible in order to combat the desire of human nature for idleness. Chadwick had certainly influenced the Poor Law *Report* in this direction, although he owed his ideas to Bentham's pleasure/pain philosophy and to his prison plan, the great Panopticon. Indeed, one should remember that Chadwick had, early in his career, been Bentham's secretary.[21]

The workhouse test was simply a way of putting the less eligibility principle into practice. The aged, ill, orphans and widows needed institutional care. These indigent and destitute people had to be looked after. But it was felt that there was no need for the able-bodied poor, those with low wages, to be looked after and that this was, in any case, contrary to the 43rd of Elizabeth. The 1834 Poor Law *Report* was concerned to deter pauperism, not to reduce poverty. The *Report* was also alarmed that the 'setting the poor to work' part of the 43rd of Elizabeth had been ignored and abused.

The workhouse test was considered vital, for it would end outdoor relief for those seeking assistance, remove the poor from subsidy by the Poor Law, and restore the principle of work. By offering relief at a lower rate than that of an independent worker, it would remove the attraction of the Poor Law. It was a development of the Nottinghamshire system whereby the deterrent workhouse would become an asylum for the able-bodied. Common welfare required, under Benthamism, that the minority should accept the conditions laid down for them. As Fraser says: 'The 43rd of Elizabeth thought in terms of involuntary pauperism; 1834 acknowledged but dismissed it.'[22] This harshness in approach was derived from a sense that the fear of the workhouse would force workers to find employment and improve themselves.

The Poor Law *Report* also reflected Chadwick's concern for administrative tidiness. Whether accurate or inaccurate, selected or typical, the fact is that the individual practices of almost 15,000 parishes suggested incompetence to Chadwick; as a result, the *Report* suggested that there should be a centralized and uniform system, whereby a central board would administer the Poor Law and have the power to frame regulations and to control local practices. To make the workhouse test viable, the principle of the Gilbert Act had to be extended and parishes were to be encouraged to join together to form unions.

The Poor Law Amendment Act was a close reflection of the main recommendations of the *Report*. It was introduced in April 1834 and became law in August with only the limited opposition of Richard Cobbett and *The Times*. As the *Report* advised, the Act was directed towards dealing with paupers rather than the poor, through the medium of the workhouse test. Parishes would be grouped into Poor Law unions which would be administered by professional and salaried officials responsible to elected boards of guardians. The parishes would pay for the relief of their own poor, but the general expenditure (widened later to include the sick, the vagrant and the immovable) was charged to a common fund, administered by the union, into which all the parishes paid. It is wise to remember that before 1860 this was a burden on the poor as well as the rich, since the Poor Law assessment was not based upon rateable value. In the cases of settlement, each parish would be responsible for its own paupers. The local unions would be subject to the unifying control of the Poor Law Commission. This was to be a three-man body, to which Chadwick was appointed secretary. Despite some differences in detail, the philosophy of the New Poor Law was that of the *Report*. Indeed, as Peter Wood has suggested: 'The New Poor Law was born out of the belief that the Old Poor law was causing a degeneration of the working classes by encouraging idleness and over-population at great expense to the ratepayer.'[23]

The New Poor Law, 1834–1870s

Yet, whilst the New Poor Law was clearly a significant event in the development of social policy, it is not at all clear what it produced. Its introduction has provoked numerous debates about its precise origins, its acceptance, and the extent of its influence upon the local unions.

One hotly debated question is why, in general, was the new structure accepted by the landed gentry? The Webbs argued that the New Poor Law was far more effective than the Old Poor Law, which was administratively inchoate and controlled by the gentry and landed interests.[24] In the 1970s Anthony Brundage challenged the assumption of a radical change and looked towards the underlying continuity of the Poor Law Amendment Act, for far from subverting the authority of the magistracy and landed interests, it actually reinforced the corporate authority of the landed élite. To Brundage, the deference of rural communities was enforced by the new arrangements.[25] This conclusion was based upon his study of the ten counties of the rural Midlands and East Anglia, where it is clear that the key landed figures were prepared to call in the assistant commissioners to set up Poor Law unions because of their concern about disturbances. Such was the case when, on 12 November 1834, Lord John Russell, his brother the Marquis of Tavistock, and Thomas Bennett of Woburn, the steward of the Duke of Bedford's estates, called in Adey, the assistant commissioner, with the intent of setting up a Poor Law union around Woburn.[26] Opposition to this and to the creation of other Poor Law unions was quickly overcome and the landed interests and leaders of society were normally positive in their attitude to the New Poor Law, helped by the fact that outdoor relief continued in the rural counties because it was cheaper than institutionalization. These landed authorities did not have their power over the guardians challenged until 1894, when the Local Government Act abolished ex-officio guardians and eliminated property qualifications, plural voting and proxy votes for elected guardians.[27]

More recently, the views of both the Webbs and Brundage have been challenged and modified. Peter Mandler argues that the New Poor Law was undeniably utilitarian in intent and accepts that it was administered in rural areas by and for the benefit of the landlords. But he goes further and suggests that the gentry were not the victims of the centralizers, nor the engineers of new structures of deference, but active agents in the process of modernization. The New Poor Law was thus not simply a reflection of new attitudes towards poverty and the primacy of the free market, but a framework which many of the gentry accepted and freely advocated.[28]

This debate continues; there has been no clear outcome, for the issue is one of degree. Nevertheless, one can establish certain points of agreement. The first is that it is no longer acceptable simply to suggest that utilitarian ideas were imposed upon an unwilling and reluctant population, for if the hostility had been widespread, and irreconcilable, the New Poor Law would have had difficulty surviving. Secondly, there remains some doubt as to whether or not there was the continuity and the implied deference that Brundage noted.[29] What was obvious is that the New Poor Law represented a change of direction in social policy. Thirdly, there is no denying that there was some strong support for the New Poor Law from the landed élite for the *laissez-faire* policy it implied rather than for the continued social control it offered. As Mandler suggests, this 'enlightened' landed élite included William Sturges Bourne, the chairman of the 1817 Select Committee and a royal commissioner in 1832–4. Thomas Frankland Lewis, the accepted author of the 1817 *Report* and the leading Poor Law commissioner after 1834, and his son George Cornwell Lewis, who also became a leading Poor Law commissioner, were both prominent landlords.

It is not surprising, given the mixture of *laissez-faire* and deferential overtones evident in the acceptance of the New Poor Law in many rural areas, that there was much local continuity between the Old and the New Poor Laws. The new guardians and relieving officers were often the same men who had operated the system before change. Given such a situation, one has to ask how responsive the local guardians were to the need to adapt and how successful was the central authority in imposing change?

The 1834 Poor Law Amendment Act was similar to the Poor Law *Report* but lacked some of the powers that the latter had recommended. Most obviously, it did not give the central authority the power to compel unions to build new workhouses, although it had powers over the extension of the old workhouses. As a result, the Poor Law Commission appears to have had mixed fortunes in establishing a measure of uniformity on the system and in imposing the workhouse test as the basis for 'less eligibility'.

There were clearly some areas of success for the Poor Law Commission/Poor Law Board. Poor Law expenditure kept to a growth of about 0.5 per cent per annum for the first thirty years of the New Poor Law.[30] Indeed, in the years 1834–43 the national Poor Law expenditure did fall to about £4.5–5 million per annum and fluctuated between £5–6 million for the subsequent twenty years. This obviously pleased the landed interests who had objected to the high level of rates, although it is not clear whether these controlled expenditure levels were due to good economic conditions in farming or to the effective introduction of the workhouse test in the southern rural counties. Nonetheless, the central authority felt that something had been achieved through the work of its assistant commissioners/inspectors.

Yet there was clearly much local resistance to change, particularly in connection with the workhouse test and outdoor relief, and this has called into question the whole balance of the relationship between central authority and the local unions as well as the effectiveness of central control. From recent research, it appears that the introduction of the New Poor Law varied enormously from area to area and from time to time and that many of its main features were not introduced in any effective manner. The New Poor Law was successfully introduced into the agricultural South of the country in the mid-1830s, with only a few disturbances, and to parts of the North, mainly the North-East. Yet in other areas, most obviously the West Riding of Yorkshire, Lancashire and parts of Wales, there appears to have been some determined opposition, since attempts to introduce it were made during the late 1830s when there was an economic depression. Why this variation occurred is not always easy to explain. Obviously, the workhouse test was geared more towards rural rather than urban areas, where temporary unemployment necessitated the provision of outdoor relief. Nevertheless, in the North-East, where there was considerable industrial employment, it may well have been the sensitivity of the Poor Law inspector that permitted its relatively amicable acceptance or the nature of the employment of the region. Both Fraser and Wood acknowledge that these inspectors could influence the acceptance of the Poor Law. The urbane Sir John Walsham secured more local co-operation in the North-East than did the antagonistic Charles Mott in Lancashire and the West Riding.[31] Alfred Power also gained no respect from the public of the West Riding, his previous position as a factory commissioner in 1833 having already soured local opinion towards him.

The most obvious resistance to the New Poor Law occurred in the industrial areas of Yorkshire and Lancashire.[32] Richard Oastler, the leader of the factory movement, carried this support into the Anti-Poor Law movement in the Huddersfield area, where he attacked the New Poor Law as the 'catechism of Hell'. Peter Bussey and the Revd. George Bull did much the same in Bradford. The result was some anti-Poor Law reaction and rioting in 1837 and 1838. The guardian elections in Oldham were successfully boycotted, there was a refusal to appoint a clerk to the guardians at Huddersfield, and riots by local ratepayers at Todmorden led to the use of the military to keep order. There was also much opposition in areas where the issue was less emotive. In Halifax, for instance, the *Halifax Guardian* opposed the New Poor Law as 'unEnglish, pernicious and wicked', encouraged the mass meeting of resistance held on Hartshead Moor, and published accounts of the ill-treatment, separation and starvation imposed by the New Poor Law.[33] It encouraged general opposition to the New Poor Law, to Mott, the assistant commissioner, and to any suggestion of construction of a new workhouse.

Some of this resistance arose from the fact that the Poor Law Commission sent an assistant commissioner to form Poor Law unions in each county. He would do this by calling a meeting of landowners, magistrates and other men of substance to give their views and by taking into consideration the existing boundaries of the unions formed under the Gilbert Act, which were not subject to the new changes, dealt with about 10 per cent of the population of England and Wales and were referred to by Driver as 'lagoons of irrationality'.[34] The assistant commissioners worked from the South to the North of England and Wales and, in their haste to ensure that the unions became the basis of the 1837 Registration Act for births, marriages and deaths, often created units which were by no means of an equal size in population or area. In fact, the standard, set at about 15,000 acres for a union, varied enormously and occasionally reached 80,000 and 100,000 acres. Therefore, much of this progress was hasty and achieved through compromise which challenged the uniformity of the system.

Despite this speed, some areas resisted unionization for some time, managed to retreat from it altogether or were forced to reorganize. In the case of Liverpool, for instance, special parliamentary dispensation was given to allow it to dissolve the new union and return to the former system of administration under its own local Act. The New Poor Law was not introduced to Leeds until 1844 and the Bradford Poor Law Union was reorganized in 1848, when the outer townships, concerned at the cost of relieving Bradford through the common fund, broke away and formed the North Bierley Union.[35] In the end, however, almost 15,000 parishes were shaped into about 600 unions and there were few retreats from the new structure. As Felix Driver suggests, this was accomplished quite quickly. Whereas in August 1835 there were 114 unions in existence, uniting 14 per cent of all the parishes and 9 per cent of the population, by August 1838 this had reached a total of 580 unions, uniting 95 per cent of the parishes and 80 per cent of the population.[36] By 1846 the largest block of parishes un-unionized by the 1834 Act was to be found in an area stretching along the western Yorkshire side of the Pennines from South to North Yorkshire, and most of these were Gilbert unions over which the Poor Law Commission found it had no control following a successful legal challenge at the Court of the Queen's Bench in 1840.[37] There were also other Gilbert parishes and local Act unions distributed throughout the rest of England and Wales.[38]

Yet the formation of Poor Law unions was a relatively straightforward affair. Other measures were rather more difficult. The building of workhouses was, for instance, contentious. The Poor Law Commission could order the extension and enlargement of an existing workhouse but not the building of new ones. Within five years of the Poor Law Amendment Act being passed, about 350 workhouses had been built, normally in a single building of a mixed workhouse type, largely in the rural South of England.[39] There were urban successes as well. The Halifax guardians were divided (18:6) about the building of a workhouse in 1838 but, with the encouragement of Power and the prospect of financial help, they agreed to build a new workhouse in November 1838.[40] This was success of a kind and both Karel Williams and Felix Driver accept that there were some triumphs in this direction.[41]

Nevertheless, it is clear that there was much more resistance in the industrial North and in parts of Wales. The Leeds guardians refused to build a new workhouse to replace the old inadequate provisions until 1859.[42] Because of the conflict between the inner and outer Bradford townships, it was not possible for a new workhouse to be built there until 1851 and it was 1858 before the North Bierley Union workhouse was opened.[43] There were delays in building workhouses in North Wales, where the Caernarfon guardians put in some determined resistance to the construction of a workhouse. Even though the Poor Law commissioners applied for strong pressure from the Queen's Bench in 1843, it was not until 1846 that the institutions came into operation.[44] On balance, then, there appears to have been some acceptance of the need to build new workhouses in the rural counties, but considerable opposition and delay in the North.

The end of outdoor relief and the introduction of the workhouse test proved to be an even more difficult task to achieve. It was soon clear that outdoor relief could not be abolished and the Poor Law Commission recognized this fact when it devised the Labour Test Order in 1842, whereby outdoor relief was given as long as some work was done. This ran against the grain of the General Order of 1841 which had been strengthened by the 1844 Outdoor Relief Prohibitory Order, issued to enforce the Orders to end outdoor relief by the southern unions, four-fifths of whom were abandoning the practice. The 1842 Order and the 1844 Order were obviously contradictory, but by 1847 there were 73.6 per cent of the unions using the 1844 Order, 11.3 per cent using the Labour Test Order and 15 per cent using both Orders.[45] Thereafter, the balance moved away from the unions ending outdoor relief and the erosion of the workhouse test continued under the Poor Law Board (1847–71). The General Order of August 1852 acknowledged the continuance of outdoor relief and required that it be given in kind to all groups. Thereafter, the number of unions operating the 1844 Order declined rapidly and by 1871 only six unions were operating under this Order alone. Indeed, the numbers receiving indoor relief were always a small minority of the total number of paupers: 14.3 per cent in 1840, 12.26 in 1849 and 15.49 in 1869.[46] The 'principle of 1834' was not being applied and the allowance/outdoor relief system continued to flourish. What this meant was that even in the rural unions of the South of

England, the workhouse test was being ignored, the rural unions moving against it, on grounds of cost, from the 1840s onwards.

The reality was that the Poor Law was a compromise between the local guardians and the central authority. On the major policy issues, such as outdoor relief and the introduction of the workhouse test, the central authority was forced to compromise and draw up regulations to allow for local practice. On other issues, such as the building of new, single-site workhouses, the central authority was more successful. There is obviously supporting evidence for all sides in the debate. Karel Williams is clearly right in suggesting that the majority of the workhouses had been built within six years of 1834.[47] Indeed, Anne Digby accepts this point. Yet both Michael Rose and Anne Digby are also clearly right when they argue that the central authority failed to impose the workhouse test in any meaningful way up to the 1870s.[48] Workhouses were built but the workhouse test was barely applied.

There were also other areas in which the central demand for uniformity and efficiency was thwarted by local practice – most notably, in connection with rating and settlement. The 1834 Poor Law *Report* had condemned the abuses of the Settlement Laws but made recommendations suggesting minor reforms only. The problem was that parochial localism was so well entrenched amongst the farmers, traders and small occupiers of the parish that it seemed impossible to change the rating and the settlement system, which implied that local parish ratepayers, rather than the union, paid for their own poor, until the financial reforms in the 1860s.

There were major problems with this continued arrangement. There were many 'chalk and cheese' unions like Bradford and York, where the outlying and country ratepayers felt that they were subsidizing the cost of the town paupers. The creation of a common fund to cover the general expenditure of each union offered the prospect of a gradual transition from parish to union rates, and was helped by the 1846, 1848 and 1861 Acts which allowed the care of the sick, lunatic and vagrant to be charged to the common fund. Even these developments did not prevent deep difficulties in financing the Poor Law in periods of distress – particularly in twenty-eight Lancashire unions facing the cotton famine in the early 1860s and London during the severe winters of 1860–1 and 1866–7. In these cases, a variety of emergency legislation – the Union Relief Act of 1862 (under which other country unions could be asked to provide funds), the Public Works Act of 1863 and the Metropolitan Poor Act of 1867 (which equalized the poor rates for London and placed the monies into the common fund) – was used to deal with the failure of parish relief.

In the end, however, it was two broader pieces of legislation that moved the basis of Poor Law finance from the parish to the union. The

Irremovable Poor Act of 1861 altered the basis of contributions to the common fund from the past levels of pauperism to the ability to pay based upon the value of property. The Union Chargeability Act of 1865 established union rating and made the relief of the poor chargeable to the common fund. At last, parish rating had been replaced by union rating and the principle of the ability to pay, based upon property values, had been established.

Settlement also proved intransigent to reform for some time. It caused dispute and litigation in the eighteenth and early nineteenth centuries and had been criticized by Malthus but remained an integral part of the New Poor Law. The Poor Law commissioners had examined and operated a variety of schemes to reduce the problem – most obviously, the attempts to encourage migration from the southern rural counties to the northern industrial counties and schemes to move poor families to the colonies – but these only dealt with a small part of the problem and were often ineffective. More important was the fact that local boards of guardians built up a network of reciprocal arrangements whereby they agreed to provide relief for the applicants of another union in return for the provision of non-resident relief. There were more than 82,000 persons receiving such relief in 1846, the year in which the Poor Removal Act conferred irremovability on those who had lived in a place for five years. This was reduced to three years in 1861 and one year in 1865. Some sense of proportion had to be instilled into a system that could be disproportionately expensive, as is illustrated by the case of the Halifax overseer who ran up a bill of £50 contesting the removal of a family from Elland, a bill which was far more expensive than that of relieving the pauper family.[49] Settlement became less of an issue as the nineteenth century progressed but, as Michael Rose reminds us, the law of settlement was more resilient than was often supposed.[50]

The need for compromise between local and central interests was always a factor that was going to inhibit the speedy introduction of central reform. Nonetheless, on the 'tidying up' issues of finance and settlement, the central authority gradually imposed some type of recognizable system, even if it could not impose the '1834 principles'. It also operated some control over petty regulations and had the power to block staff appointments and to permit certain types of expenditure. In the end, as Felix Driver has suggested, the relations between the central authority and the local Poor Law guardians were immensely complex and often varied from union to union. The central authority won on some issues but lost on others, often important ones. Yet it is difficult to conclude other than to suggest that in the early years of the New Poor Law the central authority was only able to progress at the rate allowed by the local guardians. If the local interests opposed central change, they simply ignored or bypassed its orders and regulations.

Apart from the issue of central and local control, there has also been significant discussion about the extent to which the New Poor Law was a cruel institution. The Andover scandal, which highlighted the fact that paupers were reduced to gnawing at rotting bones, and the Hoo workhouse scandal, involving the flogging of young girls, created the image of the workhouse as an instrument of cruelty wielded by the oppressive Poor Law authorities. The reality is that there is little evidence of physical cruelty being widespread. That such cases did occur is more a reflection of the fact that the Poor Law Commission and the Poor Law Board had limits to their powers.[51] Generally, indoor paupers were usually better fed and better housed than the poor who lived outside the workhouse. There were cases of local abuse but these were against the direction of central authority. Nonetheless, there is no doubt that the day-to-day regulations of the workhouse were cruel. The whole atmosphere of prison-like discipline and harsh regulations, the separation of families and the rigorous timetables were cruelties of a kind. Indeed, M. A. Crowther has suggested that the inhumanity revolved around a boring and tiresome routine.[52] Anne Digby makes much the same point. She argues that all six of the dietaries advocated for use in workhouses ensured that the inmates were better fed than the agricultural labourers in the rural South. Nonetheless, she accepts that the psychological harshness of the regime, which separated families and imposed a prison-like mentality, was cruel.[53] Ursula Henriques also suggests that the insensitivity of the system revealed a sense of cruelty.[54]

The real problems were ones of image and contradictory aims. At one and the same time the New Poor Law was to be both a deterrence and a provider of humane relief. It is true that these were to be developed in accordance with the different classifications of those to be relieved, but it is clear that this is not how the public mind perceived its presence. The workhouse soon became a forbidding institution in popular culture, to be avoided at all costs and if at all possible. Part of the reason for this was the changes in the 1860s and 1870s which paved the way to the 'principles of 1834' being applied more effectively and to the reduction in outdoor relief.

Nationally, rateable values began to grow rapidly during the second half of the nineteenth century, even if this was not necessarily the case in southern agricultural districts. They grew faster than relief expenditure and permitted the vast growth of spending that occurred in the 1860s, estimated at an average of 3.5 per cent per annum in the period between 1859–63 and 1869–73.[55] This occurred largely as a result of three pieces of legislation. Two of these, the Irremovable Poor Act of 1861 and the 1865 Union Chargeability Act, already referred to, established union rating and a rating system based upon property values. The third was the Union Assessment Committee Act of 1862 which ordered unions to form committees to supervise new valuations, and the move towards more uniform standards helped the process. The end product of these three Acts was that the cost of relief was increasingly moved from the poorer sections of society to the rich.[56] The burden of rates was also switched from the poorer to the richer parishes.[57] In addition, the 1869 Poor Law Loans Act allowed unions to increase their expenditure by extending their borrowing from twenty to thirty years.

Both Peter Wood and Michael Rose have observed that these Acts increased Poor Law spending, which provoked attempts to reduce expenditure by making it more difficult for individuals to obtain outdoor relief. The Goschen Minute of 1869 certainly provided the stimulus for change, advocating that philanthropic bodies such as the Charity Organisation Society (COS) should deal with some of those applying for outdoor relief. The fact that the number of those receiving outdoor relief was reduced markedly over the next thirty years, and that the COS took up very few cases, simply adds to the findings of both Rose and Wood. As a result, expenditure levels rose by only 0.3 per cent between 1869–73 and 1879–83 and remained broadly at the same levels until the years 1895–1914, when they rose again by 3.5 per cent per annum.[58] At the same time, the New Poor Law became more professional, as trained staff were employed to replace inmate staff and were more specifically geared towards meeting the problems of children, the old and the infirm.[59]

Conclusion

The argument offered in this chapter has already been outlined in the introduction. In all the debates the chief point to note is that there was always a tension between the central authority and the local parishes and unions in the eighteenth and nineteenth centuries which led to important compromises and variety in the application of the principles of the New Poor Law. Indeed, it was not until the late nineteenth century that the 'principles of 1834' were applied, by which time philanthropy, electoral reform and a rising humanitarian concern for the poor, particularly for children and the aged, were paving the way for further reform. In an increasingly pluralistic society, perhaps one should expect a tendency towards contradictory policies and actions and a situation in which central authority is not always able to achieve its objectives. Certainly, the universal application of one workhouse test and the principle of less eligibility proved impossible even in the 1870s. As will be indicated in later chapters, it was the state that eventually rescued the Poor Law in the early twentieth century – before abandoning it in its traditional form in 1929 and altogether in 1948.

The driving force of much, if not all, social policy was the need to tackle the failures of the Poor Law – to deal with the able-bodied unemployed, the young, the sick and the old.

Notes

1. This chapter does not deal with the Scottish Poor Law, which was run by the Board of Supervision, defined a specific role to voluntary bodies and denied relief to the able-bodied. In practice, both the English and Welsh and the Scottish system were variable and saw the accumulation of powers to the central body. For the Scottish system, see A. Paterson, 'The Poor Law in Nineteenth-Century Scotland', in D. Fraser (ed.), *The New Poor Law in the Nineteenth Century* (1976), pp. 171–93.

2. A. Digby, *The Poor Law in Nineteenth-Century England and Wales* (1982); F. Driver, *Power and Pauperism: The Workhouse System 1834–1884* (Cambridge, 1993); M. E. Rose, 'The Allowance System under the New Poor Law', *Economic History Review* 24 (1966); M. E. Rose, 'The Anti-Poor Law Agitation', in J. T. Ward (ed.), *Popular Movements (1830–1850)* (1970); M. E. Rose, *The English Poor Law 1780–1930* (Newton Abbot, 1971); M. E. Rose, *The Relief of Poverty 1834–1914* (London, 1972).

3. D. Ashforth, 'The Urban Poor Law', and A. Digby, 'The Rural Poor Law', in Fraser (ed.), *The New Poor Law*, pp. 128–48, 149–70.

4. P. Wood, 'Finance and the Urban Poor Law: Sunderland Union, 1836–1914', in M. Rose (ed.), *The Poor and the City: the English Poor Law in its Urban Context* (Leicester, 1985), pp. 20–56; P. Wood, *Poverty and the Workhouse in Victorian Britain* (Stroud, 1991).

5. K. Williams, *From Pauperism to Poverty* (1981).

6. M. E. Rose, 'The Crisis in Poor Relief in England, 1860–1914', in W. J. Mommsen (ed.), *The Emergence of the Welfare State in Britain and Germany* (1981), pp. 50–70.

7. D. Fraser, *The Evolution of the British Welfare State* (1984), p. 34.

8. Wood, *Poverty and the Workhouse*, p. 54.

9. *Ibid.*

10. Fraser, *Evolution*, p. 35.

11. J. D. Marshall, *The Old Poor Law, 1795–1834* (1968).

12. Fraser, *Evolution*, p. 38.

13. Wood, *Poverty and the Workhouse*, pp. 59–60; J. D. Marshall, 'The Nottinghamshire Reformers and their Contribution to the Old Poor Law', *Economic History Review* 13 (1961).

14. J. R. Poynter, *Society and Pauperism: English Ideas on Poor Relief 1795–1834* (1969).

15. *Annual Reports of the Halifax Workhouses, 1804–1811*, HAD, HAS 173, and *1811–1830*, HXT 191, deposited in the Calderdale Branch of West Yorkshire Archives based at Halifax.

16. Digby, *The Poor Law*, pp. 9–10.

17. M. A. Crowther, *The Workhouse System 1834–1929: The History of an English Social Institution* (Cambridge, 1983), p. 21.

18. *Report from His Majesty's Commissioners for Inquiry into the State of the Poor Laws in England and Wales*, Parliamentary Papers 1834 (44), xxvii. This has also been published, with an introduction by S. G. Checkland and E. O. A. Checkland (eds.), as *The Poor Law Report of 1834* (1974).

19. M. Blaug, 'The Myth of the Old Poor Law and the Making of the New', and 'The Poor Law Report Re-examined', *Journal of Economic History* 23 (1963) and 24 (1964); D. A. Baugh, 'The Cost of Poor Relief in South-East England', *Economic History Review*, 2nd ser., 28 (1975); D. McCloskey, 'New Perspectives on the Old Poor Law', *Exploration in Economic History* 10 (1973); J. P. Huzel, 'The Demographic Impact of the Old Poor Law', *Economic History Review*, 2nd ser., 33 (1980).

20. G. R. Boyer, *An Economic History of the English Poor Law 1750–1850* (Cambridge, 1990).

21. J. Bentham, *Pauper Management Improved: Particularly by Means of an Application of the Panopticon Principle of Construction*, ed. E. Chadwick (1812).

22. Fraser, *Evolution*, p. 47.

23. Wood, *Poverty and the Workhouse*, p. 71.

24. S. and B. Webb, *English Poor Law History, Pt. 1, The Old Poor Law* (1927), chapters 4 and 7; S. and B. Webb, *English Poor Law History, Pt. 2, The Last Hundred Years*, 2 vols. (1929), i, chapters 1 and 2. Also look at J. Redlich and F. W. Hirst, *The History of Local Government in England*, 2nd edn., ed. B. Keith-Lucas (1970, originally published 1903), pp. 103–16.

25. A. Brundage, 'The Landed Interest and the New Poor Law: A Reappraisal of the Revolution in Government', *English Historical Review* 87 (1972), pp. 27–48; A. Brundage, 'The English Poor Law and the Cohesion of Agricultural Society', *Agricultural History* 48 (1974), pp. 405–17; A. Brundage, *The Making of the New Poor Law: The Politics of Inquiry, Enactment and Implementation, 1832–1839* (1978), pp. 1–46, 105–44, 181–5.

26. Brundage, *The Making of the New Poor Law*, pp. 105–6, drawing from the Poor Law Commission Minutes, 12 and 14 November 1834, MH 1/1.

27. *Ibid.*, pp. 184–5.

28. P. Mandler, 'The Making of the New Poor Law Redivivus', *Past and Present* 117 (November 1987), pp. 131–57. Also look at A. Brundage, D. Eastwood and P. Mandler, 'Debate: The Making of the New Poor Law Redidivus', *Past and Present*, May 1990, pp. 183–201.

29. A. Digby, 'The Rural Poor Law', in Fraser (ed.), *The New Poor Law*, pp. 152–3; A. Digby, *Pauper Palaces* (1978), pp. 55–61; R. P. Hastings, *More Essays in North Riding History* (Northallerton, 1984), pp. 36–7.

30. Wood, *Poverty and the Workhouse*, p. 76.

31. D. Ashforth, 'The Treatment of Poverty', in D. G. Wright and J. A. Jowitt (eds.), *Victorian Bradford* (Bradford, 1982), pp. 81–100.

32. M. E. Rose, 'The Anti-Poor Law Movement in the North of England', *Northern History* 1 (1966), pp. 70–91; N. C. Edsall, *The Anti-Poor Law Movement 1834–1844* (Manchester, 1971); Driver, *Power and Pauperism*, pp. 112–30.

33. *Halifax Guardian*, 4 March 1837, 9 and 16 June 1838.

34. Driver, *Power and Pauperism*, p. 42.

35. Ashforth, 'Poverty', p. 92.
36. Driver, *Power and Pauperism*, p. 37.
37. *Ibid.*, pp. 38–40, 43, which contain three maps of the unionized and non-unionized areas of England and Wales. Also p. 49, quoting the case of *R* v. *Poor Law Commission* (re Allstonefield Incorporation), 11 Ad. & El. 558.
38. *Ibid.*, maps on pp. 43, 45.
39. A. Digby, *The Poor Law*, p. 16.
40. *Halifax Guardian*, 28 July and 17 November 1838, and a bundle of letters regarding a loan for the workhouse, HAS B/84/4, in the Calderdale Branch of West Yorkshire Archives, Calderdale Library, Halifax.
41. Williams, *From Pauperism to Poverty* (1981); Driver, *Power and Pauperism*.
42. Fraser, *Evolution*, pp. 52–3.
43. Ashforth, 'Poverty', p. 94.
44. J. Lindsay, 'The Problems of the Caernarfon Union Workhouse from 1846 to 1930', *Caernarvonshire Historical Transactions* 52–3 (1991–2), pp. 71–85.
45. Digby, *The Poor Law*, p. 21.
46. Fraser, *Evolution*, p. 52.
47. Williams, *From Pauperism to Poverty*.
48. Digby, *The Poor Law*, pp. 19–26.
49. M. E. Rose, 'Settlement, Removal and the New Poor Law', in Fraser (ed.), *The New Poor Law*, p. 35.
50. Fraser (ed.), *The New Poor Law*, p. 43.
51. D. Roberts, 'How Cruel was the Victorian Poor Law', *Historical Journal* (1963), p. 100.
52. Crowther, *The Workhouse System*, part II on the inmates.
53. Digby, *The Poor Law*, p. 17.
54. U. Henriques, 'How Cruel was the Victorian Poor Law?', *Historical Journal* 11 (1968).
55. Wood, 'Finance and the Urban Poor Law', p. 22.
56. Ashforth, 'Poverty', p. 91, notes that 77.4 per cent of all poor rate assessment in Bradford between 1848 and 1850 came from property with the low annual rateable value of under £6. Mills were rated very low and what was occurring is that relief was falling on the poor not the rich.
57. Wood, 'Finance and the Urban Poor Law', p. 46.
58. *Ibid.*, p. 22.
59. Crowther, *The Workhouse System*, chapter 6, pp. 135–55.

CHAPTER THREE

POLICING IN THE EARLY AND MID-NINETEENTH CENTURY

Policing became immensely important in England with the growth of industrial towns in the late eighteenth and early nineteenth centuries. At that time the modernization of the police became an urgent need to many contemporary writers and political commentators. The reason for their concern has been a matter of contentious debate. Those historians who have accepted the Whig interpretation of history, emphasizing progress and improvement, have suggested that the old parochial system was failing and that by the late eighteenth century England was facing a serious crime wave. The new police of the metropolitan force, the counties and the boroughs, were clear responses to that problem.[1] A similar view, but from an opposing political standpoint, has been presented by Marxist historians, who maintain that the police were seen as an answer to the problem of maintaining social order, rather than to curbing crime, in a rapidly growing industrial society.[2] Evidently, it was the control of the working classes and their movements that was the prime driving force behind change. Despite obvious differences, both interpretations see the police in functional terms, although the Whig traditionalists tend to stress the importance of the great men and ideas in confronting the crime wave, whilst the Marxists emphasize the class nature of the actions taken to preserve public order. In other words, the difference is whether or not the police were merely watchers or class warriors.

Although clearly not a Marxist, Stanley Palmer has also emphasized the public order function of policing, suggesting that modern policing developed to deal with Jacobins, Luddites, Chartists and the like rather than to deal with crime.[3] Research since the mid-1970s, much of which has been focused upon provincial communities, has also suggested that local conditions varied greatly and that cultural factors – such as past experience, the attitude of local officialdom, and the quality of the recruits – did much to shape the development of the new police at the local level. This research has done much to undermine the Whig notion that the metropolitan model was widely applied and has suggested that policing varied greatly in style, efficiency and effectiveness from region to region and between locality and locality.[4]

Thus the 'new police' have variously been presented as efficient policemen, class warriors, a sensible response to perceived political instability, and as a disparate group of forces which varied immensely in their efficiency and effectiveness. Recently, some of these views have been challenged by Clive Emsley.[5] The enormity of the challenge cannot be overestimated for, drawing upon recent research, he doubts that the old parochial system was inefficient or that the new police were more efficient than their predecessors, suggests that the police have always attempted to act by consent, even if they have always enforced a dominant ideology,[6] and that the perceived problem was 'a degree of social disorder and a degree of crime'.[7] In other words, he has discarded the established rival interpretations except for those which suggest cultural variability and a variety of responses.

This chapter will examine the various historical interpretations offered on the new police and will focus upon related issues such as crime statistics[8] as well as examine the ways in which government imposed discipline and social policy.[9] It will raise the issue of the effectiveness of the new policing, the character of the provincial and metropolitan forces and the degree to which the new police were accepted by the public. Its main contention is that Emsley is nearer the mark in suggesting that the parochial system was not necessarily inefficient, that the new police forces were not always dynamic and successful, and that local cultural factors greatly influenced the shape, focus and effectiveness – and acceptance – of local policing. As Emsley suggests: 'the English police developed their particular characteristics primarily because of the cultural and political environment in which they spent their formative years.'[10] It is also clear that the new police emerged because of the threat of social order just as much as the rising levels of crime.

Policing in the late eighteenth century and early nineteenth centuries: crime, public order and the old police

T. A. Critchley has made great play of the general decline of policing before 1800. He has traced the way in which constables emerged in Norman times to represent ten families, noted the changes in the twelfth and thirteenth centuries which saw the emergence of a parish watch of twelve men, and examined the rising social status of the constable in the fifteenth and sixteenth centuries and the subsequent decline of the office of constable in the eighteenth century. He has argued that, faced with an increasing concern about crime, many provincial communities applied for watching, paving and cleansing Acts – 200 towns and 100 parishes obtaining such powers in the late eighteenth and early nineteenth centuries.[11] Apparently, such action ran parallel to a growing concern about lawlessness in London which led Henry Fielding, chief magistrate of Bow Street in 1748, John Fielding, who succeeded him in that role until

1779, and Patrick Colquoun to suggest the need for significant reform. Henry Fielding attempted to raise the public awareness of police matters; John Fielding published several pamphlets, including *A Plea for Preventive Robberies within Twenty Miles of London*, which contained the idea that households should band together in groups of up to twenty to supply information on criminals to Bow Street; Colquoun published *A Treatise on the Police of the Metropolis* in 1797, which marshalled together statistics on crime and suggested the need for a preventive police force. Evidently, these reformers helped to encourage the development of the Bow Street Runners, who obtained that name in 1785, and the emergence of a small but reasonably efficient preventive force for London.

This traditional Whig view has come under stern criticism in recent years from a variety of writers and, most obviously, from Ruth Paley, who suggests that neither John Fielding nor Colquoun exerted much influence upon police reform in London: 'My own study of Patrick Colquoun suggests that he, too, was a man of little or no influence in government circles.'[12] There was, in any case, a widespread hostility to the idea of a police force, along French lines, that might threaten English liberties. Moreover, as Paley suggests, whilst the watch forces of London were fragmented into eighty or so local government units, that did not mean that they were inefficient. Indeed:

> By 1829, almost all urban parishes had reorganised their watch by means of local acts. The provisions of such acts were not uniform but the principles on which they were based were as follows: each abandoned the principle of voluntary service enjoined by the Statute of Winchester, and had substituted a force paid for the local rates.[13]

She doubts whether the Metropolitan Police Act of 1829 did much to bring about an improvement in London policing, suggesting that most of the pre-1829 force were men under 40 years of age and that the new force was faced with a high turnover of personnel, more than 3,000 in the first two years, which reduced its effectiveness and led to objections about the poor quality of the new police.[14] Indeed, the destruction of the parochial watch and the substitution of the more expensive and no more efficient new police caused great criticism. Given that the 1829 Act had little to do with the poor state of policing in London, Paley speculates that it probably had more to do with two other factors. The first is the fact that 6,000 of the 22,000 troops in England were tied down by disturbances in the northern district and the creation of the metropolitan police force helped the government to deal with its domestic difficulties.[15] The second is that much of the initiative for reform came from Peel, who attempted to apply his experience of being Chief Secretary in Ireland, where he learned to distrust local structures, to the reform of police in England.[16]

Paley has quite clearly shattered any illusion that the 1829 Act was a product of concern about policing in London. There is, undoubtedly, much evidence of concern about lawlessness and the threat to public order but little statistical evidence to suggest that there was 'a general decline in policing'. Nevertheless, there was a rising anxiety about crime and disorder in the eighteenth century. The Gordon riots of 1780, which placed London in the hands of an anti-Catholic mob for several days and saw the burning of the magistrates' Bow Street office, served to encourage such concerns.[17] More immediately, the Queen Caroline riots of 1820–1, which were seen as a popular triumph revealing the ineffectiveness of the police, intensified the need for action.

Evidence of rising crime statistics in England in the early nineteenth century also fuelled these fears. Between 1805 and 1848 'serious crime, as registered by committals to trial at assizes and quarter sessions, increased sixfold while the population doubled'.[18] These increases did not include the far more numerous petty offences, such as common assaults and drunk and disorderly behaviour. Palmer has attempted to measure the extent of crime and notes that the widening of summary offences produced twice the level of committals (the filing of criminal charges) by mid-century. Extrapolating backwards for the statistics from 1857 (following the 1856 Police Act which created a national record of indictable offences), he suggests that only three out of every five indictable offences led to committals. Thus the incidence of major crime seems to have increased tenfold rather than sixfold. Whilst there is evidence to suggest that the new metropolitan force did discourage major crime,[19] it is clear to Gattrell and Hadden that the new forces 'were scarcely effective at a national scale by the 1850s' and that the constables' vigilance, or lack of it, 'scarcely influenced at all' local rates of committals for indictable offences.[20] Nevertheless, the number of indictable offences may well have been artificially inflated by the reduction in the number of capital offences and a number of measures easing the cost of prosecution.

The fact is that industrial society appears to have brought about an increasing opportunity for crime, a rising level of larceny and the potential for even greater social conflict. This was most evident in the rising crime statistics of the industrial counties and the general trend, on a smaller scale, appears to have been evident in rural counties as well.

There was clearly a general trend towards rising crime levels. Nonetheless, recent research suggests that the parish watch was reasonably effective in dealing with normal crimes in London and that the same was also true of the parish watch throughout England. The beadles, watchmen, parish constables and JPs of the old system covered 40 English counties and 25,000 parishes. They were probably ineffective against organized criminal gangs and serious public disorder but were quite

Table 3.1   Committals for trials for Cumberland, Westmorland and Lancashire, 1811–1851 [21]

| | No. of Committals | | | Committals per 100,000 population | | | |
Year	Cumberland	Westmorland	Lancashire	Cumberland	Westmorland	Lancashire	England & Wales
1811	17	5	563	12.7	10.9	64.1	51.7
1812	53	9	661	40.0	19.8	79.5	62.7
1820	55	17	1898	36.0	33.0	180.2	115.2
1821	66	18	1963	42.3	34.3	186.4	108.3
1822	50	14	1718	32.5	27.2	163.1	99.4
1830	74	22	2028	43.8	39.8	152.4	131.2
1831	74	17	2352	43.8	30.8	168.3	140.4
1832	75	28	2624	44.3	50.7	196.4	147.0
1840	131	38	3506	73.6	67.2	210.3	172.8
1841	151	33	3987	84.8	58.3	239.1	174.3
1842	115	39	4497	64.6	70.7	269.7	194.1
1850	146	76	3340	74.8	130.1	164.4	150.9
1851	153	62	3459	78.5	123.3	170.3	155.5

Committals per 100,000 population, 1811–1851

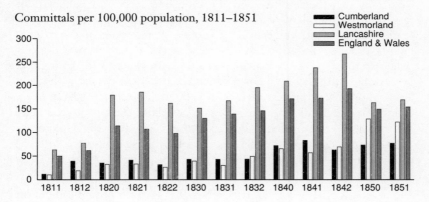

effective in dealing with the normal range of criminal activities. David Philips has noted, in his study of policing in the 'Black Country' in South Staffordshire and part of South-West Worcestershire, that:

> The image of the ... parish constable, quite inadequate for the task he had to perform, is so firmly fixed in most historical accounts that they [historians] never seem to ask why, if that was the case, the system continued to work until the 1840s without any serious breakdown of law and order in those communities which relied on parish constables. The system had many flaws, but it coped with much of 'normal' crime and small-scale disturbances. [22]

Philips also found that his Black Country constables were farmers in the rural parishes and small tradesmen and artisans in the towns, who served for many years and regarded themselves as full-time policemen. Until the 1840s the vast majority of those committed to trial in the Black Country were apprehended by parish constables; and in Staffordshire men were appointed to this office until 1865.[23] These men seem to have earned the respect of the community, often knew the name of the offenders, could call upon their neighbours for help and found that those they apprehended 'nearly always did as bidden'.[24]

It is also possible that in England as a whole the absence of public prosecutors until 1879 may reflect the efficiency of private prosecutions and of the old system of policing. The fact is that there appears to have been a well-organized system of parish constables in some areas, supported by a variety of voluntary institutions. Local constables were supported by the 450 or so Associations for the Prosecution of Felons that emerged in England between 1744 and 1856. These were funded by private subscription and run by small property owners. Yet it is not easy to establish how widespread this picture of effectiveness was, since there have been few studies of the parish constable system.

Why, then, was the new police force formed? There is the interesting possibility that the reforms were a response to increasing expectations regarding the standard of security and that previously accepted levels of disorder were no longer to be tolerated. It may well be the case, as Palmer and Paley argue and Emsley implies, that the creation of the new police of the late 1830s had more to do with the control of popular protest than with the breakdown of law and order connected with rising levels of normal criminal activity. To Palmer: 'The spur to police innovations in the 1830s was the threat of working-class protest.'[25] The events that led to Peterloo, followed by the 'Captain Swing' violence of 1830, the protests over the 1832 Reform Bill, those connected with the transportation of the 'Tolpuddle Martyrs', the protests against the New Poor Law in parts of the North and South between 1835 and 1838, especially in the smaller, unchartered towns of northern England, and the Chartist disturbances of the late 1830s and the 1840s were motive enough to encourage administrative changes. The Chartist disturbances were certainly important in the passing of the Rural Constabulary Act of 1839. Nonetheless, it is noticeable that little was said about disorder when the Municipal Corporation Act was passed in 1835.

Most certainly, the borough police emerged to replace the old system as part of the administrative clean-up that was represented by the Municipal Corporation Act of 1835 and the rural or country police forces came into existence from 1839 onwards as part of an attempt to deal with the Chartist disorders and was the brain-child of both Edwin Chadwick and Charles Rowan. Indeed, Palmer suggests that:

In this sense, the numerous petitioners of the Constabulary Force Commission (1836–9) who protested that crime in their area was under control missed the political point. If most authorities were dealing adequately, if also under increasing strain with the war against normal crime, this would help to explain why the adoption of the borough and county forces was so piecemeal, so gradual after 1835–9. In this interpretation local resistance was not simply spiteful, self-interested, or hysterically constitutional. The fear of crime, whipped up by their lurid statements in Chadwick's Constabulary Commission report of 1839 had been overplayed by most police historians. There was, however, one important duty for which, all can agree, the myriad local institutions *were* hopelessly inadequate: the control of large scale or widespread public disorder.[26]

The point is well made if one looks at the size of the pre-reform northern towns in England. The fact is that the tiny forces employed by most towns found it impossible to control crowds and riots. The Bradford force, although it had been increased slightly at the time of the Bradford incorporation in 1847, was grossly inadequate to deal with the Chartist disturbances of April, May and June 1848. It was stressed that 'The police dare not venture into it [Bradford] without being supported by the military ...'[27] An attempt to arrest the Chartist ringleaders failed because 'Briggs (Superintendent of the East Division of Morley and used in this operation because the Bradford superintendent was down with a fever) had got drunk and failed to give proper orders to special constables. One man arrested for drilling. 17 men and one woman for rioting.'[28] In the end it was the military who did most to arrest the Chartist leaders and to send them to trial at York.[29]

It was in this climate of fear about public order, as well as the rising level of crime, that the process of reform was promoted. In the first instance, there was great emphasis upon modernizing the metropolitan forces and then on the provincial forces, both urban and rural. What emerged, despite the Whiggish beliefs of some historians, was not one system of policing gradually to replace the old system, but three systems which overlapped with the remnants of the past. There was the metropolitan force, formed in 1829 and responsible to the Home Secretary; the borough forces run by the watch committees of the local borough council; and the county forces, subject to the unelected officialdom of the magistrates who were controlled by no more than the ratepayers' concerns for expenditure which might lead to petitions.

The metropolitan model

The Metropolitan Police Act of 1829 did not come out of the blue. The new police had appeared in Ireland in the late eighteenth century but

Table 3.2   Pre-reform police in northern towns in England, 1835–1838 [30]

Town	No. of constables	No. of nightwatchmen	1841 population
Liverpool	44	130	286,500
Manchester	30	150	235,000
Birmingham	30	170	182,900
Bradford	4	–	66,700
Salford	5	22	53,000
Bolton	10	–	51,000
Preston	5	–	50,900
Oldham	2	5	43,000
Blackburn	3	–	36,600
Halifax	4	–	27,500
Wigan	–	14	25,500
Rochdale	3	13	24,300
Ashton-under-Lyne	4	–	22,700
Stalybridge	6	–	20,000
Wakefield	3	11	18,800
Burnley	1	9	14,200

Liverpool, Preston and Wigan were incorporated towns in 1835; Manchester, Birmingham and Bolton were incorporated in 1838, but their charter was legally contested.

had not been imposed in England for fear of challenging and under-mining the historic rights and liberties of Englishmen. Yet a combi-nation of rising crime levels and public disorder seems to have paved the way for change. The statistics on crime which Sir Robert Peel presented to Parliament indicated a large increase in the number of people being committed to gaol.[31] Whether these figures rose due to improved policing or to increased crime must still remain a matter for conjecture, although the rising level of economic opportunity in a developing industrial society must have added to this situation largely through the periodic slumps that occurred. Indeed, Gattrell and Hadden have sug-gested that crime increased in times of depression and declined in periods of prosperity.[32]

Peel's experience as Chief Secretary in Ireland meant that he was fully aware of the new experiments in policing there and he was prepared to take action in a way that Viscount Sidmouth, the Home Secretary he replaced in 1822, was not. In December 1826 a Home Office inquiry into the London police emphasized the failures of the system and Peel came up with ideas similar to those introduced into the Dublin police in 1786 and 1808: to form a city with a single police district of ten miles' radius, to divide it into six divisions and to place a 'divisional magistrate' in charge of all constables and watchmen. The scheme foundered quickly due to the end of Lord Liverpool's administration. But with the return of Wellington's government in January 1828, Peel returned to the Home Office and revived his scheme. A select committee met between March and May 1828 and reported in July 1828. It recommended that a single metropolitan police district be formed and a police officer appointed under the immediate control of the Home Secretary. The Metropolis Police Improvement Bill was introduced into the House of Commons in 15 April 1829, went through without a division, was directed through the Lords by Wellington and received royal assent on 19 June 1829. There was very little debate on this most important piece of legislation.

This Act raised a single metropolitan rate to finance a metropolitan force to operate in the ten-mile radius from Charing Cross, except for the City of London, under the control of Colonel Charles Rowan, a retired Irish military officer, and Richard Meyne, an Irish barrister, who became the two 'Commissioners of Police'. The force was to be based at 4 Whitehall Place, which backed on to a narrow lane known as Scotland Yard, and the force was to consist of about 3,000 men. As it evolved, the new metropolitan force attempted to give the impression that it was not a standing army. The policemen were not to be armed, except with staves (although divisional inspectors could carry pocket-pistols) and the force was to consist of men under 35 years of age whose height was not less than 5 feet 7 inches and who were both physically and mentally fit. They would earn about three shillings per day or £50 per year.

Initially, the creation of the new force did not go ahead without major problems. The turnover was enormous: of the first 2,800 constables enrolled, 2,238 were dismissed – 1,790 for drunkenness.[33] Between 33 and 40 per cent of the force were dismissed each year and, with resignations, more than half the force left each year. The constables complained of long hours and low pay, and there was a lack of training, prospects of promotion and higher pay.

Nonetheless, the new metropolitan force was the most effective police force ever created, even if it was because of the sheer numbers of men rather than the improved efficiency of the individual officers. It also produced a mixed impression upon the mind. There is no doubting Storch's suggestion that the new police created working-class antagonism in many industrial towns and London. The 'Blue Idlers', 'Blue Devils', 'Blue Drones' and the 'Unboiled Lobsters', descriptions derived from their new uniforms, were unpopular amongst the poor and the working classes in London and became the object of hostile ridicule in the provinces also, where they were sent sometimes in periods of disturbance. They also sparked off some opposition from small shopkeepers and radicals on the basis that the metropolitan force was costly and unconstitutional. Indeed, the metropolitan force did cost an average of £207,000 per year between 1830 and 1832, compared with an annual cost of £137,000 for the pre-1829 parochial force.[34] They also appeared to offer a challenge to English liberties when they were used in maintaining public order in the 1830s, whether in events connected with the 1832 Reform Bill or the 1834 meeting at Copenhagen Fields held in support of the Tolpuddle Martyrs. Nevertheless, the new police were increasingly accepted by the middle classes, who began to see them as an antidote to both crime and disorder. They were probably unable to impose the social control that some interested parties expected of them but by the 1850s, when economic conditions were improving, they were nevertheless able to impose the rule of law and 'began to pierce and destroy the criminal rookeries'.[35]

There was a hope, raised by Edwin Chadwick and some of his Benthamite supporters, that the new metropolitan force would be the basis of the national system. In fact, individual rights and interests were so jealously guarded that this was not to be. Both the boroughs and the counties developed their own alternative systems.

The borough forces

The borough police forces were the result of changes from an entirely different direction and no metropolitan blueprint was applied. It was the reform of the 246 town corporations investigated by a select committee that led to the Municipal Corporations Act of 1835. Clause 76 of the Act required that borough councils each establish a watch committee, which was to appoint paid constables and watchmen. It was thus the locality, not central government, that was to exert control over policing in the provincial borough. The Home Office simply received quarterly reports about pay, appointments and regulations.

About forty years ago Jenifer Hart acknowledged that government records could not give precise figures for the early borough police forces and noted that it was not until the HM Inspectors of Constabulary Reports appeared after 1856 that accurate information became available. Nevertheless, she estimated that there were between 3,600 and 4,100 borough police in 1846, 4,325 and 4,425 in 1853 and a minimum of 4,780 policemen in 1856 – all figures which she suggests are slight underestimates, since not all boroughs have full police records.[36] She further suggested that police reform in the provincial towns was slow because of a number of reasons, including the opposition of people who felt that the new police were a challenge to English liberties, the parsimonious attitude of many watch committees, the poor quality of the recruits and other factors. This seminal work has provoked intense debate. Historians have focused upon the reasons for the formation of the new borough police, the efficiency of the new bodies and the extent to which they were accepted by the public. As already suggested, they have divided into Whig historians,[37] who saw the unreformed system being replaced with a far more efficient police force based upon the metropolitan model, and others, who have seen police reform as only part of the extension of controls over the working class which provoked popular hostility[38] or who have suggested that there was no pattern to the reform because of cultural variations. Recent research suggests that there was immense variation between one borough and another.

Clearly, some boroughs took their responsibilities more seriously than others. Liverpool had a force of 590 men in 1839 and 822 by 1848. Manchester had 343 policemen in 1839 and 447 in 1848. At the other extreme, Leeds had a force of only 20 in 1836 and 112 in 1839, and York, advised to start with a force of 24, had 12 policemen in 1836 and 27 in 1856. Some of the smaller towns had far fewer policemen. Stockport, with 13 policemen, had a ratio of 1:3,806 inhabitants in the early 1840s; Wigan, with 6 policemen, had a ratio of 1:4,097 and Bolton, with 10 policemen, had a ratio of 1:4,834. It took time for these ratios to improve, although by 1855 Middlesbrough had a ratio of 1:1,375,[39] Manchester (1853) a ratio of 1:547 and Bolton (1853) of 1:2,346. Table 3.3 also reveals the immense variation between the size and expenditure on borough forces in Yorkshire.

These variations arose from the fact that each watch committee adopted different policies. The majority appear to have acted immediately to form a police force but there were laggards. Hart has suggested that of the 178 corporations initially subject to the Municipal Corporations Act, only 108 had formed police forces between about 1835 and 1839. A total of 155 had formed police forces by 1853, the details of 17 are unknown, and 6 boroughs had no police force in 1853.

Table 3.3   Size and expenditure on Yorkshire borough forces, 1853 [40]

Borough	No. of police	Cost of police (£)
Leeds	152	9,137
York	22	1,350
Doncaster	9	556
Scarborough	5	234
Richmond	4	90
Pontefract	4	108
Bradford	111	5,005
Wakefield	21	1,263

In addition, all the 19 boroughs incorporated between 1835 and 1853 had formed forces within two years of incorporation.[41]

In some towns – such as Birmingham, where there were Chartist meetings in August 1838 and in April 1839 – the creation of a force was rapid not least because the government decided that, irrespective of the creation of municipal authorities, the Chartist threat to local order was too great to be left to the actions of a local watch committee.[42] Birmingham was granted a charter of incorporation on 31 October 1838 and was forming a police force in September 1839[43] but, like Manchester and Bolton, was subject to temporary government legislation whereby the force was headed by a police commissioner directly responsible to the Home Secretary.[44] The first pay sheet for the new force, at the end of 1839, indicates that it employed one inspector at 38s. 6d. (£1.92½p) per week, one inspector at 29s. 2d. (£1.46p), four sergeants at 21s. (£1.05p) and two constables at 17s. 1d. (85p). It developed quickly thereafter, advertising for young men under 36 years of age and more than 5 feet 8 inches in height. By 1 November 1839 the force was 260 strong.[45] On 20 November 1839 the new police force took over the policing of Birmingham. The old police and watch systems ended and the metropolitan police who had been in Birmingham since July 1839 to counter the Chartist threat returned to London. The Birmingham force was pushed up to just short of 400 before the commissioner resigned and handed over power to the Birmingham Watch Committee on 1 October 1842.[46]

Many forces did not have the size, or professional edge, of the Birmingham police. In some boroughs the new police force simply continued as the nightwatch rather than as policemen and in many the police constables were allowed to hold other jobs. Indeed, as late as 1852 the policemen of Bath and Liverpool, both quite well-organized and numerous forces, were allowed this opportunity.

Despite some obvious general features of the new borough police forces, our knowledge of their effectiveness, efficiency and public acceptance still remains rather skimpy. There have, in fact, been relatively few detailed studies of the 190 or so boroughs that had police forces by the mid-1850s. Eric Midwinter has made brief excursions into the condition of the borough police in Lancashire, and some theses have noted the changes that were brought about.[47] Beyond this, and some general regional studies, there are no more than a handful or so academic studies of the new borough police. Some of the best recent work has been undertaken by Roger Swift, who has examined policing in York, Wolverhampton and Exeter.[48] He has suggested that policing in these boroughs was immensely variable. In general, he found that the efficiency of the police was still low in the 1850s, as Jenifer Hart suggested, but that the industrial community of Wolverhampton seems to have reformed itself more quickly than did York or Exeter. Indeed, the change-over to the new police in the latter two communities was apparently more cosmetic than real, for the traditional pattern of policing, including parish and special constables, continued to function well into the mid-nineteenth century. He also argues that the fears about the new police were real but differed from community to community – although the desire for local control was always paramount. Swift's more detailed individual study of police reform in early Victorian York is also a major endorsement of Hart's view that 'in most boroughs the reform of the police was gradual ... and the level of efficiency still low in the 1850s'.[49] Financial restrictions and the intense parochialism of the city council's approach to policing meant that York's new police were badly organized and barely distinguishable from the old police.

The obvious, but difficult, question to answer is how effective were these borough forces? The changing composition of crime statistics, let alone their survival, make this difficult to measure. The fact that crime went up during economic depression and that additional numbers of police led to the increased recording of crime make it difficult to estimate whether such increases or decreases suggest improved or worsening efficiency. Studies of individual boroughs are barely more revealing, since they indicate variation between community and community, although they do tend to suggest some degree of police efficiency.

In York the crime statistics are patchy, since police occurrence books only survive for the years 1842–5, and in incomplete form. A study of quarter sessions and assize calendars, prison records and the like suggests that the York police brought 'a vast amount of crime to light between 1836 and 1856', appear to have discouraged petty crime and to have restricted serious crimes to only gradual growth between 1835 and 1856, during which time the population of York had increased by about 30 per cent.[50] The support of voluntary bodies such as the Association for the Protection of Property in York and its Neighbourhood and the decision to maintain surveillance on known criminals seem to have had a good effect and the York police were not faced with any riots or major public disturbances between 1835 and 1856. York appears to have been a relatively orderly city and the new police contributed to this by their attack on petty crime.

The situation in Middlesbrough seems to have been somewhat different. In the absence of a series of accurate crime statistics, it appears that: 'There is little evidence that the new police in Middlesbrough had a great impact on crime itself in these years [1835 to 1855], at least not until the last three years under review.'[51]

On balance, then, the borough forces appear to have been immensely variable in their organisation, size and effectiveness. Their degree of public acceptability seems to have been equally variable and confused, as a later section will emphasize. Nevertheless, one should note that whilst the metropolitan police and the borough police forces dealt with a significant urban population, there were many towns that had not been incorporated and rural districts which continued to operate the old policing system.

The rural and county forces

The concern about the resistance to the New Poor Law, the rise of Chartism and other threats to public disorder also appears to have stimulated an attempt to improve the quality of policing in the rural and non-borough districts. A government commission on policing, appointed in October 1836 at the height of Poor Law riots, reported in March 1839. This body of three commissioners was dominated by Edwin Chadwick and Charles Rowen, the London police commissioner, and its outcome, the *Constabulary Report*, was essentially Chadwick's creation. Chadwick claimed that criminals were moving from urban into rural areas to avoid the new police, a point refuted forty years ago by Hart, and suggested that the parish constables were illiterate and incapable of dealing with crime and public order.[52] The solution was to create a country-wide police force. It was to be unarmed, to consist of about 8,000 men, and to be controlled by the metropolitan police commissioners and the Home Office. Three-quarters of the cost would come from the county rates and the rest from the government.

There was an immediate reaction from the county magistrates who, by and large, suggested that the recommendations were only acceptable if the police forces remained in county hands. The County Police (Rural Constabulary) Act that emerged in August 1839 was a step back from Chadwick's personal preferences. Counties were encouraged to form forces, but it was left to the quarter sessions of each county to decide whether or not to set up a county force, the size of that force and the appointment of a chief constable (not commissioner). The government simply set a minimum height of 5 feet 7 inches for the size of policemen and stipulated that recruits should be under 45 years of age.

In fact, the permissive nature of this legislation meant that only eight counties (including Durham, Lancashire and Worcestershire) adopted the Act in 1839, twelve in 1840 and four in 1841. Only four more counties adopted the Act between 1841 and 1856. Many rural southern counties decided not to set up a force at all. Apart from the slow and patchy development of county forces, there were, as with the borough forces, great disparities between the forces as to size and effectiveness. Whilst Lancashire developed a force of more than 500 men (502 in 1839 and 593 in 1856), Yorkshire (East Riding) had a force of 9 between 1849 and 1856 and Rutland (formed in 1849) maintained a force of 1 constable.[53]

An insight into the problem of creating the county forces is given by David Foster in an article which deals with both the East and North Ridings of Yorkshire.[54] He argues that the magistrates of both Ridings were unwilling to provide Chadwick with evidence for his *Constabulary Report*, assumed that the small amount of serious crime came from thieves who issued forth from towns to commit crimes and then returned to their town bases, and rejected the Rural Constabulary Act on grounds of economic cost rather than constitutional principles. In effect, then, the magistrates decided in 1839 that the two Ridings, covering more than 3,000 square miles and about 300,000 people, would be run under the old parish constable system. Whether the old policing arrangements were inefficient, which Foster implies, must remain an open question given recent research which suggests that in London and in some towns and counties the old policing arrangements worked well in dealing with crime if not disturbance.

Reaction to the police

There is no doubt that the emergence of the new borough and rural police was greeted with some hostility and much indifference. That may have been for a number of reasons: because they seemed to challenge the rights of Englishmen, that they were dominated by ex-army officers or because they were seen to be a weapon of social control in dealing with the working classes. Certainly, some historians, such as Storch, see the police as weapons of class oppression. John Foster, a Marxist historian, has argued that the Parish Constables Act (1842) was part of the process of taking power out of the hands of the radical vestries and putting it into those of the parish constables who would be responsible to the chief constable of the particular county.[55] To Foster, the Act was clearly more than the regularization and revival of a dying system.

To Foster and Storch, the resentment of the working class towards the new police stems from the fact that, whilst minor working-class misdemeanours tended to be ignored by the old system, the police were now acting as 'domestic missionaries', picking up vagrants, proscribing loud talking and operating the 'move-on system'. It is suggested that their purpose became to transform the police into well-organized, sober and diligent workers. This view finds some support from Clive Emsley, who feels that the police were expected to act as 'domestic missionaries' and did bring about a greater strictness in the enforcement of new levels of decorum and order on the streets.[56] Nevertheless, given the work of Storch which suggests that there was resistance to this influence, and observing that the police experienced a high turnover of staff in the years between 1829 and the 1850s, it seems doubtful whether the police carried much social influence in early Victorian society. The fact is that the early police commissioners, watch committees and chief constables faced a very serious problem of domesticating their own police forces, never mind the community at large. This, according to Carolyn Steedman and Peter Bramham, does not seem to have occurred until the late nineteenth century.[57]

Nevertheless, there appear to have been marked regional and local differences in attitudes towards the police. In large industrial towns such as Leeds, Bradford, Birmingham and Oldham, there was opposition to the presence of the new police, as Storch and Foster have suggested. In other areas, where new and rapid industrial growth was less evident and where the new policing differed little from the old, the hostility may have been less. Indeed, the new police appear to have been accepted by the inhabitants of York, perhaps because they were almost the same as the old police, and there was not the popular hostility experienced in the industrial towns of the Midlands and the North.[58] According to Swift:

> the evidence suggests that the 'new police' were regarded as merely an agent of traditional authority in York, and the process of police reform in the city poses a question mark against the 'conflict view' of police history. Whilst the social control interpretation of borough policing is certainly a tenable one in the context of the great industrial and manufacturing communities of early Victorian England, it is perhaps a persuasive hypothesis when applied to those towns and cities which were relatively untouched by the Industrial Revolution.[59]

There may have been differences between the large industrial and 'traditional' urban communities, but in the end the new reformed police were accepted.[60] This was certainly the case by the 1860s and 1870s, if not in the early Victorian period. The use of the police to deal with Chartism, the 'Plug Plot' disturbances of 1842 and other public order disturbances was more than enough to explain working-class resistance and hostility to the new police until mid-century. That conflict became less thereafter, when moves were being made to provide a more comprehensive, professional and stable police force. Indeed, it appears that some 'respectable' working-class men and women welcomed the police and were prepared to use them and the legal system for their own ends. This can be seen in both the quarter session and petty session records for both Middlesbrough and the Black Country.[61]

Reform in the 1850s

The police reforms of the mid-1850s were initiated by Viscount Palmerston (Home Secretary, 1853–4), Sir George Grey (Palmerston's Home Secretary, 1855–8) and Edwin Chadwick. They were framed within the context of war and changes in the law. Post-Crimean war fears of a footloose ex-soldiery roaming the countryside and some equally real concerns following the 1853 Penal Servitude Act and the phasing out of transportation were key factors in the build-up to the 1856 County and Borough Police Act.

Palmerston had appointed a select committee on the police in April 1853. It drew evidence from fifty-seven witnesses, mainly county police officers and county magistrates who were favourable to the new police. It recommended that the police should be made compulsory in all counties, that small borough forces should be consolidated with the surrounding county forces, and that central government should help to pay for the new and extended system of policing.

The 1854 'General Police' Bill followed these recommendations by suggesting that there should be four government 'Inspectors' to supervise the borough and county forces, but this was met by strong opposition, was revamped several times and eventually withdrawn. It was revived in the spring of 1856, when Sir George Grey was Home Secretary in Palmerston's administration. He compromised on the 1856 Bill, most obviously in making it optional for any borough, whether with a population of under or over 20,000, to consolidate with the county force. The appointment of borough constables also remained with the watch committee and was not to be transferred to the chief constable. Yet the Home Office was empowered to frame 'general regulations' and the four salaried 'Government Inspectors of Constabulary' were empowered to authorize that a quarter of the cost of pay and clothing to boroughs and counties would be reimbursed by the Treasury for those forces certified as 'efficient'.

There was opposition even to this amended measure but in the end the threat of agitation posed by the return of troops after the Crimean war,[62] the rising level of disturbances and some concern about crime levels were sufficient to see the Bill onto the statute books. Both Palmer and Emsley also agreed that the experience of the new policing since 1829 had undermined the fear that the police would develop a network of spies and act as a force of oppression.[63] Indeed, Emsley concludes, in a wider perspective, that:

> The police have always enforced a dominant ideology; they have the power of coercion, but they have generally preferred to act by consent. It might be argued that the claims of the police to protect the ordinary law-abiding citizen whatever his wealth or social status are a form of deception, given that so much power in the hands of the few ... Alternatively, without accepting the Whig consensual view of English politics and society but recognising where power lay within that society, it seems more realistic to conceive of the law and the

police as multi-faceted institutions used by Englishmen of all classes to oppose each other, to cooperate with, and to gain the concessions from, each other.[64]

The County and Borough Police Act of 1856 was clearly important because it obliged all counties to set up police forces and offered a 25 per cent Treasury grant to all county and borough forces that obtained a government efficiency certificate. In other words, it ensured that there would be modern police cover for the whole country. The populous West Riding of Yorkshire was thus forced to form a force in 1856. Also, the new standards it imposed were a shock to the existing forces and did encourage improvements. This is evident in the case of York. It was widely believed that the York force would easily pass an inspection but Colonel James Woodford's visit of November 1856 did not go well. His report suggested that the force was poorly dressed and equipped, badly accommodated and failing in other respects. The York police were deemed to be inefficient. Woodford's second inspection in July 1857 was little better and he noted that 19 of the 29 constables had less than one year's experience. York then changed its attitude, declared its intention to open a new police station and was subsequently given a certificate of efficiency in April 1858. It gained its 25 per cent Treasury grant after much shock, debate and persuasion.

York was thus forced to improve its performance in order to qualify for the Treasury grant. The early returns from Her Majesty's Inspector of Police show that not all did so immediately and that there was immense variation between forces in response to the 1856 Act. David Taylor's recent research reveals that by 1862 the police and population ratios had improved considerably upon those of ten or twenty years before, as indicated in Table 3.4, although some forces were still operating at more than twice the ratios of the better-organized borough forces. Marked differences were also evident in the comments of the Inspector of Police. In 1859 the Bradford force was considered to be a 'well chosen [&] active body of men' and in 1860 they were described as

Table 3.4 Police/population ratios for some Yorkshire boroughs, 1862

Borough	Police/pop. ratio	Borough	Police/pop. ratio
Huddersfield	1:738	Halifax	1:1,000
Bradford	1:892	York City	1:1,009
Leeds	1:908	Doncaster	1:1,264
Wakefield	1:927	Scarborough	1:1,671
Sheffield	1:969		

a 'well formed, healthy and effective body of men'. However, problem forces still remained. Indeed, in 1860 the Leeds force was described as containing:

> a considerable number of men [who] do not seem to have been chosen for their qualifications or physical ability ... there are others, who from age and long service, seem to be pretty well worn out and no longer capable of officially and satisfactorily performing their duties.[65]

Although many forces still had a high turnover of manpower, in the order of 40 and 50 per cent over one and two years,[66] they were gradually and perceptibly brought into line. Eventually, as Steedman suggests, the police began to develop a sense of identity and evolved significantly between 1856 and 1880.[67]

The social composition and turnover of the police

Whilst the quantity of policing was variable and often inadequate until 1856 and beyond, the quality was also suspect. One of the major problems for any force was the high turnover of manpower. As already indicated, this was case for the metropolitan force when it was first formed in 1829. Thirty years later, in the early 1860s, the annual turnover of the force was still about one-sixth of those recruited.[68] The borough police faced a similar problem. Force Orders for Birmingham up to 4 July 1841 show that 358 men had been dismissed, 273 had resigned, died or been medically discharged. Out of 1,019 men who had been recruited since the inception of the force in 1839, only 388 remained.[69] In York there were 150 appointments between 1836 and 1856 and 104 departures. Of those who left, 58 had resigned and 42 had been dismissed.[70] The average length of service of recruits to the West Riding County Constabulary in 1856–9 was 5.9 years, but 41 per cent had left within their first year of service and 52 per cent had left after two years.[71] The situation was similar in Buckinghamshire and Staffordshire between 1856 and 1880.[72]

Part of the reason for this turnover was the high level of dismissals. Percentages of 40–50 per cent for dismissals were not uncommon, as is apparent in the case of York, although it was only 22 per cent in the newly formed West Riding County Constabulary between 1856–9.[73] In Buckinghamshire the percentage appears to have been 46–55 per cent for first-year recruits between 1856 and 1880, although dismissal levels fell rapidly with length of service.[74]

Dismissal was usually because of drunkenness, neglect of duty, being absent from the beat and other issues of corruption. In York 21 of the 42 dismissals were due to drunkenness,[75] although it only accounted for about a fifth of all dismissals in the West Riding County Constabulary in the late 1850s.[76] There were, of course, exceptional reasons for dismissals and forced resignations. Inspector Joseph Turner, who had served in the York force from its beginning, was forced to resign because he owned some cottages occupied by ladies of ill-repute.[77]

Another reason for the high turnover and dismissal rates was the fact that police pay was usually poor, the prospects for promotion were limited, and the morale was low. It would appear that many recruits saw policing as a temporary job until more suitable, less arduous and better-paid work arose. This, of course, raises the question of what type of people were attracted into policing?

Traditionally it has been argued that the largest proportion of the first new police were former agricultural labourers. This view probably arises from the fact that Superintendent F. W. Mallalieu told a select committee of Parliament in 1852/3 that the best recruits for the metropolitan police were to be found among the 'Intelligent part of the agricultural labouring community'.[78] Indeed, a survey of 300 entrants to the metropolitan police from November 1872 to February 1874 shows that 31 per cent (91 men) came from the land, and only 12 per cent from the military services and 5 per cent from other police forces.[79] This impression has been qualified by a number of historians, most obviously Carolyn Steedman, when they have looked beyond London and examined the meaning of the term 'labourer'. In analysing the social composition of the recruits in Staffordshire and Buckinghamshire between 1856 and 1880, she suggests that 27 per cent of the recruits in Buckinghamshire were labourers in 1856/7, 50 per cent in 1863 and 59 per cent in 1880. In Staffordshire 31 per cent of recruits were labourers in 1856/7, 52 per cent in 1863 and 47 per cent in 1880. Nevertheless, she adds that:

> labourers did not show themselves to be significantly more successful than other work groups in enduring until pension time. In Stafford-shire, as in Buckinghamshire, the majority of long-service men between 1856 and 1880 was always composed of ex-rural labourers, but in the more industrialised county other work groups contributed long-service men out of proportion to their numbers at recruitment.[80]

In addition, Steedman argues that the term creates many problems, for it does not necessarily mean that the recruits came straight from the land. In Buckinghamshire, for instance, of 153 recruits in 1857, 41 were labourers, but only 15 were farm labourers.[81] There also seem to have been differences between Buckinghamshire and Staffordshire, with the latter employing more local people than the former, which might have been affected by the nearness of London. In other words, it would appear that farm labourers were not necessarily as dominant in recruitment as is sometimes suggested and that local economic, social, geographical and trade cycle conditions might have determined the pattern and length of recruitment.

Bramham's analysis of the constables appointed in the West Riding County Constabulary for the late 1850s suggests that 27.6 per cent (a similar percentage to Buckinghamshire) were labourers and that a dozen or so other occupations accounted for the rest. In his analysis of those who were inspectors, he found that only 8.5 per cent were from a labouring background.[82] W. J. Lowe has also found that about 70 per cent of the recruits in the Lancashire Constabulary came from a few occupational groups, such as skilled tradesmen, cotton factory opera-tives, weavers and general labourers, although there were some railway workers, clerks, bookkeepers and miners.[83] In York, of 47 recorded previous occupations between 1835 and 1856, there were 8 labourers; 7 policemen; 4 farm servants; 3 farmers, soldiers, watermen and shoe-makers; 3 parish constables, servants and bailiffs; a variety of other occupations were represented by one recruit.[84]

There is only patchy evidence to indicate whether or not these men were local or drawn from outside the immediate community. Where research has been done, most seem to have been local men. In York most applicants appear to have been natives of York or the surrounding area.[85] In the case of the Staffordshire county force, 77 of the 135 recruits in 1873 came from that county, 18 were unknown, and many of the others came from nearby. In the case of Buckinghamshire, only 5 of the 22 recruits in 1863 came from that county, but most of the rest came from neighbouring counties. In these particular cases, the major-ity of the men were also single (70 per cent in Buckinghamshire and 96 per cent in Staffordshire) and relatively young.[86]

Thus the social composition of the early modern police suggests that they comprised a relatively young force of inexperienced men, drawn partly from the rural labourers but essentially locally based, immensely variable in geographical and social origin according to their locality and often unmarried. It was not until the late nineteenth century that the development of a system of promotion encouraged the force to become more stable, with married men becoming more evident as a career structure, pensions and the like beckoned.

Conclusion

The emergence of modern policing in England was slow. It came about not so much as a result of the failure of the old policing but as a result of the increased middle-class fear that it could not cope with the threat of public disorder posed by the anti-Poor Law riots, Chartist activities and other public disturbances in a society undergoing rapid social and economic change. The new forces that emerged were not necessarily well organized or much more effective than their predecessors, although the increased number of the police undoubtedly exerted an influence over the recording of crime and may have helped to discourage petty crime. The middle classes hoped that the police would act as the disseminators of their views, but the lack of police uniformity militated against any attempt to impose a particular set of social values. The fact that there were three forms of policing in England – the metropolitan, the borough and the county – all of which adopted different structures even when the government imposed an element of uniformity and control from 1856 onwards, cut across attempts to impose one set of social values. In addition, it is clear that all three models suffered from shared difficulties in recruitment and immense variations in both the quantity and quality of their police force. The high turnover of recruits meant that the early police forces were very inexperienced. Different communities also experienced different difficulties. Indeed, it is quite clear that cultural variation was a major factor in shaping the evolution of the new police during the first half of the nineteenth century and that there were marked differences in the extent to which the police were accepted by their community. Thus, the progress of policing was neither even nor ever simply a matter of improving social control. It evolved as communities evolved and the emergence of the new police forces themselves exerted some influence on their own evolution.

Notes

1.   T. A. Critchley, *A History of Police in England and Wales* (Constable edition, 1978).
2.   R. D. Storch, '"The Plague of Blue Locusts": Police Reform and Popular Resistance in Northern England 1840–1857', *International Review of Social History* 20 (1975), pp. 61–90; R. D. Storch, 'The Policeman as Domestic Missionary: Urban Discipline and Popular Culture in Northern England, 1850–1880', *Journal of Social History* 9 (1976), pp. 481–509.
3.   Stanley H. Palmer, *Police and Protest in England and Ireland 1789–1850* (Cambridge, 1988).
4.   P. Bramham, 'Parish Constables or Police Officers? The Development of a County Force in the West Riding', *The Journal of Regional and Local Studies* 7, 2 (Autumn 1987), pp. 68–80; D. Foster, 'Police Reform and Public Opinion in Rural Yorkshire', *The Journal of Local Studies* 2, 1 (Spring 1982), pp. 1–8; D. Foster, 'The East Riding Constabulary in the Nineteenth Century', *Northern History*, 1985, pp. 193–211; C. Steedman, *Policing the Victorian Community: The Formation of the English Provincial Police from 1856–1880* (1984); R. Swift, *Police Reform in Early Victorian York, 1838–1856* (York, 1988); R. Swift, 'Urban Policing in Early Victorian

England, 1835–1856: A Reappraisal, *History* 73 (1988); E. C. Midwinter, *Law and Order in Early Victorian Lancashire* (York, 1971); D. Taylor, 'Crime and Policing in Early Victorian Middlesbrough, 1835–55', *The Journal of Regional and Local Studies*, 11, 1 (1991), pp. 48–66.

5. C. Emsley, *The English Police: A Political and Social History* (Hemel Hempstead, 1991); F. C. Mather, *Public Order in the Age of the Chartists* (1964).

6. *Ibid.*, p. 5.

7. *Ibid.*, p. 16.

8. V. A. C. Gattrell and T. B. Hadden, 'Criminal Statistics and their Interpretation', in E. A. Wrigley (ed.), *Nineteenth Century Society* (Cambridge, 1972), p. 353.

9. M. Foucault, *Discipline and Punishment* (Harmondsworth, 1977).

10. Emsley, *English Police*, p. 6.

11. Critchley, *Police in England and Wales*, p. 25.

12. R. Paley, '"An Imperfect, Inadequate and Wretched System"? Policing London before Peel', *Criminal Justice History* 10 (1989), pp. 97–8.

13. *Ibid.*, p. 102.

14. *Ibid.*, pp. 114–17.

15. *Ibid.*, p. 121.

16. *Ibid.*, p. 125.

17. Palmer, *Police and Protest*, pp. 85–7.

18. *Ibid.*, p. 381, and look at table 10.3 on p. 382.

19. J. Hart, 'Reform of the Borough Police 1835–1856', *English Historical Review* 70 (1955), pp. 414–15.

20. Gattrell and Hadden, 'Criminal Statistics', p. 353.

21. Parliamentary Papers 1826–7, vi, pp. 62–3; 1826–7, xvii, p. 185; 1831–2, xxxiii, p. 2; 1835, xlv, p. 20; 1846, xxxiv, p. 66; 1851, lxi, p. 64.

22. D. Philips, *Crime and Authority in Victorian England: The Black Country, 1835–1860* (1977), pp. 61, 77.

23. *Ibid.*, pp. 59–63, 78–81.

24. William Derrincourt, *Old Convict Days* (1899), p. 10, referring to Darlaston in the 1830s, quoted in Philips, *Crime*, p. 53.

25. Palmer, *Police and Protest*, p. 385.

26. *Ibid.*, p. 384.

27. PRO, Home Office Papers, HO 45/2410, letter from the West Riding JPs to the Home Office, 19 May 1848.

28. *Ibid.*, letter from the Bradford mayor and the West Riding JPs to the Home Office, 29 May 1848.

29. *Ibid.*, report to Home Office, 10 July 1848, and a letter from Mossman, a solicitor, 1 August 1848.

30. Palmer, *Police and Protest*, p. 397.

31. L. A. Radzinowicz, *A History of English Criminal Law and its Administration from 1750*, 4 vols. (1948–68), iv, p. 70, suggests that the number of committals per 100,000 rose between 1811–13 and 1825–7 by 124 per cent in the provinces and by 53 per cent in London and Middlesex.

32. Gattrell and Hadden, 'Criminal Statistics', pp. 368, 378.

33. Palmer, *Police and Protest*, p. 302.

34.   *Ibid.*, p. 308.
35.   Phillip Thurmond Smith, *Policing Victorian London: Political Policing, Public Order, and the London Metropolitan Police* (Westport, Conn., 1985), p. 207 This deals with the policing in London between 1850 and 1868, when Sir Richard Mayne was solely in charge of the London police after the retirement of Sir Charles Rowen in 1850.
36.   Hart, 'Borough Police', pp. 417–18.
37.   Critchley, *Police in England and Wales*; J. J. Tobias, *Crime and Industrial Society in the Nineteenth Century* (1967); C. Reith, *A New Study of Police in History* (1956).
38.   Storch, 'Blue Locusts'; Philips, *Crime and Authority*; A. Donajgrodzki, *Social Control in Nineteenth Century Britain* (1977).
39.   Taylor, 'Crime and Policing in Middlesbrough', p. 54.
40.   Bramham, 'Parish Constables or Police Officers?', p. 71.
41.   Hart, 'Borough Police', p. 416.
42.   J. W. Reilly, *Policing Birmingham* (Birmingham, 1989), p. 5.
43.   *Ibid.*, pp. 4, 9–12.
44.   Palmer, *Police and Protest*, pp. 420–1.
45.   Reilly, *Policing in Birmingham*, p. 11.
46.   *Ibid.*, p. 16.
47.   A. Elliott, 'The Establishment of Municipal Government in Bradford 1837–57', PhD dissertation, University of Bradford, 1976.
48.   Swift, 'Urban Policing in Early Victorian England; Swift, *York*.
49.   Hart, 'Borough Police', pp. 420–1.
50.   Swift, *York*, pp. 27–36.
51.   Taylor, 'Crime and Policing in Middlesbrough', p. 63.
52.   Hart, 'Borough Police', pp. 411–15. Hart's view is accepted by Mather, *Public Order*, p. 128, and Critchley, *Police*, pp. 74–5. This view is rejected by Tobias, *Crime and Industrial Society*, pp. 74–5.
53.   Palmer, *Police and Protest*, p. 442. This indicates the size of the county forces. Gloucestershire had a force of 250 in 1839 and 1856, Wiltshire one of 201 on both dates and Staffordshire one of 210 in 1842 and 279 in 1842. Westmorland had a force of 1 in 1846 and 8 in 1856.
54.   Foster, 'Police Reform and Public Opinion in Rural Yorkshire'.
55.   J. Foster, *Class Struggle and the Industrial Revolution: Early Industrial Capitalism in Three English Towns* (1974), p. 60.
56.   Emsley, *English Police*, pp. 70–2.
57.   Steedman, *Policing the Victorian Community*; Bramham, 'Parish Constables or Police Officers?'
58.   Swift, *York*, pp. 36–7.
59.   *Ibid.*, p. 41.
60.   Swift, 'Urban Policing', p. 237.
61.   I am indebted to Dr David Taylor (University of Huddersfield) for this information; Philips, *The Black Country*.
62.   Emsley, *English Police*, p. 51, refers to the concern about the fear of Tommy Atkins brutalized by the Crimean campaign.
63.   Palmer, *Police and Protest*, p. 515.
64.   Emsley, *English Police*, p. 5.

65. This, and Table 3.4, is information gathered by Dr David Taylor and taken from his recent work on the HMI Police returns.

66. Bramham, 'Parish Constables or Police Officers?', pp. 73–4; Steedman, *Policing the Victorian Community*, pp. 92–105.

67. *Ibid.*, part II.

68. Emsley, *English Police*, p. 26.

69. Reilly, *Birmingham Policing*, pp. 15–16.

70. Swift, *York*, p. 23.

71. Bramham, 'Parish Constables or Police Officers?', p. 74.

72. Steedman, *Policing the Victorian Community*, pp. 93–5.

73. Bramham, 'Parish Constables or Police Officers?', p. 73.

74. Steedman, *Policing the Victorian Community*, p. 94.

75. Swift, *York*, p. 6.

76. Bramham, 'Parish Constables or Police Officers?', p. 75.

77. Swift, *York*, p. 23.

78. Parliamentary Papers 1852–3 (715), xxxvi, *Second Report of the Select Committee on Police*, q. 2872.

79. Smith, *Policing Victorian London*, p. 46.

80. Steedman, *Policing the Victorian Community*, p. 71.

81. *Ibid.*, p. 73.

82. Bramham, 'Parish Constables or Police Officers?', pp. 72, 74.

83. W. J. Lowe, 'The Lancashire Constabulary 1845–1870: The Social and Occupational Function of a Victorian Police Force', *Criminal Justice History* 4 (1983), pp. 41–62.

84. Swift, *York*, p. 13.

85. *Ibid.*

86. Steedman, *Policing the Victorian Community*, chapter 3.

CHAPTER FOUR

THE FACTORY QUESTION
c.1802–1870s

The 'factory question' of the early and mid-nineteenth century had a great deal to do with tackling the problem of child labour but also related to the concern that other factory workers, men as well as women, were working excessive and intolerable hours in the new woollen, worsted and cotton textile factories that were springing up in the industrial North, particularly in Lancashire and the West Riding of Yorkshire. By the second half of the nineteenth century this concern to restrict the hours of work had been widened to include other factories and industrial work as well. What is evident in the first three-quarters of the nineteenth century is that the state became increasingly involved in the control of factory conditions due to a variety of factors, including the extra-parliamentary pressure of the factory movement, the parliamentary pressure of both Whig and Tory MPs, the dynamism created by the factory inspectors, and the strong streak of paternalism emerging from protectionist Tories. There was, perhaps, no single driving force to factory reform and many of those who were responsible for the humanitarian outcome were not necessarily driven by the same objectives. Factory reform thus represented a combination of traditional landed values, Benthamite thought and administrative incrementalism.

From the start it was obvious that there were two movements pushing forward for factory reform. On the one hand there was the 'factory movement', or Short Time movement, which was simply concerned to restrict the hours of work for children, youths and women, that wished for no state intervention beyond the restriction of working hours to ten per day. Secondly, there was the factory reform taken up by the Whigs, and some Tories, which sought to set up a regulatory system based upon inspection. This was to be more intrusive, assumed a level of state surveillance and went far beyond what Richard Oastler and the 'factory movement' sought to achieve. Whilst the Ten Hours Act of 1847 could be seen as the achievement of the first movement, the 1833 Factory Act and most of the other legislation of the 1830s and 1840s was seen to be a product of the second movement.

The features of early factory legislation, 1802–1831

Early factory legislation was characterized by two related factors. Firstly, there was the concern that children who fell on the Elizabethan Poor Law of 1601 should be apprenticed out to industry. Secondly, there was the related concern that such children should have both their health and morals protected, especially if they began work in the larger industrial establishments. Evidence that the health of Poor Law apprentices was far from adequate prompted the government to introduce the Health and Morals of Apprentices Act of 1802, sponsored by Sir Robert Peel, who was a cotton spinner and the father of the future Prime Minister of the same name. This Act applied to all parish apprentices, whose hours of work were to be limited to twelve per day, who were not to work at night, who had to be provided with adequate sleeping facilities and who had to receive a minimum of two hours' education per day. The Act proved to be unworkable, since the local JPs, sometimes manufacturers themselves, were reluctant to enforce it. In any case, it was only applicable to manufacturers in cotton and wool who employed more than twenty persons.

Interest in the whole question of factory legislation was not revived for more than a decade. In 1813 Robert Owen, a social reformer and factory master, began a campaign to improve the conditions of factory children and this encouraged the formation of a House of Commons committee in 1816, chaired by Sir Robert Peel. Lord Kenyon chaired a similar committee in the House of Lords in 1818 and 1819. Peel's Commons committee drew upon a wide range of evidence. James Pattison, a director of the East India Company and a silk manufacturer at Congleton, Cheshire, suggested that the health of children employed in mills was good and that there was no reason for educational provision or inspection. This contrasted with the evidence presented by Theodore Price, a Warwickshire JP, who stated that he would prefer to send his four daughters to a Warwick Bridewell rather than a cotton mill for seven years.[1] Despite the contrasting nature of the evidence, Peel's Act of 1819 forbade children under 9 years of age to work in cotton mills and restricted those children over 9 to twelve hours a day.

This legislation, though well intended, could not be policed effectively in the absence of an inspectorate. Subsequent legislation in the 1820s took matters little further. John Cam Hobhouse, the Whig-Radical MP for Westminster, promoted the 1825 Act, which did prohibit night work for children, and the 1839 Act, which made minor amendments to the 1825 Act. Yet much more effective action was required and this came in the 1830s.

The pressure for state action, 1830–1833

The demand for a widening of state action came from several directions. John Wood, John Rand, J. G. Horsfall and several other of Bradford's large worsted spinners and manufacturers had begun to campaign for the restriction of children's hours of work in the 1820s. John Doherty, who was organizing cotton trade-unionism from the mid- and late 1820s, also identified with the need to reduce the working hours of children. There were further humanitarian efforts in Parliament. Yet what gave such demands an impact was the outburst of activity and campaigning associated with Richard Oastler (1789–1861).

Oastler, known as the 'Factory King' or 'King Richard', was an evangelical Anglican and a land agent at Fixby Hall, Huddersfield. He had been born in Leeds, educated at the Moravian school at Fulneck and had taken over from his father as steward or agent at Fixby.[2] It was not until September 1830 that John Wood, a wealthy Bradford manufacturer, revealed to Oastler the appalling conditions in which children laboured. As a result he wrote a letter in the *Leeds Mercury* attacking the 'Yorkshire Slavery'. He wrote that:

> The very streets which receive droppings of an 'Anti-Slavery Society' are every morning wet by the tears of innocent victims of the accursed shrine of avarice, who are compelled (not by the cart-whip of the negro slaver driver) but by the dread of the equally appalling thong or strap of the over-looker, to hasten, half-dressed, but not half-fed, to those magazines of British infantile slavery – the worsted mills in the town and neighbourhood of Bradford!!![3]

Events moved quickly. Oastler created a stir and soon found that he had to abandon writing for the Liberal *Leeds Mercury* and had to send his letters to the *Leeds Intelligencer* and the Radical *Leeds Patriot*. By the spring of 1831 Short Time committees had set been set up in the West Riding, Lancashire and Scotland. Soon afterwards, in June 1831, Oastler met with a deputation of operatives and agreed to lead a campaign for shorter hours in what was called the 'Fixby Hall Compact'. A few months later Oastler emphasized that the arrangement was designed to support the introduction of 'Ten Hours a day and a Time-Book Bill'.[4]

This campaign was supported by a wide range of people who held different opinions. John Doherty, the trade-union leader of the Lancashire cotton operatives, was active in the National Regeneration Society in the early 1830s and advocated the eight-hour day through his *Herald of the Rights of Industry*.[5] In contrast there was much support from Tory manufacturers such as Bradford's John Wood, who allegedly spent £40,000 on the cause and was toasted in the popular broadsheets of the day, such as *The Factory Girl*;[6] there were Anglican vicars such as the

Revd (Parson) George S. Bull of Bradford. These Tories and Anglicans had been hostile towards the 1832 Reform Bill but felt that legislation was required to protect children because they were not ' free agents' and were being exploited. Indeed, there were many Tory landlords, such as William Busfeild Ferrand (1809–89) of Bingley, who wished to extend the protectionism offered by the Corn Laws to workpeople and children. There were also some Whigs and Liberals, such as John Fielden (1784–1849), a cotton manufacturer from Todmorden and the Radical MP for Oldham from 1832 to 1847, who wrote *The Curse of the Factory System* (1836). Other supportive manufacturers included Charles Hindley (1800–57), MP for Ashton, and Joseph Brotherton (1783–1857), MP for Salford. A small group of nonconformist ministers in Lancashire also espoused the ethic of progress and improvement. The most famous was Joseph Rayner Stephens (1805–79), a Methodist preacher who stimulated the Lancashire side of the Short Time movement from about 1835 onwards.

Recent work suggests that there was some medical support for the movement, although medical opinion was divided.[7] Such support could, of course, be traced back to Dr Percival of Manchester and several other eighteenth-century doctors but was also evident in the ten hours campaign. A majority of medical opinion in Lancashire and the West Riding of Yorkshire appears to have been drawn to the ten hours movement, but they tended to have strong local connections and to be linked with the local institutions in the towns. Where the link was not so firm, and particularly amongst surgeons with higher qualifications and less of a link with the local populace, there appeared to be opposition to the ten hours movement.[8] Nevertheless, medical influence appears to have been marginal.[9]

The Short Time, or factory, movement was thus composed of a variety of individuals and groups, representing different interests, who agreed to bury their differences in the cause of achieving the ten-hour day. Their movement was active during the early and mid-1830s but after a number of years of relative dormancy, particularly between 1838 and 1841, it revived its activities and was vigorous until the passing of the Ten Hours Act in 1847.

Such extra-parliamentary activities gave strong support to those who were striving for ten hours legislation in Parliament. Initially, it was Michael Thomas Sadler, an evangelical Tory from a Methodist background, a Leeds linen merchant and sometime member of Leeds Corporation and MP for the Duke of Newcastle's pocket borough of Newark, who took up the cause of the ten-hour day when Hobhouse's 1831 Bill was weakened. After a mass pilgrimage to York on Easter Monday 1832 which led to a petition to Parliament signed by over 130,000 people, Sadler was asked to chair a select committee to take evidence in connection with his Ten Hours Bill. This committee, famed for its bias, and Sadler gathered evidence that children suffered ill health from excessive amounts of work. However, the work was cut short by the 1832 general election which followed the 1832 Reform Bill. This swept away Sadler's seat, then at Aldborough, and forced him to contest the Leeds election of 1832. Standing against John Marshall Jnr, heir to a flax-spinning empire, and T. B. Macauley, the Whig orator, it was obvious that, as Hobhouse remarked: 'The factory question is mixed up with party politics in Yorkshire and more especially in the town of Leeds.'[10] Defeated in the election, Sadler was replaced by Lord Ashley, later the seventh Lord Shaftsbury, as the parliamentary leader of the ten hours movement. In March 1833, two months after the publication of the Sadler Report, Ashley reintroduced Sadler's Bill for the ten-hour day.[11] The Sadler Report, bringing together the evidence of more than eighty witnesses, strongly supported the need to protect children from long hours of work. The London meeting of the Society for the Improvement of the Conditions of Factory Children on 23 February 1833, which brought together Ashley, Oastler, Robert Owen and Daniel O'Connell, the Irish patriot and agitator, encouraged developments in that direction. Nevertheless, the government felt that the employers, who had not been heard, should be consulted and delayed the Bill until a Factory Commission, led by Southwood Smith and Edwin Chadwick, examined the question in more detail.

These commissioners attempted to gather evidence throughout the country but came into conflict with Oastler and his supporters in the West Riding of Yorkshire. On Thursday 16 May 1833, having arrived three days earlier, the factory commissioners were met by 1,000 opera-tives organized by the Short Time committee and 1,000 operatives who regarded 'the object of their visit as an expensive plot to delay the passing of the great measure introduced into parliament by M. T. Sadler'.[12] A poster published in June recorded their treatment in the West Riding:

Get Away!!!

Get Away!!! [13]

Said 'KING RICHARD'

THE COMMISSIONERS

have obeyed the Royal Word!!! Having *seen* in Leeds, and *felt* in Bradford, and everywhere, that they have disgusted all honest Men, and having been sickened by the Songs and terrified by the Groans, and haunted by the withered Forms of the Factory Slaves, they are off to London to get their £200 for this bad Job, and to seek a better *if they can find it*. They set off from Bradford at Half-past Seven on Thursday Evening. The Road Ticket was made out for Keighley, but

after they had ordered the Carriage the Ticket was altered for
Wakefield and the London Road. The Secretary of the Bradford
Short Time Committee, who had taken good care of them in
Bradford, kindly followed them out 34 Miles to Doncaster, and
joined them and warmed himself along with them at the Kitchen Fire
of the Inn, at Two in the Morning!!

After such Rest as they could get, and a Saunter in Doncaster, and
after trying to 'commissioner' the Bradford Secretary in vain, their
Worships went off to London at One o' Clock on Friday Afternoon
as cross as old patch, when the Representatives of the Short Time
Committees of Yorkshire bade them a Long, Long Farewell!!!
'Confound their Politics, Frustrate their Knavish Tricks.'
Live 'King Richard' and the Ten Hour Bill!!!

The 1833 Factory Act

Despite such hostility, the Factory Commission proved to be more
enlightened than Oastler expected. In June 1833 it produced a report
which, whilst accepting some of the opposition of factory masters to
state intervention, maintained that children were not 'free agents' and
thus needed protection, whilst adults did not need protection since they
were free to leave their employment. Within a month Ashley's Ten
Hours Bill was defeated but, in August, Althorp, the Whig Chancellor,
introduced his own Bill which became law. It applied to all textile mills,
except for silk and lace, barred children from working under the age
of 9, limited those between 9 and 13 to no more than eight hours per
day and forty-eight hours per week, and restricted those young persons
under 18 to twelve hours per day and a maximum of sixty-eight hours
per week. In addition, two hours of education were to be provided for
children and the Act was to be enforced by four factory inspectors.
These inspectors were to be aided by a body of resident superintendents
who could initiate prosecutions. They also had judicial power, which
they used rarely, but this was withdrawn in 1844.

The 1833 Act was obviously an important piece of legislation in the
evolution of state welfare. It extended the state responsibility to protect
children beyond that of the Elizabethan Poor Law, created an effective
mechanism for enforcement and imposed an element of Benthamism
when dealing with children without impairing the individualism of
adults. What is equally clear is that it was not well received by most
of the interested parties.

Oastler and the factory movement were far from happy with an Act
which allowed young persons to work long hours and which imposed
the dreaded prospect of a state bureaucracy and centralization. All that

his movement wanted was a ten-hour day and a time book by which children would sign in, do their ten hours and sign out.

The factory masters were little happier, for they felt that state intervention would impair their ability to compete and many regarded the 1833 Act as a 'Tory plot' to pay back the middle classes for their success in pushing the 1832 Reform Bill through Parliament. Nassau Senior (1790–1864) reflected their views when he wrote that: 'The manufacturer is tired of regulations – what he seeks is tranquillity – *implore pace.*'[14] From time to time the factory masters attempted to get the legislation amended, without much success. Nonetheless, Leonard Horner, a factory inspector, wrote to his daughter that: 'They [the mill owners] naturally dislike the Act, like any other interference, but they say that as they were to have one, that which has been passed was very little open to objection, and they see no difficulty in carrying it into effect.'[15]

The factory inspectors varied in their response to the 1833 Factory Act. Oliver MacDonagh makes the point that most of them were retired from their occupations and suggests that many of them and their assistants were ignorant, pluralists into the bargain.[16] Only Leonard Horner knew anything about mills and for the first three years he and his three colleagues served only the interests of the employers. Looking back from 1848, Thomas Howell, a factory inspector, reflected that:

At that period I had no practical experience of the factory system, or of the working of the Act of Parliament, which did not come into full operation till 1836, inasmuch as under our instructions we were at this period in communication exclusively with the employers, with a view to making the law acceptable to them, and from some of whom we unwarily adopted suggestions which appeared plausible enough on paper at the time, but which on very short practical acquaintance with the factory system in the cotton district, when the law was afterwards fairly launched, caused me to repent, and which I gladly seize the present opportunity to repudiate.[17]

Nonetheless, the factory inspectors soon widened their scope and became more critical. Leonard Horner offered what was perhaps the most balanced account when he wrote a report, which became a pamphlet, *On the Employment of Children, in Factories and Other Works in the United Kingdom, and in some Foreign Countries* (1840). He criticized the exclusion of the silk mills from the 1833 Act, suggested that further state involvement was necessary in order to protect the health and morals of children and argued for better application of the educational provision for children working in factories. His argument was that the 1833 Act was a successful measure but that it needed to be built upon:

The Act of 1833 has been productive of much good: it has put an end to a large proportion of the evils which made the interference of the legislature then necessary. But it has not done nearly all the good that was intended: it has not by any means accomplished all the purposes for which it was passed. The failures have mainly arisen from the defects in the law itself; not in the principles it lays down, but in the machinery which was constructed for the purpose of carrying the principles into operation ... it was in some degree legislating in the dark; a great part of the mechanism adopted was entirely of a novel description, of a kind that had never been tried in former factory acts; and after it was set to work, much of it was found to have been ill-contrived, and some so bad that it obstructed, and to a great degree prevented, the attainment of the object.

Dissatisfaction with the 1833 Factory Act may have been rife but it produced its own momentum of change. In 1840 Ashley was appointed to chair a committee to look into the working of the 1833 Act. It highlighted the defects to which Leonard Horner and other inspectors had pointed and demanded further state intervention. However, it was the 1842 Report of the Royal Commission on the Employment of Children which proved to be more effective. Written by Thomas Tooks, John Southwood Smith, Leonard Horner and John Saunders, it revealed the extent of child labour in coal mines and produced the famous woodprints of semi-naked children working in coal passages. It suggested that there was 'nothing in the nature of employments included under the present inquiry distinctly injurious to health' but that long hours interrupted the proper nutrition of the children.[18] In its wake, Ashley promoted a Coal Mines Bill in 1842 which suggested that children become free agents at 13 years of age but this was reduced to 10 years by the House of Lords. Nevertheless, the final Act admitted that women were 'unfree' agents and removed them from working underground.

Sir James Graham, the Home Secretary, also tried to implement the educational provisions that Horner had sought in his 1843 Factory Bill but, as a result of the hostility of Edward Baines Jnr and the dissenting opinion of Yorkshire, 'the Yorkshire Voluntaryists', the decision to promote parish schools to provide education for the factory children was abandoned and the 1844 Factory Act merely established that such children were subject to half-time attendance at schools, that they could start work at 8 years of age but were to work half-time and no more than six and a half hours daily. The administration of the Act was tightened and machinery was to be fenced. In addition, the unfree agent idea was extended to include women who, like young persons, would not be allowed to work more than twelve hours per day. Factory legislation was extended but the ten-hour day, the prime and only concern of the factory movement, had not been achieved.

The ten-hour day

The ten-hour day was the most controversial of issues and produced some of the most determined differences of opinion. The critics of the measure argued that it would reduce the wages of workers, that parental authority would be impaired and that a relatively unfettered factory system was essential to the economic well-being of Britain. Indeed, it was felt by some, such as John Bright, that Britain's exports would be drastically affected by a reduction of working hours.[19] In any case, there were those who still maintained the eighteenth-century attitude that legislation was not the proper domain of government. As Lord Melbourne stated in 1836: 'the duty of a Government is not to pass legislation but to rule.'[20]

In contrast, the supporters of the ten-hour day used a variety of arguments to substantiate their cause. It was felt that women would be 'unsexed' if separated from their families, that children needed to enjoy a wholesome childhood and that excessive labour poisoned the relations between masters and workmen. The ten-hour day was seen as an ameliorative measure that could solve the physical, social and political problems imposed by the factory system in society and that would bring about social harmony. The purpose of the Bills was not, as *The Times* stated, to limit industry 'but only to exert a sort of parental control over useless labour and consuming toil'.[21] In the 1840s Oastler offered the variant that the ten-hour day would help to keep the economy of the country balanced:

> The universal cry now is, 'we are ruined because we produce too much' – my cry has been for many years, 'Produce less.' Had my advice been taken ten years ago, the present losses of the factory masters would have been prevented.[22]

The fourteen years between the 1833 Factory Act and the implementation of the 1847 Ten Hours Act saw the Short Time movement wax and wane. In the immediate wake of the energetic extra-parliamentary reform of 1830–3 there was something of a lull. The supporters of the movement got caught up in the anti-Poor Law protests and Oastler faced financial problems which led to his imprisonment in the Fleet debtors' prison in 1840.

Nevertheless, the demand for the ten-hour day was always just beneath the surface and could be rekindled as the moment required. The Revd George S. Bull and Richard Oastler issued a circular under the title of *Faithful Advice and Warning: To the Factory Workers (Old and Young) of Yorkshire and Lancashire* in February 1836. It was an attempt to raise support for the repeal of the 1833 Factory Act currently being presented as a motion to Parliament and suggested that, given the political in-fighting that was going on, it was sensible to try to exclude all children under 10 from the mills, to defend the eight-hour principle for those up to 13 and to restrict the hours of work to less than ten for those between 14 and 21 years of age.

When this political debate had blown over, the Short Time movement more or less blended in with the anti-Poor Law movement and other popular protest groups. Its sense of continuity was maintained by the fact that Ashley attempted to attach a ten hours clause to any Factory Bill that was considered, but unsuccessfully so, as in 1838, 1839 and 1841. At more or less the same time Leonard Horner became a powerful advocate of the ten-hour day. Yet it was not until 1844 that the extra-parliamentary movement and the parliamentary movement began to combine their efforts again.

At the beginning of this chapter it was recognized that the ten-hour day gained political support from all sections – from Tories, Whigs, Liberals and Radicals. In other words, it was an issue that cut across party divides. Within each party and political grouping there were sections who supported one case or the other. These political divisions became far more tense in the 1840s as society and its values began to change.

The most obvious development was the formation of the Anti-Corn Law League, which sought to remove the protective Corn Laws and succeeded in its efforts in 1846 with the help of such new Conservatives as Sir Robert Peel, the Prime Minister, and Sir James Graham. Behind their action was the implication that free trade would bring about the end of child labour. Sympathetic to the ideas of the middle class, Peel opposed the ten-hour day and made the twelve-hour day an issue of confidence which led to the defeat of Ashley's ten hours clause in the 1844 Act. When Peel opposed Ashley's Ten Hours Bill in January 1846 and reversed his policy of protectionism by removing the Corn Laws, Ashley resigned and left the parliamentary section of the ten hour movements in the hands of John Fielden.

At the same time the ten hours movement was stirring itself throughout the country. Indeed, the circular of the Keighley Short Time Committee to Members of Parliament in March 1844 stated that:

AT A MEETING Of the short Time Committee of Keighley, in the West Riding of the County of York, held on Friday evening, March 8th, 1844, the following resolution was unanimously adopted to which we beg respectfully to draw your attention, in the hope that you may be pleased to give Lord Ashley your cordial support in the effort he is about to make to obtain a Law to protect Young Persons employed in Factories, from being worked in them more than Ten Hours per Day for Five Days in the Week, and Eight on the Saturday.

Joseph Vickers, Secretary

Resolved – That this Meeting is deeply convinced that the just claims of the Factory Population require that the Hours of Labour for all Young Persons under 21 Years of Age, employed in Factories, should be limited to Ten per day, for Five days of the Week, and EIGHT on Saturday.[23]

At the end of May 1845 the central Short Time committee issued a notice and circular to the factory operatives of the United Kingdom calling for a conference of representatives from:

every town in the manufacturing districts, to consult together what is the best course to be adopted under the existing circumstances. On Sunday, June 18th, 1845, a Meeting of Delegates will therefore be held at York Taverne, York Street, Todmorden, at Eleven o'clock, to which meeting every district is particularly requested to send, at least, one delegate.[24]

What is clear is that there was a strong revival of the Short Time movement – even if it appears to have lost the immense vigour of its youth.

With the revival of the movement, more emphasis was placed upon the demand for the ten-hour day throughout 1846 and 1847, culminating in the Ten Hours Act of 1847. The reason for this success has been subject to some speculation. Three major explanations have been put forward. First, the traditional explanation has been that the Ten Hours Bill became law because the Conservative protectionists sought revenge for the repeal of the Corn Laws in 1846. At the other extreme, Karl Marx viewed it as the first success of the working class. There is also a third explanation, offered by W. C. Lubenow and William O. Aydelotte, and that is that the ten-hour day was an issue which divided all political parties and that after Peel's repeal of the Corn Laws, the Conservative protectionists were no longer restrained and simply voted according to their instinct to turn the balance in favour of the Ten Hours Bill.[25] Indeed, Lubenow states that: 'It was only after the fall of Peel's government that Conservative MPs could join with the Liberals and Radicals, having their own political perspective, to pass the ten-hours bill.'[26]

All three explanations are plausible. The traditional argument is supported by the fact that there was a switch in the voting of the Conservative protectionists, although it is difficult to measure the extent to which revenge was the prime concern. Marx's argument is supported by the revived extra-parliamentary movement, although it carried less vitality and energy than it had enjoyed in the early 1830s, despite being led once again by Richard Oastler. Above all, however, there was evidence that there was a shift in the voting behaviour. The voting pattern on the ten hours question in 1844, 1846 and 1847 reveals that all the political parties and their sub-groups had a section that favoured the ten-hour day. Of the Conservative MPs, whether protectionists, Peelites or others, 46 per cent voted in favour of the ten-hour day in 1844, 50 per cent in 1846 and 78 per cent in 1847. Of the Liberals, the equivalent percentages were 57 per cent, 47 per cent and 58 per cent, respectively. The opinion of the Whigs, Liberals and reformers remained reasonably constant but what had changed was the vote of the Conservative protectionists. Of these, the percentages were 57 per cent, 70 per cent and 94 per cent. The Conservative protectionists, a body of between 98 and 130 Members in this period, tipped the balance in favour of the Ten Hours Bill. Many of these MPs would have voted for the Bill in 1844 had Peel not made the twelve-hour day a matter of confidence. Indeed, the extent of the confusion and overlapping of politics at this time was commented upon by Charles Cavendish Fulke Greville when he stated: 'I never remember so much excitement as has been caused by Ashley's Ten-Hour Bill, nor a more curious political state of things, such intermingling of parties, such a confusion of opposition ...'[27]

It was in this politically molten atmosphere that the Ten Hour Bills were discussed. John Fielden pushed forward a Bill in 1846 which was lost in May of that year. But the political events surrounding Peel's defeat and the poor trade conditions which meant that many people were working a ten-hour day created more opportunities in 1847, when John Fielden reintroduced the Bill and it was passed.

The 1847 Factory Act proposed that young persons and women would be restricted to eleven hours of work per day during its first year of operation and ten in the second. Oastler and Bull had achieved the objectives which they had outlined in their *Faithful Advice and Warning* circular of 1836. Whilst maintaining an interest in raising the minimum age of employment to 13 or 14, they recognized that a reduction of the excessive hours of work for women and young persons was an effective way of keeping the hours of work for children at a low level.

The Ten Hours Act was a major landmark in the development of state intervention but it was not immediately effective. Employers found loopholes and got round the Act, most obviously by varying meal breaks and using children in relays. By such means, the working hours of adult males could be extended beyond twelve, and even if the working hours of children and youths were not extended, they often had to be available for more than twelve hours. In February 1850 Baron Parke, judging on a test case, found the relay system to be legal. Ashley supported the 1850 Act which amended the law to the original intention of the ten hours movement but the factory lobby secured a ten-and-a-half-hour day. But the Act did not indicate the parameters within which children had to work their hours and it was left to the 1853 Factory Act to ensure that children were not allowed to work beyond 6 p.m. By that Act, the normal working day became 6 a.m. to 6 p.m. Children had to work their six and a half hours within these limits and young persons and women had to work their ten-and-a-half-hour day within these times. This meant that adult male free agents would be restricted to a ten-and-a half-hour day.

The effectiveness of inspection

In recent years the major debate about the Factory Acts has focused upon the effectiveness with which they were implemented. The problem has already been alluded to. There were obviously too few inspectors (there being only James Stuart, Leonard Horner, T. J. Howell and R. J. Saunders in the first instance) and superintendents, with most inspectors having 1,500 or more mills to inspect and Leonard Horner covering more than 2,000 in Lancashire and Westmorland. A similar situation occurred in the case of mining.

In the first three or four years of operation of the 1833 Factory Act it is clear that inspectors were increasingly concerned to establish a working relationship with employers. Thereafter, they appear to have been more concerned to apply the law. Nevertheless, there were many problems in doing this. The fines were too low, even if they could be multiple, defendants could often get off the charge by exploiting the conflicting clauses of the different factory Acts, and the responsibility for breaking the Factory Acts could be passed on to the workers who were sub-contracted to complete the work. Indeed, this third point is reflected in one case brought by Superintendent Robert Baker:

Yesterday, Mr John Howard, carpet manufacturer, was summoned before the sitting magistrate, Dr Williamson and James Musgrave, Esq., at the Court House, Leeds, charged by Mr Superintendent Baker with having worked a boy under thirteen years of age more than nine hours a day. Mr Howard acquitted himself of any liability in the matter, by showing that he had several times given orders for the Act to be strictly observed in his works, and left the execution of it to his workmen. The information was discharged as to Mr Howard, but the slubber who employed the boy and who paid his wages and had power to discharge him was fined five shillings and costs. [Slubber: person responsible for the preparatory spinning before the finer spinning commences.] It appeared that the boy was sent to school for two hours every forenoon and that the working time was very little more than forty-eight hours a week.[28]

The inspectors varied in background and whilst the factory inspectors were men of a liberal background, the mining inspectors tended to be more technically qualified. In addition, the factory inspectors were inclined to act independently – Horner being inflexible as to principles whilst Saunders was far more pragmatic.

The administration and success of the factory and coal mines legislation has been the basis of substantial research in recent years. The current debate began in 1980 when Bartrip and Fenn suggested that the inspectorate was ineffective in ensuring that there was proper fencing and safety at work.[29] It built upon previous work which had suggested, though not necessarily proved, that the magistrates were wilfully obstructive because they were either sympathetic to, or drawn from the ranks of, the manufacturers.[30] MacDonagh has noted that 'successful prosecutions under it [1833 Act] were few but some there were', whilst Martin has suggested that 'Factory owners could nullify the intentions of the Act and make fools of the Inspectors.'[31] Ursula Henriques also suggested that magistrates moved from bench to bench to frustrate the efforts of the inspectors, whilst Thomas noted the way in which the Justices applied the 'sovereign remedy, a fine of twenty shillings for each offence'.[32]

This minimalist view of the effectiveness of inspection was subsequently taken to task by Peacock, who examined the prosecutions under the Factory Acts in Lancashire and the West Riding of Yorkshire and found that about three-quarters of factory prosecutions were successful and that success rates often exceeded 90 per cent – the Manchester magistrates dismissing only 4 per cent of cases and the Leeds ones only 7 per cent.[33] Examining the records of 450 magistrates, 7,400 offences and 2,700 different defendants, he suggests that there was considerable co-operation between the factory inspectors and the magistrates to ensure that the Factory Acts were properly enforced. Indeed, he argues that magistrates did not flout the law and that many of those fined did pay more than one pound, with multiple offences increasing the fine considerably. These views have been partly endorsed by Clark Nardinelli, drawing on the work of Howard Marvel, who has suggested that the magistrates enforced the law because they were often themselves larger manufacturers who found that the 'burden of the Factory Acts was small' to them.[34]

Nevertheless, the effectiveness and the enforcement of the Factory Acts is still open to question. Only a small percentage of those who infringed the regulations appear to have been taken to court, there is plenty of evidence that the inspectors criticized magistrates, and Peacock has included in his 'successful prosecution rates' those employers who paid costs to avert prosecution, which rather assumes guilt when none was established.[35] Also, Fraser suggests that the low prosecution rate may have been because Horner suggested that only winnable cases should be prosecuted and because the factory inspectors themselves were highlighting notorious acquittals in order to create a climate which would encourage further legislation.[36]

Though there is no clear picture of how effectively the factory legislation was applied, the evidence suggests that inspectors might have been successful in prosecution even if this success only related to a small number of factories. Even by the end of the century the environment of many factories was not being properly controlled, as the report on the woolcombing industry in Bradford and other similar surveys indicated, and the fact that women's conditions of employment were not properly dealt with.[37] There was probably a general improvement in factory conditions but there were always factories that were less than vigilant in applying the standards.

Gap filling

The work of the Short Time committees was at an end by the 1850s, but factory legislation continued to be developed and extended. Ashley, who became the seventh Earl of Shaftsbury in 1851, pressed for the extension of factory legislation beyond textile factories and encouraged the formation of the Children's Employment Commission to examine conditions in the unregulated trades. It had produced five reports by 1866, which were acted upon by the minority Conservative government in 1867. The Factory Extension Act of 1867 widened the existing legislation to factories employing more than fifty workers in a range of trades including metalworking, printing, paper and glassworks. Children under 8 years of age were not allowed to work and older children were supposed to have ten hours' education per week. The 1867 Hours of Labour Regulation Act applied to those, including private houses, with fewer employees.

Once again, it was the Conservative party that was to deliver the final surge of significant factory reform in the 1870s. Paul Smith has traced this development in detail.[38] Whilst A. J. Mundella had failed to get Parliament to accept his Nine Hours Bill on several occasions in the early 1870s, Disraeli, who had won the 1874 general election partly on the issue of social reform, decided to act. His Home Secretary, R. A. Cross, introduced the 1874 Factory Act which established a ten-hour day and raised the age of half-time employment from 8 to 10 and full-time employment from 13 to 14. Women and young persons had a ten-hour day and, therefore, adult males had effectively the same hours. At the same time Cross set up a Factory Acts Commission which led to the 1878 Factory Act, an Act which consolidated existing legislation. This provided the basis for the regulations of factories until the mid-1930s.

With the 1878 Act, major factory legislation in the Victorian age came to an end. There was, of course, such legislation as the Workmen's Compensation Act of 1897, but the 1878 Act represented the completion of the substantial factory reform of the nineteenth century. That is not surprising; Disraeli's death in 1881 signified the end of immediate Conservative interest in factory reforms and the regulation of hours, and the economic deflation of the late nineteenth century and the increased level of foreign industrial competition made the possibility of the extension of factory controls unlikely. Thereafter, the reduction of hours and the changes in working conditions were to be of a much more gradual nature. Indeed, in the 'fair trade' movement of the 1880s such prominent advocates of the tit for tat relationship in trade as Samuel Cunliffe Lister, the owner of Manningham Mills at Bradford, were firmly of the opinion that the tide of factory reform had to be rolled back rather than pushed forward.

Conclusion

The ten hours movement was not about the state control of industry but the limitation of hours and the controversy was between those who wished to reduce hours, to provide education and to improve conditions and those who felt that the market should determine the demand for labour and the need to employ children. In the end, those who wanted limitations and controls won. The political support for these ideas came from all political parties and political interest groups but most readily from the Conservative party and its protectionist – and paternalistic – wing. It was an unusual combination of interests that produced this situation. The battle between the contending forces, although it was most obvious in the early 1830s, extended over nearly half a century. However, epoch-making factory legislation came to an end in the late 1870s when the fluctuating interests of the manufacturing classes, the commitment of the Conservative party and the economic depression and deflation all led to the conclusion that major factory legislation had come to an end. Nevertheless, it was in this sphere that the state established a new primacy of responsibility alongside that which had already been established in the area of poor relief. Other state action, in public health and education for example, took much longer to exert an impact.

Notes

1. *Report of Minutes of Evidence Respecting the State of Health and Morals of Children Employed in Manufactories* (1816), evidence of James Pattison and Theodore Price.
2. C. Driver, *The Life of Richard Oastler* (1946).
3. *Leeds Mercury*, 16 October 1830.
4. Quoted in a letter 'To the Working Classes of the West Riding of the County of York' which appeared in the *Leeds Intelligencer*, 20 October 1831 and the *Leeds Patriot*, 22 October 1831.
5. John Foster, *Class Struggle and the Industrial Revolution: Early Industrial Capitalism in Three English Towns* (1974), pp. 110–11.
6. *The Factory Girl* was dedicated to John Wood, Esq., written by Robert Dibb of Dewsbury, published by E. Willan of Dewsbury and cost 1d. (0.4p) It was a one-sheet poem which described the sufferings of 'Jane the Factory Girl' and the profits went to the Ten Hours Bill. There are copies of it in the Short Time Committee Collection in the West Yorkshire Archives Service, Bradford.
7. Robert Gray, 'Medical Men, Industrial Labour and the State in Britain, 1830–50', *Social History* 16 (1991), pp. 19–42; R. Gray, 'The Language of Factory Reform', in P. Joyce (ed.), *The Historical Meaning of Work* (Cambridge, 1987).
8. Gray, 'Medical Men', pp. 22–4.
9. *Ibid.*, p. 27.
10. *Leeds Mercury*, 26 November 1831, quoted in D. Fraser, *The Evolution of the British Welfare State* (1983), p. 19.
11. G. F. A. Best, *Lord Shaftsbury* (1965); E. Hodder, *The Life and Times of the Seventh Earl of Shaftsbury*, 3 vols. (1886).
12. Look at J. T. Ward, *The Factory System*, ii. *The Factory System and Society* (Newton Abbot, 1970), pp. 104–5, for documents on this and J. T. Ward, *The Factory Movement, 1830–1855* (1962); J. T. Ward (ed.), *Popular Movements, 1830–1850* (1970); B. L. Hutchins and A. Harrison, *A History of Factory Legislation* (first edition, 1903, other editions and 1966 Cass reprint of third edition, 1966); M. W. Thomas. *The Early Factory Legislation* (1962); D. Roberts, *Victorian Origins of the British Welfare State* (1960).
13. From a large poster in the Short Time Committee Collection. It was published by H. Wardman, Printer, 6 Chapel-Lane, Bradford, 15 June 1833.
14. Nassau Senior, *Letters on the Factory Act, as it Affects the Cotton Manufacturer Addressed to the Right Honourable the President of the Board of Trade* (1837).
15. Quoted in Oliver MacDonagh, *Early Victorian Government 1830–1870* (1977), p. 5. Also look at B. Martin, 'Leonard Horner: A Portrait of an Inspector of Factories', *International Review of Social History* 14 (1969).
16. MacDonagh, *Early Victorian Government*, pp. 55–77.
17. *Report of Factory Inspectors*, Parliamentary Papers 1849 [1017], xxii, quoted in MacDonagh, *Early Victorian Government*, chapter 4.

18. *Report of the Commission for Inquiry into the Employment and Conditions of Children in Mines and Manufactories*, Parliamentary Papers 1843, xiii, p. 424.
19. William C. Lubenow, *The Politics of Government Growth: Early Victorian Attitudes towards State Intervention 1833–1848* (Newton Abbot, 1971), p. 158.
20. Quoted in MacDonagh, *Early Victorian Government*, p. 5.
21. *The Times*, 21 April 1847.
22. Oastler, *Fleet Papers*, i, p. 165.
23. A copy can be found in the Short Time Committee Collection.
24. *Ibid.*
25. Lubenow, The *Politics of Government Growth*, p. 176; William O. Aydelotte, 'Voting Patterns in the House of Commons in the 1840's', *Comparative Studies in Society and History* 5/2 (1963).
26. Lubenow, The *Politics of Government Growth*, p. 176.
27. *Ibid.*, p. 146.
28. *Leeds Intelligencer*, 15 December 1838. Also quoted in Ward, *The Factory System*, ii, p. 162.
29. P. W. J. Bartrip and P. T. Fenn, 'The Administration of Safety: The Enforcement Policy of the Early Factory Inspectorate 1844–1864', *Public Administration* 57 (1980), pp. 87–102.
30. Thomas, *Early Factory Legislation*, p. 116; J. Pellow, *The Home Office 1848–1914* ((1982), p. 125.
31. MacDonagh, *Early Victorian Government*, p. 49; Martin, 'Leonard Horner', p. 14.
32. Ursula R. Q. Henriques, *The Early Factory Acts and their Enforcement* (Historical Association Pamphlet in Appreciation in History, 12; 1970), p. 16.
33. A. E. Peacock, 'The Justices of the Peace and the Prosecution of the Factory Acts 1833–1855', PhD thesis, University of York, 1982; A. E. Peacock, 'The Successful Prosecution of the Factory Acts, 1833–55', *Economic History Review*, 2nd ser., 37/2 (1984), pp. 97–120.
34. Clark Nardinelli, 'The Successful Prosecution of the Factory Acts: A Suggested Explanation', *Economic History Review*, 2nd ser., 38/3 (1985), pp. 428–30; Howard P. Marvel, 'Factory Regulation: A Reinterpretation of Early English Experience', *Journal of Law and Economics* 20 (1971), pp. 379–402.
35. Peter Bartrip, 'Success or Failure? The Prosecution of the Early Factory Acts', *Economic History Review*, 2nd ser., 38/3 (1985), pp. 423–7.
36. Fraser, *Evolution*, p. 30.
37. Bradford Trades and Labour Council, Report of Evidence of the Enquiry Conducted by the Bradford Trades and Labour Council into the Conditions in the Woolcombing Industry, 1897–8, now located in the West Yorkshire Archives Services, Bradford.
38. P. Smith, *Disraelian Conservatism and Social Reform* (1967).

CHAPTER FIVE

HEALTH, TOWNS AND THE STATE
c.1800–1914

The history of public health in nineteenth-century Britain has often been presented as evidence of the Whiggish belief in progress.[1] Great thinkers and administrators such as Edwin Chadwick (1800–90) and Sir John Simon (1816–1904) are supposed to have shaped the attitude of the state and to have forced change on to a reluctant body of local authorities. Obviously, there is evidence to support this viewpoint and it has provoked a classic, though now almost redundant, debate between those who maintain that Benthamite thinking was the driving force for reform and others who feel that intolerable conditions forced the state to intervene.[2] As in many other areas of social policy, there is now substantial evidence in favour of the second viewpoint which suggests that local bodies were far more receptive to public health reforms than had previously been supposed and that in nineteenth-century Britain the battle had less to do with confrontation between the state and the locality than with the enormous problems that were being faced by the early and mid-Victorians, challenged by a staggering array of legal and technical problems which had not been tackled before. Indeed, Anthony Wohl has written:

> though ... it is certainly pertinent to talk in terms of *laissez faire*, local autonomy, and low rates, the often hesitant or erratic progress was as much to do with inexperience and uncertainty bred of ignorance as with any conscious political or economic philosophy. The early and mid-Victorians were, quite simply, pioneers faced with a set of problems that were novel not only in their form but in their magnitude.[3]

Later, writing of the 'cliché' of 'corruption, innate conservatism, and ... parsimony of local government', Wohl argues that 'the engineering and fiscal problems involved in sewerage schemes, the bewildering technological difficulties and the fears associated with committing the budget to relatively untried and unproven experiments could act as a legitimate deterrent.'[4] Other writers have expressed similar views.[5]

This chapter will suggest that the traditional confrontational viewpoint of public health reform is exaggerated. Rather than a Benthamite-driven state in conflict with reluctant localities, it would appear that many forces established a dialogue to meet the challenge of worsening public health and that local initiatives and perceptions were just as important as the pressure of administrators and thinkers, even if Chadwick and Simon did raise the pace of health reform. Ultimately, the 'sanitary idea' did gather its own momentum, even though improvements in health standards and the decline of death rates awaited the improved living standards of the working classes. In the realm of public health, the majority of the nineteenth century was taken up with the creation of an administrative structure rather than with tackling the worst causes of ill-health and death.

The problem

Public health has always been a problem but it became immeasurably more important with the onset of rapid industrialization in the late eighteenth and early nineteenth centuries. This encouraged rapid population growth and Britain's population doubled between 1801 and 1851. Much of this occurred in the new industrial towns. Whilst (excluding London) there were only 13 towns with more than 25,000 people in 1801, there were 40 by 1841. Bradford's population increased from 29,000 in 1801 to 77,000 in 1831. Manchester's rose from 75,000 in 1801 to 202,000 in 1831 and 376,000 by 1851. Other industrial towns experienced similar rates of growth.

With these high levels of population growth, housing provision was inadequate. Cellar dwellings, back-to-back houses and cheap housing of various kinds mushroomed but could not keep up with demand. The inadequacy of housing provision meant that many people sought accommodation in overcrowded lodging-houses. Yet the major concern was the fact that the majority of houses did not have an adequate drainage, sewerage and water supply. Water was vital to all these necessary provisions and its shortage led, in many industrial towns, to the use of local rivers which were invariably open sewers. The Aire, which supplied Leeds, was one such:

> It is charged with the contents of about 200 water closets and similar placed, a great number of common drains, the drainage from dunghills, the Infirmary (dead leeches, poultices for patients, etc.), slaughter houses, chemical soap, gas, dung, dyehouses and manufactories, spent blue and black dye, pig manure, old urine wash,... amounting to about 30,000,000 gallons per annum of the mass of filth with which the river is loaded.[6]

The poor administrative structure of local communities in early Victorian Britain meant that there was little or no effective control of building, sewering and the piping of water and that many of the perceived health problems were perpetuated. Since many of the new

industrial towns did not have modern local government until the late
1830s or 1840s, the cleansing, watching and lighting of the streets was
normally undertaken by the 'improvement (or paving) commissioners',
appointed under a local Improvement Act, of which there were about
300 by the early nineteenth century, or by the 180 or so boroughs or
municipal corporations that existed in 1800. Since each borough
remained distinct and did not necessarily share common responsibilities, it was normally the numerous local improvement commissioners
who provided the basis of early public health reforms,[7] but even their
duties were immensely variable. There were also thousands of other
local Acts connected with turnpike trusts, enclosures, the poor law and
other activities that impinged upon public health matters.

Most of the local Acts of the late eighteenth and early nineteenth
centuries made some basic provision for public health. Many established
the obligation to provide sewers under the streets instead of allowing
drains to run in the channel in the middle of a street.[8] The removal of
the resultant muck, soil or dirt was usually auctioned out to the highest
bidder, the 'muck majors' who cleared it out of the towns and sold it
to the farmers.

The rapid growth of the industrial urban population overstretched
the powers and means of the unreformed system of local government.
Death rates rose to phenomenally high levels in these towns. Even
the state found its efforts to tackle the problem thwarted by its own
hesitancy, some local resistance and inexperience, technical ignorance
and political volatility. In effect, public health reform was a slow and
painstaking affair and there was no real structure to tackle health
problems in a uniform and meaningful fashion until 1875. Indeed, it
took thirty or forty years of effort before local administration was
sufficiently developed to make deep inroads into the mass of ill health
that persisted into the late Victorian years. The Municipal Corporations
Act of 1835 created ratepayer democracy but it did not immediately
apply to all industrial towns when it was passed and contained no
specific recommendations regarding public health provision. Initially,
until responsibilities were thrust upon them by the state, municipal
corporations had to use local Acts to take action on public health. It was
not until the late 1840s that this situation was changed.

Nevertheless, reform came from many directions and local effort was
significant. Forty years ago Bryan Keith-Lucas indicated that there were
two main factors responsible for health reform. First, there were the
many local groups concerned with improving their own conditions.
Secondly, the outbreak of cholera was a great inducement to action.[9]

The state was always reluctant to become involved in health reforms
and only did so as a result of the onset of epidemics. A short-lived Board
of Health was formed by the Privy Council in 1806–7 due to a threat

Table 5.1 Death rates per 1,000 in the major industrial towns, 1831 and 1841

Town	1831	1841
Birmingham	14.6	27.2
Leeds	20.7	27.2
Bristol	16.9	31.0
Manchester	30.2	33.8
Liverpool	21.0	34.8
Average	20.69	30.8

of yellow fever. More serious were the outbreaks of cholera in 1831–2, 1848–9, 1854 and 1866–7. Cholera was a water-borne disease which was indiscriminate. It led to the formation of the Central Board of Health in June 1831 and the formation of 1,200 local boards by an Order in Council. The Cholera Act of 1832 legalized the procedures and empowered local boards to finance their anti-cholera provisions from the poor rates.

Nevertheless, cholera, which killed large numbers of people in epidemics, about 130,000 in all, was relatively insignificant when compared with the general domestic fevers that killed the working classes. Typhus, caused by a poor environment, was almost endemic amongst the working classes, as was tuberculosis. As a result, death rates were high: probably below 19 per 1,000 before 1831, they had risen to about 22.4 per 1,000 in 1838 and, as a result of cholera, to over 25 per 1,000 in 1849.[10] Death rates in the major industrial towns are indicated in Table 5.1.

Table 5.2 Comparative chances of life in different classes of the community: average age of deceased (years)[11]

Town	Professional	Trade	Labourers
Truro	40	33	28
Derby	49	38	21
Manchester	38	20	17
Rutland	52	41	38
Bolton	34	23	18
Bethnal Green	45	26	16
Leeds	44	27	19
Liverpool	35	22	15
Whitechapel	45	27	22
Strand	43	33	24
Kensington	44	29	26
Kendal	45	39	34

The differences between occupational groups, social class and industrial and non-industrial towns are indicated in Table 5.2. It reveals that there are marked differences in the average age of death between professional, trade and labouring populations and that this age was lower in the new industrial towns than in the old urban centres.

It was evident to all that the health of the nation was worsening in the early years of the Victorian age. But what was to be done? The state could intervene if pressed, as Chadwick and cholera were to do during the 1840s. Nevertheless, the immediate responses came from the locality rather than the centre.

Local responses to public health concerns

Physicians of the early eighteenth century were already well aware of the dangers posed by bad sanitation and poor housing. From the 1770s onwards public health was examined in a statistical manner by a group of physicians and dissenting clergymen who, by and large, were friends of Joseph Priestley. They included Dr John Haygarth of Chester, the Revd John Aikin of Warrington, Dr Matthew Dobson of Liverpool, the Revd Richard Price of London and Dr Percival of Manchester, who began to inquire into the problem of public health. They were helped by the bills of mortality published for Manchester and other towns, which recorded the causes of death more accurately.[12] Some of this group began to investigate the conditions in Manchester and to produce articles in *Memoirs of the Manchester Literary and Philosophical Society* and in the *Philosophical Proceedings of the Royal Society*. The latter included a paper by Dr Price on 'Differences between the Duration of Human Life in Town and Country Parishes and Villages', Dr Thomas Percival's article on the state of population in Manchester, and other similar papers by Aikin and Haygarth.[13]

These statisticians proved that industrial towns were having a bad impact upon human life. They also put their experience and knowledge to good effect. In 1784 an outbreak of fever at Radcliffe prompted the Lancashire quarter sessions to call in Dr Percival to help them and he urged them to turn their attention to the sanitary conditions in the cotton mills. A few years later Percival put forward a scheme for improving the sanitary conditions of the poorer parts of Manchester. In 1796 a Board of Health was formed and similar boards were established elsewhere.[14]

Percival and his colleagues were attempting to measure the disease with the object of controlling its spread by improving the condition and health of the labourers. They were, in fact, anticipating the concerns and developments that were to occur almost half a century later.[15] This included the improvement of the homes of the poor, better sanitation, the inspection of factories and many other arrangements. In addition, Dr Ferrier, who became the principal medical worker with the Manchester Board of Health, attempted to control the spread of disease through common lodging-houses.

Similar developments occurred in other towns such as Liverpool, which submitted a Bill to Parliament in 1802, which was defeated, to control court and cellar dwellings. Nevertheless, the sanitary provisions contained within the numerous Improvement, or Paving, Acts did help the situation. Indeed, Keith-Lucas's appeal that more detailed research be undertaken to establish the link between local initiatives to improve public health has partly been fulfilled and the evidence suggests that there was a vast amount of such activity before the 1840s. However, the focus of debate has been placed upon the health propaganda developed by Edwin Chadwick and others in the 1840s and early 1850s which directed local efforts into a more meaningful movement.

The age of Edwin Chadwick

The formation of the Poor Law Commission in 1834 and the creation of the office of Registrar-General in 1837–8 led to the production of a mass of statistical evidence on the issue of public health. Chadwick's work suggested to him that many of those who fell on the Poor Law were widows and orphans whose male breadwinner had died from disease. The illness produced by disease also threw families onto the Poor Law. As a good Benthamite, Chadwick believed in efficiency and noted that unnecessary ill health and death had the direct result of increasing the cost of poor relief. This led to Chadwick's report on sanitation, which began life in 1838 in response to the fact that government auditors had disallowed the expenditure incurred by guardians in the East End of London in the removal of nuisances. Lord John Russell, the Whig Home Secretary, asked the Poor Law Commission to run a sort of pilot study on the link between the environment and disease in the worst areas of London. Three doctors – James Kay, James Arnott and Southwood Smith – were employed on this and their work led to Chadwick's wider sanitary inquiry. These 'fever' reports were responsible for the Poor Law commissioners giving Chadwick leave of absence to produce a more substantial inquiry. Chadwick then sent questionnaires to Poor Law assistant commissioners and drew evidence from about 1,000 boards of guardians, relieving officers, prison officers, Registrar-General returns and many other sources.

Chadwick's progress was checked by a number of factors, including R. A. Slaney's Select Committee Report on the Health of Towns, which had appeared in 1840 and dealt mainly with the overcrowding of cemeteries. Unfortunately, its existence led Lord Normanby (Home Secretary,

1839–41) to forbid Chadwick to complete his work. However, Sir James Graham, the new Tory Home Secretary appointed after the 1841 general election, allowed Chadwick's work to be published. It appeared in July 1842 as the *Report on the Sanitary Condition of the Labouring Population of Great Britain*, a document of 372 pages of text and 85 appendices. It reproduced much of the statistical material contained in the Registrar-General returns, as already indicated, and stressed the statistical differences between death rates in industrial towns and other urban centres, thus producing evidence that disease and environmental conditions were linked. Given that there were also differences between occupational groups, it was confirmed that insanitary housing, which dominated the new industrial towns, was the cause of much disease. As a good Benthamite, Chadwick drew evidence to suggest that unnecessary loss of life was a waste of money. His solution was the creation of a powerful central administration that would introduce schemes for sewage removal through glazed round pipes and demand improvements in the supply of water: 'That for all these purposes, as well as for domestic use, better supplies of water are absolutely necessary.'[16]

Chadwick's report sold more than 100,000 copies and was a clear indictment of the poor sanitary condition of Britain, even if Chadwick's work itself had little immediate impact, unlike his work on the police and the Poor Law. Indeed, there were too many technical, financial, ideological and political problems in its way. Chadwick believed, as many doctors did at the time, in the miasmic theory that smells transmitted disease. Even if that was not so, the removal of nuisances would certainly reduce disease levels. A bigger problem here was that civil engineering was not sufficiently developed. There was a shortage of civil engineers due to the railway boom, and the sheer scale and cost of sewerage schemes inhibited action. The financial concern was very real and Chadwick complained that: 'I am crying out Pestilence and for the relief of the masses but can get no one to hear of means which will affect the pockets of small owners ... who set up the cry of self-government against any regulations which may lead to the immediate expenditure for putting in better condition the houses for which they exact exorbitant rents.'[17]

There was also the problem of vested interests. Inevitably, it would be the middle classes who would be faced with the rates to provide sewerage schemes and the removal of nuisances and many felt that they were being asked to pay for something that was not their concern. Of the provision of a municipal water supply, one comment was that: 'All they want is to expand other people's money and get popularity by letting what *they may call poor* have the water for nothing and also accommodating themselves and tenants at other people's expense.'[18]

Faced with such difficulties, Chadwick was forced to propagandize for health reforms. His hand was strengthened by the Duke of Buccleuch's Royal Commission on the Sanitary State of Large Towns and Populous Districts, which he unofficially directed. It produced three published reports on the environmental and administrative problems of towns. The Bradford Board of Surveyors gave evidence to this body on 22 March 1844 and noted that, since the board had to retire from office at the end of the year and seek re-election: 'they are aware that ... a strong party may assemble and that a new board (may be elected) who may be either totally ignorant of their duties or who ... being averse to the present Board may suspend the improvements going on ...' They also reported upon the appalling health problems, most particularly the fact that the Bradford Canal is supplied with water from the Beck: 'This noxious compound is conveyed through the sluice to the canal where it undergoes a process which renders it still more offensive ... so that the waters of the canal are scarcely ever cool in summer and constantly emit the most offensive gases ...'[19]

Other developments also increased support for Chadwick's health reforms. Dr Southwood Smith helped to organize the Provincial Health of Towns Association, formed in December 1844, which produced special reports on six towns including Liverpool, Preston and Huddersfield. Chadwick also began his ill-ventured Towns Improvement Company and the Public Health Association also added to the debate.

This campaigning led to a spate of minor legislative reforms such as the Nuisances Removal Act of 1846, which allowed the justices in petty sessions to prosecute those responsible for nuisances, and the 1847 Town Improvement Clauses Act and the Town Police Clauses Act, which consolidated and defined the obligations of towns to lay water supplies and main drainage schemes and to control nuisances. There was also legislation connected with cemeteries, public washhouses and the like. Nonetheless, Chadwick always found that there were vested interests to be dealt with and that the many different bodies involved in public health either blocked effective legislation or created administrative chaos.

Water commissioners, commissioners of sewers, Poor Law guardians, highway surveyors, select vestries, street commissioners and improvement commissioners all contributed to public health, and private water companies and other commercial concerns had interests to protect. In London there were in fact about 300 bodies administering local Acts. Chadwick wrote to Ashley in 1844:

> frequently interested parties are seated at Board of Guardians who are ready to stop anything which may lead to expenditure for the proper repair of the dwellings of the labouring classes.
> Where measures of drainage are proposed and the works carried

out by Commissioners of Sewers are found to be defective a cry is raised nothing must be done for fear of offending the Commissioners ... When additional supplies of water are called for ... one cry raised is 'Oh the interest of the companies is too powerful to be touched'.[20]

Above all, there was resentment at the suggestion that local bodies should lose their powers to some central administration. The localities wished to run their own affairs, whilst Chadwick felt that, if they did so, local democracy would lead to inactivity. As a result of the threat of centralization, many of the largest towns and cities obtained their own Acts to administer local health reforms.

Nevertheless, many of these local Acts were produced with the desire to avoid central government legislation. The Leeds Improvement Act of 1842 emerged from an attempt to avoid the obligations contained within the general Acts being discussed in 1841. Manchester and all the other large cities did similarly. One of the most important of these Acts was the Liverpool Sanitary Act of 1846, which made the corporation a health authority and obliged it to appoint an engineer, an inspector of nuisances and a medical officer of health. W. H. Duncan became Liverpool's medical officer of health, the first such in Britain.

Thus a variety of factors obtained to check the propaganda campaign which Chadwick had mounted. Some of these blocks came to the fore when Lord Morpeth, a minister in Russell's government, discussed the possibility of a Public Health Bill in 1847. An attempt to introduce a Bill was made in 1847 but failed. Morpeth introduced the Bill again in 1848 but was again opposed by those who feared centralization and the loss of local self-government and came in for particular criticism from Joshua Toulmin Smith, who wrote in the *Morning Chronicle* and attacked centralization in his book *Centralisation or Representation*. As a result of these attacks, the 1848 Act was reduced in both power and scope. The only redeeming feature was that a report in 1848 led to the formation of the Metropolitan Commission on Sewers, out of which the London County Council was to emerge.

The 1848 Public Health Act was in fact a permissive piece of legislation and there was no compulsion for local health boards to be established and to take action until death rates reached 23 per 1,000. However, petitions from 10 per cent of the ratepayers in communities where death rates were less than 23 per 1,000 could lead to the formation of a local health board. There were in fact 284 applications to form local Boards of Health between 1848 and 1853, 168 from those with a death rate of less than 23 per 1,000. The Act also established the General Board of Health in London, with Chadwick as its salaried commissioner. However, it was essentially an advisory and co-ordinating body and not an initiator of reforms. It was the cholera epidemic of 1848 and 1849 that extended its powers, although most of the larger cities applied for their own Acts in order to limit the ability of the General Board to direct their activities.

The cholera outbreak of 1848 gave the Act rather more significance than it would otherwise have had, for it forced politicians to take the issue of public health seriously. As *The Times* reflected: 'The Cholera is the best of all sanitary reformers, it overlooks no mistake and pardons no oversight.'[21] Its impact was not because it was a major killer but because it was a shock disease that affected the middle classes just as much as the working classes, although it was often the working-class areas that suffered most.

The propelling influence of cholera was evident in the less heavily, as well as the newly, industrialized towns. In Reading it was the southern part of the town, the working-class district, that was most affected in 1849 and here it was Silver Street that was 'likely to be prejudicial to health ... for cholera is a health inspector that speaks in a language nobody can misunderstand'.[22] Even though Reading was not a major sufferer from cholera, it did encourage a relatively dormant council to take action to deal with the 3,000 cesspools that dominated the town's health problems in the 1850s and 1860s. Indeed: 'Cholera was a disease that few ignored in [the] nineteenth century and the reaction to cholera in Reading's council was typical of a wider, national reaction invoking issues of political power, knowledge and legitimate government.'[23]

Temporarily, at least, the General Board exercised increased power and influence. Yet by 1854 only 184 boards had been firmly established and only 13 of these had initiated waterworks and sewerage schemes. The fact is that the General Board lacked real influence and support. This was particularly the case in London, where the Treasury refused to provide the finance for the General Board to purchase cemeteries in London. The 1852 Water Act also allowed the existing water companies to continue to sell water. This provoked *The Times* to reflect that:

> The simple truth is, not that the Board of Health has neglected its duties but that it has misconceived its opportunities and miscalculated its scope. It originally acquired unnatural licence from extraordinary circumstances of popular fear, but instead of subsiding into sentiment of practical decorum as the public cooled down it foolishly pushed the notions and pretensions to a height more preposterous than before ... The cholera has departed out of sight and mind and we have relapsed into indifference or something beyond. Everything we ought to have done, we have left undone.[24]

The real problem was that there were too many vested interests. The case of London demonstrates this point. A Metropolitan Commission reported on, and was theoretically responsible for, health in London between 1847 and 1850 and, although Chadwick managed to control some of its sub-committees, the entrenched vested interests would not permit the commission to yield to the General Board. Chadwick changed tack and encouraged the formation of a Royal Commission on the Sanitation in London in 1850. This examined the cut-price competition that went on between the eight water companies in the metropolitan district and recommended that the 300,000 houses involved in London should be supplied by stand-pipes at a rate of between 1 to 20 and 1 to 30 houses. It also further maintained that the Thames should be abandoned as a water supply, that the existing companies should be abolished and that there should be a wider supply to houses. In other words, this was an attack upon the inactivity and failures of the Metropolitan Commission.

But the government was not prepared to implement the full Royal Commission report. In 1850 the General Board was given only half of the London area to control. It was to be given the rest in the Water Bill of 1851 but the Treasury brought this to a halt by its refusal to finance the purchase of the eight water companies at a cost of £250,000. The water companies, with joint capital of about £5,000,000, had opposed the water scheme of the General Board and the government decided to defer its decision about a Chadwickian water supply system for London. Other legislation anticipated for London was also blighted.

Outside London there were similar problems for the board. Eric Midwinter has demonstrated that the 1848 Public Health Act was only taken up by 26 Lancashire townships between 1848 and 1858 and thus, by 1858, that only about 400,000 Lancastrians out of more than 2,500,000 were subject to the 1848 Act and the General Board.[25] Midwinter also added that many of the local Boards of Health were run by a few uninspired persons who were underpaid and inefficient. Also, there was little in the way of a link between the local Boards of Health and the General Board of Health.

The General Board continued until 1858, although a second board had been formed on 12 August 1854, with Sir Benjamin Hall as its permanent salaried secretary. In effect, the General Board of Health ceased to carry weight in 1854 once Chadwick, dubbed the 'grand lama of sanitary reform', was dismissed.[26]

The age of Simon

In the twenty or so years that followed the dismissal of Chadwick the leading spirit in public health reform was Dr (later Sir) John Simon. Unlike Chadwick – who attempted, but failed, to create a centralized system of administration – Simon attempted to work with the local administrations, to such an extent that he obtained a uniformity of provision which went some way towards Chadwick's aims.

Simon was a London doctor who had been appointed London's first medical officer of health in 1848 and became medical officer of the General Board of Health in 1855. In 1858 the functions of the General Board of Health were divided between the Local Government Act Office and the new Medical Department of the Privy Council, which appointed Simon as its first medical officer. In this post, Simon effected improvements in the administration of health within a permissive framework of legislation. He encouraged the adoption of the large number of local Public Health Acts that were being sought in these years.

There was in fact a confusing array of bodies responsible for public health, ranging from Poor Law guardians to town councils, improvement commissioners and select vestries. Their responsibilities were often overlapping. As Derek Fraser suggests, their were four main types of legislation in the public health field: straightforward Public Health Bills that gave local boards the powers to appoint officials; Nuisance Removal Acts setting national guidelines; water supply and sewage disposal legislation (Sewage Utilisation Act, 1865); and legislation dealing with epidemics, such as the Disease Prevention Acts of 1848 and 1855. 'These four Areas of public health law – sanitary, nuisance, sewer and disease prevention also competed with the whole range of local Acts which individual areas had procured.'[27]

Simon could only *encourage* the development of public health measures, given that his powers were restricted to the sanctioning of loans. As a result, there were no powers to force new houses to be connected to mains sewers. He therefore focused his attention upon producing statistical evidence in health. His *Papers Relating to the Sanitary State of the People of England*, published in 1858, collected information on the appalling sanitary situation still prevailing in England and drew attention to four types of disease – diarrhoeal, fever, pulmonary infections and infantile disorders. Simon's work was given added impact by the fact that 1858 was the year of the 'great stink', when the Thames reached an all-time high in terms of pollution.

These concerns about health led to the 1859 Public Health Act, which created a National Vaccine Establishment, allowed the Privy Council to investigate all matters of public health, transferred some powers to the Privy Council, and stated that medical officers of health should, from time to time, report to the Privy Council.

The Medical Department of the Privy Council operated from 1859 until 1871 but found that its influence was watered down by the fact that the Home Office, the Board of Trade and other departments of government had overlapping health responsibilities. Yet, influenced by Simon, the Medical Department undertook numerous medical surveys: the

Greenhow Survey on tuberculosis, dietary surveys in Lancashire, typhus surveys, and the like. It developed social survey techniques to a fine art.

Yet by 1865 Simon had came to the conclusion that permissive powers must be replaced by obligatory powers and he stated in his annual report:

> I venture to submit that the time has now arrived when it ought not any longer to be discretional in a place whether that place shall be kept filthy or not. Powers sufficient for the local protection of public health having been universally conferred, it next, I submit, ought to be an obligation on the local authorities that these powers be exercised in good faith and with reasonable vigour and intelligence.'[28]

As a result of this report, the Sanitary Act of 1866 was passed.

This 1866 Act made sanitary powers, previously restricted to the local Boards of Health, available on a universal basis; it enlarged the jurisdiction of those authorities responsible for nuisance removal, because it included houses for the first time; and it enjoined all nuisance-removal authorities to perform their functions efficiently. Effectively, it extended the influence of central government over local government. It allowed the Medical Department of the Privy Council to encourage more towns to appoint a medical officer of health; in 1866 only 22 of the 68 large towns outside London had such a post. It also permitted Simon to be more influential in supporting the extension of the Contagious Diseases Acts, promoting vaccination and encouraging more social surveys.[29] Under his stewardship, there was a gathering pace of government loans to local authorities for sanitary purposes. Over £11,000,000 was loaned between 1848 and 1872, a sum which rose to £22,000,000 between 1873 and 1880.[30]

Notwithstanding such developments, the 1866 legislation was badly drafted. As a result of pressure throughout the country, the Royal Sanitary Commission, a Royal Commission, was set up in 1869. Its report of 1871 shaped the subsequent debate between the Liberal and Tory parties over health reform. The 1871 Local Government Board Act established the new Local Government Board, which consolidated the functions of the Local Government Board, the Registrar-General's Office, the Medical Department of the Privy Council and the Poor Law Board. The 1872 Public Health Act created a local version of this by establishing sanitary authorities, whose duties were obligatory, throughout the country. There were to be town councils and local boards in urban areas and guardians in rural areas. They had, for instance, to appoint a medical officer of health. What Liverpool had done in 1847 now became universal, as Chadwick had wanted it to do in 1842.

Simon therefore presided over substantial changes in the administration of health in Britain. He worked for the state on health matters from 1855 until 1876 when, at the age of 59, he left public service. During his period of responsibility he had brought about gradual change by building up confidence between local and central government and had achieved more than the far more radical Chadwick.

Progress or failure? The painstaking consolidation and failures of the late nineteenth and early twentieth centuries

Wohl has stressed that there were over 1,000 sanitary districts in England and Wales in the second half of the nineteenth century and that very few have been subject to any detailed research.[31] Therefore, it is difficult to assess accurately what was achieved in the field of public health in the twenty-five or thirty years leading up to the 1875 Act. Nonetheless, it is clear that death rates in the 1870s were lower, but not significantly so, than they had been in the 'filthy forties'. The national statistics – although they may have been subject to under-registration until 1874, when registration became compulsory – certainly suggest only minor improvements and the national infant mortality rate seems to have stuck at about 152 or 153 per 1,000 between the 1840s and 1870s, with levels in many industrial towns being well over 200 per 1,000. The 'massacre of the innocents' continued despite increasing expenditure on public health. More precisely, Barbara Thompson has suggested that Bradford's incorporation in 1847 had partly been due to the demand for sanitary reform and that over one million pounds had been paid by ratepayers between 1847 and 1872 to promote improvements in public health. Yet the results of this expenditure were far from impressive.[32] Why, then, were major health improvements not achieved, despite a rising level of public health expenditure and an improving organizational structure?

Thompson suggests that in Bradford the faltering improvements in public health were due to a variety of factors, at the centre of which was the slow and limited action of the local authorities, whose improvements were designed to benefit the middle rather than the working classes. Indeed, the middle classes and the 'minority of muck' delayed or prevented the municipal authority from dealing with the smoke problem from the steam engines that drove the worsted mills and the Bradford Water Company and its supporters were able to delay the municipalization of the water supply until October 1855. In the end, the municipality had to be in tune with the demands of its ratepayers and Thompson concludes on the Bradford experience that: 'no Town Council could afford to be in advance of the opinion of its ratepayers. The 1848 Public Health Act, of which so much had been expected, turned out to be a damp squib so far as the incorporated towns were concerned.'[33] In any case, the powers of town councils were often less than supposed.

In the early 1850s they could only turn down plans for houses on the grounds of inadequate drainage, not because they were back-to-back or cellar dwellings, and it was not until 1858 that town councils could compel house builders to provide sinks. The ratepayers had limits which all town councils had to respect and the new public health reforms moved very slowly. In some cases this may have been bad for the towns, but in the case of Bradford, whose water supply was limited and whose sewerage arrangements were defective, the introduction of a water closet system may well have presented more dangers than a continued reliance upon smelly privy middens, which at least did not foul the water supply.

The case of Bradford was by no means unique. Many towns experienced similar delays. In Liverpool an Act of 1854 permitted the council to demand that house-owners convert to WCs but it was three years before Liverpool had the water supply to meet such demands. It was another six years before moves towards the provision of water closets began in earnest.[34] Leeds and other towns also made halting attempts to embark upon financially expensive and politically unpopular public health schemes.[35]

For many urban areas, then, there was only a gradual improvement in the administrative infrastructure of health in the years between 1840 and 1875. There were some early landmarks, such as Dr Joseph Bazalgette's scheme to provide pipes and main sewers to the North of the Thames and a covered reservoir at Barking Green, and the work of James Simpson (1799–1869) to develop the slow sand filter in Glasgow in the 1820s and to pipe clean water from Long Ditton, ten miles upstream of the Thames, down to the centre of London for the Lambeth Water Company. The work of Dr John Snow in connection with cholera also emphasized the need to control the quality of the water supply. All these developments helped to improve the sewerage and water supply of London and paved the way for clean, filtrated water. The subsequent move towards building reservoirs also made a big impact upon water quality. Yet it was not until the late nineteenth century, when an effective and uniform administrative structure was in place and when the Local Government Board began to sanction more loans for public health (£267,000 in 1871, £3,098,000 in 1878 and £7,267,000 in 1893), that real health improvements occurred.[36] This was evident in the infant mortality figures, which fell from approximately 150 per 1,000 to around 100 per 1,000. This all-round improvement in child death rates can be seen in the case of Bradford (see Table 5.3), although Bradford's rates were much higher than the national averages and the economic depression of the mid-1880s to the mid-1890s offset some of the earlier improvements. Nevertheless, the mid-1870s appear to have been some type of watershed in the public health of Britain: new health changes were afoot.

Table 5.3   Death rates per 1,000 in Bradford during the late nineteenth century [37]

Years	All ages	Infant mortality rate	1–4 Years	5 and over
1871–5	26.7	203	50	15.6
1876–80	23.8	167	44	14.7
1881–5	19.9	161	29	13.6
1886–90	21	170	35	14.3
1891–5	19.8	176	32	14.3
1896–1900	18	166	26	13
Change	−33%	−18%	−48%	−17%

The Public Health Act of 1875 codified previous legislation and provided the basis of public health activity up to 1936. Richard Cross, Disraeli's Home Secretary, also introduced the Artizans' and Labourers' Dwellings Act in 1875, which enabled local authorities to replace insanitary housing. They were already empowered to register, inspect and even to set up common lodging-houses under an Act of 1851 and an 1866 Act did permit councils to borrow money at low rates of interest to provide working-class housing. W. M. Torrens's Artizans' and Labourers' Dwellings Act of 1868 allowed councils to demand that owners improve their property and to purchase and demolish insanitary properties. But this Act dealt with individual properties, whereas the 1875 Act envisaged the redevelopment of whole areas, such as Corporation Street in Birmingham. Both Acts were permissive and limited in their effectiveness and, as a result, had to be amended in 1879.

Some councils took these responsibilities seriously, though the majority did not. Liverpool did develop an experimental block of council cottages in 1869 and cities such as Leeds and Birmingham went in for redevelopment and house building in the mid-1870s. Still, it was not until the 1890s that more councils began to take an interest in housing improvements and council-house building. The 1890 Housing of the Working Classes Act, although still permissive, gave councils the powers either to deal with individual houses or to redevelop areas under its A and B sections. Nevertheless, such actions were expensive, likely to be resisted by the Defence of Property League and did not lead to much house building except in one or two towns; it was not until 1907/8 that 'progressive' Bradford obtained its first council houses.

The provision of municipal housing in Bradford was indeed a slow and painstaking affair. It had been the plank of many Independent Labour party (ILP) municipal programmes and their representatives raised it before the sanitary committee (later the health committee) in connection with the clearance of the Longlands Street area, a notorious housing and health black spot in Bradford. In 1898 Fred Jowett, a member of the Independent Labour party and vice-chairman of the sanitary committee, persuaded the Bradford medical officer of health to make an official representation to the committee about Longlands which, under the 1890 Housing Act, compelled the council to submit an improvement scheme. Jowett hoped that such a scheme would be introduced quickly and would offer working-class families at least a basic corporation house of two bedrooms, a bathroom and WC at the reasonable rent of 4s. 6d. per week. But he had not reckoned with the trenchant opposition of the property owners and the Liberty and Property Defence League.

They objected because their compensation under the 1890 Act would be less than under the compulsory purchase terms of street improvement schemes.[38] The scheme which the council put forward in 1899 was instantly rejected and sent back to the health committee, of which Jowett was now chairman, and a new scheme was drawn up and presented to the council in October 1899. It proposed to deal with the Longlands area, a piece of land of 22,650 square yards which contained 284 houses and 1,360 persons, a density of 301 persons per acre compared with the city average of 21.6 per acre. It was an area where the death rate was 50.8 per 1,000, compared with the Bradford average of 17.54. Despite the evidence, the scheme was only passed by one vote and was quickly rescinded by the Tories after the municipal elections.[39]

Although further attempts were made to press forward with the Longlands scheme, it was not until August 1901 that Bradford City Council agreed to clear the area, that tenements to accommodate 432 persons would be erected and that small 'through' houses would be built in Faxfleet Street for the 925 displaced persons.[40] Limited as this scheme was compared to the total slum problem of Bradford, it was still strongly disapproved of by Tories and some Liberals, who fought to prevent any further extension of municipal housing. Independent Labour party leaders later argued that:

> The leader of the Liberal party in Bradford, Alderman H. B. Priestman, has recently been claiming that his party is just as anxious to remove slums and remedy poverty as the Socialists. Whilst we do not doubt that in the main both Liberals and Tories have the kindliest feelings towards their poorer fellow citizens, yet we feel compelled to point out that when it comes to an actual conflict between the sacredness of human life and the sacredness of property, they are generally to be found on the side of property.[41]

The trenchant opposition of the Liberals and Tories had not been dissipated before 1907 and the Labour group's demand for a solution to the housing problem had to await new legislation after the First World War.

The public health problems of the nation were thus dealt with slowly and almost grudgingly. Because the state adopted a policy of almost nudging the local administrative structures into action, the pace of development was inevitably variable. The Civic Gospel movement of the 1850s and 1860s, nurtured by Christian Socialists such as the Revd Charles Kingsley and the Revd F. D. Maurice, worked in tandem with the efforts of groups of Liberals and Nonconformists in Birmingham, such as Joseph Chamberlain, George Dawson and Robert Dale, to foster new responsibilities amongst the borough authorities. By the 1860s the civic ideal was catching the public mood. Indeed, Robert Dale, the Birmingham Nonconformist minister, stated that:

> Towards the end of the 'sixties a few Birmingham men made the discovery that perhaps a strong and able Town Council might do almost as much to improve the conditions of life in the towns as Parliament itself ... speakers ... dwelt with glowing enthusiasm on what a great and prosperous town like Birmingham might do for its people. They spoke of sweeping away streets in which it was not possible to live a healthy and decent life; of making the town cleaner, sweeter, brighter; of providing gardens, parks and a museum; they insisted that great monopolies like the gas and water supply should be in the hands of the corporation; that good water should be supplied without stint at the lowest possible prices.[42]

It was the municipal revolution and the emergence of what was called 'gas and water socialism' that paved the way for the improvements in public health towards the end of the nineteenth century. Nevertheless, the health of the nation remained an issue of serious concern at the turn of the century, not least because infant mortality remained almost intractable at a very high level.

The public health problems of Britain at the beginning of the twentieth century are dealt with in detail in Chapter eight. Yet it needs to be established in this chapter that the 'national efficiency' debate and the problem of high infant mortality rates were at the forefront of political and social debate in the first decade of the twentieth century. Infant mortality, which had been around 150 per 1,000 for England and Wales in the mid-nineteenth century, remained stubbornly resistant to reductions. It remained well over 100 per 1,000 in the Edwardian years before coming down to 88 per 1,000 in 1920 and 53 per 1,000 in 1938.[43] Yet such figures hid a great deal of regional and occupational diversity. Between 1896 and 1905 infant mortality averages were high in most

Lancashire towns: 166 per 1,000 in Bolton, 220 (233 in 1903) in Burnley, and 208 in Preston.[44] Death rates did come down considerably in all these towns over the next few years – although they were still in the 120–60 per 1,000 range for most Lancashire towns on the eve of the First World War. At this time great emphasis was placed upon the need to improve mothering skills and great interest was shown in the Huddersfield scheme of Alderman Broadbent, which provided a financial incentive for parents to register their children and to keep them alive through the first year of life. It was claimed that this had helped to reduce infant mortality in Huddersfield from an average of 142 per 1,000 between 1895 and 1904 to an average of 117 per 1,000 between 1905 and 1907. Indeed, the 1907 figure had fallen to 97 per 1,000. Along with tuberculosis, infant mortality was considered to be one of the scourges of the early twentieth century.

One of the great concerns of politicians was that despite vast expenditure on new sewerage and water schemes in the late nineteenth century, there had been no major downward movement in infant mortality and death rate figures – only the most gradual of reductions from the 1870s onwards. In searching for explanations, great emphasis was placed upon the need to educate people about ill health and the failures of mothers to appreciate what was necessary for their children. The Broadbent scheme was an attempt to make mothers more aware of the need to look after their children more carefully. The fact that the vast majority of working-class housing was of a poor and often insanitary nature and that piped water was not readily available does not seem to have entered into the calculation.

Certainly the Edwardian years saw a concerted campaign by voluntary organizations and the municipality to tackle the poor state of public health. The Guild of Help, a philanthropic organization committed to community action to deal with poverty which soon outstripped the Charity Organisation Society in national importance, began to work with other philanthropic bodies, the Agenda Club and many local authorities to organize 'health weeks'.

The Agenda Club, formed in 1911, was a national organization of men who realized that 'all is not well with England'.[45] Formed by E. V. D. Birchall of Birmingham, who became the honorary secretary of the National Association of the Guilds of Help, it saw itself as the English Samurai, invited a Japanese official to its first annual meeting and proclaimed respect for 'these Samurai, careless of material gain'.[46] It was this body which appealed to guilds and other charity organizations to focus upon health by holding one week in the year – 28 April–4 May (1911) – as a time when public health measures would be raised throughout the country. In the first year its appeal was taken up by ten London boroughs and thirty provincial towns.

Municipal and voluntary bodies worked together to produce these weeks. In Bolton the Guild of Help revived the tuberculosis committee of 1911 and organized a health week in 1912 in which health problems were highlighted, special lessons on hygiene were offered in schools, board of guardians and sanitary committee leaflets were distributed, visits were organized to the Wilkinson sanatorium where 'the methods of fighting the white scourge' (tuberculosis) were demonstrated, there were visits to the sewage works and the corporation waterworks, and numerous other activities.[47] A second health week was organized in Bolton and in other towns from 6–12 April 1913.

Indeed, philanthropic bodies were very deeply involved in health provision. The County Borough of Bolton Guild of Help did, for instance, provide an open-air shelter for consumptives.[48] But their relationship with municipal and local authorities was not always easy. At the national conference of the Guild of Help in 1913 L. V. Sharp, of Leeds, suggested that: 'One of the difficulties in the way of voluntary service was a certain nervousness on the part of the municipal and local authorities as to accepting co-operation with voluntary agencies.'[49] The relations between the guild and the local authorities were eased, however, by the fact that the eighty or so guilds that emerged usually had the local mayor as their president. By 1911 two-thirds or more of the guilds existing at that time were acting in concert with local health departments and education committees.[50] There was, indeed, co-operation between health visitors and inspectors. The Bradford health inspectors and the Bradford Guild of Help worked together to deal with families on the milk lists and those who lived in dirty houses.[51]

It is, of course, difficult to establish the extent to which improvements occurred as a result of philanthropic and municipal efforts. The Liberal reforms that will be discussed in Chapter eight obviously left some mark on public health. However, what is clear is that standards did improve from about 1904 onwards, although the real pace of public health improvement seems to have begun after the First World War.

Conclusion

For the vast majority of the nineteenth century public health was slow to improve. Local administrative structures lacked uniformity and effectiveness, despite the efforts of some individuals, whilst central government lacked commitment. Chadwick had a vision of a central authority administering public health to some uniform standard but found that local resistance made such a concept untenable in a nation concerned with the preservation of individual liberties. Nevertheless, much was achieved as a result of central government encouraging and directing local authorities to accumulate powers and responsibilities. By 1875 a public health system had emerged but the nation was far from healthy. Although deaths arising from some diseases and conditions had fallen, death rates generally still remained high and infant mortality proved resistant to all the expensive water and sewerage engineering projects that were developed in the late nineteenth century.

The 'national efficiency' debate of the early twentieth century focused the attention of both private and public interests on the need to tackle infant mortality, tuberculosis and other health problems more effectively. The Liberal reforms helped to tackle ill health, but in the end improvements in public health depended upon raising the standard of living for the majority. The First World War did this for the poorest section of the community and the inter-war years saw a remarkable improvement in the quality of housing. There were still problems of income and, as we shall see, unemployment made its contribution to persistent ill health. But improving public health depended upon improving the environment and income and job prospects.

The nineteenth century had concentrated upon achieving a public health administration that was consistent with both local democracy and individual rights. However, by 1900 it was becoming obvious that even the most expensive engineering schemes could not bring about a major breakthrough in health unless the living standards of the majority were also improved.

Notes

1. S. E. Finer, *The Life and Times of Sir Edwin Chadwick* (1953); Royston Lambert, *Sir John Simon, 1816–1904, and English Social Administration* (1963).
2. Oliver MacDonagh, 'The Nineteenth-Century Revolution in Government: A Reappraisal', *Historical Journal* 1 (1958), pp. 52–67; S. E. Finer, 'The Transmission of Benthamite Ideas 1820–1850', in Gillian Sutherland (ed.), *Studies in the Growth of Nineteenth-Century Government* (Totowa, NJ, 1972), pp. 11–32; E. C. Midwinter, *Social Administration in Lancashire 1830–1860: Poor Law, Public Health and Police* (Manchester, 1969); Lambert, *Sir John Simon;* Robert M. Gutchen, 'Local Improvements and Centralisation in Nineteenth-Century England; *Historical Journal* 4 (1961).
3. Anthony S. Wohl, *Endangered Lives: Public Health in Victorian Britain* (Cambridge, Mass., 1983), p. 3.
4. *Ibid.*, p. 169.
5. Midwinter, *Social Administration in Lancashire*, pp. 107–8; Christopher Hamlin, 'Muddling in Bumbledom: On the Enormity of Large Sanitary Improvements in Four British Towns, 1855–1885', *Victorian Studies* 32 (1988), pp. 55–83.

6.   *Leeds Intelligencer,* 21 August 1841.
7.   B. Keith-Lucas, *The Unreformed Local Government System* (1984), chapter five.
8.   *Ibid.,* p. 116.
9.   B. Keith-Lucas, 'Some Influences Affecting the Development of Sanitary Legislation in England', *Economic History Review* (1953–4).
10. D. Fraser, *The Evolution of the British Welfare State* (1984), p. 60.
11. E. Chadwick, *Report on the Sanitary Condition of the Labouring Population of Great Britain* (1842; 1965), pp. 219–27.
12. Bills of mortality were first published for London in the sixteenth century and were published for other towns in the late eighteenth century.
13. *Philosophical Transactions of the Royal Society* 64, pp. 54, 438; 65, pp. 85, 322, 424.
14. *Works, Literary Moral and Medical, of Thomas Percival, MD* (1807), p. cxcix.
15. Keith-Lucas, 'Sanitary Legislation in England', pp. 291–2.
16. Chadwick, *Report on the Sanitary Condition,* p. 424.
17. R. A. Lewis, *Edwin Chadwick and the Public Health Movement 1832–1854* (1952), p. 108; also quoted in Fraser, *Evolution,* p. 66.
18. Thoresby Society (Leeds) 22B10, 'Projected Leeds Waterworks', MS note, quoted in Fraser, *Evolution,* p. 67.
19. *Second Report of the Commissioners for Inquiries into the State of Large Towns and Populous Districts,* ii (1845), pp. 182–8.
20. Lewis, *Chadwick,* p. 110. Also quoted in Fraser, *Evolution,* pp. 68–9.
21. *The Times,* 5 September 1848. About 32,000 people died of cholera in 1831–2, 62,000 in 1848–9, 20,000 in 1853–2 and 14,000 in 1866–7.
22. Klause-John Dodds, 'Much Ado about Nothing? Cholera, Local Politics and Public Health in Nineteenth-Century Reading', *Local Historian* 21/4 (1991), p. 171, quoting from the *Berkshire Chronicle* for 1849, though no precise date is given.
23. *Ibid.,* p. 175.
24. *The Times,* 21 June 1852.
25. Midwinter, *Social Administration in Lancashire,* pp. 83–4.
26. Lewis, *Chadwick,* p. 369.
27. Fraser, *Evolution,* p. 73.
28. Lambert, *Sir John Simon,* p. 370.
29. There were 74 local enquiries between 1856 and 1866 and 232 between 1867 and 1872. There were also about 3,700,000 vaccinations between 1867 and 1874.
30. Wohl, *Endangered Lives,* p. 162.
31. *Ibid.,* p. 166.
32. Barbara Thompson, 'Public Provision and Private Neglect: Public Health', in D. G. Wright and J. A. Jowitt (eds.), *Victorian Bradford* (Bradford, 1981), pp. 137–64.
33. *Ibid.,* p. 146.
34. Wohl, *Endangered Lives,* p. 102.
35. *Ibid.,* pp. 104–5.
36. *Ibid.,* p. 162.
37. Thompson, 'Public Provision and Private Neglect', p. 157.

38. F. Brockway, *Socialism over Sixty Years: The Life of Jowett of Bradford* (1946), p. 51. Also K. Laybourn, ' "The Defence of Bottom Dog": The Independent Labour Party in Local Politics', in Wright and Jowitt (eds.), *Victorian Bradford*, pp. 235–7.

39. Brockway, *Jowett of Bradford*, p. 52; *Bradford Observer*, 28 October 1899.

40. Brockway, *Jowett of Bradford*, p. 52.

41. *Forward*, 18 October 1907.

42. A. W. W. Dale, *The Life of R. W. Dale* (1899), p. 401.

43. K. Laybourn, *Britain on the Breadline: A Social and Political History of Britain between the Wars* (Gloucester, 1990), pp. 55–8.

44. *County Borough of Bolton Guild of Help Magazine* 2/7 (April 1908), p. 88.

45. *The Helper* (Bolton) 6/4 (April 1912), p. 49.

46. *Ibid.*

47. *Ibid.*, pp. 49–50.

48. County Borough of Bolton Guild of Help, *Seventh Annual Report* (year ending November 1912), p. 31; County Borough of Bolton Guild of Help, Minutes, Finance and General Purposes Committee, 26 July 1913.

49. *County Borough of Bolton Guild of Help Magazine* 7/29 (October 1913).

50. *Ibid.*, 12 June 1911, p. 5, reporting on the annual conference of the Guilds of Help at Birmingham, 1911.

51. Bradford City Guild of Help, *Seventh Annual Report* (1910–11).

CHAPTER SIX

EDUCATION
c.1800–1944

In the course of the nineteenth century the state assumed increasing responsibility for the education of the working classes in England and Wales. Whilst it did attempt to increase the efficiency, effectiveness and probity of the secondary and public schools, through the work of the charity commissioners and the Clarendon and Taunton Commissions of the 1860s, it was more concerned with the improvement of the education of the general population. As the century progressed, the state accepted that educating the working classes was desirable, decided that it could not rely upon voluntary effort alone and, in the twentieth century, began to make decisions about how far up the educational ladder the working classes could go. From barely recognizing the need for workers to receive an education at the beginning of the nineteenth century, the state had come to accept, in a formal sense, that every child should receive both an elementary and secondary education as of right by 1944. There were many elements which shaped this dramatic transformation in the role of the state, but two dominating factors existed in the form of the industrial challenge from Britain's industrial competitors and the extension of democratic political rights to the working classes, an action which demanded the development of both economic and social as well as political citizenship.

Education and the lower orders, c. 1800–1833

When, in 1807, Samuel Whitbread MP attempted to create pauper schools throughout the country, he failed because of the intense opposition of such people as Davies Giddy, who proclaimed that the scheme would:

> be found to be prejudicial to the morals and happiness of the labouring classes; it would teach them to despise their lot in life, instead of making them good servants in agriculture and other laborious employments to which their rank in society has destined them; instead of teaching them subordination it would render them factious and refractory as was evident in the manufacturing counties; it would enable them to read seditious pamphlets, vicious books and publications against Christianity; it would render them insolent to their superiors ...[1]

This view did not persist once it became clear that industrial growth was creating a mass of people who clearly lacked educational provision. With educational destitution evident for all to see, some members of the middle classes began to push for the provision of a Christian education which could inculcate the right attitudes amongst the labouring population.

The main spokesman for the education of the labouring population was Henry Brougham, who was a Whig Lord Chancellor in the early 1830s. One of the political giants of his age, he was – above all – the great founder of the idea of state intervention in education. He was acquainted with James Mill and Jeremy Bentham and was committed to Benthamite/utilitarian notions about the need for an efficient, educated and effective workforce. Brougham developed many of his ideas in the *Edinburgh Review,* of which he was the editor in 1810. He advocated the fourfold plan of investigating educational provision, offering state support to voluntary educational societies, encouraging parents to pay for the education of their children, and examining whether charity endowments for the 'education of the poor' were being used properly.

Brougham's ideas were influential and the commitment to both voluntary effort and parental responsibility were to become major features of state support for education in England and Wales throughout the nineteenth century. Indeed, the Anglicans set up their National Society – to provide cheap charity education for the working classes – in 1811 and the Nonconformists formed the British and Foreign School Society – which evolved out of the Royal Lancastrian Society of 1808 – in 1814. Both societies were supported by Brougham and were influenced, respectively, by the ideas of Andrew Bell and Joseph Lancaster, the Quaker who ran his own school in Borough Road, London. They developed schemes whereby children acted as monitors to other groups of children who had been set exercises under the overall supervision of a teacher.

A Charity Commission was set up and revealed the misuse of funds in the 1820s, but it had no powers to rectify the situation. More directly, however, Brougham investigated the level of educational destitution in Britain. Between 1816 and 1818 he chaired a parliamentary Committee of Inquiry on the Education of the Lower Orders in the Metropolis and Beyond. Its report, produced on 20 June 1816, concluded that a very large number of children were without any form of education, even though their parents were 'very desirous of obtaining that advantage for them', and that charitable donations should be investigated. In its second report, in 1818, it suggested that private subscriptions should be raised but that, where these were not forthcoming, the parish school system could be developed. Despite the fact that the committee found that only 7 per cent of the population were attending day schools, Brougham's Parochial Schools Bill of 1820 was defeated.

State or voluntary education? 1833–1870

Nevertheless, pragmatism prevailed as it became clear that the state had to encourage the voluntary schools to take action to supplement the educational efforts of parents. In 1833 Viscount Althorp, the Whig Chancellor, provided £20,000 to be granted to voluntary societies on a quid pro quo basis. The state was now attempting to finance voluntary education not according to educational need, but according to the scale of voluntary subscriptions raised.

Over the next three decades the state moved quite rapidly, at least after the first few years, towards subsidizing and encouraging voluntary educational effort. It tried to make good the educational weaknesses in the system, most notably by tackling low school attendance, the shortage of teachers, the lack of suitable textbooks and the deficiency of suitable buildings.

The 1833 Education Act was essentially a short-term building grant of up to £20,000 per year and the formation of a Committee of Council for Education, a committee of the Privy Council, in 1839 helped to ensure that this provision continued. This committee had been formed at the express wish of Queen Victoria, who instructed Lord John Russell to advise Lord Lansdowne that 'your lordship, with four others of the Queen's Servants, should form a board or Committee, for all matters affecting the Education of the People'.[2] This same letter also suggested that an inspectorate should be set up and that non-denominational training colleges (normal schools) might be established. The Tory-Anglican alliance blocked the non-denominational college idea and government control over teacher training was delayed a few years, but the committee was responsible for the founding of such denominational colleges as York St John and Battersea in 1843 and the emergence of a school inspectorate which was very much under the wing of the Anglicans.

Apart from the training of new teachers, the committee attempted to deal with teacher shortage through the creation of a pupil teacher minute, implemented by an Order in Council, on 25 August 1846. This created a system of grants whereby able children could carry out five extra years at school as paid monitors or pupil teachers. These pupil teachers could be appointed to schools where there were competent masters to teach them. They had to be 13 years of age, fluent readers and neat writers, and able to repeat the Catechism if they were Anglicans. They were to be inspected by the inspectors of education during their five-year apprenticeship and would be paid on a rising scale of £10–20 over this period. The schoolmasters and mistresses were also to be paid at the end of the year if their pupil teachers were considered satisfactory – at the rate of £5 for one, £9 for two, £12 for three, and

£3 for every additional pupil teacher after that. Those pupil teachers who were most proficient would be able to obtain a Queen's scholarship which would allow them to go to a normal school or training college. The whole scheme was a remarkable one for the ending of the monitorial system, the creation of an adequate teacher supply and the development of teacher training.

The early voluntary schools continued to use the Bible, and literature related to it, until the government recognized the need to provide book grants from the late 1840s onwards, which is when Longman, Green & Co. began to produce secular school textbooks.[3] Capitation grants were paid to rural and urban schools, respectively, in 1853 and 1856, thus encouraging teachers to improve attendance. Despite the voluntary nature of school attendance, these grants did increase the numbers at day schools. Other factors outside the immediate domain of the committee also encouraged educational attendance. Most notably, the 1844 Factory Act had demanded half-time education for all those children who worked in textile factories. The measure was extended to other types of industrial establishments in the 1860s.

Such state involvement in education created problems. One immediate concern was the cost of education. This rose from the £20,000 allocated in 1833 to more than £200,000 by 1850 and to just over £813,000 by 1861.[4] Educational expenditure appeared to be rising unchecked. A second problem concerned the influence of the Church of England, which claimed a privileged position with regard to education, and a third was the campaigning of the dissenters and Nonconformists, alarmed at the power of the Church of England.

It was the strength of the Anglican Church that posed the immediate problem. With its comprehensive parish system, it was able to raise more money than the dissenters and Nonconformists to trigger the pound for pound formula under the 1833 Act. In 1839 the Anglican Church had shaped the responsibilities and functions of the Committee of Council for Education and on 10 August 1840 its powers were confirmed by the same Order in Council which recorded the concordat with the Archbishop of Canterbury and gave the Archbishops of Canterbury and York the authority to appoint school inspectors and the automatic right to a report on any inspected National Society or Church of England school. Combined with the support of the Tory party in the House of Commons and the presence of bishops in the House of Lords, there was little doubt that the Church of England was in a position to exert substantial control over education.

Dissent also exerted its own considerable influence. Congregationalists, Unitarians – even Methodists and Roman Catholics – joined together in the 1840s to resist Anglican influence. Led by Edward Baines Jnr, editor of the *Leeds Mercury* and MP for Leeds in the 1860s, they petitioned Parliament to resist the 1843 Factory Bill which intended to create a half-time system and a parish system of schooling. So powerful was this extra-parliamentary lobby that the 1844 Factory Act omitted any reference to the supply of a comprehensive parish school system. The Yorkshire Voluntaryists, led by Baines, resisted all state education on the grounds that it was likely to be controlled by the Anglicans. Baines did not change his mind until the late 1860s, and then only temporarily. The Voluntaryists therefore insisted that religious denominations should provide their own education.

Inevitably, the state was faced with difficulties with developing any effective policy towards education. Yet it did introduce the policies already outlined under the guidance of Dr James Kay, later Sir James Kay-Shuttleworth, who was appointed the first Secretary of Education in 1839 and worked in that post for ten years. He had been a doctor in the Manchester slums and a Poor Law official and used this background to influence teacher training and to appoint an experienced group of educational officials. His concern for raising educational standards won increasing support, not least from some of his early opponents and most notably from W. F. Hook, vicar of Leeds, who began to see the need for compromise in education. Hook admitted in 1846 that:

> The Church has no more claim for exclusive pecuniary aid from the State or for any pecuniary aid at all, than is possessed by any other of those many corporations with which our country abounds. To call upon Parliament to vote any money for the exclusive support of the Church of England is to call upon Parliament to do what is unjust. The taxes are collected from persons of all religions and cannot be fairly expended for the exclusive maintenance of one.[5]

It was this changed attitude that encouraged Kay-Shuttleworth to develop the pupil–teacher training scheme, which found support from Anglicans, Wesleyans and Roman Catholics although not from Congregationalists and Unitarians, who opposed the development of state education in the 1847 general election.

Nonetheless, religious attitudes were changing. Some dissenters continued to oppose the state control of education and over 350 dissenting schools had been opened by 1851, but during the 1840s many Anglicans had come to accept that 'Popular education must be an affair of the State' and that 'The schoolmaster must become a public functionary, duly qualified for his office and under due control.'[6]

Kay-Shuttleworth resigned in 1849 and was replaced by R. R. W. Lingen, who remained in post until 1870, becoming secretary of what was renamed the Education Department after 1856. Widely regarded as a humourless administrator, Lingen strengthened the control of the state. The scale of expenditure rose dramatically: there were more than 15,000 pupil teachers in 1859 and more than 22,000 teachers receiving the appropriate teaching fee. Horace Mann's *Census of Education for 1851*, published in 1854, indicated that great strides had been made in education – day school attendance having risen from 477,000 in 1818 to 1,544,000 in 1833 and to more than 2,447,000 in 1851. Such growth and success was achieved, however, in a climate of concern about public expenditure.

The cost of the Crimean war and the rising level of public expenditure alarmed both MPs and administrators. A review of educational costs was in order and this was undertaken by a Royal Commission on Popular Education, chaired by the Duke of Newcastle, which was formed in 1858 and reported in 1861, issuing six volumes of evidence and findings.

Apart from the Duke of Newcastle, the commission consisted of Sir John Coleridge a (High-Churchman), Edward Miall (a dissenter and an opponent of state intervention), Nassau Senior (an economist who had served on the Poor Law Commission), the Revd William Rodgers (a leader in London education) and Revd W. C. Lake and Professor Goldwin Smith (both university lecturers). It investigated schooling provision in various districts and eventually provided the most detailed study of educational provision in England and Wales to date.

It found that the proportion of the population receiving education had risen from about 1 in 17 in 1818 to 1 in 7.6 by 1861, although that was still short of the objective of 1 in 6. More worrying was the fact that 38 per cent of the children attended schools for less than a year and that few extended their education beyond the age of 11. The standards of education were also low and few children of 10 or 11 appear to have developed the ability to read a newspaper or write a letter. In order to rectify this situation, the Newcastle *Report* suggested that there was a need to provide 'sound and cheap elementary instruction' and that there should be an element of payment by results for teachers: 'There can be no sort of doubt that if one teacher finds that his income depends on the condition that his scholars do learn to read, whilst another is paid equally well whether they do so or not, the first will teach more children to read than the second.'[7] Although the government was not inclined to support its other suggestions of setting up borough and county Boards of Education, drawing money for these from the rates, the commission's emphasis upon payment by results appealed to both Robert Lowe, the vice-president of the Education Department, and to Ralph Lingen. The principle was applied in the so-called 'Revised Code' of 1862, which came into operation on 1 August 1863.

Under the Revised Code, the government continued to provide building grants but also paid four shillings (20p) to all those children who attended 200 half-day sessions in schools per year and offered an additional eight shillings (40p) to those children who passed the appropriate standard, from one to six, in reading, writing and arithmetic – the three Rs. For passing each of these subjects, the pupil would earn one-third of the amount of money allocated to the three Rs. It was argued that, under this system, teachers would be forced to increase their efforts to improve the standards of education for fear of failing the annual inspection and thus losing income. As Robert Lowe informed the House of Commons in a much misquoted statement: 'I cannot promise the House of Commons that this system will be an economical one and I cannot promise that it will be an efficient one but I can promise that it shall be either one or the other. If it is not cheap it shall be efficient, if it is not efficient it shall be cheap.'[8]

There has been considerable debate about the impact of the Revised Code upon education. Contemporaries such as Matthew Arnold, who was a school inspector, suggested that it simply swept away many grants that were essential and encouraged rote learning: 'The work of teaching in school is less interesting and more purely mechanical than it used to be.'[9] Its defenders suggested that it would force teachers to spend as much time with the weakest children as well as the cleverest: 'Now, we press as clearly into the grounding work of the junior classes as we do into the more interesting instructions of the elders.'[10] In more recent times there has been a conflict of opinion between Mary Sturt, who has been critical of the Revised Code, and John Hurt, who has seen it as an essential part of the process whereby the state established its supremacy over the Church of England.[11]

Whatever the debate, it appears that Lowe achieved both parts of the equation, for his reforms made popular education both cheap and efficient. In 1861 the average attendance at schools to which the government paid grants was 855,077 and the parliamentary grants came to £813,441. By 1865 the average attendance was 1,016,558 and the parliamentary grant had fallen to £636,806. Both attendances and costs began to rise thereafter.[12] The salary of certificated masters fell from £94 10s. 3d. in 1861–2 to £86 10s. 9d. in 1865–6; those of the certificated mistresses fell from £62 15s. 5d. to £55 0s. 2d. in the same years; and the number of pupil teachers fell from 16,277 in 1861 to 10,955 by 1866. The number of resident students at training colleges also fell. Therefore, in the short term, there were financial reductions in educational spending, although the costs began to increase in the late 1860s.

The Revised Code had transformed the pattern of educational spending, strengthened the hand of the state and prepared the way for more unbroken education for the working classes. Yet it was the 1870 Education Act which established the right of every child to receive some form of schooling. Introduced by W. E. Forster, who had been in

Gladstone's Liberal ministry between 1862 and 1870, the 1870 Education Act was a product of many developments in the 1860s. In the first instance, the second Reform Act of 1867, with its enfranchisement of some of the better-off sections of the working classes, encouraged the state to look more positively upon the provision of elementary education. Secondly, the Paris Exhibition of 1867, which saw other nations taking some of the gold medals for industrial development, certainly encouraged industrialists to contemplate the need for universal educational provision. Thirdly, the formation of educational societies further nurtured improvements in this sphere of activity. In 1869 the National Education League was formed in Birmingham with the express intention of promoting a universal state system of education through local authorities: 'The establishment of a system which shall secure the Education of every Child in the Country'.[13] During the same year the rival National Education Union was formed in Manchester to demand more financial aid to enable the voluntary societies to do their educational job more effectively. Despite the fact that their views were diametrically opposed, it was evident that both societies saw educational destitution as still existing upon a wide scale in the cities and towns of England and Wales.

Forster did in fact acknowledge the above pressures when he confirmed the gravity of the situation to the House of Commons in early 1870:

What is it that we have not? More or less imperfectly about 1,500,000 children are educated in the schools that we help – that is, they are simply on the register. But, as I had the honour of stating last year, only two-fifths of the children of the working classes between the ages of six and ten years are on the registers of the Government schools, and only one-third between the ages of ten and twelve. Consequently, of those between six and ten, we have helped about 700,000 more or less, but we have left unhelped 1,000,000; while of those between ten and twelve, we have helped 250,000, and left unhelped at least 500,000. Some hon. Members will think, I daresay, that I leave out of consideration the unaided schools. I do not, however, leave them out of consideration; but it so happens – and we cannot blame them for it – that the schools which do not receive Government assistance, are, generally speaking, the worst schools ...

[Y]et the result of the State leaving the initiative to volunteers is, that where the State help has been most wanted, State help has been least given ... In helping those only who help themselves ... we have left unhelped those who most need help.

... Our object is to complete the present voluntary system, to fill the gaps, sparing the public money, procuring as much as we can the assistance of parents ...

We must not delay. Upon the speedy provision of elementary education depends our industrial prosperity.[14]

Indeed, the 1870 Education Act was to provide the basis of an increased commitment to state intervention in the provision of a universal system of education in England and Wales.

The dual system of education: from the 1870 Education Act to the 1902 Education Act

The 1870 Education Act did not introduce universal free or compulsory education but it did provide the basis out of which such policies emerged over the next two decades. It created what was known as the 'dual system' of education. On the one hand, it permitted voluntary schools to continue with increased grants. At the same time, all areas of England and Wales had to be surveyed and those where educational provision was considered inadequate had to set up school boards, *ad hoc* bodies that were to be elected by ratepayers, who would have as many votes to cast as there were places to be filled, with powers to raise an education rate from the local population in order to build and operate 'board schools'. These school boards could also obtain government grants. However, they were not allowed to use the Catechism or the religious formularies of any religious groups in their teaching and children could be withdrawn, on parental demand, from any religious instruction offered in either a board or voluntary school which received government grants. The state had thus created two systems of education which operated independently of each other and which, despite the compromises, were mutually hostile to each other. It was this hostility and conflict which dominated the development of education over the next three decades.

The inadequacy of educational provision meant that many areas of England and Wales set up school boards in the early 1870s, but mainly in 1871. Indeed, in the 1870s there were about 2,500 school boards in England and Wales and about 2,600 by 1902. Board schools provided about 16 per cent of places for the elementary school population in 1880, rising to 54 per cent in 1900.[15] Yet, despite this growth, there were still many voluntary schools operating within school board areas – and subject to some of their by-laws – and many areas, like Wakefield, where educational provision was deemed sufficient not to need a school board.

As was their right, many of these school boards passed by-laws in the 1870s to make education compulsory. Yet it was the Sandon Education Act of 1876, which set up school attendance committees, and A. J. Mundella's Education Act of 1880 which made attendance compulsory for children aged between 5 and 10 years. The process of providing free education took another ten years. By the early 1880s parents were paying about 3d. (1.25p) per week in school fees, although many school boards waived such fees for needy children. The 1891 Fee Grant Act practically established free education and only about one-sixth of elementary school children were paying fees in 1895.

Free and universal elementary education combined with changes in the approach to teaching to bring about substantial improvements in education. The Cross Commission, which dealt with elementary education in 1886–7 and reported in 1888, suggested that the 'payments by results' system was now out of date and that education should be based upon the teaching of knowledge rather than facts. The principles of the 1862 Revised Code were removed in 1890.

Such developments did not ease the tensions and debates within education. The fact is that the Anglicans, the Catholics and, to a lesser extent, the Wesleyan Methodists protested against the formation of school boards, since it was their schools who would face competition from the board schools. By and large they were, politically, Tories, although the Catholics were mainly Liberals. They felt that the school boards were unnecessary, objected to the rate support that they received and opposed what they saw as superfluous and extravagant public expenditure. At the other extreme, many Nonconformists and dissenters, who identified with the Liberal party, were supportive of the school boards and felt that there ought to be a comprehensive state system of elementary education throughout England and Wales.

It was these two viewpoints, embellished with some political eddies, that formed the basis of the conflict over the school boards and made for triennial trials of strength in elections to them. In Nottingham it was noted that the Conservative candidates were likely to do well in the first school board elections:

On Sunday several electioneering sermons were preached, and yesterday there was a good deal of canvassing in several of the wards on behalf of the Conservative candidates … It is to be regretted that the contest should recently have assumed so much of a party character. The Five who have held meetings [under the presidency of Dr Ranson, a Liberal] to protest against what they call dictation seem likely to lose votes, because the impression prevails that instead of utilising the existing schools (which by the time-table conscience clause, that religious instruction must be given at the beginning or the end of school hours, and that any child can be withdrawn from instruction if the parents desire it), this party desires to erect new ones to enter into competition with those, and, if possible, bring them to 'painless extinction'. As this would be a costly experiment to the ratepayers, already too heavily burdened, it may be easily believed that Messrs. Rothera, Richards and others (though well known as clever manipulators of party elections) may lose votes which from their former party connexions they may think themselves fairly entitled.[16]

The report, whilst purporting to be even-handed, clearly favoured the Conservative Anglicans rather than the Liberal Nonconformists. Its final appeal was for the electorate to select men who were likely to work together for the common good and not to place their cumulative votes in the hands of one or two popular candidates.

School board elections often became bitter local contests. In Bradford the Liberal 'eight' normally held the balance of power over the six Conservatives and one Catholic, and a kind of political balance was achieved. This was thrown out of gear when the Independent Labour party, taking advantage of the fact that each ratepayer could cast fifteen votes however they wished, tried to get its supporters to divide their votes between the two candidates. As a result, W. H. Drew was returned in 1891, Margaret McMillan in 1894 and Margaret McMillan and the Revd R. Roberts in 1897.[17] However, the intrusion of the ILP did nothing to mollify the hostility between the two groups. Whilst the Liberals – and particularly Alfred Illingworth, a Bradford MP and the lionesque figure of Liberalism – did much to resist challenges to the school boards through the North of England Education League (formed in 1895), Anglican and Catholic opinion in Bradford was hostile. The Reverend Carmonti Gallacher stated that 'The Board Schools had failed to get half their children into the schools. They had only succeeded in widening the gulf between the Voluntary and Board Schools.'[18] Exaggeratedly, he added of the Bradford School Board that:

It had developed precocity, the spirit of contempt for authority, and disobedience and wilfulness. It had taught children to despise their parents, to be rude to their elders and to disregard the work of others. These were everyday complaints. A mother told him the other day that she had occasion to say to her little girl, nine years of age, that steam was coming out of the kettle. The child replied 'It isn't steam its vapour (laughter).' This was what the Board schools had done. They had filled little children with conceit, and turned steam into vapour (laughter).

Similar events occurred in Huddersfield, where the Liberal dissenters usually held the balance of power on the school board under the leadership of the Revd Dr Bruce, minister of Highfield Congregational Chapel. The Conservative Anglicans criticized the Huddersfield School

Board's abandonment of religious assemblies for offering only a minimum of religious teaching and were alarmed at the competition to the Church schools; the cry of 'Heathen Huddersfield' was never far from their lips.[19] The situation was summed up by D. F. E. Sykes, Huddersfield's historian of the nineteenth century, who wrote that:

> The election was contested between the parties of the sectarian and the unsectarian education, and since that time there had been a triennial trial of strength between those on one side who approve of definite and dogmatic religious instruction to the teaching of Bible History or Gospel morality ... Up to the present the Undenominational candidates have always obtained the majority on the Board, the ratepayers being largely tinged with dissent and possibly suspecting that a majority of the Churchmen might perceive a duty divided between church schools and those of the public at large ...[20]

The fact is that there was bitter conflict between those who owned schools, and therefore objected to the competition of the school boards, and those who did not and wished to see the extension of public and state responsibility for schooling. In a political sense, it tended to represent a conflict between the Conservatives and the Liberals. The Conservatives and Anglicans, in particular, were opposed to state provision of elementary education and the extension of school board activities into areas, such as secondary education, into which they were not supposed to stray. However, in the end it was a combination of administrative, religious and political developments that brought an end to the school board era.

The Royal Commission on Elementary Education (the Cross Commission) reported in 1888 that three-quarters of school boards had the minimum of five members and that 25 per cent of school board districts had a total population of less than 500. The smallness of the areas of these small school boards made it impossible for them to raise sufficient rates to provided a good education. The message was clear: school boards had to be amalgamated into larger areas or possibly brought under local government control. This was a view which was strengthened by the Bryce Report (a Royal Commission on Secondary Education) of 1895, which suggested that there was a need for larger and more effective units of local educational organization. The Education Act 1902 (introduced in 1903) could in many respects be seen as a consequence of these suggestions, with the formation of 328 local education authorities in the place of 2,600 school boards. The 1899 Education Act, which created the Board of Education as the one national body, responsible for all education, can also be seen as part of this tendency towards administrative tidiness and efficiency and also arose out of the recommendations of the Bryce Report. By 1903, then, one central government department ran elementary, and some secondary, education through 328 local education authorities in England and Wales.

This need for administrative tidiness, which was nurtured by government administrators such as Robert Morant, was strengthened by other campaigns. The Church of England was, for instance, unhappy about the fact that some school boards began to offer secondary education and that their own schools, dependent upon grants and fees, were starved of finance and unable to compete against them in providing cheap secondary education. All these concerns became more important when Salisbury's Conservative government came to power in 1895, committed to restricting the school boards and to strengthening voluntary schools. The 1897 Education Act provided extra grants to the voluntary schools and the 1902 Education Act got rid of the school boards. Before the latter Act, however, there was substantial political debate over the activities of the school boards. One of the major concerns was the development of the 'higher grade' schools.

The 1870 Education Act suggested that school boards should provide elementary education, although there was the possibility of the provision of some secondary education for higher classes as long as it did not represent the majority of education offered in a school. But some school boards began to gather older and more able students together into higher grade schools which were effectively secondary schools. The Royal Commission on Elementary Education (Cross Commission) reinforced this by suggesting that some aspects of secondary education might be offered in grades V and VI of elementary education. In addition, the Bryce Report (on Secondary Education) in 1895 surveyed such schools, thus legitimizing their existence. The Department of Science and Art gave technical grants to such schools before it was absorbed into the Board of Education in 1899. On the whole, the development of higher grade, or secondary, schools within school boards was not hindered by the various government education departments. Indeed, by 1895 there were 66 higher grade schools/departments educating about 25,000 scholars. The bulk of these were to be found in the North of England, six being in Bradford and one in Huddersfield (it was formed in 1893).

The Anglicans objected to the higher grade schools for seeming to represent a cheaper form of secondary education for the better-off working-class child who might otherwise have been tempted to take the modern type of syllabuses being offered at Anglican grammar schools. This type of pressure was evident in June 1899 when the School of Art in London complained to Cockerton, the auditor of the London School Board, that money was being spent on offering secondary education in evening classes that was not sanctioned by the 1870 Education Act. Cockerton refused to approve this expenditure in his audit and his decision was upheld in the courts of law in December 1900. This meant that school boards were limited to providing elementary education, although Robert Morant allowed them to continue through his 1900 minute which imposed strict restrictions upon the age of those who could be offered higher-grade education.

By 1900 there was, effectively, a full-scale attack being mounted against the school boards. The Church of England had also made a new concordat with the government whereby the Church would find its educational opportunities extended. In 1901 there was a determined effort to pass an Education Bill which would confine the school boards to elementary education. But eventually, in December 1902, the Education Act was passed. It was a twenty-seven-page document which brought about fundamental changes in public education. It abolished the school boards and transferred their powers, and those of the school attendance committees, to the local education authorities (LEAs).[21] It gave the LEAs powers to provide technical and secondary education and permitted rate-assistance to voluntary schools of all descriptions as long as one-third of the governors (normally two out of six) were appointed by them.

The 1902 Education Act provoked intense debate. The Nonconformists and dissenters opposed it, some going so far as to refuse to pay the education part of the local rates. The emergent Independent Labour party tended to support this opposition, generally complaining that the 1902 Act represented taxation without representation and failed to provide adequately for the secondary education of the working-class child. To W. H. Drew, the secretary of the Bradford Trades and Labour Council: 'The bill would arrest the progress of education.'[22] Fred Jowett, opposing the 1902 Bill at the tenth annual conference of the Independent Labour party at Liverpool, stated:

> That this conference enters its emphatic protest against the Government Education Bill, inasmuch as it withdraws education from public control, subsidises denominational education without giving anything but nominal control, and deprives women of the right to be directly elected or even to sit on local education authorities ...[23]

Conservative opinion was directly opposed to such views. Mr Quarmby, Conservative leader on the Huddersfield School Board, suggested that the school board had been an endowment to Nonconformity: 'because the amount of religious teaching given in the Board Schools was evidently sufficient for Nonconformists. Voluntary schools had suffered a great injustice by the Board Schools being carried on for the benefit of Nonconformists.'[24]

Notwithstanding such conflict of opinion, the 1902 Education Act was introduced in 1903 – once the new LEAs had been formed with a balance of councillors and co-opted members which could be approved by the Board of Education. The new arrangements, despite the controversies they raised, did encourage a much more effective system of administration. Indeed, despite Liberal insistence that they would remove the 1902 Act when they came to power, it remained the basis of education in England and Wales when they returned to office. The Birrell Education Bill, the School Feeding Act and the Education Act concerned with medical provision, all passed in 1906 or 1907, simply attempted to improve opportunities for the educational advancement of the working classes. They did alter the system. As a result, rate-assisted secondary schools were committed to providing free education to the 25 per cent of their pupils who would come through the LEAs, and in some LEAs a school feeding system was established and local medical departments were set up to monitor the health of schoolchildren. The 1902 Act was a landmark in the educational history of England and Wales.

Labour and education

From the beginning of the twentieth century the working classes began to exert considerable influence upon educational reform in England and Wales. However, their initial influence was focused upon the physical condition of education and it was not until the First World War that more far-reaching policies, aimed at extending secondary and even higher education to the working classes, were developed.

In the 1880s the quasi-Marxist Social Democratic Federation had emphasized the importance of an educated working class in the struggles ahead. In 1893 the national Independent Labour party had also declared its concern about public educational provision. Indeed, the ILP in particular was to exert a major influence upon the Labour Representation Committee/Labour party from 1900 onwards and ultimately helped to shape and influence the evolution of its policy.

The link between the Bradford Trades Council and the Independent Labour party was one of the vital factors in the development of Labour's education policy. The Bradford Labour Union/ILP was effectively in control of the Bradford Trades Council from mid-1892. The Bradford ILP had, as already noted, stressed the need to improve the quality of life of the working-class child and Margaret McMillan did note, in respect to school feeding, that 'Education on an empty stomach was a waste of money.'[25] She had developed this adage as a result of her experiences when helping with the physical examination of pupils in the Bradford board schools in the mid-1890s, when she attended the school inspections of Dr Kerr, medical officer of health for Bradford.

The Bradford ILP built upon such work between 1904 and 1907 when the issue of school feeding had became a central feature of its educational policy.[26] It campaigned from 1904 to 1906 to get the municipal authorities to introduce a school feeding programme, with free meals for those children in need. It was opposed by a local Liberal party which objected to 'municipalising poverty'[27] and strongly advocated voluntary effort for children starving 'by no fault of their parents' and the Poor Law for 'neglectful' parents.[28] That opposition only broke down as the Liberals began to feel that their position on the boards of guardians and the city council was threatened, and when Dr Crowley, the son-in-law of H. B. Priestman (the Liberal leader who was a Quaker and the brother of Arthur Priestman, the ILP leader), surveyed the nutritional standards of children as the medical superintendent to the Bradford Education Authority. Crowley's studies, presented in a series of lectures to the Northern Educational Conference held in Bradford between January and March 1907, suggested that at least 6,000 children in the Bradford area were underfed and that a further 15,000 children had 'nourishment below the normal'.[29] It was therefore not surprising that the Liberal party changed its position and gave its support to the local implementation of the Education (Provision of Meals) Act passed in December 1906.

By October 1907 Jonathan Priestley, headmaster of Green Lane School and father of J. B. Priestley, was serving school meals at White Abbey Dining Room, one of the five dining-rooms opened simultaneously by the Bradford Education Authority.[30] This was considered to be a great achievement, for Fred Jowett, Bradford's first Labour MP, had been involved in the campaign to get the legislation through the House of Commons and other activists, such as J. H. Palin and Willie Leach, had also campaigned strongly for it.[31] Indeed, Fred Jowett, MP for Bradford West, reflected upon the success of his school feeding campaign:

> And the school dinners. What a world of difference to the physical welfare and comfort of the thousands of children concerned this institution will make this winter. Think how, a few years ago, the proposal to provide food for the underfed children at the public cost was met with bitter opposition. But who, having a heart to feel, would turn back now? One might go on to speak of school baths, the development of the system of medical inspection of school children, and other things, as to which the most encouraging feature is that the public mind has been changed, the community conscience awakened.[32]

The ILP was also involved in many other related campaigns. It fought, successfully, for medical inspection in schools and to get rid of the half-time system which, by the early twentieth century, had become a block to good education in a period when full-time education was the norm. It may have influenced the Labour party's educational policy.

During the First World War the Labour policy on education was developed further. In recent years, however, the origins of the Labour party's educational policy have come under scrutiny. For many years it was argued – by the ILP and, later by Brian Simon – that policy was a product of the work of the Bradford Trades and Labour Council and the Bradford ILP, whose 'Bradford charter' was accepted in its entirety by the Labour party.[33] More recently, this view has been challenged. J. R. Brooks has argued that the Labour party policy did not originate with the ILP and the Bradford Trades and Labour Council but emerged from several programmes of reform, only one of which was the Bradford charter.[34] None of them was a final policy statement, just contributions to the debate. He also argues that if it had not been for a pamphlet, *What Labour Wants for Education* (1916), issued to all local Labour groups by the Workers' Educational Association, there would have been no Bradford charter.

It is true that there was a veritable paper-chase of being which did shape the Labour party's thinking, but it is equally true that the ILP was developing many of the ideas that were to emerge in the Bradford charter. This point has been made by both Carolyn Steedman and Clive Griggs.[35] Steedman, in particular, stresses that a trawl of ILP conference reports suggests that the party was already recommending the raising of the school-leaving age in 1895, advocating state maintenance of children 'while under teaching' in 1897 and supporting the end of child labour at the same conference.[36] She suggests that it was this type of background that William Leach, one of the chief architects of the charter, was drawing upon rather than the WEA pamphlet.[37] Griggs also notes the way in which socialist groups influenced the Trades Union Congress along the same lines and played upon the sense of educational deprivation that many trade-union leaders felt they had experienced.[38] He argues that these influences flowed back into the ILP and the Labour party during the First World War. On balance, the evidence tends to support the arguments of Steedman and Griggs.

In October 1916 the Bradford Trades Council organized a conference to discuss 'Education after the War' which was to be dominated by the policies 'formulated by local trade unionists'.[39] This became known as the Bradford charter, reflected many of the ideas developed by the TUC and the ILP and added the even more radical proposal that there should be compulsory secondary schooling for all children until they were 16. This secondary education was to take place at a common secondary school and within the framework of a national system of education which would extend from nursery school to university. There was also to be a great extension in medical facilities, the provision of school meals and the creation of a system of graded allowances to enable children to stay on at school until they were 16. There were also various other suggestions, including that the Treasury bear a greater proportion of the cost of education and pensions for secondary teachers.

This charter was campaigned for by William Leach, a leading ILP and an employer, and was discussed by trades councils, MPs and the Board of Education. It was accepted at the Labour party conference in February 1917, where it was proposed by Meredith Frank Titterington of the Bradford Trades Council.[40] The ILP discussed the policy at their conference in Leeds in April 1917, where it was referred to the National Administrative Council. The charter never actually became official ILP policy, although it was always identified with the ILP.[41] Indeed, Carolyn Steedman has reconstructed the way in which the Bradford ILP and the Bradford Trades Council operated together with William Leach, Fred Jowett, and others to develop many of the policies that emerged in the Bradford charter.[42] Her only concern is that the charter became absorbed into the post-1917 discussion on education, where it, and its advocates, 'were the victims of the new regime of the educational "expert"'.[43] Nevertheless, the Bradford charter appears to have emerged from the activities of members of the Bradford ILP and the Bradford Trades Council, even if it was never officially accepted by the national ILP.

Education, c. 1918–1944

Despite some comments to the contrary, the 1920s and the 1930s were years in which some fundamental decisions were made about education.[44] It is true that important legislation was rather thin on the ground – the two really important measures, the 1918 'Fisher' Act and the 1944 'Butler' Act, having occurred in wartime. Nevertheless, there was serious debate about education at this time – particularly about the extent to which secondary education would be made available to the working classes. Indeed, it is obvious that the Hadow Report of 1926 greatly influenced the policies that were officially accepted in 1944.[45]

The post-war years had begun well with the government intention to implement the 'Fisher' Act of 1918. This Act was supposed to extend educational opportunities as part of the post-war reconstruction. It abolished half-time education from 1921, intended to provide working-class children with the opportunities to advance their skills at educational colleges, and raised the school-leaving age to 14. Along with the Young Report, which advocated an increase in secondary provision from less than 400,000 places to 2.25 million, it was clear that the Fisher Act was designed to be the dawn of a new age in education. But the idea of extending secondary education to the working classes was aborted when the financial crises of the early 1920s led to the 'Geddes axe' on public expenditure. Education suffered badly as a result.

Notwithstanding such financial restrictions, it is clear that substantial headway was being made towards the provision of secondary education for the working classes. At the beginning of the inter-war years secondary education was essentially the prerogative of the middle classes, although some working-class children had ascended the educational ladder offered by scholarships in those secondary schools receiving state assistance and in the higher grade schools. There were schemes to extend this system but they expired as the Geddes axe fell.

Yet the inter-war years saw a widening of the debate on secondary education and developments towards a less demanding form of education for the working classes. Further stimulus in this direction had been given by R. H. Tawney, who had been largely responsible for a document entitled *Secondary Education for All: A Policy for Labour* which was produced in 1922 by a Labour party advisory committee.[46] Along with Tawney's book *Equality*, this served to suggest that universalism ought to be the basis of education.

It is often argued, as Brooks maintains, that *Secondary Education for All* was influential in shaping the policies recommended by the Hadow Report of 1926. Yet the Hadow Report would appear to owe less to Labour's education policy than is often supposed. It is true that it was the Labour government of 1924 which set up the Hadow Committee, even though it reported to Stanley Baldwin's Conservative government in 1926. It is also true that Tawney was a member of the Hadow Committee. Nevertheless, Labour influence did not seen to run very deep. Hadow decided against advocating the principle of universalism and suggested that students should be subject to a selective system decided at the age of 11 by an examination that was to become known as the 'eleven-plus': 'We are disposed to believe that we may safely recommend the institution both of an entrance examination, on the lines of the present examination for scholarships and free places in secondary schools, to determine the conditions of entry into selective modern schools ...'[47] At this stage, according to ability, children would either go to grammar schools, the higher schools formed by the LEAs after the 1902 Act, or to modern schools, which were the old senior departments of elementary schools. The school-leaving age was to be raised to 15, and the modern school student would leave school at that age, whilst the grammar school pupil would go on to 16 and the old established grammar schools would take pupils on to 18 in anticipation of their entry to university. Apart from its selectivity of approach to secondary education, therefore the Hadow Report recommended that 15, not 16, should be the new school-leaving age. Neither of these recommendations was Labour party policy.

The Conservative government did not officially accept the Hadow recommendations but, rather, encouraged LEAs to introduce them if they so desired. In fact, the raising of the school-leaving age was not acted upon until the 1936 Education Act, which recommended its implementation from September 1939, an action that was delayed until 1945 due the outbreak of the Second World War.

LEAs took individual action and Bradford was the first authority to reorganize along Hadow lines and establish 'Hadow' schools. William Leach explained this when he wrote that Bradford was 'more alive to the real meaning of the war of the classes, as expressed in terms of education than in any other part of the country'.[48] Although the Bradford LEA was increasingly dominated by the Labour party, it was the ILP which, to a large extent, determined the agenda. The ILP Commission on Education (1927) produced a number of reports and recommendations for the entire range of educational provision. It suggested that 'the nursery school repudiates punishment and external discipline' and advocated that children should be taught through experience.[49] The Bradford ILP's attitude towards the Hadow Report was that it did not offer universalism but equality of opportunity – which, from an unequal base, would inevitably be unequal. It also felt that the new schools would be secondary schools under primary regulations. In other words, the post-Hadow secondary schools would effectively be elementary schools under a new name for those aged 11 and over. Nevertheless, it supported the Bradford City Council's decision to reorganize along Hadow lines. The ILP felt that this would provide more time for the development of the physical aims of secondary education, something which it had highlighted in its evidence to the Hadow Committee.

Ironically, it was the Anglican Church which showed most hesitation about the Hadow proposals. S. C. Cannon argues that religion was a force for progress in education during the early twentieth century but that the Anglicans, in being cautious about Hadow, were in fact being cautious about the ILP's interpretation of it. To Anglicans, education had to be about religious choice and the Bradford ILP, the Labour party and the city council appeared to be restricting that choice in creating grammar schools and modern schools.[50] Anglicans felt that a progressive curriculum was about individual personal development.

Bradford was the first of many LEAs to adopt the Hadow recommendations for the introduction of an eleven-plus test and secondary reorganization. Indeed, by the late 1930s about three-quarters of children in the public sector were attending post-Hadow schools.

There were also other developments in the pipeline. The Spens Report of 1938 suggested some modifications by adding the notion of technical schools to secondary education. There were other similar developments in 1943, when the Norwood Report suggested that there were three types of pupil who would fit into the three types of secondary institution available – grammar, technical and modern.

How much progress was made, of course, is a matter of debate. When G. A. N. Lowndes first wrote his *Silent Social Revolution* in 1937 he measured the developments over nearly seventy years and was amazed at how far education had come.[51] Brian Simon was not so convinced. Whilst he recognized that the Labour party had done as much as it could to extend educational opportunity, particularly given that it was never able to form a majority government, he felt that the educational life of working-class children had not altered greatly during the inter-war years.[52] For working-class children, the school-leaving age was still effectively 14, in most cases they were still taught in the old elementary school buildings and there had only been relatively minor changes in the curriculum, the most important being that secondary subjects were taught separately rather than collectively after 1926. Indeed, despite the efforts of LEAs, the government had not formally committed itself to secondary education for all.

R. S. Barker is even more critical than Brian Simon and feels that the Labour party and its two inter-war governments did not do enough to develop a socialist education policy. As a result, he feels that little changed and that, for the inter-war years: 'The tragedy of English education is the tragedy of English social life. It is organisation of education upon lines of class.'[53]

The Second World War altered this position only marginally, although it did see the legal acceptance of secondary education for all. R. A. Butler had produced a White Paper entitled *Educational Reconstruction* in 1943 which formed the basis of the 'Butler' Education Act of 1944. This Act created the post of Minister of Education and invested the occupant of that post with the duty of providing a comprehensive and wide-ranging educational system. The term 'elementary' disappeared and LEAs were given responsibility for primary, secondary and further education. It committed the government to providing different types of education for different types of pupils. All three kinds of secondary schools – grammar, technical and modern – were to be given equal status but would be geared to the individual needs of different types of children. In addition, fee-paying was abolished at all local authority secondary schools (though not at direct grant schools) and the school-leaving age was, at last, to be raised to 15 in 1945. The Act did not in fact legislate for the tripartite division of secondary education – such divisions had already emerged as a result of the Hadow and Spens Reports and the Norwood Committee. The new secondary structures never worked well; the technical schools failed to develop or to provide the skills considered essential for the more intelligent working-class child. Indeed, the division of secondary education has remained a controversial issue ever since. Nevertheless, asked recently whether or not the 1944 Act was the greatest single advance in the history of education in England and Wales, Professor A. H. Halsey answered:

> Yes ... and I've thought carefully about this. There is rather an important competitor in the 1902 Act. But everything considered, I choose the 1944 Act as long as it is not seen as legislation but as a declaration of social intent. If so, then that was the great Act. By comparison we can't even remember any of these stupid Acts that we've had lately.[54]

Conclusion

Great strides in public education were made between 1800 and 1944. During these years the need to educate the working-class child had been established, the state had assumed direct responsibility for education and it was accepted that secondary education would be available to all, not simply to the middle classes. Of course, equality of opportunity based upon an unequal social system did not mean that the working classes received equal treatment in the provision of education. Indeed, it will be seen in a later chapter that education continued to be a controversial area of social policy, with debates over the issue of comprehensives versus grammar schools and with the rising demand for university education. As democracy emerged, the educational policies of the state were forced to respond to the will of the majority, but it is surprising how class-based public education remained and how slowly it responded to the democratic challenge. The slow and meandering development of state educational policy in England and Wales is demonstrated by the fact that secondary education did not become a legal requirement until 1944, even though a majority of children received something purporting to be of secondary standard before that date.

Notes

1. Quoted in M. Sturt, *The Education of the People* (1967), p. 5. See also D. Fraser, *The Evolution of the British Welfare State* (1973), pp. 72–3, and J. Hurt, *Education in Evolution: Church, State and Society and Popular Education, 1800–1870* (1971).
2. Extract from a letter of Lord John Russell to Lord Lansdowne, 4 February 1839, quoted from Sturt, *The Education of the People*, pp. 77–8. This itself is quoted from J. Kay-Shuttleworth, *The School in Relation to the State, the Church and the Congregation* (1847), chapters 1 and 2.
3. J. M. Goldstrom, *Education: Elementary Education 1780–1900* (Newton Abbot, 1972), particularly pp. 92–7, deals with the type of school textbook that was being produced.

4. D. W. Sylvester, *Robert Lowe and Education* (1974), includes many tables on the cost of education and how it was reduced in the 1860s.

5. W. F. Hook, *A Letter to the Lord Bishop of St Davids* (1846), p. 38.

6. *Quarterly Review*, September 1846.

7. The Royal Commission on Popular Education (Newcastle Commission), *Final Report: Recommendations*, vol. 1 (1861), p. 157. There were six reports in all.

8. Hansard, *Parliamentary Debates*, Third Series, clvx, col. 229, 13 February 1862.

9. *Report of the Committee of Council on Education (1867–8)*, p. 291.

10. *Report of the Committee of Council on Education (1869–70)*, p. 67, from the comments of the inspector, the Revd Du Port.

11. Sturt, *The Education of the People*, and Hurt, *Education in Evolution*.

12. Sylvester, *Robert Lowe*.

13. National Education League Handbill, c. 1870.

14. Hansard, *Parliamentary Debates*, Third Series, cxcix, cols. 438–44, 17 February 1870.

15. Fraser, *Evolution*, (1973), p. 81.

16. *Nottingham Journal* , 29 November 1870.

17. K. Laybourn, '"The Defence of the Bottom Dog": The Independent Labour Party in Local Politics', in D. G. Wright and J. A. Jowitt (eds.) *Victorian Bradford (Essays in Honour of Jack Reynolds)* (1981), p. 226.

18. *Bradford Observer* (soon to be the *Yorkshire Observer*), 24 April 1902.

19. M. Dewsbury, 'The Teaching of Religion and the Huddersfield School Board', *Journal of Educational Administration and History* 11/2 (July 1979), and M. Dewsbury, 'Huddersfield Board Schools, 1870–1903', M. Ed., University of Sheffield, 1971.

20. D. F. E. Sykes, *History of Huddersfield and its Vicinity* (1898).

21. Education Act, 1902 (2 Edw. 7, Ch. 42), part III, 5, 3.

22. *Bradford Observer* (soon to be the *Yorkshire Observer*), 23 April 1902.

23. *Ibid.*, 2 April 1902.

24. *Huddersfield Daily Chronicle*, 7 May 1902.

25. *Yorkshire Daily Observer*, 30 November 1904.

26. K. Laybourn, 'The Issue of School Feeding in Bradford, 1904–1907', *Journal of Educational Administration and History* 14/2, (1982) p. 37.

27. *Bradford Daily Telegraph*, 1 December 1904.

28. The comments of W. E. B. Priestley, which appeared in *Bradford Portraits* (1912), p. 52.

29. *Forward*, 7 October 1907. Also *Bradford Daily Telegraph*, 7 January, 6 and 27 March 1907. On 6 March 1907 Dr Crowley is quoted as saying that: 'He thought that the whole requirements of the twentieth century could be summed up in the shibboleth "Civic Control and Voluntary Help".'

30. F. Brockway, *Socialism over Sixty Years: The Life and Times of Jowett of Bradford* (1946), p. 6.

31. J. H. Palin, *Bradford and its Children: How they are Fed* (1908); *Forward*, 29 October 1904.

32. Bradford Trades and Labour Council, *Year Book for 1909* (1910), p. 55.

33. B. Simon, *Education and the Labour Movement 1870–1920* (1965),

pp. 208–46. Also look at B. Simon, *The Politics of Educational Reform 1920–1940* (1974).

34.   J. R. Brooks, 'Labour and Educational Reconstruction 1916–26: A Case Study in the Evolution of Policy', *History of Education* 20/3 (1991), p. 246 (article pp. 245–59).

35.   C. Steedman, 'The ILP and Education: The Bradford Charter', in D. James, Tony Jowitt and K. Laybourn (eds.), *The Centennial History of the Independent Labour Party* (1992), pp. 277–98; C. Griggs, *The Trades Union Congress and the Struggle for Education, 1868–1925* (Falmer, 1983).

36.   Steedman, 'The Bradford Charter', p. 278.

37.   *Ibid.*, p. 283.

38.   Griggs, *Trades Union Congress and Education*, pp. 214–33.

39.   *Times Educational Supplement*, 19, 26 October 1916.

40.   Labour Party, *Report of the Annual Conference of the Labour Party held in Albert Hall, Peter Street, Manchester, on Tuesday January 23rd, and the three following days* (1917), pp. 135–6.

41.   ILP, *Report of the Annual Conference held at Leeds, April*, (1917), p. 76; *Report of the National Administrative Council: To be Presented to the Conference of the Independent Labour Party, on April 1st and 2nd, 1918* (1918), pp. 27–8; *Report of the Twenty-Sixth Annual Conference, Leicester, April 1918* (1918), p. 82; *ILP Summer School, Bryn Corach, Conway, N. Wales, June 30th to July 13th 1917* (1917).

42.   Steedman, 'The Bradford Charter", pp. 285–92.

43.   *Ibid.*, p. 292.

44.   Fraser, *Evolution*, p. 190, suggests that education was 'a minor concern of Governments in the inter-war years …'

45.   *Report of the Consultative Committee of the Board of Education: The Education of the Adolescent, 1926* (Hadow Report) (1926).

46.   Labour Party, *Secondary Education for All: A Policy for Labour* (Hambledon Press edn., 1988).

47.   Hadow Report, introduction.

48.   Bradford Trades and Labour Council, *Year Book for 1926* (Bradford, 1927), incorporating the Annual Report for 1926, p. 49.

49.   Bradford Independent Labour Party Commission on Education, *Draft of the Interim Report on Nursery Schools*, 1927, p. 6.

50.   S. C. Cannon, 'The Influence of Religion on Education Policy 1902–1944', *British Journal of Educational Studies* 12/2 (1964), pp. 143–60. See also M. Cruikshank, 'The Denominational Schools' Issue in the Twentieth Century', *History of Education* 18/2, (June 1972).

51.   G. A. N. Lowndes, *The Silent Social Revolution: An Account of the Expansion of Public Education in England and Wales 1895–1965* (2nd edn., 1979).

52.   Simon, *Politics of Educational Reform*.

53.   R. S. Barker, *Education and Politics 1900–1951: A Study of the Labour Party* (Oxford, 1972), p. 103.

54.   *Guardian*, Education Supplement, 18 January 1994, the day before the fiftieth anniversary of the 1944 Education Act.

CHAPTER SEVEN

THE ROLE OF THE STATE, PHILANTHROPY, AND THE TREATMENT OF POVERTY IN THE SECOND HALF OF THE NINETEENTH CENTURY

The second half of the nineteenth century was, as José Harris has revealed, an immensely complex period for the evolution of social policy which does not give itself easily to a simple categorization – it was far too pluralistic for that.[1] In this period both the Liberal and the Conservative parties gradually extended social responsibilities whilst continuing the Victorian commitment to a minimal state. Alongside this, and operating within a liberal economy, state power continued to work through the locality and great reliance was imposed upon the philanthropic contribution of the local community and its citizenry, particularly in the sphere of education. In other words, social policy often revealed conflicting tendencies that operated along distinctive and separate routes. No easily decipherable pattern of social policy emerged; instead, there was a constant interplay between various forces operating within a particular social and political structure. There is no obvious trajectory to the development of social policy in the Victorian period; a balance of forces and interests determined what emerged at any particular time.

The role of the state in these periods was the subject of substantial debate in the 1950s and the 1960s. On the one hand, it was argued that the state developed an increasing willingness to intervene, particularly in the 1830s and 1840s, because of the influence of Benthamism. At the other extreme, it has been suggested that social reforms had more to do with a humanitarian concern to tackle problems which took on their own momentum through the emergence of an administrative structure. These conflicts will be examined later in this chapter but seem almost redundant today in a climate of opinion that tends to accept the pluralism of society in the development of social policy. It would appear that the state introduced social reforms at the pace permitted by the commitments of political parties, employers, ideology and effective public opinion. Even parliamentary socialists in the early twentieth century were prepared to accept that their collectivist ideas could not run ahead of public opinion if they were to succeed.

Not surprisingly, then, Britain could still lay claim to be one of the most philanthropically orientated of societies in the late nineteenth century. Its charitable contribution was immense and very much, though not entirely, focused upon the need to tackle the problem of poverty and the various crisis points in life that could lead to the social and economic decline of the 'respectable' working classes. Changing attitudes meant that by the end of the century the chief problem of society was seen to be poverty and not the pauperism that the 1834 New Poor Law had been geared towards tackling. It was this that edged the Liberal governments of 1906–14 to introduce social reforms and to consider the structure of the Poor Law. Nevertheless, there was still an enormous reliance placed upon philanthropy and the commitment of its representatives, such as the Charity Organisation Society, to self-help before that date.

The role of the state in Victorian society

There is an enormous literature on the changing role of the state, especially for the period from the sixteenth century onwards. Historians have written of the 'mercantilism' of the sixteenth to eighteenth centuries, in which the state assumed some responsibility for the social welfare of its citizens. They have noted the impact of Adam Smith's *Wealth of Nations* (1776), which rejected the regulations that had emerged in the interest of free competition. They have equally examined the associated ideas elaborated by David Ricardo, Nassau Senior and others. The essential question in all these contributions is: what was the role of state to be? For eighteenth-century figures, this produced much debate and concern but there appears to have been a remarkable degree of consensus between writers and politicians throughout the nineteenth century.

Politicians, by and large, were adamant that, whilst the state would be strong, it would, at the same time, be limited in its social activities. Pat Thane suggests that: 'It was in the 1820s that a strategy of constructing a minimal but firm regulatory state within which a free economy and free individuals could flourish clearly took precedence in government circles.'[2] Thereafter the Whig tradition of 'judicious intervention in social questions' was revived in the 1830s, Peel moved for liberalization in the 1840s and revived the concept of the minimalist state, and, after some loss of direction in the 1850s, Gladstone revived the minimalist ideas that had been developed earlier.[3] In other words, there were slight changes in direction and more positive state intervention when the Whigs were in power but, in essence, politicians only encouraged state intervention when they were forced to do so in order to encourage the development of an individualistic society.

This trend was amended slightly in the late nineteenth century, when Conservative governments held office for twenty-three years in between 1874 and 1906. Under Disraeli and his Conservative successors, the dominant theme was stability and some rejection of social values based on individualism and a doctrine of natural rights. The essential concern was to curb greed and to encourage the care of the community – although this was to be achieved through an adaptation of existing facilities and through local administration wherever possible. In other words, the Conservatives were more inclined to encourage social intervention than the Liberals had been under Gladstone, but not to any significant or radical degree.

The political attitudes of the different parties have obviously shaped the extent to which state intervention developed during the nineteenth century. Nevertheless, there were many other factors at play. There is, for instance, no doubt that Jeremy Bentham and his supporters exerted some influence. Bentham recognized that community interests might have to be catered for. This meant that the state would have to intervene on some occasions for the good of the community to ensure efficiency and effectiveness in the interest of the individual. The Benthamites, sometimes known as utilitarians or philosophical radicals, were concerned to establish harmony between natural interests and happiness for the majority within a freely competitive society. The commitment to government intervention was thus determined by necessity. John Stuart Mill, for instance, expressed these view in his *Principles of Political Economy* (1848), arguing that the government should depart from the ideal of *laissez-faire* only in those exceptional cases where there was a compelling reason for state intervention.

The views of Benthamites, as indicated in previous chapters, were carried forward by such men as Edwin Chadwick, Leonard Horner and James Kay-Shuttleworth. They clearly exerted an influence within the government. Yet there were also many other forces at work. Roy Hay and Joseph Melling have both suggested that the role of the employers should be considered as an essential part of the evolution of social policy between 1870 and 1914.[4] A recent article by Hay suggests that, apart from a small group of Quaker businessmen and philanthropists such as Charles Booth, little attention had been focused upon the business influence. He rectifies this omission by reference to the evidence given by some employers, most notably the Birmingham Chamber of Commerce and the Association of Chambers of Commerce, to the Royal Commission on the Poor Laws, 1905–9. The Birmingham Chamber's proposal for a national scheme of labour exchanges seems to have influenced the plan that eventually emerged.[5] In other words, Hay notes, the leading figures in the business sector supported some of the Liberal reforms because they believed that this was one way of controlling labour. This elaborated upon a view he had already expounded in the late 1970s.[6]

Joseph Melling takes these ideas well back into the nineteenth century and suggests that during the second half of the nineteenth century, as well as in the Edwardian period, British industrialists' relations with labour remained their principal concern when evaluating the state's policy proposals and that the development of industrial welfare in the later nineteenth century contributed to their assessment of the prospects for policy innovations.[7] Rejecting Patrick Joyce's suggestion that the Lancashire manufacturers ensured industrial passivity and cultural dominance between the 1850s and the 1890s, Melling argues that there was conditional compliance between employers and workers, based partly upon the fact that many factory owners in both Lancashire and Yorkshire provided their own welfare benefits.[8] Nevertheless, British industry was slow to develop in this direction in comparison to American industrialists and management control techniques were less sophisticated, tending towards the housing provision and superannuation benefits which were offered to 280,000 employees in Britain in 1910.[9]

Welfare was clearly provided by some of the larger employers as a way of establishing some type of workplace control. Employers also dealt with the state and were obviously concerned with anything that threatened the relations between management and workers, even though they were not able to prevent the passing of the Employers' Liability Act of 1880. Employers – and particularly the big railway lobby, which had representation within both the major political parties – were able to act as pressure groups on any aspect of social policy that affected their interests. Some opposed Joseph Chamberlain's Workmen's Compensation Act of 1897 and were suspicious of reforming civil servants such as William Beveridge. Above all, they were concerned to shape the social insurance reforms that emerged in 1911. Whilst Lloyd George seems generally to have ignored the employers' lobby and the multitude of suggestions that it brought forward, the employers themselves seem also to have gone for a less than vociferous campaign of establishing understandings and a working policy with civil servants.

The differing attitudes of politicians, Benthamites, civil servants, businessmen – and even the Labour party and the trade unions in the early twentieth century – have ensured that there could never be a straight pathway to social reform in the mid- and late nineteenth century. Apart from the minimalist state attitude, with periods of slightly more assertive policy, it is clear that pluralism meant that there were many twists and turns in the development of social policy.

What does this mean for the variety of historical interpretations that have emerged over the past thirty or forty years and which dominated debate in the 1950s and 1960s? The debate which raged between those who have emphasized the influence of Benthamism and those who have emphasized the administrative build-up, often in some incremental manner, no longer seems as relevant as it once was. Both explanations have their place and both fail to provide a full explanation of the evolution of social policy.[10]

Until the 1950s there were numerous studies of the work of social reformers in the early and mid-nineteenth century which suggested that their ideas owed a considerable debt to the Benthamites. One of the leading works was S. Finer's study of Sir Edwin Chadwick.[11] Such approaches were challenged by Oliver MacDonagh, who published an article in 1958 in which he suggested that whilst the function and the scope of the executive was changed profoundly in the early nineteenth century, it was neither revolutionary in kind or quantity.[12] In particular, he felt that the influence of Bentham and his disciples had been exaggerated and that there were other forces at play. He developed a famous five-stage model for an administrative explanation which allowed for the cumulative effect of gradual change at the margins. Apparently, public exposure of problems led to legislation, which was followed by more effective administration, which in turn revealed that new legislation was necessary before, finally, leading civil servants were given the freedom to deal with problems as they arose. Many other writers acknowledged this type of analysis. Royston Lambert, whilst accepting that Sir John Simon was influenced by Benthamite ideals, was nonetheless attracted to MacDonagh's views, noting that civil servants became part of a self-expanding administrative process which developed its own momentum and helped to carry state intervention forward with or without the overt support of politicians.[13] A few years later MacDonagh's views were extended by Dr Lubenow, who argued that Victorians did not perceive conflicts between theory and practice, nor between collectivism and individuals, as important. Instead, they focused upon the conflict between a traditional model of politics which placed faith in the historic right and past practice of English government, with the prime emphasis upon local self-government, and the attack posed by centralization upon the traditional freedom of English institutions. Incrementalism was the end product of the continual conflict between these options and constant changes at the margins.[14]

These challenges did not go unanswered. Henry Parris responded, attacking MacDonagh's interpretation of Benthamism and, more importantly, arguing that each individual adherent did not need to know Bentham's name and ideas: 'one Chadwick (whose Benthamism Dr MacDonagh admits) counted for more than many hundreds of rank and file public servants'.[15] He further argued that MacDonagh's model fitted the Passenger Acts but fell down in its application elsewhere and suggested an alternative five-stage model. This maintained that there was a governmental revolution in response to social and economic changes, that the nineteenth century therefore falls into two periods, pre-1830 and post-1830, that Benthamism dominated the second period, that the application of the principle of utility led to the simultaneous extension of *laissez-faire* and state intervention, and that once executive

officers were appointed, they played an increasing role in the development of their own powers. He thus concludes that Bentham's ideas
were influential because they derived from the background processes of
change around him.

This alternative line of argument has had significant support. Jenifer
Hart attacked MacDonagh's view because of his tendency to generalize
from the emigrant regulations and for a variety of reasons put forward
by Parris, most notably the insistence that Bentham's ideas could only be
effective amongst those people who had read his works. She also doubts
whether the driving force of what she refers to as a 'Tory interpretation
of History', with its emphasis upon the Christian conscience and a
general humanitarian desire to tackle social evils, can be proved.[16]
More recently, Pat Thane has suggested that MacDonagh's 'progressive
model allows too little space for the setbacks experienced to administrative momentum in the 1840s and, still more, in the 1850s'.[17] The fact
is that the independent Poor Law Commission, proposed by Chadwick,
acquired such a bad reputation that it was wound up in 1847 and
Chadwick himself was removed from the General Board of Health and
its powers somewhat dissipated in the 1850s. In any case, localism, the
local organization of state provisions in the interests of local bodies and
to the detriment of central control, severely circumscribed the powers
of civil servants. Administrative momentum and incrementalism there
may have been, but, just like Benthamism, they had their limits and
should not be too rigidly applied by historians. Both Benthamism and
administrative momentum had their part to play and most historians
today would tend to accept that there were many forces working
towards the development of social policy.

Historians have therefore failed to impose a clear and unchallenge-
able structure of development upon the emergence of state intervention
in the nineteenth century. Quite clearly, many factors were at play here
also – ideas, political parties, civil servants, employers and an element of
incremental growth. Pluralism was dominant and the blend of influences changed from time to time. In any case, fundamental to the final
mixture was the way in which Victorians saw their society operating.
Their moral code was a factor which conditioned change and the limits
of state action. The moral code of the politically dominant middle
classes was based upon a commitment to self-help. Samuel Smiles's
Self Help (1859) captured the spirit of the age in suggesting that self-help
'is the root of all genuine growth in the individual; and, exhibited in the
lives of many, it constitutes the true course of national vigour and
strength.'[18] It served many functions, justifying the existing economic
system, legitimizing the economic success of individuals and offering
the possibility that all might rise through their own efforts.

Such an outlook soon permeated most sections of society, despite the alternative viewpoints that emerged from time to time, socialist or otherwise in origin. Such was its success that the alternative collectivist ideas of the Social Democratic Federation, the Socialist League, the Fabians and the Independent Labour party which emerged in the 1880s and 1890s were clearly anathema to the vast majority of the population, and especially to the organized and institutionalized working classes. Indeed, self-help had already become a feature of working-class life through the friendly societies, which had more than four million members by the 1870s. The co-operative movement also tended to confirm the faith of the working class in self-help, albeit through collective action. Working-class involvement in savings banks, building clubs and other similar activities confirmed this commitment to self-help.

In the early Victorian period, then, individualism and a commitment to self-help shaped public opinion. But they ran side by side with the type of state intervention already discussed, including the limiting of hours and employment for women and children, health controls and the state maintenance of paupers. This is a paradox, but quite obviously understandable in a pluralistic society in which many interests were vying for support. Derek Fraser has speculated that this inconsistency might be attributed to five main reasons – the difference between theory and practice, the difference between the social and the economic spheres, the fact that Benthamite utilitarianism is a mixture of both *laissez-faire* and collectivism, that Benthamism had no central role to play (partly based upon the ideas of MacDonagh), and that state intervention had little to do with ideas and owed more to the emergence of an incremental approach to welfare policy.[19] Yet one can speculate for ever about the reasons for such inconsistency. The real point is that such inconsistencies should be expected in a pluralistic society. There is nothing unusual in individualism and *laissez-faire* operating alongside a meandering and gradual extension of essentially minimalist state intervention.

By the 1870s state intervention was emerging in many different ways and for many different reasons. First, it was often a pragmatic response to some deficiency. Secondly, it often assumed the form of a conflict between centralization and local government which normally meant that the state granted permissive powers before it imposed obligatory duties. Thirdly, there was an element of self-generating administrative momentum, although it was not always clearly evident and active, as in the late 1840s and the 1850s. Fourthly, there was also an increasing tendency to combine both voluntary and state action: there were elementary schools, dispensaries, hospitals and reformatories in Victorian England that were state-aided but run by private philanthropy.

All these factors were evident in the late nineteenth century, although the last feature was particularly evident between about 1870 and 1900. As Frank Prochaska has stressed: 'No country on earth can lay claim to a greater philanthropic tradition than Great Britain. Until the twentieth century philanthropy was widely believed to be the most wholesome and reliable remedy for the nation's ills ...'[20] In the late nineteenth century charity worked alongside the state in attempting to tackle poverty and to impose the values of self-help that were to be considered the antidote to social revolution.

Philanthropy and poverty, c. 1870–c. 1900

Although the nation seemed committed to self-help as a virtue, the ubiquity of philanthropy recognized that this could not be achieved by all. Charitable action was evident at every level of society, covering all the classes. Every community had its own charitable organizations and numerous national organizations began to emerge in the late nineteenth century to attempt to co-ordinate some of their activities, the most famous being the Charity Organisation Society (COS) which was formed in London in 1869. Naturally, the COS has drawn the greatest attention but one should not be misled by its activities, for it was essentially a London-based and southern organization and carried relatively little influence amongst philanthropic bodies in the rest of the country. It was important, but not all charities adopted its style or were reluctant to work with the local representatives of state activity.

The sums gathered and distributed in the form of charity were vast and incalculable.[21] Nevertheless, one can gain some glimpses of the scale of the financial operation. For instance, in 1861 there were about 640 charities in London with an annual income in excess of £2,500,000, even excluding individual donations. This was, in fact, more than was spent by the Poor Law authorities in London. Widened to the nation as a whole, it would not be surprising if charity greatly exceeded national Poor Law expenditure, especially given that Liverpool, Birmingham and other large cities also had very well-organized charity relief organizations.[22]

The range of charity provision was immense. As Frank Prochaska stresses, much charitable contribution went unrecorded because the first line of defence for many poor people was their own family. Thereafter, it spread out into working-class philanthropy, about which there are few records.[23] The West Birmingham Relief Fund, established in 1892 by working men, apparently gave advances to the disabled and paid rent for deserving cases.[24] The Mansion House Funds, which relieved the unemployed, often included working men and women as subscribers, and many of the better-off working men helped the poor by running provident societies, savings banks, boot clubs, lying-in and other similar types of charities. A working man's pastoral aid society in Liverpool had 2,000 subscribers.[25]

There was, of course, more obvious charitable provision. Most religious denominations offered provisions for the poor and in 1859 the Jewish Board of Guardians was set up to run its own sectarian Poor Law. Visiting societies, which aimed to bridge the social gap, were set up and included the Anglican-based Metropolitan Visiting Relief Association formed in 1843. In addition, there were many denominational missions that distributed religious tracts and provided social 'work care. For instance, the Mill Hill Unitarian Chapel of Leeds was set up in 1844:

> to assist in the diffusion of religion and morality among the poor of Leeds, to promote education, temperance, cleanliness, comfort in their homes, to extend consolation, advice and assistance to them in times of sickness and trouble, and to aid in the general ameliora-tion of their habits and moral and physical condition.[26]

As a result, the Unitarians, focusing particularly upon Holbeck and New Wortley, provided Sunday schools, evening improvement classes, home visiting and pressured the local authorities to improve the health and housing conditions of the slum areas with which they dealt.

Housing charities such as the Peabody Trust emerged to provide cheap housing for the poor and Octavia Hill conducted housing experi-ments with the destitute. There was the National Benevolent Institution, which granted pensions to needy gentlemen, the RSPCA, the YMCA, Dr Barnardo's and numerous other institutional developments as well. There were numerous charitable acts by large manufacturers. Caroline Colman, a member of the Colman family which ran its business empire from the Carrow Works, Norwich, became involved in providing tech-nical classes for up to 200 men, sewing classes for women, Sunday schools and similar activities.[27]

There were also notable city-based developments. The Charity Organisation Society was formed in 1869 to deal with the alleged threat of moral deterioration spreading across London as a result of the cunning poor hoodwinking the traditional charities into subsidizing them. Ostensibly, it emerged to create order and structure out of the chaos of London charity.[28] In Liverpool William Rathbone, who became an MP in 1868, was one of a group of prominent local citizens who pushed for the creation of the Central Relief Committee in January 1863 to co-ordinate charitable activities in a more effective manner than bodies such as the Distribution Committee of 1855, the District Provident, the Strangers' Friend and the Charitable Society had done. He wrote of the transformation that was brought about in his book, *Method and Muddle in Charitable Work* (1867), which was later published under the title of *Social Duties, Considered in Reference to the Organisation of Effort in Works of Benevolence and Public Utility*, by a 'Man of Business',

in 1867. The initial idea of the Central Relief Committee was to save
the deserving poor from having to apply for parish relief and to control
mendacity but, as with the COS, its direction was soon to change as
theory and practice conflicted with experience.[29]

One of the major questions is: why was charity given so readily?
Frank Prochaska would tend to argue that it stemmed more from
kindness, religious or otherwise, and a desire to do something for one's
fellow man and that it owed less to social control. Indeed, he maintains
that:

> The concept of 'social control' which has been introduced to explain
> charitable action is rather murky and reductionist, for the wish to
> make others conform to the same values and speak the same language
> is implicit in social relations generally from family to family life in
> national politics. When associated with concepts such as 'bourgeois
> hegemony' it may also be misleading, for it begs the question whether
> there was a revolutionary proletariat in need of control. Historians
> find it difficult to deal with 'social control' when it is implicit and
> unconscious. And as a conscious philanthropic motive it is easily
> overplayed. Fear of social unrest cannot explain the persistence of
> charitable subscriptions through changing political circumstances....
> If fear of domestic revolution was a crucial consideration, the ruling
> classes could have done a more effective job of controlling their social
> inferiors by passing general statutes. To rely on the chaos of *ad hoc*
> charitable institutions, many of which were rivals and at cross-
> purposes, was not a very efficient form of subduing the disaffected.[30]

This contrasts with the views of many other historians who either half
accept his point or reject it altogether.[31] The fact is that, efficient or
inefficient as it may have been, philanthropy was just one of the many
means by which social relations were maintained; it was certainly in the
mind of the middle classes, who felt that it could be used to tidy over
major crisis points as they occurred.

There is no doubt that there were many other concerns at play.
There were genuine religious motives and the need to salve one's conscience about the gulf between wealth and poverty. There may also have
been a degree of social assertion to be gained from being listed as a
prominent contributor on one of the many thousands of contribution
lists which covered Britain. The fact is that the reasons for charitable
contribution – then, as now – can be extremely variable and amorphous.
Social control was merely one of the items on the hidden agenda of
charity, albeit an important one.

Perhaps more revealing is the attitude of the middle classes and the
'respectable' in Victorian society towards the recipients of charity.

There is no doubt that there was a growing body of opinion which recognized that poverty – and the unemployment that sometimes caused it – was involuntary. Nevertheless, there was also the persistent belief that poverty was the result of the personal failing of the feckless and idle poor. It was believed that charity could bring about a moral change and help to create a self-help mentality. The COS argued that there was 'no doubt that the poverty of the working classes in England was due, not to their circumstances ... but to their own improvident habits and thriftlessness'.[32] C. S. Loch, the secretary from 1875 until 1913, therefore saw philanthropy as an educational tool, for 'Charity is a social regenerator ... We have to use charity to create the power of self-help.'[33]

The problem was that this did not seem to be working. The proliferation of largely uncoordinated charity in the early part of the nineteenth century left the impression that charities were inefficient, badly organized and likely to encourage, rather than discourage, poverty. The COS felt that the lack of co-operation and organization between charities meant that funds were dispensed indiscriminately.

The COS was formed to tackle these problems. It was concerned at the moral decay and the unscrupulous misuse of charities by some of the working classes, but it was more concerned with 'bringing about co-operation between the Charities and the Poor Law, and amongst the Charities'.[34] In effect, the COS intended to act as a co-ordinating agency for London. Each Poor Law area would have one committee to represent all the local charity agencies and a second one, a 'charity office', to compile a register of all relief applicants, who would be investigated by the committee. The committee would look at cases and institute scientific methods of social casework. In effect, then, the COS wished to curb charitable expenditure by maintaining some type of record of what was given and by introducing procedures to ensure that cases of poverty were properly examined and that appropriate and uplifting assistance was given. The casework approach had already been well developed in some German towns and had at least the advantage of establishing the real needs of the poor and of not removing them from their familiar environment. If families wished to emigrate or seek other forms of help, the COS could refer them to other charitable societies, thereby acting as some type of clearing house. In these ways it was felt that mendacity would not be countenanced and indiscriminate provision avoided.

These aims were almost religiously applied and advertised by Charles and Helen Bosanquet, Edward Denison, Octavia Hill and C. S. Loch. The COS advocated a visiting system and developed, from various precursors, social casework into a vigorous enquiry. Unlike many other organizations, they were quite prepared to turn the 'undeserving away'

– particularly the hopeless cases of the alcoholic, the depraved and the chronic idler. They looked for cases where there was genuine evidence of self-help and independence. To these people they would give cash payments as a temporary expedient; they might provide a mangle for a widow so that she could take washing in, for example.

The COS was strongly opposed to the provision of state help, since they felt it to be enfeebling. Instead the man of the household should prepare for all the normal contingencies of working-class life – in particular, illness, unemployment and old age – and the COS would simply step in when the distress was too great. In essence, the COS maintained that personal initiative could avoid poverty, that social and economic conditions were almost irrelevant, that philanthropy could deal with whatever problems arose and that state intervention was not necessary. This view was nicely summarized in its eighth annual report:

> The principle is, that it is good for the poor that they should protect against all the *ordinary* contingencies of life, relying not upon public or private charity, but upon their own industry and thrift, and upon the powers of self-help that are to be developed by individual and collective effort. Ample effort will still be left for the exercise of an abundant charity in dealing with exceptional misfortune ...[35]

From the outset, the COS was clearly out of touch with the times; it soon found its own principles being ignored or fudged and its effectiveness was rather blunted by the small number of cases with which it actually dealt. As the century progressed, it became clear from social surveys that poverty was far more widespread than the COS had calculated. Equally, it is clear that the COS was only dealing with the tip of the iceberg. In fact, it only found about 800 jobs for those people it dealt with in London between 1886 and 1896. Even more problematic was the fact that many members of the COS found it difficult to abandon the poor to destitution or the Poor Law, no matter what their official position was. The Settlement House movement, very much influenced by Samuel Barnett and the formation of Toynbee Hall in 1884, was one critical departure. Barnett had been a founding member of the COS and was convinced that it did not understand the real problem of poverty and helplessness. The idea that he put forward was that there should be residential settlements for young university graduates who would work amongst the poor in their spare time – attempting to teach them art, music and other subjects and earning their respect. The idea was not to patronize the working classes.

In recent years Robert Humphreys has provided the most comprehensive demolition of the COS position. His main criticisms are that it was out of tune with the times, for other charities recognized that poverty was not necessarily the personal fault of the poor, that it often practised what it did not preach when it came to financial aid for the poor, and that it was disdainful and contemptuous of the Poor Law and other charitable activities whilst often adopting similar principles of operation. Humphreys' argument is that the COS leaders were more concerned with rhetoric than deed and that by 1890 they were rejecting most applicants for relief, knowing that they would end up in the workhouse.

The influence of the COS over other relief agencies seems to have been exaggerated. Despite its claims to be a co-ordinating agency, it found that local guardians and charitable bodies did not respond enthusiastically to them. Indeed, Thomas Mackay, the Poor Law historian, and COS supporters admitted that 'with few exceptions, Poor Law authorities have remained impervious to the influence of the Society'.[36] Equally, the COS seems to have been reluctant to take on the cases created by the impact of the Goschen Minute of 1869, issued by the Poor Law Board, which recommended that Poor Law unions tighten up on their provision of outdoor relief. The Stepney Poor Law Union reduced the number of applicants receiving outdoor relief from 4,347 in April 1868 to 224 in 1876 but the COS only felt that there was one case 'considered deserving', and this was a pattern repeated in most other Poor Law union areas.[37] In the end, Humphreys concludes that: 'No matter how the COS Council blustered about their efficiency as an organising Society it is clear that in practical terms they failed miserably to rationalise relief to London's poor' or to make good the cases created by the Poor Law's more miserly attitude to the poor.[38]

The COS also failed in other departments. Its original intention had been to recruit capable volunteers to examine cases methodically and avoid 'impulsive charity'. In the event, both in and outside London the COS had to employ salaried agents to lead investigations. These agents seem to have hardened the policy of the COS, for the metropolitan branch dismissed an increasing proportion of applicants as time went on. In 1871, of 12,506 applicants, 34 per cent were dismissed as ineligible or undeserving, 31 per cent were referred and 35 per cent assisted. In 1880, of 20,770 applicants, 45 per cent were dismissed, 23 per cent referred and 32 per cent assisted. In 1890 the COS restructured the presentation of information and all that can be gleaned easily is that, of 21,402 applicants, 54 per cent were dismissed.[39] Dismissal was usually because the applicant was a beggar or was drunk. For instance:

M. D., Homeless, applied for assistance, would not say where she lived last. Stated she had stopped in Whitechapel, where she had paid 1s. 6d. a week. Her statement was so rambling, that but little value could be attached to it. On enquiry at the place where applicant slept on the previous night it was ascertained that she was a beggar.[40]

Because the COS received little support from other relief agencies, it became involved in making its own financial provision. To distinguish it from other forms of relief, it was to be 'individual, personal, temporary, and reformatory' and only given to industrious applicants.[41] The COS was not interested in dealing with the impotent poor, since this would open them to a life of idleness and debauchery. In other words, it was opposed to the provision of doles for those who had little prospects of developing their independence. Guardians usually paid between three and four shillings in outdoor relief to a deserving adult pauper – worth about two shillings for a wife and 1s. 6d. for each child. The COS claimed to be unhappy with such arrangements but, nonetheless, found itself attempting to provide hand-outs on equal lines.

More specifically, the COS argued that the Poor Law was inappropriate 'for the impotent poor, and financially inadequate for the active poor'.[42] Examining its grants, loans and pensions, the three main ways in which the COS offered assistance, Humphreys argues that its rhetoric about the Poor Law was meaningless in the light of its own provision. Apparently, by 1890 pensions were the main form of financial relief and yet they were worth less than the Poor Law doles that the COS criticized.

The COS offered loans in the 1870s on the basis that they would be paid back, but these declined in importance because of default. Between 1883–4 and 1889–90 the number of loans fell from 852 to 686, the cost declining from £1,480 to £472 and the average value from £1. 14s. 10d. (£1.74p) to 13s. 10d. (69p). Grants – to buy clothing, mangles for women to take in washing, for removal to other areas and the like – also followed a similar pattern of decline. Taking the same time period as above, grants declined from 6,314 to 4,920, their cost fell from £4,360 to £3,111 and the average value of them fell from 13s. 10d. (69p) to 12s. 7d. (63p). This was despite the fact that many of the examples of grants that the COS published were higher. Ironically, it was in the area of pensions – which the early COS was critical of, since it felt that they would discourage people from saving for the future – that it made its biggest contribution. Faced with many worthy cases and special claims, the various districts of the London COS paid more out on pensions than on any other item of relief: £10,836 in 1883–4 and £17,693 in 1889–90. There are no accurate figures for the number and cost of pensions provided in the whole of London, but in South St Pancreas the average per week for 18 pensions was 5s. 4d. (27p); Tower Hamlets Pensions Committee averaged about 2s. 8d. (13p) for its 100 pensions. These figures hide a wide variety of pension levels, the highest in South St Pancras being 12s. 4d. per week or £32. 1s. per year, whilst the lowest annual total was £1. Humphreys' point is that these totals were generally lower than the outdoor relief levels paid out by the metropolitan Poor Law authorities, which usually varied, as weekly rates, between 3s. and

4s. for adult applicants, with the addition of 2s. for a wife and 1s. 6d. for each child.[43] Humphreys stresses that: 'This recognition that COS pensions were frequently worth no more than the meanest Poor Law provision, strikes at the very heart of COS propaganda which repeatedly ridiculed the alleged inadequacy of the statutory dole.'[44]

In the final analysis, the COS carried little real weight and influence and dealt with only a small proportion of the poverty that it intended to oversee and co-ordinate. Its attitude and inconsistency meant that its true influence in London was limited and, as will be suggested in the next chapter, its influence outside London was barely evident and was easily swept away by the Guild of Help. What is clear is that, unlike other philanthropic bodies, it was not really facing up to the realities of poverty, which were becoming all the more evident as social surveys began to reveal its true and enormous extent in Britain.

Poverty surveys

The second half of the nineteenth century saw increasing revelations about the extent of poverty in British society. Although there was a constant concern and interest in the topic throughout the period, it was not until the last twenty years of the century that it began to reach fever pitch.

Yet there had been some earlier interest in the 1850s. In 1851 Henry Mayhew, a London journalist who wrote for the *Morning Chronicle*, published a selection of his articles under the title *London Labour and the London Poor* which was also reissued a decade later. He described the conditions of the working class of London, their accommodation and their social problems. There was some interest in the subject but no tremendous campaign to do something about it, although charities began to form themselves into national organizations and the government did attempt to control the overcrowding of lodging-houses and other problems.

Nevertheless, it was not until the 1880s that the issue came to the fore. At this stage Britain was experiencing an economic deflation and depression of the economy and both agriculture and trade were subjected to royal commissions. Whilst these conditions created concern, it was a combination of other social factors that seem to have produced a greater interest in poverty.

On the one hand, there was the rebirth of socialism in Britain, through the Social Democratic Federation, the Socialist League, the Fabian Society and the Independent Labour party (ILP), all of whom began to stress the social inequality in Britain and called for the mustering of social facts. Some of these bodies, particularly the ILP, became involved in local investigations. The Bradford ILP, for instance, was involved in a survey of unemployment in 1893 and 1894. It held a number of public meetings with the Fabians and the newly formed Social Reform Union, a body of prominent Nonconformist ministers, and the Trades Council. A committee was formed on 20 December 1893 and began to organize a social enquiry into the unemployed in Bradford, excluding the floating population and the inmates of the workhouse. It discovered that 58,558 people, or 27.1 per cent of the population of Bradford, were suffering the effects of unemployment: 9,689 were wholly unemployed, 11,914 were partially unemployed and 36,745 were dependents.[45]

Such socialist interest was stimulated by a spate of publications in the 1880s. Henry George's *Progress and Poverty*, which did much to stimulate an interest in socialism, was published in Britain in 1881 and focused attention upon poverty. Andrew Mearns, a Congregationalist minister, published a short pamphlet entitled *The Bitter Cry of Outcast London* (1883) which presented the case of the London slum dwellers. W. T. Stead publicized the need for housing reform in his *Pall Mall Gazette* and G. R. Sims gathered together a collection of his articles in *How the Poor Live in Horrible London* (1889).

One of the major contributions was made by William Booth, founder of the Salvation Army, in his book *In Darkest England and the Way Out* (1890). He exposed the awful social conditions that existed in England and advocated agricultural schemes, emigration and the work of the Salvation Army to save bodies and souls. The largest shock waves, however, came from two social surveys by Charles Booth and Seebohm Rowntree.

Charles Booth was a Liverpool merchant who, between 1886 and 1902, surveyed poverty in London. Initially, two pilot studies were done on Tower Hamlets in 1886 and East London and Hackney in 1887, and these revealed that about a third of the population lived below Booth's estimated 'poverty line'. Gathering together the impressions of school board visits, checking these against the impressions of informed local people and employing his own investigators, including Beatrice Potter, the later Mrs Beatrice Webb, he was able to produce seventeen volumes of material on working-class budgets, industry and employment and religion in London. Defining poverty as 'having no surplus' to guard against the costs of unemployment, sickness or death in the family, he came to the conclusion that about 30 per cent of the population of London were living in poverty. These were divided into eight classes, of whom A (the lowest class of occasional labourers and the like), B (the very poor casual earners), C (the intermittent earners) and D (the small regular earners) made up the 30 per cent.

Initially, these levels of poverty and the techniques involved were rejected by the COS and other interested parties. Yet they were soon to be confirmed by Seebohm Rowntree's survey of York entitled *Poverty: A Study of Town Life* (1901). Rowntree started from the presumption that, since York was typical of most of the provincial towns in England, what occurred there would be a fair reflection of what existed elsewhere. In 1899, a period of average prosperity, he employed investigators to survey every working-class household in York (11,560) to establish the levels of family income and expenditure. This information was checked against the records of wages which his own firm and others kept. It was then related to Rowntree's own poverty line, based upon a less generous diet than was available in the workhouse but one sufficient to ensure the 'physical efficiency' of the individuals. It also included a calculation for clothing, rent, light and fuel and established that the minimum income required for a family of five was 21s. 8d. (£1. 8p) per week, composed of 12s. 9d. food, 4s. 0d. rent and 4s. 11d. clothing, light, fuel and other items. Like Booth, he divided the working-class population into classes. Class A, the lowest, with families of four to six living on less than 18s. (90p) per week, represented 2.6 per cent of the working population; class B, chiefly the unskilled labourers, constituted 5.9 per cent of the population; and class C, about 20.7 per cent of the total population, were those whose conditions varied between insufficient and barely sufficient. It was from these three categories that it was estimated that 7,230 people of York, or 9.91 per cent, were living in 'primary' poverty and 13,072 people, or 17.93 per cent, were living in 'secondary' poverty.

By finding that about 28 per cent of the population of York were living in some degree of poverty, Rowntree confirmed the clear message of Booth's work that up to one-third of the inhabitants of many towns were suffering poverty of some description. His calculations were, of course, controversial. His 'primary' poverty referred to those below the poverty line he had calculated and thus, by definition, without enough food to live on. Those in 'secondary' poverty were living above his poverty line but obviously in want and squalor because they could not manage their expenditure efficiently.

The calculation of the 'poverty line' and 'secondary poverty' drew some criticism. Nevertheless, there was much substance in this survey, most obviously because it attempted to examine the causes of poverty. It calculated that, of those below the 'primary' poverty line, 51.96 per cent were there due to regular but low wages, 22.16 per cent due to large families (of more than four children) and 15.36 per cent due to the death of the chief wage-earner. Illness accounted for 5.11 per cent, unemployment of the chief wage-earner for 2.31 per cent and irregularity of work for another 2.83 per cent. The survey also established that the life of a labourer was marked by a poverty cycle of five alternating periods of want and plenty, three of which – early childhood, the raising of a family and old age – were dominated by poverty.[46]

No matter what criticisms emerged, however, it is clear that the issue was to the forefront of social concerns by the late nineteenth century. Even a minimalist Welfare State had to think about how to tackle poverty and its causes.

Poverty and politics

The extensions of the parliamentary franchise in 1867 and 1884, changes in the terms for municipal candidature and voting in the 1880s, and the effective removal of all but the twelve-month residence qualification for voting in the guardian elections from 1894 onwards – all these things made central government sensitive to the working-class voter and the need for social reform as never before. Out of these changes came the possibility of the emergence of an independent Labour party, especially as the financial qualifications for candidates were reduced and removed, thus permitting the poorer, working-class-based parties to put forward municipal and parliamentary candidates. Trade-union membership also rose rapidly to over a million by the beginning of the 1890s and to about two million by 1900.

These types of pressures added to other political developments which were encouraging greater municipal and state action. Most notably, Disraeli had shown some interest in social reform in the 1870s, particularly in respect of health and factory legislation. Lord Randolph Churchill also pushed the Conservative party in that direction. Equally, the radical Liberal Joseph Chamberlain, who was mayor of Birmingham between 1873 and 1875, was pushing the Liberal party in a similar direction. Chamberlain's involvement in the Civic Gospel movement prepared him well for his future national role in social policy after entering Parliament in 1876. Between 1880 and 1885 he was president of the Board of Trade in Gladstone's second ministry and became the effective head of the social reform movement. In 1885 he mounted a very strong campaign against the property owners for depriving the rest of the population of their historic rights and offered the so-called 'unauthorized programme' in the general election campaign to deal with the evil of 'the excessive inequality in the distribution of riches'.

It was the serious unemployment problem of 1886, which had led to riots by the unemployed in London on 8 February 1886 and to much socialist agitation, that provided the context in which Chamberlain, as president of the Local Government Board in Gladstone's short-lived third ministry, issued the Chamberlain Circular in March 1886. It authorized municipal public works schemes to relieve unemployment and was a dramatic change in government policy – both because it was an admission that unemployment was not necessarily a personal failing and because it was an attempt to avoid forcing individuals on to the Poor Law. Within twenty years this had paved the way for the Unemployed Workmen's Act of 1905.

Thereafter, Chamberlain's social contribution was limited. He left the Liberals and helped to form the Unionist party over the Home Rule crisis in 1886, drifted into the Conservative party as a result and was a member of Salisbury's Unionist Cabinet in 1895. Although Chamberlain was Secretary for the Colonies, he pressed for the passing of the Workmen's Compensation Act of 1897, which made employers fully liable for the accidents of their employees while at work.

Apart from Chamberlain's efforts, one must note that municipal 'gas and water socialism' was becoming a feature of all urban centres. Birmingham developed its housing, sewerage, water and gas schemes in the early 1870s and Huddersfield had a municipal tramway by 1882. Most other towns and cities followed suit and the government seemed to follow their lead. The 1875 Artizans' Dwelling Act, the 1885 Housing of the Working Classes Act, following the 1885 Royal Commission on the Housing of the Working Classes, and the 1890 Housing of the Working Classes Act all permitted the public provision of houses for the working classes. The 1890 Act, which was divided into two parts, covered both the individual clearance of slums and larger-scale slum clearance and the building of new working-class houses. It was this Act which was used by Bradford City Council to clear the Longlands district of Bradford and to build tenements for 432 people and new housing at Faxfleet Street for the 925 displaced persons.[47] Nevertheless, it took ten years, 1897–1907, to introduce the scheme, largely because of the opposition of the local branch of the Liberty and Property Defence League (formed in 1882).

Yet at this point one has to return to José Harris's pluralistic society. Whilst it is quite clear that there were some minor developments towards recognizing the need to extend state intervention in poverty and housing, it is also clear that the state was attempting to reduce its financial commitment in some directions and was prepared to allow philanthropy to assume an enhanced role. This has already been suggested. It has been seen that Goschen's Minute of 1869 led to the restriction of outdoor relief over the next few years (the number of female outdoor relief applicants was reduced from 166,407 in January 1871 to 53,371 in January 1891) on the assumption – false, as it proved – that the COS and voluntary bodies would screen, and assume some responsibility for, applicants before they ever reached the relieving officer.

By the later years of the century it was clear that both philanthropy and the Poor Law were failing to tackle the social problems of society in any effective manner. The sick, children, lunatics and the elderly were gradually being dealt with more sympathetically by the Poor Law, but those receiving inadequate wages and forced to apply for outdoor relief were not, as suggested above, being treated any better. Indeed, Michael Rose was probably correct to suggest that the deterrent Poor Law was a product more of the 1870s than the 1830s.[48]

Conclusion

The late nineteenth century had seen the gradual extension of the minimalist state within the context of a pluralistic society which was developing social policy in different directions and along several fronts. Despite the slowness of change, it is clear that there had been a fundamental change of perception between the 1830s and the 1890s. Poverty was now the dominant force driving social policy. It was recognized that about 28–30 per cent of the population lived in a state of poverty, even though only 2 or 3 per cent were paupers. By the 1880s the concern about pauperism, which had developed in the 1830s, had given way to the concern about poverty. By the early twentieth century the concern about national efficiency had raised the issue of poverty to a new level and was forcing a compromise between the role of the state and philanthropy.

Notes

1. José Harris, *Private Lives, Public Spirit: A Social History of Britain 1870–1914* (Oxford, 1993).
2. P. Thane, 'Government and Society in England and Wales, 1750–1914', in F. M. L. Thompson (ed.), *The Cambridge Social History of Britain 1750–1950*, iii. *Social Agencies and Institutions* (Cambridge, 1990). p. 12.
3. *Ibid.*, pp. 15, 25, 29.
4. R. Hay, 'Employers and Social Policy in Britain: The Evolution of Welfare Legislation, 1905–14', *Social History* 2 (1977), pp. 435–55; J. Melling, 'Welfare Capitalism and the Origins of Welfare States: British Industry, Workplace Welfare and Social Reform, 1870–1914', *Social History* 17/3 (1992), pp. 453–78.
5. Hay, 'Employers and Social Policy', pp. 445–7.
6. R. Hay, 'Employers' Attitudes to Social Policy and the Concept of "Social Control", 1900–1920', in P. Thane (ed.), *The Origins of British Social Policy* (1978), pp. 107–25.
7. Melling, 'Welfare Capitalism', p. 458.
8. P. Joyce, *Work, Society and Politics* (Brighton, 1980); Melling, 'Welfare Capitalism', pp. 459–60.
9. Melling, 'Welfare Capitalism', p. 462.
10. For the former ideas, look at S. E. Finer, *The Life and Times of Sir Edwin Chadwick* (1952). For the latter, look at O. MacDonagh, 'The Nineteenth-Century Revolution in Government: A Reappraisal', *Historical Journal* 1 (1958); O. MacDonagh, *Early Victorian Government* (1977); O. MacDonagh,

The Passenger Acts: A Pattern of Government Growth (1961); and W. C. Lubenow, *The Politics of Government Growth* (Newton Abbot, 1971).

11.   Finer, *Chadwick*.

12.   O. MacDonagh, 'The Nineteenth-Century Social Reform: A Tory Interpretation of History', *Past and Present* (1965), pp. 39–61.

13.   R. Lambert, 'Central and Local Relations in Mid-Victorian England: The Local Government Act Office, 1853–1871', *Victorian Studies* 6 (1962); R. Lambert, *Sir John Simon, 1816–1904, and English Social Administration* (1963).

14.   Lubenow, *Government Growth*.

15.   H. Parris, 'The Nineteenth-Century Revolution in Government: A Reappraisal Reappraised', *Historical Journal* 1 (1958), p. 28; V. Cromwell, 'Interpretations of Nineteenth-Century Administration: An Analysis', *Victorian Studies* (1966), pp. 245–55.

16.   J. Hart, 'Nineteenth-Century Social Reform: A Tory Interpretation of History, *Past and Present* 31 (1965), pp. 39–61.

17.   Thane, 'Government and Society', p. 21.

18.   S. Smiles, *Self Help* (1859), p. 1.

19.   D. Fraser, *The Evolution of the British Welfare State* (1983), pp. 111–17.

20.   F. Prochaska, 'Philanthropy', in F. M. L. Thompson (ed.), *The Cambridge Social History of Britain 1750–1950: Social Agencies and Institutions* (Cambridge, 1990), p. 357.

21.   *Ibid.*, pp. 357–8.

22.   M. Simey, *Charity Rediscovered: A Study of Philanthropic Effort in Nineteenth-Century Liverpool* (Liverpool, 1992; formerly published in 1951 as *Charitable Effort in Liverpool in the Nineteenth Century*).

23.   *Ibid.*, pp. 360–70.

24.   *Report of the Royal Commission on the Aged Poor*, Parliamentary Papers 1895, xv, pp. 885, 888, quoted in Prochaska, 'Philanthropy', p. 364.

25.   Prochaska, 'Philanthropy', p. 33.

26.   Mill Hill Chapel Subscription Book, 1844 (in custody of Mill Hill Chapel), quoted in E. A. Elton, 'A Victorian City Mission: The Unitarian Contribution to Social Progress in Holbeck and New Wortley, 1844–78', *Thoresby Society Miscellany* 16 (1977), part 4, p. 316.

27.   Prochaska, 'Philanthropy', p. 372.

28.   R. Humphreys, *Scientific Charity in Victorian London: Claims and Achievements of the Charity Organisation Society, 1869–1890* (London School of Economics & Political Science, Working Papers in Economic History 14; 1993).

29.   Simey, *Charity Rediscovered*, pp. 81–96.

30.   Prochaska, 'Philanthropy', pp. 371–2.

31.   Note, for instance, Fraser, *Evolution*, pp. 126, 128.

32.   *Charity Organisation Reporter*, 24 February 1881, p. 50, quoted in Humphreys, *Scientific Charity in Victorian London*, p. 1.

33.   *Charity Organisation Reporter*, 27 September 1884.

34.   *Ibid.*, 26 March 1873, p. 55.

35.   *Eighth Annual Report of the Charity Organisation Society* (1876), appendix iv, p. 24.

36. *Charity Organisation Review* (1889), p. 25, quoted in Humphreys, *Scientific Charity in Victorian London*, p. 7.
37. *Charity Organisation Review*, 14 December 1876, p. 61, quoted in Humphreys, *Scientific Charity in Victorian London*, p. 8.
38. Humphreys, *Scientific Charity in Victorian London*, p. 10.
39. *Ibid.*, p. 16.
40. *Ibid.*, p. 17, quoting from *1st Annual Report: Poplar, Bow, and Bromley COS* (1873), p. 27.
41. K. Woodroffe, *Scientific Charity to Social Work* (1968), p. 39.
42. Humphreys, *Scientific Charity in Victorian London*, p. 5.
43. *Ibid.*, pp. 18–36, and particularly table 3, p. 22, and table 4, p. 30.
44. *Ibid.*, p. 32.
45. *Manifesto of the Bradford Unemployed Emergency Committee, 1894* (Bradford, 1894), p. 6.
46. E. P. Hennock. 'The Measurement of Poverty: From the Metropolis to the Nation, 1880–1920', *Economic History Review* 40 (1987), provides an excellent review of the whole development of poverty surveys and their significance for the study of poverty.
47. K. Laybourn, '"The Defence of Bottom Dog": The Independent Labour Party in Local Politics', in D. G. Wright and J. A. Jowitt (eds.), *Victorian Bradford* (Bradford, 1982), pp. 235–7. Also, *Bradford Labour Echo*, 14 January 1899; *A Brighter Day, 1899*, Series 1, copy in Deed Box 13, Case 52, West Yorkshire Archives, Bradford; *Forward*, 18 October 1907.
48. M. E. Rose, 'The Crisis of Poor Relief in England', in W. Mommson (ed.), *The Emergence of the Welfare State in Britain and Germany* (1981), pp. 50–70.

CHAPTER EIGHT

VOLUNTARY HELP AND THE STATE
c.1900–1914

The emergence of state intervention, through the medium of the Liberal social reforms of 1905–14, was the most important development in the decade before the First World War, largely because it challenged both the undermined local control and the philanthropic efforts that had been the basis of British social policy until that time. Indeed, Derek Fraser reflects that: 'Whatever historical perspective is used, one cannot escape the conclusion that Liberal social policy before the First World War was at once at variance with the past and an anticipation of radical changes in the future.'[1] Nevertheless, one should be cautious of suggesting that there was any clean break between the past and the present, for the two styles of social policy overlapped for a number of years and the state tended to strengthen the responsibilities, if not the independence, of local administration. In addition, the voluntary and charitable sector was mixed in its response to the state. The London-based Charity Organisation Society (COS) was reluctant to accept that poverty was anything other than a personal failing and was hostile to David Lloyd George's state insurance scheme which was forcing voluntary bodies to become an authorized sub-service of the state.[2] In contrast, the Guild of Help, a new philanthropic body that emerged in 1904 and quickly superseded the COS, recognized the challenge that was coming and its 'new philanthropy' contained an inherent commitment to working with public bodies. Its aim was to check the pace of state intervention by demonstrating the way in which voluntary help could become more efficient, effective and progressive in acting as the friend of the poor. Yet neither the approach of the COS nor that of the Guild of Help succeeded, for state intervention absorbed and controlled voluntary efforts as it assumed predominance in a society which had, hitherto, been primarily based upon local control and private charity. Both the COS and the Guild of Help were swallowed up by the state in the vortex of war, when they became mere adjuncts to, rather than partners in, state social welfare. The state became ubiquitous as the traditional and philanthropic means of dealing with poverty – and its kindred causes of ill health and unemployment – became less relevant and potent. For a decade or more, however, there was the possibility of overlap and co-operation between the state and charity as local authorities became more geared towards the needs of Whitehall than to their immediate electorate.

The Edwardian years were clearly ones of transition which saw the state assume new and wider responsibilities. But why did state intervention widen? In recent years historians have tried to explain the emergence of the Liberal Welfare State in a variety of ways. Some have seen the explanation of state growth in the influence of ideas and idealists.[3] Others have focused upon the failures of the philanthropic and traditional forces in society, which necessitated state involvement no matter how reluctant administrators and government might have been to intervene. C. F. G. Masterman, journalist and Poor Law guardian and MP, described Rowntree's *Poverty: A Study of Town Life* (1901) as a 'thunder clap' and 'one of the most important pieces of detailed social investigation ever undertaken'.[4] Others have suggested that welfare capitalism might have exerted an impact, although a declining one, on the evolution of the British Welfare State.[5] A fourth group have been at pains to challenge any notion that the Liberal Welfare State emerged as a result of pressure from a newly enfranchised working class. Rightly, however, they point out that the working class was initially suspicious of the new state intervention because of a variety of experiences and associations, one of which was the link between state intervention and the operation of the feared Poor Law. Evidently, it was only once the new Liberal reforms were at work that attitudes changed.[6] To some writers it was the concerns of the middle classes, rather than the working classes, that led to efforts to patch up poverty rather than to tackle it. Pat Thane focuses upon the concerns of David Lloyd George and the new Liberals to support the existing political and economic system.[7] David Vincent has also commented perceptively on this middle-class, rather than working-class, concern, and noted that it imposed its own limits:

> Henceforth it was evident that for the most part reform would not extend far into the realm of low wages, nor far beyond the capacity of insurance to deal with the failure of charity and the Poor Law. Increasing national prosperity would be the means rather than the end of legislation. The task was to find a more efficient way of dealing with poverty, not a way of dealing with poverty which was to promote a more efficient economy.[8]

In this whirl of ideas and debates it is becoming obvious that many forces helped to shape the evolution of the Welfare State, although Liberal governments appear to have convinced themselves of the need both to tackle the obvious social failings of society and to stem the threat from the Labour party and socialism, whose vision of social change was far wider than anything they would contemplate. However, the evolution of state intervention through the Liberal reforms did not follow one trajectory. There were many political and social eddies which modified its direction. Indeed, philanthropy made its contribution, albeit declining and failing, in the decade prior to 1914 in a desperate attempt to convert the state to its ideas about how society should tackle poverty.

The voluntary and charitable sector: the past and the future

The early twentieth century saw a debate within both the philanthropic community and government as to the best way of dealing with poverty. As the old philanthropy gave way to the new, there was serious debate and overlapping concerns on such issues as unemployment, old-age pensions, national insurance, the future of the Poor Law and other related issues, all of which became the focus of attention from David Lloyd George, Winston Churchill and Liberal governments. Although philanthropic influence was limited, due largely to both its inability to form an effective pressure group and to the immense social problems that it encountered, it did contribute to the whirl of ideas that influenced the role of the state before 1914 and, indeed, to the policies that were developed. Philanthropy was considered to be an essential part of the process by 'which individuals and political groups found themselves pulled in several contrary directions at once'.[9] The older philosophy of the nineteenth century was not immediately swept away by the newer one of the twentieth century and the Guild of Help, at least until 1914, attempted, with limited impact, to balance the two forces of philanthropy and the state.

This impending replacement of philanthropy, whether new or old, by state action was recognized by B. Kirkman Gray, who wrote that:

> The change from philanthropy to social politics has been great – private philanthropy cannot provide a remedy for wide-spread want which results from broad and general social causes; that it ought not to be expected to do so; that the provision of such remedies is the proper responsibility of the State and should be accepted as such.[10]

Yet even he accepted that there were openings for philanthropy through delegation, co-operation or some other form of arrangement. In other words, he recognized that the concept of the new philanthropy was a viable proposition. Nonetheless, there were varied responses from the guilds as to how they would work with the state and new legislation. At one extreme there was the Bradford City Guild of Help's eternal optimism that the new legislation would provide it with varied and increased opportunities by releasing it from unnecessary burden. At the other extreme there was the pessimism of the Halifax Citizen's Guild, which, despite its commitment to working with public authorities and the state, was worried that the role of the Guild of Help was being minimized by new legislation and saw little prospect for future development. This tension within the Guild of Help movement became more evident with the rising tide of social legislation and particularly with the debate surrounding the Poor Law and the National Insurance Act, although the introduction of other legislation played its part in shaping attitudes. In the end, state legislation was inevitable given the Edwardian concern about national efficiency and the problem for philanthropy was to determine its precise position in relationship to the state.

This was not easy, given that the old philanthropy was almost totally opposed to the state – its attitudes being very much shaped by the COS – whilst the new philanthropy of the Guild of Help sought to establish a working relationship with the state in dealing with health, unemployment, pensions, and the Poor Law, although its efforts were febrile. F. Prochaska has written that:

> No country on earth can lay claim down to a greater philanthropic tradition than Great Britain. Until the twentieth century philanthropy was widely believed to be the most wholesome and valuable remedy for the nation's ills, a view that is not without its adherents today.[11]

Undoubtedly, he is right. In London alone the 1,000 most prominent charities had received over £7,000,000 by the 1890s.[12] The King's Fund, founded in 1897 under the patronage of the Prince of Wales, soon to become Edward VII, raised between £100,000 and £150,000 per year – gathered from bequests and voluntary contributions. Its assets exceeded £1,800,000 in 1910 and the income from investments stood at over £77,000.[13] Between 1897 and 1948 it disbursed £4,444,242 to twelve general hospitals in London with medical schools, including Charing Cross, Guy's and King's, and a total of £12,413,253 in all.[14]

Yet it is clear that all the efforts of the old philanthropy had done little to reduce the death rates of the nation or to improve the general health or condition of its population, a situation that was highlighted by the poor conditions of the Boer War recruits. Combined with the rising unemployment of the early years of the twentieth century, this led many people to feel that the old philanthropy had failed. In any case, its influence outside London and Liverpool was negligible; there were only 26 COS organizations, with 44 paid and 235 voluntary organizers, in the North of England, serving about 3.5 million people in the various towns at a cost of £16,000 per year. By 1908 the COS had expanded to 33 organizations, 64 paid and 500 voluntary organizers, serving a population of 4.5 million at a cost of £23,000.[15] Its influence was not great and its opposition to state pensions, the National Insurance Act of 1911 and other areas of Liberal legislation meant that it was unsympathetic to the state. Indeed, it was positively hostile when the Lloyd George scheme forced voluntary bodies to become an 'authorized sub-service' of the state.[16]

This hostility partly derived from the fact that the COS saw poverty as evidence of personal failure and not as a failing of society. It spent much of its time in anti-mendacity campaigns which echo the more recent attempts to root out the scrounger in the Britain of Margaret Thatcher and John Major. Effectively, the COS was harsh and unsympathetic towards the unemployed and the poor.

In contrast, the Guild of Help was far more concerned with recognizing some of the failings of British society. It showed far more respect for the impoverished individual and accepted that it was often economic circumstances, rather than personal failings, that caused poverty.[17] Indeed, a central feature of the Guild of Help was its commitment to working with public bodies in a partnership to tackle poverty – and its emphasis was always placed upon action by the local community. In Bradford this connection was reflected in the fact that F. H. Bentham, the chairman of the Bradford Board of Guardians and a member of the Royal Commission on the Poor Laws, was also a founder member of the guild, a member of its executive committee and a vice-president during the First World War. The Bradford Guild also noted that, in 1908, 28 per cent of its cases had been reported by official bodies such as the guardians and the local education authority.[18] Thereafter, relevant information was passed between the two bodies. In Bradford, Halifax and in many other communities the guilds participated in the arrangements to provide free school meals to children during the severe economic depression that occurred in the winters of 1905 and 1908.

The whole purpose of the guilds was to build up an effective community structure with which to tackle poverty and unemployment. Indeed, according to *Help*, the organ of the Bradford Guild:

> The Guild of Help is the practical expression of the civic consciousness and the embodiment of the new philanthropy. The old, was clearly associated with charity in a narrow sense, and between those who gave and those who received was a great gulf fixed; the 'lady bountiful' attitude has received its death blow, the Guild worker does not go in as visitant from another world but as a fellow creature to be helpful.[19]

Apart from an extensive pattern of social casework designed to alleviate the sufferings of the poor by giving advice, arranging necessary health, clothing and holiday provision, it sought to act as a form of labour exchange. The idea was to rescue the poor and to prevent destitution.[20] This desire led guilds into a wider range of activities. Indeed, the Halifax Guild encouraged the local authority to appoint health visitors and, as noted above, in Bolton, Bradford and Halifax, as well as other areas, the guilds contributed to the provision and the distribution of school meals. In Bradford there was also a short-lived attempt to operate a land colony at Eccleshill, and subsequently at Guiseley, which went under the title of the Bradford Land Settlement Co. Ltd.[21] In Bolton there was relief for consumptives, the provision of spectacles for children, a scheme to deal with juvenile offenders who would otherwise be imprisoned, and one which provided maternity kits for mothers-to-be.[22] Habits of thrift were encouraged amongst the poor, including the membership of friendly societies and trade unions, and health weeks and anti-beggar campaigns were also organized. These, and a vast array of other activities, with numerous local variants, formed the very stuff of the many guilds that were formed.

In order to undertake these activities, the guilds created an administrative structure based upon divisions and districts, with the districts equating to municipal wards. In some cases there was an executive committee or central board in control of the guild but often, as in the case of Bolton, it was a finance and general purposes committee that effectively ran the guild. The case of the Bradford Guild illustrates one common pattern, although there were variations. The Bradford City Guild of Help was launched in September 1904. It was organized into four divisions, with ten districts within each division. There was an executive committee which presided over the entire scheme and a central board, consisting of all the district heads, appears to have met from time to time. Ideally, there were to be ten helpers within each division, apart from the district head and secretary. Theoretically – and, indeed, in practice – this meant that the Bradford Guild would have at least 450 helpers. These people would deal with the 500–1,000 applicants per year who were referred for help from the helpers and the central office of the guild through individuals such as ministers of religion or through the guardians, Education Department or similar official bodies.

The new philanthropy's range of activities differed little from those of the old philanthropy. Both forms undertook casework and had many other activities in common. Indeed, Charles Loch of the COS commented: 'It seems to me that in the work of the Guilds we find many of our own experiences repeating themselves. Their statements of object are often very much like our own. They appear to spring from an undercurrent of thought which is familiar ...'[23] Despite this view, contemporaries and historians have noted at least three major points of difference between the old and the new philanthropies which were more than mythological distinctions. The first was that the guild movement had a more positive attitude towards working with public bodies. As Elizabeth Macadam wrote: 'the new philanthropy ... [was] a unique partnership ... a system of combined statutory and voluntary service, which has grown up in the last forty years.'[24] Secondly, the London-based COS was far more centralized than the guild movement which, despite national developments, remained a collection of autonomous bodies whose emphasis upon civic consciousness might be regarded as almost inimical to national organization. Thirdly, it is suggested that the guilds showed far more respect for the individual than the COS did and accepted that society was often to blame for poverty. The three factors together were deemed to represent a 'scientific approach' to dealing with poverty.

Yet, in the end, the Guild of Help failed to provide the answer to poverty, since its approach was chiefly designed to endorse the existing class distinctions, the moral responsibility of the middle classes for the poor and the moral discipline of the recipient. In other words, the guilds were more concerned with palliatives than solutions. Indeed, the thinking of many members of the Bradford Guild was revealed by the comment that: 'It is, after all, a more important matter to inculcate habits of providence and thrift than merely to tide over periods of distress.'[25] This attitude naturally drew criticism from socialists, who emphasized the need to redistribute wealth rather than to patch up the failings of Edwardian capitalist society. Yet even the most supportive of commentators would have to acknowledge that the Guild of Help and the new philanthropy failed to make any decisive impact upon the social problems of the day.

The new philanthropy was unable to tackle the high levels of poverty resulting from unemployment that occurred in many northern towns during the Edwardian years, and the Halifax Guild had to admit that, after dealing with 1,398 cases in 1908–9, it had consciously kept the number down to less than 600 in 1909–10, due to the 'feeling that in the previous year much of our resources and strength were expended in attempting too much'.[26] In addition, a quick perusal of a small sample of the 5,682 casebooks which survive for Bradford for the years 1905–21 suggests that, in any case, it was not the really poor who were being dealt with, for many of the recipients of help seem to have been families whose joint incomes exceeded £1, and often £1. 5s. (£1.25p) per week. This is an impression strengthened by the fact that some of the poor districts of Bradford, such as the two Bowling Back Lane Districts, found it difficult to attract helpers and maintain a consistency of organization.[27]

G. R. Snowden, who investigated the Guild of Help movement in 1911, also suggested that it was a worthy but undeveloped movement and implied that it had a long way to go to fulfil its objectives: 'The ideal which the Guilds of Help have set before them is a high one, and is only to be reached by a long, patient and often discouraging process of hard work.'[28] And he recognized that 'the normal resources of the Guild of Help are insufficient to cope' with unemployment in times of distress.[29] This situation was certainly not helped by the reluctance of the

Bradford Guild to set up a fund to provide relief, due to the fact that its motto was 'Not Alms but a Friend'.[30] Yet most guilds do appear to have avoided that particular problem on the grounds of expediency, even though they never had enough funds to tackle poverty and its causes in an effective manner.

The Guild of Help also failed in three other respects, two of which are associated with the fact that it sought to be a community response to poverty. In the first place, it did not gain the full support of the whole community even in those areas where registers of the unemployed were set up. Local civic consciousness was riddled with dissent and tensions. There were poor relations between the guilds and the COS and there were many problems with religious charities. The Church of England and the dissenting and Nonconformist religions often possessed their own organized system of district visitors and tended to object to the guild helper as an intruder.[31] Few local trades councils were represented; the secretary of the Bolton Trades Council was a prominent member of the Bolton Guild, but such an association was rare and more typical was the situation in Poole, where Mr Bishop, of the Federated Trade Union, ignored the invitation to join the League of Help's executive committee.[32]

A second, and consequential, weakness of this lack of community spirit was the fact that the guild was not able to draw widely upon the support of the whole local community. According to G. R. Snowden: 'The helpers are drawn from all classes of society: in a few Guilds half or more than half of the men and women were of the working classes.'[33] Margaret Brasnett, developing the theme, asserts that, of the 450 helpers active in Bradford: 'Many of them were working-class people, for Bradford was the home of the working-class movements and the cradle of the Labour Party.'[34] Michael J. Moore is more cautious, writing that: 'Solidly based in the middle classes, their appeals, however, reached well into the ranks of the working class making more attractive the idea of philanthropic service as an obligation to the community.'[35] Nevertheless, the fragmentary evidence suggests that even the cautious Moore may have exaggerated the extent of working-class involvement in the movement. Only Farnworth Guild of Help, a small guild located near Bolton, appears to have had about 50 per cent working-class membership,[36] and the main guilds, such as Bolton, Bradford and Reading, of whom at least 205 of its 300–400 members were professional or middle class,[37] all drew their support largely from the middle classes. Indeed, a very large proportion of the guild members appear to have been the daughters of the middle classes.[38] This failure to attract working-class support may have been connected to the fact that a very large proportion of the working classes were living in poverty and that the emerging trade unions and political Labour movements were generally hostile to the aims of the movement. To aspiring socialists, the Guild of Help was seen as offering limited attempts to reduce poverty rather than a commitment to change by the redistribution of wealth. Not surprisingly, then, some socialists were critical of the 'Gilded Help' that 'won't get rid of poverty in a billion years on present lines'.[39]

A third failure was that the Guild of Help was never able to establish its relationship with the state in a full and effective manner. The guilds did act as sub-contractors in school feeding,[40] did work with boards of guardians and with medical officers of health and other local agencies. In other words, there were attempts to work with the local agencies of state. They also expressed an interest in the activities of the state. Nevertheless, their influence was limited. They lacked an effective national organization from which to influence the central state and were limited in their impact upon the local agencies of state activity. At the national conference of the Guilds of Help in 1913 L. V. Sharp, of Leeds, admitted that: 'One of the difficulties in the way of voluntary service was a certain nervousness on the part of the municipal and local authorities as to accepting co-operation with voluntary agencies.'[41] G. R. Snowden also noted in 1911 that, whilst there were about 60 guilds in existence, there were 600 Poor Law unions and parishes in England: 'Moreover, in no case has the Poor Law Union been adopted as the area in which a Guild is to act, and in very few cases are the services of the Guild available through the whole area of a Union.'[42] There were some successes, particularly amongst the larger guilds, but in general the comments of Sharp and Snowden were correct and the nearest that most guilds got to working with the state was when they were absorbed into the 300 or so more genuinely locally based local representative committees which emerged during the First World War to help administer the National Relief Fund. In practical terms, that led to the extinction of some guilds and the absorption of the remaining ones into the National Council of Social Services in 1919.[43]

Neither the old nor the new philanthropies were able to deal with the rising pressures of unemployment and poverty that afflicted Edwardian society. The old philanthropy had failed to obtain sufficient support and resources to deal with the massive social problems which Victorian and Edwardian societies faced, whilst the new philanthropy was unable to elicit enough local support or resources in its endeavour to work with the state in dealing with those problems. Nevertheless, the Guild of Help, as the representative of the new philanthropy, had made a forthright attempt to tackle poverty.

The Edwardian years were ones of transition. They reflected a new consensus which was emerging to deal with the social surveys of the day, the development of women's suffrage, the issue of Labour and the consequent development of a 'new' Liberal ideology. The Guild of Help was at the centre of these activities. It wished to act as a half-way house, using voluntary help to control and influence the direction of state intervention, keeping Edwardian society within a restricted and recognizable mould. Many of its members did support the Bishop of Ripon when he maintained that the rich existed to help the poor, even though they recognized that the poor were often victims of the environment and society in which they operated and had failed due to their own personal inadequacies. It was prepared to tackle the consequences of the failure of capitalist society but not to change that society. Its efforts to engender community consciousness were one response to the problems of poverty but, in the end, local initiative was not enough. Although the attitude of the state was little different, it had the resources to ease the burden of poverty in Edwardian society even if it did not have the will to create a society in which poverty would be tackled by the redistribution of income.

The state and the Liberal reforms of 1905–1914

A. Causes of reform

The Liberals had not come to power on the issue of social reform and poverty but on a variety of other issues, such as 'Chinese slavery'. Nonetheless, social reform became the hallmark of the Liberal governments of 1905–14. The reason for this development has been the subject of intense debate, with suggestions ranging from the impact of the emergent Labour party on new Liberalism, the need to deal effectively with the failings of the Poor Law and the rising concern about those whose needs were not being met through voluntary help. All these factors undoubtedly contributed to the final blend of reforms.

The issue of new Liberalism has, of course, assumed immense importance in the debate that has focused upon the rise of Labour and the decline of Liberalism. It is argued that L. T. Hobhouse, J. A. Hobson and David Lloyd George attempted to retain working-class support within the Liberal party by offering a variety of social reforms and compromises to the working classes which became known as new Liberalism.[44] It is further maintained that their prime concern was to reconcile the demands of labour with the need for Liberal party unity, an equation that was never going to be easily arranged given Liberal reliance upon industrial and capitalist wealth. They offered conciliation for industrial conflict, public ownership to serve the demands of efficiency and communal responsibility over sectional interests.[45] The distinctive feature of these and other new Liberal policies was that they offered a framework whereby harmony, rather than class or sectional conflict, would be promoted. Indeed, Lloyd George stressed to the

National Reform Union in 1914 that: 'it is better that you should have a party which combined every section and every shade of opinion, taken from all classes of the community, rather than one which represents one shade of opinion alone or one class of community alone'.[46] Community, compromise and agreement were thus seen as the alternative to a socialist-type Labour party committed to changing society in favour of the working class. New Liberalism was to be the referee in British society, not the harbinger of class interest.

P. F. Clarke has been the clearest exponent of the view that new Liberalism was responsible for the Liberal revival before the First World War. His regional study of Lancashire suggests that the improving fortunes of the Liberal party in the country were very largely a product of the new Liberal ideas which were offered to the electorate. But one must remember that the Liberals did not fight the December 1905 general election on the issue of social reform and that there is little evidence to suggest that new Liberalism carried any meaningful presence in the provinces or outside Westminster.[47] Yet, as Pat Thane has suggested, one should not assume that the type of social reform developed by the Liberals was at the top of Labour's political agenda.[48] Indeed, issues such as fair wages and the right to work carried far more weight in the first four years of the Liberal administration when a considerable amount of work was done in connection with social reform. This view has been endorsed by G. R. Searle, who also feels that those who stress the significance of new Liberalism have been guilty of exaggerating the importance of social reform within the Liberal party and the alienation of its traditional business supporters. He argues that, far from turning themselves into social democrats, the Liberals remained strongly reliant upon the income supplied by the 'Radical Plutocrats'.[49] New Liberalism – and the social reform that it implied – might thus have been untypical of Liberal party attitudes at this time and out of tune with the concerns of the working classes and their institutions.

Even if new Liberalism did not necessarily confer political advantage, it could also be seen as a working-out of the tensions between the old Gladstonian Liberalism of free trade and individualism and the new Liberal tendency towards collective and state responsibility for social reform. The latter was particularly concerned with the question of national efficiency and its cause was clearly pushed forward by the poor quality of the British volunteers for the Boer War and Rowntree's work on poverty in York.

The importance of new Liberal ideas is clearly under scrutiny, even though they must have contributed to the general thrust for social reform. The emergence of the Labour party – with 29, soon to be 30, MPs – made state action by the Liberal government even more imperative, because of the need both to obtain Labour's political support and to defuse its potential claim to the working-class vote. The Liberal government was obviously not dependent upon Labour's political support in 1906 but became increasingly so from 1910 onwards. Indeed, given the Liberals' thumping parliamentary majority of 356, it would be surprising if they had thrown anything other than a nominal nod in the direction of Labour, at least until 1910. Thane develops an argument here which Henry Pelling first presented in the 1960s, that the working classes were hostile to state intervention because they saw it as reflecting the experience of the Poor Law and the middle-class control which that represented and that, until the legislation was introduced, the only real pressure for reform came from Liberal politicians such as Asquith and Lloyd George. She suggests that the evidence of friendly societies and socialist organizations such as the SDF tends to endorse this viewpoint.

Whilst Lloyd George and his immediate supporters obviously felt – rightly or wrongly – the need to respond to what they saw as a serious Labour challenge, there were also more pressing factors – such as the greater awareness of social problems and the obvious failures of the Poor Law and philanthropy – driving the new Liberals to advocate social reform. One contemporary writer had suggested in 1908 that: 'in the course of the last two generations the State had been forced again and again to take over tasks for which private philanthropy had found its resources insufficient.'[50] Yet it was the Poor Law in combination with philanthropy that presented the major problem. The 1834 New Poor Law offered a solution to destitution, not to poverty, and there was now increasing evidence, from Rowntree and others, that between 25 and 30 per cent of the population of England and Wales were living in a state of poverty. This revelation came at a time when the Poor Law was in serious crisis, soon to become the subject of a Royal Commission investigation. Thus, concerned by the failures of philanthropy, threatened by the burgeoning Labour party and faced with an obvious concern about the health and well-being of the nation, David Lloyd George, Winston Churchill, and others took expedient action not to solve poverty, but to reduce its virulence. As Fraser suggests:

> electoral advantage, New Liberal ideology and national efficiency – combined with humanitarian concern, bureaucratic initiative, social investigation and popular demand to produce a comprehensive programme which, some Liberals today assert, represented the 'creation of the Welfare State'.[51]

As David Vincent has noted, the poor could not rely upon philanthropic help and had to develop their own strategies for survival. Effectively, this meant women depriving themselves of food and clothing for the benefit of husband and children, taking work into the home, depending upon neighbours, and the careful and constant management of the family income, with all that this implied about the use of credit and the pawnbroker.[52] The work of other authors, such as Carl Chinn and J. White, have endorsed Vincent's findings.[53] However, the survival strategies of the poor were not enough to protect them against the high unemployment that was conspicuous in the winter months of the Edwardian years. The state had to intervene to reduce the burdens of a Poor Law faced with enormous levels of destitution and imminent collapse.

Yet state intervention, no matter how justified, was likely to create tensions in a society that was still largely based upon local action and in which moves were being made towards extending democracy. Indeed, the poverty legislation of the Liberal governments led Hilaire Belloc to note that:

> The future of industrial society, and in particular of English society, left to its own direction, is a future in which subsistence and security shall be guaranteed for the Proletariat, but shall be guaranteed at the expense of the old political freedom and by the establishment of that Proletariat in a status really, though not nominally, servile.[54]

The 1904 Inter-Departmental Committee on Physical Deterioration had already telegraphed this concern when it stated that: 'in the last resort the State acting in conjunction with the Local Authority would have for its own sake to take charge of the lives of those who, for whatever cause, are incapable of independent existence up to the standard of decency which it imposes.'[55] There was certainly strong contemporary concern that state intervention would restrict individual democratic rights. Yet this seems to be something of a false dichotomy when one notes that only about 60 per cent of working-class men and no women had the parliamentary franchise. The traditional political freedoms did not extend very far and state intervention, though initially suspect to the working classes, was ultimately seen to confer important benefits. Nevertheless, these apparently contradictory views dominated attitudes in pre-war and Edwardian society. The possibility that fundamental social reform and income redistribution would actually create genuine freedoms within an expanding state was never seriously considered except by such socialists as Fred Jowett, the ILP/Labour party MP for Bradford West in 1906, who reflected in *The Socialist and the City* that:

> The future must grow out of the present; it cannot be created to fit with a plan.
>
> The Socialist, in the city life of today, is painfully trying, amidst many difficulties and much misunderstanding, unfortunately accompanied also by a considerable amount of misrepresentation, to change the municipal institutions at present in existence and add to their

number, so as to bring them into harmony with the social gospel which he preaches in accordance to his convictions.

He cherishes his ideals because they help him to decide which way true progress lies, but the necessity for carrying public opinion with him at every step confined his power within very narrow limits. Sometimes the Socialist municipal reformer is inclined to chafe at the limitations which the indifference of public opinion imposes upon his activity, since being himself, at his best, moved by strong convictions, he is naturally impatient of delay. But, being by conviction a demo-crat, his inclination to chafe soon gives way to the feeling that on the whole it is better so, because progress in advance of the public opinion of the day rests on very unsafe foundation ...[56]

As Philip Snowden emphasized in his famous lecture 'The Individual under Socialism', collective action could guarantee working-class fami-lies sufficient income to take advantage of the individual rights they were supposed to enjoy.[57] Indeed, both Jowett and Snowden, leading figures in the Independent Labour party, were committed to gradual change and each was prepared to 'work his passage' at a local level rather than to press on with some preconceived plan without public support.

The Liberal reforms were not really part of a preconceived plan, although they were conditioned by the need to improve the lot of the working classes, to tackle poverty and do something about the parlous state of the Poor Law, and to obtain political advantage in the perceived threat from the Labour party. The first welfare reforms of the December 1905 Liberal government – the provision of school meals in 1906 and the medical inspection of school children in 1907 – arose from campaigns that had been going on before the return of the Liberals and made only a marginal difference to poverty.

B. The Poor Law

The pivotal problem was the condition of the Poor Law. The 1834 Poor Law Amendment Act – and the New Poor Law that it bequeathed – was no longer relevant to the Edwardian age and the twentieth century. To discourage the poor by imposing a workhouse test was no longer feasible in a climate where the extension of democratic rights was on the political agenda and when the Guild of Help recognized its inability to get the community to rescue the poor, if not the destitute. The 1834 Poor Law seemed even less appropriate after 1894, when any ratepayer could vote to stand for election and when the socialists began to bid for seats on the boards of guardians in Poplar, Bradford and other areas. The new Liberal reformers were forced to accept that they had to intervene and organize a coherent attack upon poverty and inequality. The opportunity arose as a result of the deliberations and findings of the Royal Commission on the Poor Laws (1905–9), although for a variety of reasons, such as the timing of events and the divisions within the commission, Liberal governments chose to tackle poverty with measures that lay outside the Poor Law structure but which tended to reduce its burden.

The Royal Commission had been set up by a Conservative government which had seen high unemployment force more than two million people per year on to the Poor Law in the early twentieth century. The poor economic conditions of the winters of 1902–3 and 1903–4 led to the nationwide creation of Lord Mayors' funds and the use of public funds to bring about relief. In this situation the labour test seemed inappropriate, but government was reluctant to acknowledge that unemployment, and consequent poverty, was of an involuntary nature. However, faced with unemployment demonstrations, Walter Long, president of the Local Government Board, persuaded the government to introduce the Unemployed Workmen's Act of 1905. Under this Act, distress committees could be established in all metropolitan boroughs and in all urban districts with a population of more than 50,000. In other areas they could be set up at the discretion of the Local Government Board when distress was acute. Yet this did not mollify the Trades Union Congress and the demonstrations of the unemployed continued, especially since the Act only applied for three years, demonstrating the unwillingness of government to take permanent responsibility for the unemployed. It was in this context that in early August 1905 A. J. Balfour announced the formation of a Royal Commission on the Poor Laws and the Relief of Distress which would report on: 'Everything which appertains to the problem of the poor, whether poor by their own fault or by temporary lack of employment'. Apart from the obvious problem of unemployment, the commission was provoked into existence by the fact that Poor Law expenditure had risen from £8.1 million in 1881 to £8.6 million in 1906. The commission finally reported to the Liberal government in February 1909.

The Majority Report of the Royal Commission on the Poor Laws, signed by the chairman, Lord George Hamilton, and fourteen members but mainly influenced and largely written by Helen Bosanquet, effectively accepted that the Poor Law could remain an all-embracing social institution and sought to reverse the trend towards removing categories of social need from it. Yet, acknowledging that the Poor Law was held in bad odour, it decided that all social services would be united under Public Assistance Committees (PACs), composed of elected councillors and co-opted members drawn from philanthropic agencies. The PACs were to make effective use of voluntary charities and social casework agencies. The indelible mark of the COS was on this report, stamped there by C. S. Loch and Helen Bosanquet.[58]

The Majority Report was clearly critical of the existing arrangements for dealing with poverty and destitution, noting the immense local variation that had occurred. In common with the Minority Report, it was concerned about the overlapping duties of local authorities and boards of guardians. Yet it also sought the high ground in desiring the moral rescue of the poor. F. H. Bentham, chairman of the Bradford guardians, a member of the Bradford Guild of Help and a member of the Poor Law Commission, speaking before the publication of the Majority Report on 'The Guild of Help and Civil Status', felt that the £15 million [sic] spent on the Poor Law each year could be better spent and that no effort was made to restore people to a 'higher status of life'. Indeed, he argued that:

> If we are to prevent people from sinking to such a condition as to need legal relief we must look to other sources of help, and this brings us to consideration of the field of voluntary help – the work of the Guild of Help and similar organisations.
> … We find that people sink in to poverty through misfortune but also through a kind of moral decay. There is no other way of arresting this decay than by bringing a stronger character to the help of the weaker.[59]

Both the Majority and Minority Reports, produced in February 1909, were critical of the existing system and advocated the introduction of labour exchanges and the raising of the school-leaving age in order to reduce the size and increase the quality of the labour market. On other matters, they varied greatly. The Minority Report wanted to break up the Poor Law into specialist bodies (dealing with sickness, old age and the like) administered by a committee of the elected local authority, but recommended that unemployment, a vast problem beyond the means of local administration, should be dealt with by central government.

The Minority Report was written by Beatrice Webb (helped by Sidney Webb) with the support of George Lansbury, Francis Chandler and the Revd Russell Wakefield, Dean of Norwich. Unlike the Majority Report, it was dismissive of charitable activities. Beatrice Webb reflected, legitimately, that: 'It is no use letting the poor come and go as they think, to be helped or not as the charitable choose.'[60]

In the end, it proved impossible to change the Poor Law before the First World War. There was resistance from the civil servants of the Local Government Board and there were problems in adapting local finance to bring about rate equalization between different areas. In the end, the Poor Law was dismantled by removing responsibility for needy groups by a series of measures on old-age pensions, the creation of labour exchanges, the introduction of the National Insurance Act of 1911, and legislation on children.

C. Old-age pensions

The demand for old-age pensions had emerged in the late nineteenth century. A scheme based upon compulsory contributions from workmen had been developed by Canon William Blackley in 1878. Although this did not go very far, Charles Booth and Joseph Chamberlain gave their support to similar schemes in the 1880s and early 1890s – Booth suggesting a scheme financed out of taxation and Chamberlain suggesting a contributory arrangement. Unfortunately, the contributory basis of Chamberlain's scheme met with opposition from the friendly societies, whilst Booth's non-contributory scheme was ruled out because of the enormous cost it would impose upon the state.[61]

This impasse was not resolved by the various reports produced in the 1890s – the Royal Commission on the Aged Poor of 1893, the Treasury committee of 1896 or the Commons Select Committee which included Lloyd George and gave official recognition to the idea of a non-contributory pensions arrangement.[62] At this point Booth mounted a national campaign for pensions that was supported by the Fabians, the Labour Representation Committee, the TUC and the co-operative movement. Faced with this campaign, the friendly societies and the COS, who had implacably opposed a non-contributory state scheme, began to accept the need to provide pensions – although the COS felt that they should be contributory. In this light, the new Liberal administration began to consider the need to develop a non-contributory scheme and David Lloyd George finally introduced such a plan in 1908, to become effective on 1 January 1909. It offered 5s. (25p) per week at the age of 70 and introduced a sliding-scale arrangement for those with incomes from 8s. to 12s. (40–60p) per week, or £21–£31 10s. per annum, provided that they had not been imprisoned for any offence, including drunkenness, during the ten years preceding their claim. These pensions were to be paid through the Post Office rather than through the Poor Law. In other words, pensions were given as a right of citizenship and were not tainted with the moral stigma of the Poor Law.

As Pat Thane suggests: 'It was a pension for the very poor, the very respectable and the very old.'[63] In fact, this meant that a relatively small number of people qualified for the pension, whose level was too low to provide more than the absolute minimum for survival. At best the sliding-scale pension was a supplement for those who had some means of subsistence, and at worst it kept a small number of the aged from the Poor Law. Nevertheless, more people qualified for pensions than was originally estimated: in the first year the cost was about £8 million, compared with the £6.5 million expected by the government. In many towns about 2 per cent of the population seem to have qualified. In Halifax, for instance, there were 1,499 claimants in the first year, of whom 1,442 were accepted. Of these, 1,284 were allowed 5s., 59 4s., 70 3s., 15 2s. and 14 1s. On this basis it was estimated that the old-age pension would, in 1909, cost £17,966 in Halifax alone.[64] The Halifax Guild of Help estimated – somewhat exaggeratedly, as it proved – that the total national cost of old-age pensions would be £11,600,000 in the first year.[65] Nevertheless, even £8 million was a considerable sum and the Halifax Guild was able to declare: 'What a great blessing this Pension Act has been proved by many cases brought under the notice of our Helpers.'[66]

D. Children

Liberal legislation also attempted to tackle the problems of child poverty. The concern for national efficiency, provoked by the poor physical condition of recruits in the Boer War, was one of the key events in forcing the state to ensure that a new generation of school children were properly fed and maintained in a healthy condition. Public concern at the so-called 'national deterioration' was further aroused in 1903, when a Royal Commission on Physical Training in Scotland recommended that both education authorities and voluntary bodies should combine in order to provide school meals. The Report of the Inter-departmental Committee on Physical Deterioration the following year recommended that medical inspection and feeding should be undertaken by the state educational system. In fact, all that the Tory administration did was to suggest that the guardians should take up responsibility for school feeding – something that was done very badly in Bradford.[67] Yet it was not until the Liberals came to power that this matter was considered seriously. Towards the end of 1906 local authorities were empowered to provide free school meals for needy children up to the cost of a halfpenny, after efforts had been made to raise money from the community. This provision was extended in 1914, when the Exchequer agreed to meet half the costs of the measure through the Education (Provision of Meals) Act. The implication of these developments is that the state was accepting responsibility for feeding those school children whose parents were not able to provide for them. Nonetheless, parents who were not impoverished were expected to feed their children properly and recent research has suggested that this attitude was supported by Ramsay MacDonald and the Labour party.[68] Indeed, it has been suggested that the Labour party, under MacDonald's leadership, saw children as central to the evolution of social policy and had a clearly thought-out strategy which rejected state maintenance as an objective, for MacDonald had a 'continuing distrust of the state, at least under capitalism, and a belief in a morally active citizenry'.[69]

The Physical Deterioration Report of 1904 also suggested the need for school medical inspection and a measure to this effect was passed in 1907 as part of the Education (Administrative Provisions) Act, paving the way for school clinics and grants for medical treatment from 1912 onwards. Indeed, the Act enabled the Board of Education to establish a medical department under Dr (later Sir) George Newman. He attempted to create a free health service for children but was opposed by the British Medical Association, who feared local authority control and wanted treatment by independent doctors, so many authorities found themselves inspecting rather than treating children, although some set up clinics with trained doctors. Indeed, by 1914 214 out of 317 local authorities were providing some form of medical treatment for children.[70]

Pressures from the Guild of Help, the Agenda Club, local authorities and other interested organizations began to force the government to mount a serious assault upon the high rate of infant mortality in the Edwardian years. Infant mortality was still over 140 per 1,000 in England and Wales in 1900.[71] It averaged 166 per 1,000 in Bolton between 1896 and 1905, which was in fact one of the lowest levels in Lancashire, with Burnley averaging 220 per 1,000 (233 in 1903) and Preston 208.[72] This pressure worked, for infant mortality fell to about 110 per 1,000 by 1913, although it was 76 for the upper and middle classes and still 153 for the unskilled.[73]

As indicated in an earlier chapter, a national campaign on health was mounted by the Agenda Club, an organization covering all parts of the country which was formed in February 1911, because 'all is not well with England'.[74] Its members saw themselves as the English Samurai, invited a Japanese official to their first annual meeting, and proclaimed respect for 'these Samurai, careless of material gain'. The Agenda Club encouraged towns to hold an annual health week, the first being from 28 April to 4 May 1911. The idea was taken up by ten London boroughs and thirty provincial towns, including Bolton and Bradford. As a result of this and other initiatives, such as the Broadbent Scheme in Huddersfield, which encouraged parents to register their children with them and gave them a guinea if the child was still alive at the end of the year, the government was forced to take action. The Notification of Births Acts of 1907 and 1915 helped to ensure that a closer check was maintained upon infant mortality rates.

The most significant development, however, was the introduction of the Children's Act of 1908. This complex Act consolidated and codified twenty-one Acts and portions of seventeen others. It established separate juvenile courts, set up remand homes with Treasury grants, and prevented children under 16 from being placed in an adult prison. The Act also formalized the Poor Law responsibility for visiting and supervising, both in their own and other institutions, children who had been subject to cruelty proceedings. The Act imposed penalties for the neglect of children as well as cruelty towards them, and children were to be protected from immorality and immoral surroundings. It also dealt with 'infant life protection' and demanded that any person taking reward for the nursing and maintenance of a child under 7 years of age had to inform the local authority within forty-eight hours.[75]

Indeed, child care became the great focus of the Act and in 1909 the Local Government Board fulfilled its responsibilities by obliging each Poor Law union to set up a boarding-out committee. Two years later it was decided that a third of the members of these committees should consist of women, who were assumed to be more sensitive to the needs of children. The boarding-out committees were to appoint salaried female employees to visit those children who were boarded out and to visit women with children who were receiving outdoor relief. They also undertook the life protection visiting required by the Act. The Local Government Board then appointed a female inspector to supervise all these activities.

The number of boarded-out children had increased from 2,799 in 1885 to 11,596 in 1914, representing about 14 per cent of all children in care. There were 70,676 children in voluntary institutions in 1913, compared with 58,991 in 1906.[76] The responsibilities of the post of female inspector increased thereafter, for in 1913 the Poor Law Institutions Order prohibited children between the ages of 3 and 16 from remaining in a mixed workhouse for more than six weeks, although children under 3 were to remain with their mothers.

The Children's Act of 1908 unleashed a whole range of improvements in the position of children, designed to encourage parental responsibility and to focus the efforts of the state. This was the intention of the Liberal administration, but it was also a wider progressive view which obtained the Labour party's full support. Indeed, Thomas Summerbell, a Labour MP speaking in the debate during the passage of the 1908 Children's Act, stated that Parliament had to 'recognise the necessity of putting within reach of every parent the economic opportunity of looking after the welfare of his or her own children'.[77]

E. The National Insurance Act, 1911: health

The old-age pensions removed a small number of people from the Poor Law and the Children's Act removed one of the largest groups directly associated with it. David Lloyd George went further and attempted to reduce the large number of respectable people thrown on to it because of ill health.

The stimulus for action came from Lloyd George's legendary five-day trip to Germany to investigate the German national insurance system in August 1908. Starting with high ambitions, however, Lloyd George was forced to moderate his expensive plans of providing widows' and orphans' pensions and other benefits, and had to confine himself to offering more affordable insurance to the working man.

On 4 May 1911 Lloyd George, as Chancellor of the Exchequer, offered his scheme to the House of Commons, stating that: 'In this country ... 30 per cent of pauperism is attributable to sickness' and noting that a considerable number would have to be added for unemployment.[78] Stressing that death was an event for which the working classes attempted to make financial contingency, he pointed out that: 'Sickness comes in the next order of urgency in the working-class mind. Between 6,000,000 and 7,000,000 people in this country have made some provision against sickness, not at all adequate and a good deal of it defective.' However, he observed that a very high number of sickness insurance policies lapsed and he emphasized that, to obtain death, sickness *and* unemployment insurance, a working-class man would have to provide at least 1s. 6d.–2s. per week, which was clearly beyond his means. Lloyd George concluded, referring to both part I of the scheme (health insurance) and part II (unemployment insurance), that:

> I do not think there is any better method, or one more practicable at the present moment, than a system of national insurance which would invoke the aid of the State and the aid of the employer to enable the workman to get over all these difficulties and make provision for himself for sickness and, as far as most precarious trades are concerned, against unemployment ...

Lloyd George's health scheme did, however, work within strict constraints. The vested interests of friendly societies, trade unions and the 'House of Industrial Insurance interest' operated the scheme. The insurance companies had 80,000 agents and called upon most houses in the country each week, managing to manipulate opinion to protest at any risk to the insurance companies and the agents who had 'bought their books'.[79] However, the existing system did provide a cheap and established system of insurance and could be supplemented by the purchase of stamps through a post office for those workers who were not in a friendly society or a trade union. Now the general supervision of the scheme fell under the control of Robert Morant and the 'approved' societies were guaranteed that the state would not intervene with their traditional business.

For those workers who were insured, there was full medical treatment by a doctor whom they would select from a local list or 'panel'. They were eligible for free treatment in TB sanatoriums but were not entitled to free hospital treatment. The doctors would be paid on a per patient basis. The contributors had to pay 4d. per week (3d. for females), the employer 3d. per week and the state 2d., which would be paid into an accumulating fund to finance benefits. They were to be between the ages of 16 and 65 and had to earn less than £150 per year. When it came into operation on 15 January 1913, the scheme provided sickness benefits of 10s. (50p) per week for men and 7s. 6d. for women for the first thirteen weeks of sickness, although nothing was paid for the first three days. After the first thirteen weeks, 5s. per week was paid to men and women. There was a disability pension of 5s. per week and a maternity benefit of 30s. (£1. 50p) was paid to the wives of insured men.

Again, there is no doubt that National Health Insurance did alleviate the burden upon the Poor Law. It is true that the dependents of the contributors were not covered, and that there was a high level of claims from women – which provoked the formation of an inquiry which reported, in July 1914, that women were subject to a high rate of previously untreated illness – but the health scheme was a vast improvement on anything that had gone before. According to Pat Thane, the cumulative effect of the measures for the aged and the sick was to reduce the number of paupers from 916,377 in 1910 to 748,019 in 1914.[80] The Poor Law was finding its burden dramatically eased even in good economic conditions.

Also, as Frank Prochaska has stressed, the National Insurance Act brought about a shift in the role of voluntary hospitals which was to have important repercussions for their finances and propaganda.[81] As a consequence of the Act, large numbers of patients were insured. Increasingly, hospitals expected to be paid for treating them, which was not easy to square with charitable traditions. Insured patients, on the other hand, saw themselves as 'receiving medical care more as a right and less as charity'.[82] Having brought voluntaryists together to defend their position, the Act forced them into a fresh examination of their role. Advances in Poor Law medical provision and the rising pace of social legislation made it clear that they could not operate in isolation, for they needed to be aware of the political thinking of government and the opposition of political parties. Prochaska feels that the King's Fund adapted well to the changing climate of public and government opinion.

Nevertheless, the King's Fund clung tenaciously to the idea of independence from the state. The growing uncertainty in the voluntary hospital movement after the passage of the National Insurance Act increased demands for government money, though not government control. For its part, as Prochaska suggests, the fund rejected the idea of financial assistance from the state, thinking that it would be a dangerous precedent.[83] Outright state control, though it had advocates on the medical and political fringes, was certainly not a serious political possibility at the time. The Royal Commission on the Poor Laws had not been uncritical of the voluntary hospitals, but neither its Minority nor its Majority Reports had suggested that they should be nationalized. It had had little to say about the precise nature of the relationship between voluntary and public hospitals and even the Minority Report, whilst calling for a unification of the public health and Poor Law services, insisted that this need not interfere with voluntary or private medical practice.

F. National Insurance Act, 1911: unemployment

Health insurance certainly helped to reduce the burden upon the Poor Law but there remained the problem of unemployment. The Conservative government's Unemployed Workmen's Act of 1905 had done little to relieve the situation and Ramsay MacDonald, Ernest Bevin and the emergent Labour party were campaigning in favour of the 'right to work' in 1908. It was at this point that the young William Beveridge emerged to provide a clear policy for tackling the problem of the unemployed.

Beveridge was a university student who had spent the years 1903–7 as a sub-warden of the Toynbee Hall East End settlement, where university graduates worked amongst the poor in their spare time. He felt that, whilst the settlement movement exerted little impact upon unemployment and poverty, it did provide opportunities for research. His work at Toynbee Hall put him into contact with the Webbs, George Lansbury and many others who were equally concerned about unemployment. His voluminous correspondence bears witness to the value of his research and contacts.

In 1906 and 1907 Beveridge was a member of the Colonies Committee, a voluntary body concerned about unemployment, along with George Lansbury, a prominent Labour leader. Whilst on good personal terms with Lansbury, Beveridge found that there was a fundamental disagreement between them. Lansbury felt that Beveridge's ideas on labour exchanges simply emptied the reservoir of unemployed on a temporary basis, and he wrote that:

I cannot see how your system is going to prevent the creation of the unemployed. You seem to imagine that the unemployed are where they are for reasons other than the real ones. The unemployed are unemployed simply because there is not enough employment to go round. ...

In conclusion remember that my difference with you is this: you think that once you have got the problem stated and set out in an understanding manner there will be left a multitude of people who emigration or colonies must deal with and that so far, the problem has been settled. On the other hand, I contend that while production is carried on for profit, there must be and will be a margin of unemployed labour on which the employer can draw whenever he pleases, and which will enable him to determine wages ...

As I have already said, there is no way out of this except in State organisation of industry ...[84]

Beveridge was also closely involved with Beatrice Webb, who attempted to draw upon his expertise to counter the COS's negative attitude towards the able-bodied unemployed when reporting to the Royal Commission on the Poor Law.[85] He was also concerned in the efforts to finance the Outer London inquiry into poverty mounted by Canon Barnett, a founder of Toynbee Hall, and Frances W. Buxton. The aim was to raise £600–700 in order to examine the 'Life and Labour in Extra-Metropolitan areas, particularly West Ham which had a population of 300,000, the great majority of them being poor'. Effectively, this was to be a survey of the poor and casual labour.[86]

Drawn into the study of poverty and unemployment at many levels, Beveridge quickly became the expert on unemployment. His ideas greatly influenced the Majority and Minority Reports of the Royal Commission on the Poor Laws, both of which accepted that there were differences between the temporary unemployment of skilled workers in periods of depression and the permanent underemployment of the unskilled or semi-skilled in an overstocked labour market. Both reports proposed the establishment of national labour exchanges at which all unemployed workmen would be registered and where all vacancies would be notified; the Minority Report suggested programmes of public works and the Majority Report accepting such measures as necessary only in times of depression. Industrial retraining in the colonies was recommended by the Minority Report for those who refused to work but was less enthusiastically accepted by the Majority Report. It advocated unemployment insurance, whilst the Minority Report sought non-contributory benefits.

Obviously, Beveridge influenced the Poor Law Commission but Winston Churchill, who was to become president of the Board of Trade in 1908, was already contemplating a package of changes, including labour exchanges, the decasualization of the docks, training for juvenile workers and other related activities. Beveridge's mark was plainly visible here, for Churchill recruited him to the Board of Trade in July 1908 with the responsibility for bringing these proposals into being. The Commons approved the formation of labour exchanges and by June 1909 they had become a reality. There were 423 such exchanges by February 1914, with appointed management boards containing worker representatives. Their managers were drawn from a variety of backgrounds, and voluntary bodies such as the Guild of Help provided their fair share of recruits. Indeed, Harry Smith of the Bradford ILP, the Bradford Cinderella Club and the Bradford City Guild of Help became the first manager of the Halifax Labour Exchange.

It is debatable how successful they were. By 1914 they were registering over two million workers per year and finding 3,000 jobs per day. Nevertheless, three-quarters of the registered never got their jobs through the exchanges and the trade unions were always suspicious that the labour exchanges could be used for strike-breaking. It is certainly questionable whether or not they achieved the 'organised fluidity of labour' claimed by Beveridge in his book *Unemployment: A Problem of Industry* (1909).

In 1909 Churchill introduced the Trades Boards Act, establishing boards of employers and employees to fix minimum wages in the unionized 'sweated trades'. Again, the effectiveness of this legislation is debatable. Less so was the introduction of unemployment insurance which became part II of the 1911 National Insurance Act. Once again, the idea came from Beveridge, who felt that unemployment insurance could be provided for most workers, if not for the chronically unemployed. Aided by H. Llewellyn Smith, Beveridge developed the idea that certain trades should be covered by a compulsory system of contributory insurance. Churchill presented their ideas to the House of Commons on 19 May 1909 in the speech in which he outlined his plans for labour exchanges in the following manner.

So I come to unemployment insurance. It is not practicable at the present time to establish a universal system of unemployment insurance ... We have to choose at the very outset of this subject between insuring some workmen in all trades and insuring all workmen in some trades. That is the first parting of the ways upon unemployment insurance. In the first case we have a voluntary system and in the second a compulsory system. If you adopt a voluntary system of unemployment insurance, you are always exposed to difficulty. The risk of unemployment varies so much between man and man, according to their qualities ... and the risk varies so much between man and man that a voluntary system of unemployment insurance which the State subsidises always attracts those workers who are most likely to be unemployed. That is why all voluntary systems have broken down when they have been tried, because they accumulate a preponderance of bad risks against the insurance office, which is fatal to financial stability. On the other hand a compulsory system of insurance, which did not add a contribution from outside, has always broken down, because of the refusal of the higher class of workers to assume unsupported a share of the burden of the weaker members of the community. We have decided to avoid these main difficulties. Our insurance scheme will present four main features. It will involve contributions from the workpeople and from the employers; those contributions will be aided by a substantial sub-vention from the State; it will be insurance by trade, following the suggestions of the Royal Commission; and it will be compulsory within the trades upon all unionists and non-unionists, skilled and unskilled, workmen and employers alike.[87]

The Act followed Churchill's outline faithfully, even though he had moved to the Home Office before it was introduced. Each insured workman contributed 2½d. (1p) per week, as did each employer, and the state provided approximately 1¾d. (0.6p). The scheme was compulsory for certain industries (such as building, mechanical engineering and iron-founding), and benefits were to be 7s. (35p) per week for up to fifteen weeks, with the possibility of subsidies to trade unions who ran their own schemes. In the final analysis, about 2.25 million men were to be protected against unemployment and the whole scheme came on to the statute book without much parliamentary rancour. The first contributions were paid on 1 July 1912, and the first benefits from 1 January 1913.

Nevertheless, there was some opposition in the country, with some trade unionists still feeling that it was part of the attempt to regiment labour and to break strikes. In the end, like George Lansbury, many workmen felt that the scheme was not a solution to unemployment but just a shifting around of the problem. The insurance scheme only dealt with a small part of the unemployment problem but it did make an attempt to reduce its impact. Nonetheless, Pat Thane rightly points out that it increased the burden on the poor rather than the rich. She estimates that a poor family on 18s. (90p) per week would be paying 10.2 per cent of its income in indirect taxes (7.1 per cent), national health (2 per cent) and unemployment contributions (1.1 per cent), whereas a family on a wage of 35s. per week was paying only 5.27 per cent in taxes and contributions (3.65 per cent in indirect taxes). Part of the cost of the new state legislation came from the pockets of the poor but, nevertheless, the state had committed some considerable sums of money to its new social reform ventures.

G. The 'People's Budget', 1909

Although some measures, such as the National Insurance Acts, involved a contributory arrangement, the state contribution to insurance, old-age pensions and other measures, as well as rising naval expenditure, did involve a considerable increase in state expenditure. As the new

Chancellor of the Exchequer, Lloyd George faced a £16 million deficit, which he sought to recover by his controversial budget of 1909. This was resisted by the House of Lords and not passed until April 1910, amidst a constitutional crisis. Once passed, this budget raised the basic rate of income tax on earned income to 1s. 6d. in the pound (7.5p) and imposed a super tax on incomes above £3,000 per annum. Death duties were also increased on estates of over £5,000 and taxes were levied on land. It was these land taxes that provoked the wrath of the Lords, for they raised 20 per cent of the unearned increment on land values, levied on the sale of land. In order to help families on lower incomes, Lloyd George also introduced a £10 tax allowance for each child under 16 for taxpayers earning £500 per annum or less. This established firmly the principle of progressive taxation. He also set up a development fund to increase job opportunities by financing such measures as afforestation and the provision of smallholdings in the countryside. This was part of Lloyd George's commitment to diminishing rural poverty and offering some wider ownership of land in the countryside, building on his Small-holdings and Allotments Act of 1908.

The 'People's Budget' was clearly designed to make some small move towards redistributing the wealth of the country through taxation and was indicative of the Liberal commitment to reducing the poverty of the masses by a relatively modest taxing of the rich. Indeed, at the end of the budget speech, Lloyd George stated that:

> This is a War Budget. It is for raising money to wage implacable warfare against poverty and squalidness. I cannot help hoping and believing that before this generation has passed away we shall have advanced a great step towards the good time when poverty and wretchedness and human degradation which always follow in its camp will be as remote to the people of this country as the wolves which once infested its forests.[88]

It provoked the opposition of the House of Lords, and led to two general elections in 1910 (one connected with the budget and the other with the power of the House of Lords). But eventually, faced with the Liberal government's threat to create new peers, the Lords agreed in 1911 that their absolute veto on legislation should be reduced to a blocking power for two years and that money Bills would be passed automatically.

Conclusion

The years between 1900 and 1914 saw not only the immense extension of the role of the state in social reform but also a process whereby old and new values were sifted to produce a new balance between the state and philanthropic bodies in the determination of social policy in Britain. It was accepted that voluntary and philanthropic efforts were insufficient to deal with the immense scale of poverty, despite the attempts of the Guild of Help to create a community response to replace the almost uncaring approach of the Charity Organisation Society. Yet, faced with high levels of poverty and unemployment and a Poor Law that was obviously wilting under the strain of the economic depression of the Edwardian years, the pre-war Liberal governments decided to introduce a set of measures to reduce the burden upon the Poor Law rather than to reform it. Although the pressure of the Labour challenge may have been one incentive for these reforms, it is also clear that something had to be done about the situation of the poor. Unable, due to a variety of political, social and economic restraints, to implement either the Majority or the Minority Reports of the Poor Law Royal Commission, the Liberal governments opted for a compromise that was to prove of temporary duration. Driven by a commitment to new Liberal ideas, the concern for national efficiency, and the hope of political advantage, the Liberal governments of the immediate pre-war years produced something which, in that hackneyed phrase, became recognized as the 'foundations of the welfare state'. The new approach was further legitimized by the experience of war.

Notes

1. D. Fraser, *The Evolution of the British Welfare State* (1973), p. 163.
2. M. J. Moore, 'Social Work and Social Welfare: The Organisation of Philanthropic Resources in Britain, 1900–1914', *Journal of British Studies* (Spring, 1977), p. 96.
3. J. Harris, 'Political Thought and the Welfare State 1870–1914: An Intellectual Framework for British Social Policy', *Past and Present* 135 (May 1992).
4. C. F. G. Masterman, 'The Social Abyss', *Contemporary Review* 81 (January 1902), p. 24, quoted in D. Vincent, *Poor Citizens: The State and the Poor in Twentieth-Century Britain* (1992), p. 1; J. H. Veit-Wilson, 'Paradigms of Poverty: Rehabilitation of B. S. Rowntree', *Journal of Social Policy* 15/1 (1986), pp. 71–4.
5. J. Melling, 'Welfare Capitalism and the Origins of Welfare States: British Industry, Workplace Welfare and Social Reform, c. 1870–1914', *Social History* 17/3 (1992), pp. 453–78.
6. H. Pelling, 'The Working Class and the Welfare State', in H. Pelling, *Popular Politics and Society in Late Victorian Britain* (1968); P. Thane, 'The Working Class and State "Welfare" in Britain, 1880–1914', *Historical Journal* 27/4 (1984), pp. 877–900.
7. Thane, 'The Working Class and "State Welfare"'.
8. Vincent, *Poor Citizens*, p. 44.

9.   J. Harris, 'Society and State in Twentieth-Century Britain', in F. M. L. Thompson (ed.), *The Cambridge Social History of Britain 1750–1950*, iii. *Social Agencies and Institutions* (Cambridge, 1990), p. 70.

10. B. Kirkman Gray, *Philanthropy and the State, or Social Politics* (1908), pp. ix–x.

11. F. K. Prochaska, 'Philanthropy', in Thompson (ed.), *Social Agencies and Institutions*, p. 357. In the rest of the article Prochaska emphasizes the social goodness that comes through philanthropy as well as the social groupings of family, neighbourhood, the poor and institutions. He challenges the murky reductionist notions of social control.

12. F. K. Prochaska, *Philanthropy and the Hospitals of London: The King's Fund, 1897–1990* (Oxford, 1992), p. 2.

13. *Ibid.*, p. 47.

14. *Ibid.*, p. 289.

15. E. W. Wakefield, 'The Growth of Charity Organisation in the North of England', *Charity Organisation Review* 34 (1908), p. 40.

16. Moore, 'Social Work and Social Welfare', p. 96.

17. M. B. Simey, *Charitable Effort in Liverpool* (Liverpool, 1951), pp. 124–36.

18. Reported in the minutes of the Borough of Poole League of Help, 13 April 1908.

19. *Help* (journal of Bradford City Guild of Help) 4/2 (November 1908).

20. Poole League of Help, minutes, 18 November 1907.

21. *Help* 1/12 (September 1906).

22. County Borough of Bolton Guild of Help, *Third Annual Report* (November 1907), pp. 5–10.

23. *Helper* (journal of the County Borough of Bolton Guild of Help) 7/3 (March 1913), report of a paper by C. S. Loch at a conference of COS societies, 24 January 1913.

24. E. Macadam, *The New Philanthropy* (1934), p. 18.

25. *Help* 1/4 (January 1906).

26. Halifax Citizen's Guild of Help, *Fifth Annual Report 1909–10*, p. 4.

27. Bradford City Guild of Help casebooks, 1603, 1620, 1908, 2205, 2359, 2523, 2561 and 3378. See also K. Laybourn, 'The Guild of Help and the Changing Face of Edwardian Philanthropy', *Urban History* 20/1 (April 1993), pp. 43–60, and K. Laybourn, *The Guild of Help and the Changing Face of Edwardian Philanthropy: The Guild of Help, Voluntary Work and the State, 1904–1919* (Lampeter, 1994).

28. G. R. Snowden, *Report to the President of the Local Government Board on Guilds of Help in England* (Cd. 56664; 1911), p. 19.

29. *Ibid.*, p. 7.

30. Laybourn, 'The Guild of Help', pp. 42–3.

31. Snowden, *Guilds*, p. 11; *Help* 2 (September 1910).

32. Poole League of Help, minutes, 20 January 1908.

33. Snowden, *Guilds*, p. 5.

34. M. Brasnett, *Voluntary Social Action: A History of the National Council of Social Services 1919–1969* (1969), p. 6.

35. Moore, 'Social Work', pp. 91–2.

36. *Croydon Guild of Help Magazine* 20 (July 1912), p. 98.

37.   *The Citizen* (organ of the Reading Guild of Help) 1/2 (July 1912).
38.   Laybourn, 'The Guild of Help'; Laybourn, *The Guild of Help*, chapter 3.
39.   *Forward*, 10 March 1906, the letter of E. R. Hartley.
40.   *Help* 1/2 (November 1905), quoting from the first annual report of the Bradford City Guild of Help, 11 October 1905.
41.   *County Borough of Bolton Guild of Help Magazine* 5/8 (June 1911), pp. 182–4, from a report of the annual conference of the Guild of Help, Birmingham, 1911.
42.   Snowden, *Guilds*, p. 2.
43.   Brasnett, *Voluntary Social Action*.
44.   K. Laybourn and J. Reynolds, *Liberalism and the Rise of Labour* (1984), chapter 1; P. F. Clarke, *Lancashire and the New Liberalism* (Cambridge, 1971); D. Powell, 'The New Liberalism and the Rise of Labour, 1886–1906', *Historical Journal* 19/2 (1986).
45.   Powell, 'The New Liberalism', pp. 376, 379, 382.
46.   *Manchester Guardian*, 7 November 1914.
47.   K. Morgan, 'The New Liberalism and the Challenge of Labour: The Welsh Experience', in K. D. Brown (ed.), *Essays in Anti-Labour History* (1974); A. W. Purdue, 'The Liberal and Labour Parties in North-East Politics, 1900–1914: The Struggle for Supremacy', *International Review of Social History* 26/1 (1981), pp. 1–24; P. Thompson, *Socialists, Liberals and Labour: The Struggle for London 1885–1914* (1967), p. 170.
48.   Thane, 'The Working Class and State "Welfare"'.
49.   G. R. Searle, 'The Edwardian Liberal Party and Business', *English Historical Review* 98 (1983).
50.   Gray, *Philanthropy and the State*, p. 2.
51.   Fraser, *Evolution* (2nd edn., 1984), p. 174.
52.   Vincent, *Poor Citizens*, pp. 5–22.
53.   C. Chinn, *They Worked All Their Lives: Women of the Urban Poor in England 1880–1939* (Manchester and New York, 1988); J. White, 'Campbell Bunk: A Lumpen Community in London between the Wars', *History Workshop* 8 (Autumn 1979); J. White, *The Worst Street in North London* (1986).
54.   H. Belloc, *The Servile State* (1912), p. 183.
55.   *Report of the Inter-Departmental Committee on Physical Deterioration*, Parliamentary Papers 1904, xxxii, p. 17.
56.   F. W. Jowett, *The Socialist and the City* (1907), pp. 2–3.
57.   P. Snowden, *Individual Under Socialism* (Keighley ILP Pamphlet, 1903).
58.   A. M. McBriar, *An Edwardian Mixed Doubles: The Bosanquets versus the Webbs* (Oxford, 1987).
59.   *Help* 3/9 (June 1908).
60.   M. E. Rose, *The Relief of Poverty* (1972), p. 46.
61.   P. Thane, 'Contributory *versus* Non-Contributory Old Age Pensions', in P. Thane (ed.), *The Origins of British Social Policy* (1978).
62.   Fraser, *Evolution* (1st edn., 1973), pp. 140–1.
63.   P. Thane, *The Foundations of the Welfare State* (1982), p. 83.
64.   *Help* (Journal of the Halifax Citizen's Guild of Help) 1/1 (January 1909), pp. 4–5.
65.   *Ibid.*, 1/8 (October 1909), pp. 8–11.

66. *Ibid.*, 1/2 (February 1909).
67. K. Laybourn, 'The Issue of School Feeding in Bradford, 1904–7', *Journal of Educational Administration and History* 14 (2 July 1982), p. 32.
68. J. Stewart, 'Ramsay MacDonald, the Labour Party, and Child Welfare, 1900–1914', *20th Century British History* 4/3 (1993), pp. 105–25.
69. *Ibid.*, p. 108.
70. Thane, *Welfare State*, (1982) p. 78.
71. A. S. Wohl, *Endangered Lives: Public Health in Victorian Britain* (1983); R. Woods, 'Mortality Patterns in the Nineteenth Century', in R. Woods and J. Woodward (eds.), *Urban Mortality in Nineteenth-Century England* (1984), pp. 37–64.
72. *County Borough of Bolton Guild of Help Magazine* 2/7 (April 1908), p. 88.
73. *74th Annual Report of the Registrar General* (1913), table 288.
74. Plymouth Civic Guild of Help, *Seventh Annual Report* (1913–14), p. 5.
75. *Help* 1/2 (February 1909), pp. 6–8.
76. Thane, *Welfare State*, p. 79.
77. *Hansard*, Fourth Series, clxxxvii, col. 580.
78. *Ibid.*, 4 May 1911.
79. Sir Henry N. Bunbury (ed.), *Lloyd George's Ambulance Wagon: The Memoirs of William J. Braithwaite, 1911–1912* (1957).
80. Thane, *Welfare State*, p. 91.
81. Prochaska, *King's Fund*, p. 76.
82. *Ibid.*, p. 129.
83. *Ibid.*, p. 130.
84. Papers of William Henry Beveridge, deposited in the British Library of Political and Economic Science in 1959, Private and Personal papers, Ib 6, letter from George Lansbury to Beveridge, 1 February 1907.
85. *Ibid.*, Ib 6, letter from Beatrice Webb to Beveridge, 4 May 1907.
86. *Ibid.*, Ib 6, circular on the Outer London inquiry, January 1907.
87. *Hansard*, 19 May 1909.
88. *Ibid.*, 29 April 1909, quoted in Fraser, *Evolution* (1st edn., 1973), pp. 145–6.

CHAPTER NINE

THE FIRST WORLD WAR
AND THE INTER-WAR YEARS
1914–1939

The decade prior to the First World War had seen a dramatic extension of the role of the state, even if philanthropy had continued to play a rather more important part in social policy than has often been assumed. Yet the First World War necessitated an even more dramatic intervention, for this was the first war to involve mass warfare and to demand the enlargement of the functions of the state to meet the requirements of national defence. With millions under arms and the whiff of social reconstruction in the air, there was great optimism that the post-war years would see a more enlightened age, when social security would meet the needs of a modern democratic society. The problem was that, whilst the First World War and the extension of the franchise in 1918, which increased the electorate from seven million to twenty-one million, made social reform an essential part of the programme of every political party, it is clear that the high levels of unemployment meant that poverty and ill health were a long way from being tackled in an effective manner. The First World War extended the administrative structure and responsibilities for social relief, but the high levels of unemployment, poverty and ill health of the inter-war years caused serious problems for the social policy of all governments.

In the final analysis, the years between 1914 and 1939 saw the end of the policies on destitution that had dominated Victorian thinking and the development of selective policies to deal with the problems of specific social groups. However, faced with a high level of unemployment, successive inter-war governments created a confused and complex pattern of social security which barely alleviated the condition of a large proportion of the unemployed and the poor. The inter-war years confirmed that British society was not ready for the redistribution of income and wealth. It was not until the Second World War that the mood changed and universalism became the dominant theme. The years between 1914 and 1939 can thus be seen as some type of transition period between the destitution policies of the Victorians and the universalism of Beveridge and post-war Labour governments.

The First World War

The First World War affected the balance of the new relationship that was being struck between the voluntary sector and the state in pre-war years. It ensured that the state became dominant and the voluntary sector subsidiary.

Voluntary societies found themselves drawn together, both to each other and public organizations, in tackling the immense problems of poverty and social disruption that resulted from immediate wartime dislocation. Many of them, particularly the local organization of the Guild of Help, abandoned their social casework and co-ordinating activities and moved to act as part of a vast relief effort. Within four years they had become an important adjunct, though not a partner, to the state. Indeed, the wartime experience forged many of the voluntary societies, including the Guild of Help and the Charity Organisation Society, into the National Council of Social Service in 1919, the fore-runner of the present National Council of Voluntary Organisations.

The immediate and widespread dislocation of military men and the plight of their dependents led to the Prince of Wales's appeal to volun-tary societies on 6 April 1914, as a result of which the National Relief Fund was formed. New volunteers joined existing societies and helped to form over 300 local representative committees (usually known as LRCs, although they often went under the slightly varied titles of 'Mayor's Committee', the 'Lord Mayor's Relief Committee' or the 'City Representative Committee') in urban, borough, and country districts to administer its monies and to co-ordinate relief. Responsible for the relief of civilian and military distress, the LRCs brought together vol-untary and public agencies in a programme of investigation and relief. Their efforts were encouraged by the government Committee for the Prevention and Relief of Distress. Out of this, voluntary societies were now forced to co-operate more effectively than ever before. As M. J. Moore wrote: 'The pressures of war had forced the co-ordination that had previously eluded voluntaryists, and they recognised a valuable chance to build an effective national organisation.'[1]

The Guild of Help strengthened its national association by employ-ing a full-time paid secretary and creating regional organizations. Two almost unknown societies moved to the forefront of relief. They were the Soldiers' and Sailors' Families Association (SSFA) and the Soldiers and Sailors' Help Society (SSHS), the former being the more important of the two and subject to rapid growth in most towns. Their brief was to ensure that the families of soldiers and sailors were not left destitute and to check upon those who qualified for war pensions. In Liverpool the SSFA rose from a body of thirteen members with no subscription lists to a body with 29 district heads, some 700 voluntary workers, and an expenditure of £1,000 per week within the first four weeks of the war.[2] Many of those already connected with the guilds and other relief agencies offered their services free and in the first year of war 20,000 or more new workers entered the field of personal casework.[3]

About a quarter of the LRCs and many of the SSFAs and SSHSs were run by the 83 local Guilds of Help that existed in wartime. In London the LRC was regarded as a sub-committee of the borough council. Elsewhere this was not always the case and the LRC was often seen as simply a co-ordinating committee for both public and private relief. One contemporary survey of 55 guilds indicated that 25 of them were doing virtually the whole work of the LRC, and in at least four cases the local guild had been asked to undertake the work by the local mayor.[4] In 27 other cases there were reported to be close relations between the guilds and the local branch of the SSFA and in 16 of these cases the guild was doing practically all the work. Indeed, Frederick D'Aeth wrote of the first thirteen months of war:

> There is one solitary record of the Guild being totally ignored. It is a striking testimony to the place of the Guild in the towns that in spite of personal intrigue and party and other influences so frequently present in situations such as those negotiated in August, 1914, this young body should have achieved such recognition.[5]

The effect of this was that many guilds simply suspended their pre-war activities and practically ceased to exist as they assumed responsibility for other relief organizations. The honorary secretary of the Poole Guild, which had fewer than a hundred members, suspended its normal activities from 10 August 1914 for the duration of the war: 'He felt that it would be quite impossible and impracticable for the Guild of Help to do its normal work simultaneously with that of the Mayoral Committee, which would work under a different system with different though over-lapping purpose ...'[6] He added that: 'We have to act now as if the Guild, in its charitable capacity, had never existed.' In effect, the guild no longer existed as a separate body but had given its organization to the Mayor's War Distress Relief Committee, 'acting in conjunction with the Prince of Wales' Fund and the Soldiers' and Sailors' Family Association and several other organisations'.[7] By the end of the war the Poole Guild had become the Poole Guild of Help and Council of Social Welfare *en route* to the wider organization of philanthropy.

Other guilds, such as Middlesbrough – whose helpers 'had served in the trenches of the town hall' – Croydon, Reading, Wimbledon and Bolton, all retained a semblance of independence.[8] Yet they all became involved in the voluntary activities already suggested and also assumed other responsibilities.

All the voluntary societies were actively involved in the massive scale of relief activities. They distributed relief from government and local bodies on a unprecedented scale. The Guild of Help illustrates this point. The Bolton Guild distributed relief to more than 8,000 families, representing about 32,000 people, during the first year of the war. Their relief was distributed by 1,200 volunteers.[9] The government added to the responsibilities of these voluntary bodies by passing the War Pensions Act in July 1916, which effectively transferred many of the responsibilities for pensions and payments that had been assumed by the SSFA and the SSHS to the Local Statutory Committee for War Pensions, which was composed of representatives of voluntary and public bodies. For the Bolton Guild, this now meant that, apart from working for the Prince of Wales Fund, the SSFA and other bodies, it now became a 'handmaiden of the War Pensions Committee' and dealt with 1,400 cases on its behalf in the first year following the Act.[10]

A summary of the activities of voluntary or philanthropic organizations suggests that they became an adjunct, or 'handmaiden', of the state during the First World War. Voluntary organizations abandoned their opposition to mass relief work, submerged themselves in local community activities and took on many state responsibilities, including the assessment and distribution of war pensions. The main advantage of this wartime experience is that it broadened the horizons of local guilds, encouraged co-operation with other bodies, strengthened the regional and national movements and prepared the way for the creation of wider organizations of local help to which most voluntary bodies eventually gravitated in 1919 and the early 1920s. War provided a challenge to voluntary organizations which forced them to unite and transform. Yet it was the state which transformed its function most and became the dominant force in social policy.

In 1914 Parliament passed the Defence of the Realm Act (DORA), which greatly extended the powers of the government. It allowed government to control the railways, the coal industry and many other sectors of the economy and to make munitions work a priority above private orders. Because of the huge profits that could be made, the government also imposed controls on food prices, coal prices and rents.

War imposed an immense financial burden upon the state. Public expenditure rose rapidly and the national debt rose from £650 million to about £7,500 million between 1914 and 1918. But, even more important, it imposed a demand upon manpower. After the early attempt to supply the army with volunteers and to get men to attest under the Derby scheme, the government imposed military conscription in January 1916 and began to make good the shortfall of labour through the employment of more women – 'dilutees' as they were referred to – in munitions factories and engineering works. This prompted the Labour party and the wider Labour movement to demand the 'Conscription of Riches' – since life was being conscripted, so must wealth and income.[11]

The Lloyd George coalition government, formed in December 1916, was certainly alarmed at the way in which the trade unions were increasing their power and the Labour party was dominating the domestic debates. As a result, it set up a Ministry of Reconstruction in 1917 under Dr Christopher Addison. David Lloyd George once informed the Labour party that the world was in a state of flux and that it would have to mould the new society. He attempted to subvert that possibility by developing his own policies.[12] The Ministry of Reconstruction and its various committees began to develop ideas and legislative proposals. Most obviously, it began to look at proposals for health, housing, education and unemployment.

The proposals for education have been dealt with in an earlier chapter; essentially, they consisted of raising the school-leaving age to 14, ending the half-time system and providing continuous education. The 1918 Education Act achieved some of these reforms but the financial cuts of the 1920s put an end to dramatic legislative reform, even if there was plenty of discussion about future educational developments.

Health reform was quite another matter. The state had already committed itself to the promotion of health insurance before the First World War. However, the war exposed the continued health deficiencies of the nation. Only one in three conscripts was fit enough for the army and the responsibilities for overseeing health were clearly too diffuse. Dr Christopher Addison advocated the establishment of a Ministry of Health and was supported in his view by Lord Rhondda, head of the Local Government Board, who informed the Cabinet that the public were demanding a vast improvement in health conditions and that one centralized ministry, formed as a 'war emergency measure', could be directed towards improving maternity, infant welfare and other services.[13]

Unfortunately, the Ministry of Health was not formed until after the end of the war, largely due to the fact that the vested interests of the 'industrial insurance companies and friendly societies, wished a new Ministry of Health to be restricted to the Poor Law, and related activities, and not to have their responsibilities for insurance interfered with in any way'. When it was formed in 1919, the Ministry of Health brought together the old Local Government Board and the Insurance Commission and thus retained the Poor Law under its control. However, it was soon to become involved in making up the shortage of housing brought about by the wartime conditions. The full employment achieved by wartime demands also encouraged the view that unemployment insurance should be extended.

Thus the Ministry of Reconstruction paved the way for future social policies, cultivating the so-called 'wartime socialism'. David Lloyd

George's election pledge of 'Homes Fit for Heroes' had a genuine ring to it in 1918, but the post-war years and the economic dislocation that occurred for the staple industries – and thus for governments – ensured that social policy was an area characterized by expediency rather than by continuity and clear structure.

Unemployment in the inter-war years, 1918–1939

In the years following the end of the war the economic recovery of the post-war boom sustained an optimism for the future of social provision. As a result, Lloyd George's coalition decided in 1919 that the 1911 unemployment insurance scheme should be extended to all workers – except for a few groups, including agricultural labourers – with earnings up to £250 per annum. There were thus about twelve million people eligible for unemployment insurance. It was at this moment that the bubble burst and unemployment rose sharply to the 'intractable million' that provided the base of much heavier unemployment from time to time during the inter-war years. Many were unemployed even before they had provided sufficient contributions to be entitled to benefit. In fact, it was at this time that the government began to provide extended or uncovenanted benefit, better known as the 'dole'. It was a form of outdoor relief without the Poor Law.

Frightened by the prospect of revolution, possibly led by the returned soldiers and the National Unemployed Workers' (Committee) movement, the Lloyd George coalition government brought in a system of dole which cut across the insurance principle but relieved the Poor Law from having to deal with mass unemployment. The problem was that the sheer cost of saving the Poor Law and providing benefits for the unemployed was beyond the means of the nation. Nevertheless, some means of subsistence had to be found and various governments became involved in providing expenditure for the unemployed and in attempting to bail out the unemployment fund from which insurance benefits were paid. But the government was faced with both cyclical and structural unemployment. Whilst the first could be dealt with by unemployment insurance, based upon the principle that those unemployed could find work, the long-term structural unemployment created by the decline of the old staple industries could not be dealt with in this way. Additional expenses had been laid upon this system of unemployment relief by the 1921 Unemployed Workers' Dependents (Temporary Provisions) Act which provided additional benefits of 5s. (25p) for a wife and 1s. (5p) for each child.

It was this system, with its changes in the level of benefits and nomenclature – the 'dole' being known as uncovenanted benefit (1921), extended (1924) and transitional benefits (1927) and then as transitional payments (1931) – which survived until the 1934 Act created the Unemployment Assistance Board and attempted to separate the long-term from the short-term unemployed. This whole structure was spelt out in Acts that were inconsistent and which varied according to the political party in power. Indeed, benefits tended to go up when Labour came into office and to go down or be more stringently applied under Conservative and Conservative-dominated governments.

This was apparent under the Labour government of 1924 which raised unemployment benefit to 18s. (90p), reversing the temporary decision to reduce it from 20s. to 15s. in 1921. The Labour administration also decided that all the unemployed should have limitless access to unemployment benefit and that uncovenanted or extended benefit would be relieved of its previous time-limits. In fact, the Liberal supporters of the Labour administration took exception to this attack upon the insurance principle and forced the Labour party to think about these changes for two years, during which time it had lost office and Stanley Baldwin's government had set up the Blanesburgh Committee to inquire into the insurance scheme.

The Blanesburgh Committee tackled the issue of uncovenanted benefit in the report that it produced in 1927. It recommended that there should be a new standard benefit of unlimited duration which would be secured by a minimum of thirty contributions in two years. Thus it rejected the 1911 scheme's requirement that the length of benefit should be proportional to the total amount of the contributions. In other words, the burden became that of the total insurance fund and thus of all those in work. For those who did not qualify for unemployment insurance, there was to be a temporary transitional benefit that was drawn of right but was unrelated to any insurance contributions. It attempted to offer an actuarially sound scheme based upon 6 per cent unemployment at the same time as offering transitional payments for those who could not meet the '30 in 2' contribution requirements. William Beveridge was convinced that this was wrong, since it ended the distinction between covenanted and uncovenanted benefit and thus undermined the 1911 scheme. He said that: 'It was the Conservative Government of 1927 which on the bad advice of the rather stupid Blanesburgh Committee made the insurance benefit unlimited in time and formally divorced the claim of benefit from payment and contributions.'[14]

The Baldwin government's 1927 Unemployed Insurance Act allowed this more generous treatment of the unemployed but did tighten the administrative aspects of the scheme with its 'genuinely seeking work test'. As Labour had argued in 1924, the purpose of this device was to prevent abuse and to eliminate the 'scrounger'. Under the 1911 legislation, the proportion of benefits to contributions had been 1 in 5, which was reduced in 1920 to 1 in 6. It was felt that this would prevent abuse. With the creation of the uncovenanted, or 'dole', arrangements, the principle of proportionality had been destroyed and it was felt that the 'genuinely seeking work test' had to be applied. This meant that claimants had to be making personal efforts to find work; they could not merely register for work at an exchange and wait for work to be thrust upon them. Those not doing so could be deprived of benefit as from March 1921. The Labour government of 1924 strengthened this measure and the percentage of rejections rose from 10 to 17 per cent between 1924 and 1927; the Baldwin government tightened it up further under the 1927 Act and rejected one in three claims, since the test was now applied to those seeking standard benefits as well as transitional benefit. About three million claims were rejected during the life of the test between March 1921 and March 1930.[15] It disappeared in 1930, as the Labour government kept its 1929 election promise to abolish it. The transitional benefit was now a charge on the Treasury and not upon the insurance fund. The Labour government thus made benefit easier to claim at a time when unemployment was rising fast in the world depression that followed the Wall Street Crash of 1929 and removed the 'genuinely seeking work' clause by placing the responsibility upon officials to prove that the applicant was *not* genuinely seeking work.

It was at this moment that the Poor Law's traditional form was amended to make it part of an attempt to deal with unemployment in a more comprehensive manner. Even at the beginning of the 1920s determined efforts were being made to keep the Poor Law within the principles of 1834. And, indeed, it was stressed by the Ministry of Health that: 'The amount of relief given in any case, whilst sufficient for the purpose of relieving distress, must of necessity be calculated on a lower scale than the earnings of the independent workman who is maintaining himself by his labour.'[16] However, faced with horrendously high levels of unemployment and poverty, guardians attempted to stretch regulations to ensure that improved scales of relief were given to the 350,000–400,000 unemployed – 1,500,000 in 1926 – who normally received outdoor relief. In offering such benefits and often refusing to apply a means test, conflict between some boards of guardians and the government became inevitable. This is best illustrated by the case of the thirty Labour guardians and councillors of the district of Poplar, in London, who were imprisoned in 1921 for using generous relief scales to deal with the unemployed and for ignoring the rules and regulations governing the provision of relief.

As Noreen Branson has explained, there were many other issues which were subsumed under the term 'poplarism', and the fight against low benefits and the Household Means Test, plus the demand for the equalization of rates throughout London to help the poorer boroughs, lasted well into the 1920s and 1930s.[17] In 1919 Labour gained control of the Poplar Borough Council and local board of guardians. Immediately, the guardians ignored the specific relief rates and in May 1920 the council agreed to set a minimum wage of £4 for all municipal employees, well above the previous minimum of £3 4s. 0d. They felt that the workers and the paid municipal employees should have high enough incomes for a healthy life. They also paid increased benefits for outdoor relief and refused to curb expenditure, despite the inadequacy of finance and the problem of levying rates. For more than a year there was protracted debate over financial matters both within Poplar and with government departments before matters came to a head with legal action which led finally to the arrest of the councillors and guardians in September 1921. They refused to compromise in prison and, after six weeks, were released. At a subsequent London conference to try and equalize the burden of poor relief they were successful in obtaining arrangements whereby the richer London boroughs contributed more to the Metropolitan Poor Fund than the poorer boroughs, who would then be allowed to spend on outdoor relief a sum agreed by the Minister of Health. Poplar's Poor Law expenditure was reduced by a third as a result of this action.

What this action demonstrated was that the Poor Law was no longer capable of dealing effectively with the problem of high unemployment. It was also obvious to the government that, in an increasingly democratic age, it was quite possible for the local electorate and their representatives to flout the law in an atmosphere which recognized the need to be generous to the unemployed. This was evident in the case of West Ham, Chester-le-Street and Bedwelty, in the wake of the general strike of 1926. In the last three cases Neville Chamberlain, Minister of Health, assumed powers to control and run the local Poor Law. The ministry had come to recognize how difficult it was to ignore the plight of the unemployed and the poor:

> there has been a great increase in the proportion of the population applying for assistance to the Guardians of the Poor. There has also been, in view of the size of the problem and the comparative difficulty of any other means of dealing with it, a new and general tendency on the part of the Guardians themselves to grant, even to able-bodied persons, unconditional allowances of outdoor relief, in amounts which often approximate to, and may even exceed, the normal earnings of the applicant when he is in full work.[18]

Faced with this type of excess, Chamberlain replaced the guardians in West Ham, Chester-le-Street and Bedwelty under the Guardians' Default Act of 1926.

However, Chamberlain felt that the whole Poor Law was in need of an overhaul and that it had to be fitted more closely into an attempt to rationalize unemployment insurance. The traditional structure of the Poor Law was dismantled in 1929 and 1930. Chamberlain's Local Government Act of 1929, plus a similar Act for Scotland, and the 1930 Poor Law Act brought the existing Poor Law arrangements to an end. As a result, Poor Law unions and the boards of guardians were replaced by local authority bodies known as Public Assistance Committees (PACs) for the relief of the destitute and the poor. The Poor Law hospitals were also to be handed over to the local authorities in this transfer of responsibility.

Although it might appear that the government was making the Poor Law system more representative, the whole tone of the legislation was actually directed towards ensuring that the government could exert more control than it had hitherto been able to achieve, since the 1930 Act laid down the conditions upon which outdoor relief could be applied. In addition, the government provided about 50 per cent of the expenditure, which meant that it had more control over the level of overall expenditure than it had previously been able to do. Indeed, the PAC system of relief must have appeared even more Draconian than the Poor Law system, with the widespread application of the Household Means Test by relieving officers who, in most cases, had also operated the Poor Laws.

The early 1930s gave an added impetus to concern about how to deal with unemployment. Following the Wall Street Crash at the end of 1929, unemployment rose throughout the world as markets declined. In Britain the number of unemployed insured workers rose from 1,334,000 in December 1929 to 2,880,000 by January 1931 and 2,950,000 by January 1933.[19] The financial impact devastated the economy and finances of Britain and led to the large budget deficit which provoked the political crisis and saw the end of the second Labour government in August 1931.

Although such high levels of unemployment would have been difficult to avoid, it is clear that none of the inter-war governments was prepared to offer expansionary and interventionist policies along the lines laid down by J. M. Keynes, the Liberal party's *We Can Conquer Unemployment* (1929) or the 'Mosley Memorandum' passed around Labour government circles in 1930.[20] The fact is that such interventionist policies, designed to manage and regulate the economy, were anathema to governments who were committed to free trade and, later, to protectionist policies within the confines of balanced budgets.

The main desire in the 1920s was to get back to the gold standard and free trade and then to operate under such conditions, as occurred between 1925 and 1931, because it was felt that such policies would revive world trade, stimulate the world economy and remove unemployment. Within this scenario, all that was required was small-scale

public works schemes to tide over the worst periods and areas of unemployment. When these policies failed in the early 1930s, Britain moved
towards protectionism and cheap money policies, within the context of
balanced budgets. This saw falling unemployment figures, largely due
to these measures, which stimulated a private house-building boom
and consumer demand for cars and the new light industrial products.
Nevertheless, there were still more than 2,000,000 unemployed in early
1936 and more than 1,800,000 in January 1938. There was serious
unemployment in many northern industrial black spots and government
policy seemed to be designed towards offering a small amount of public
works in the winter months to tide the economy over until the summer,
a policy which operated within tight budgetary constraints.[21]

If the economic policies to deal with unemployment were so inadequate, so were the social policies. By 1930 there were three types of
benefit. First, there was insurance benefit, paid out of an unemployment
insurance fund to anyone who had made thirty contributions in the previous two years. Secondly, there was transitional benefit, paid by the
Treasury to those who were entitled to unemployment benefit but who
had made contributions to the fund. Within two months of having made
this a charge to the Treasury and easing the regulations, the number
receiving transitional benefit had increased from 140,000 to 300,000
and cost the Treasury £19 million in the first year. Thirdly, there was
public assistance, which was paid to those who had depended upon the
Poor Law until the late 1920s. Half the cost of this was borne by the state
and the other half by the local authority and it was paid through a Public
Assistance Committee connected with the local authority.

By 1930 the Labour government was faced with an exhausted insurance fund, the mounting payment of transitional benefits, and the rapidly
rising cost of PAC expenditure. Ramsay MacDonald had to avert an
impending financial crisis. In June 1930 he took over the special responsibility for unemployment from Thomas and set up a committee of
five economists under J. M. Keynes to report to him on the matter.
In October 1930 they suggested that unemployment benefits should
be restricted, that public works schemes should be financed and that
a general tariff should be introduced.

Philip Snowden, Labour's Chancellor of the Exchequer, was opposed
to tariffs and hesitant about public works, but he agreed with the need
to restrict unemployment benefits. The task of examining the whole
issue of such benefits was left to a Royal Commission set up under Judge
Holman Gregory in December 1930. When it first reported in June
1931, it argued that the unemployment fund should be balanced by a
30 per cent cut in benefits, that 'anomalies' should be eliminated, that
unemployment benefits should be rigidly confined to twenty-six weeks
per year, and that applicants for transitional benefit should be means

tested. Given the political sensitivity of these issues within the Labour party, all the Labour government did was to introduce a Bill to deal with the 'anomalies', allowing for variation in the conditions, amount and period of benefit for casual, seasonal and short-time workers and for married women.

Notwithstanding the Labour government's retreat from the Gregory Report, the reduction of unemployment benefit was now central to British politics. As the financial crisis worsened, the government was forced to accept the creation of an all-party committee, headed by Sir George May, which was to advise Snowden on how to reduce national expenditure in such a way as to ensure a balanced budget. When it produced its findings in June 1931, it noted that there would be a budget deficit of £120 million for 1931–2 and that £97 million would be saved by increasing unemployment insurance contributions, limiting benefit to twenty-six weeks in a year, reducing standard benefit by 20 per cent and introducing a means test on transitional benefit. In the event, on 23 August 1931 the Labour government was divided on the issue of a 10 per cent cut in standard unemployment benefit and was replaced by Ramsay MacDonald's new national government. In September 1931 it introduced the Household Means Test on transitional payment, formerly transitional benefit, thus making an effective return to Poor Law principles. This was to be administered by the PACs of the local authorities. In addition, unemployment insurance was reduced from 17s. (85p, set in 1928) to 15s. 3d. (76p) and standard benefit was restricted to twenty-six weeks.

These new measures, and particularly the introduction of the Household Means Test, created a situation whereby those who had run out of standard benefit would be subject to a means-tested transitional benefit. This meant that the 'deserving' old poor, protected since the First World War by the right to insurance, could now be subject to means testing on a par with the Poor Law. Effectively, they were now being classed as the 'undeserving' poor. Indeed, by the end of 1931 400,000 people who were entitled to benefit up to November 1931 were now subject to the means test.

At this stage unemployment was getting worse not better. Towns such as Jarrow, which lost its shipyards, found unemployment rising to between 60 and 70 per cent. The full extent of the problem was indicated by a number of unemployment and poverty surveys, such as Ellen Wilkinson's *The Town that was Murdered* and the Pilgrim Trust's *Men Without Work*, as well as in the surveys of B. S. Rowntree, H. Llewellyn Smith and Herbert Tout.[22]

In an economic sense, the national governments did little to tackle unemployment. There was some public works, some juvenile 'instruction' centres and the Special Areas Act of 1934, which established special-area status for Southern Scotland, the North-East, West Cumberland and South Wales. Even this last measure, easily the most important, was limited. Two commissioners were appointed to spend £2 million a year to help local authorities with amenity schemes and attract firms into their areas. Although the sums were increased from 1936 onwards, David Lloyd George assessed the situation correctly when he made a biblical reference to it in the House of Commons on 6 December 1934:

> The age of miracles is past. You cannot feed the multitude with two Commissioners and five sub-commissioners. The new Commissioners are being sent on their apostolic mission not without purse or script, but pretty nearly that – just with a little bit of cash to deal with a problem costing £100,000,000 a year.[23]

Not surprisingly, the results were disappointing and it has been estimated that fewer than 50,000 jobs were created in the North-East, in areas where over 350,000 were registered as being unemployed in January 1935.

With unemployment continuing at such a level, it is not surprising that the national governments were keen to keep expenditure on unemployment under control. Neville Chamberlain, Chancellor of the Exchequer in MacDonald's government, was principally concerned to control the PACs, since most of them were considered to be too generous in their assessment of transitional payments. Secondly, he wished to distinguish between the short-term and long-term unemployed. In these endeavours he was supported by the Royal Commission on Unemployment Insurance, chaired by Holman Gregory, which, in its final report in December 1932, argued that the unemployment question had to be taken out of politics, removed from inconsistent local control, and that the insurance scheme proper should be separated from the issue of the long-term unemployed.

The Unemployment Act of 1934 reflected these concerns. Part I of the Act put the unemployment insurance scheme on a sounder footing and established the Unemployment Insurance Statutory Committee to act as a supervisory body. It also set up a separate agricultural scheme, so that by 1937 about 14.5 million workers were covered by specific provisions. The employer, employee and the state paid equal contributions to the fund and the right to benefits was exhausted after twenty-six weeks. The whole idea of the scheme was to make it self-supporting by dealing only with those who were temporarily unemployed.

Part II of the Act set up the Unemployment Assistance Board (UAB), which took up responsibility for the long-term unemployed. PACs were no longer to deal with the able-bodied and the UAB was to act as a centrally based body operating a means-tested system of benefits. It was to offer a new form of destitution relief to all the able-bodied on a national basis and was to take responsibility for about 800,000 people receiving transitional payment from the PACs and then for 200,000 more who received poor relief from the PACs.[24] It effectively removed these people from 200 PACs, with their 1,000 or so sub-committees, leaving the PACs to deal with the sick and the aged. The UAB was allowed to produce its own regulations, scales of benefit and means test. It was quickly found that its benefit levels were going to be lower than those operated by the PACs and, due to the protest, the 'standstill' Act was introduced in 1935 for two years, permitting the long-term unemployed to choose whichever benefit was the more favourable – that of the UAB or the PAC. The Unemployment Assistance Act of 1934 was not properly introduced, therefore, until April 1937, when the able-bodied became the responsibility of the UAB.

As a result, the PACs, the effective administrators of the Poor Law, lost all their able-bodied adult males and became a general relief agency, providing a last resort general assistance service. About 13 per cent of those receiving poor relief were the institutionalized old, young and sick and the other 87 per cent received domiciliary relief in cash, kind or service. Those assisted at home included the sick, old, deserted wives, widows and any unemployed not catered for by the UAB.

The UAB took up the social problem of the long-term unemployed until it widened its functions at the beginning of the Second World War by becoming the Assistance Board, en route to becoming the National Assistance Board in 1948. Initially, the board consisted of six members chaired by the Rt. Hon. Lord Rushcliffe. The only woman on the board was Miss Violet Markham, who had a very interesting career in social service. She was born in 1872 (and died in 1959), was a member of the Chesterfield Education Authority for many years, helped to organize the Anti-Suffrage movement between 1908 and 1912, married Lt. Col. Carruthers in 1915, was a member of the executive committee of the National Relief Fund in the First World War and was a member of the UAB (later Assistance Board) between 1934 and 1946. She was its deputy chairman between 1937 and 1946. During that time she became involved in a wide variety of activities, particularly in connection with bombed towns and cities during the Second World War. In 1938 and 1939, however, she focused her efforts on attempting to tackle the problem of long-term female unemployment. She set up pilot schemes to interview such women in Liverpool, Birmingham, Glasgow, South Wales, and many other urban centres and attempted to provide some work experience on the basis of these assessments. Whilst she conducted some of the interviews herself, she chiefly relied upon regional interviewers and their reports.[25] Many of these reports have survived, indicating the occupational background of these women, the difficulties they posed and the limited solutions that were offered to their predicament. What emerges is the extent to which the problem seemed insoluble. The special enquiry on Liverpool is indicative of the situation that had to be faced. Liverpool had 3,700 women in receipt of UAB allowances, just over 8 per cent of the total long-term unemployed. The UAB dealt with 36 per cent of all the unemployed in Liverpool. In other words, unemployment in Liverpool, covered by unemployment insurance and UAB allowances, was on the grand scale, well over 100,000. The main problem was that a lot of women's work was of a casual and seasonal nature and whilst there was a considerable amount of casual employment for women aged 25–40, there was little realistic possibility of employment for older women. One report noted that:

> With the older women sympathy is the paramount feeling around. Many of them have a substantial record of employment in the district past, but work was lost usually between the ages of 35 and 40 years. Efforts to get back into wage earning employment have been genuine as is evidenced by the number of short periods of work obtained during the more recent years. These older women have deteriorated in health and general stamina, or have genuine ailments which lower their vitality and gradually they have to all appearances become practically unemployable.[26]

This assessment was reflected in the fact that all that could be offered to these women was a few weeks at a training centre for housecraft and domestic duties. The Housecraft Training Centre, Bedford Street, Liverpool, offered a twelve-week course for between thirty and forty fit women aged 18–38 between 9 a.m. and 4 p.m. Greycourt, near Lancaster, offered two types of residential domestic courses, of eight and eleven weeks each, for a small number of older women. The problem was, of course, that there were too few centres, too many long-term unemployed women, and too limited a variety of training.

It was only the shortage of labour in the Second World War that gave these women opportunities for work, for they were not to benefit from the slow revival of the economy in the late 1930s and the rearmament programme. For them, and for many others, the reality was that they had been put into the category of the unemployable, or the undeserving poor. In the 1920s the creation of 'dole', in its various guises, had blurred the division between insured and uninsured workers. The unemployment fund could not stand the financial strain, and was about £100 million in debt by 1930. With the ending of the traditional New Poor Law structure, extra financial burdens were imposed which forced the national government to distinguish, once again, between the employable and the unemployable, the deserving and the undeserving poor. Financial expediency, rather than logic, was the winner in inter-war unemployment policy.

Health, housing, pensions and other areas
of social policy, 1918–1939

Charles Webster has recently argued that, whilst general standards might have improved, the health of a significant majority of those who were unemployed and in poverty probably deteriorated during the inter-war years.[27] More recently, Margaret Mitchell has tended to endorse Webster's view that health problems were rooted in the economic disadvantages which were caused by unemployment.[28] These opinions are at variance with those presented by C. L. Mowat, D. H. Aldcroft, John Stevenson and Chris Cook in what has been referred to as the 'received opinion'.[29] This controversial debate has raised the issues of balance, of the extent to which governments hid the levels of ill health from the public records, and questions the accuracy of the official statistics. In the end, both sides accept that general health conditions improved but differ about the significance of the problems of a sizeable minority of the population, largely based in the declining industrial North and the Celtic fringes. They accept the findings of B. S. Rowntree, particularly that living standards rose by about 30 per cent between 1889 and the mid-1930s. The other poverty surveys of the time suggested similar improvements.[30] There is little doubt about the downward direction of many of the vital statistics. The question is one of degree – the pervasiveness of such improvements. Whatever the outcome of that debate, and there is evidence that the improvement in conditions was exaggerated and that those faced with unemployment had a 50 per cent higher death rate than those who were employed, it is clear that there were structural improvements in health provision during these years.[31]

As Noel Whiteside has suggested recently, a steadily rising incidence of sickness and disability among working people was running parallel to growing unemployment during the inter-war years in Britain, and economic factors helped to influence contemporary perceptions of sickness and health in such a way as to ensure that both those who were genuinely sick, as a result of unemployment, and those who regarded themselves as being so were able to obtain health insurance.[32] Indeed, he adds to the debate about the health of the nation in the inter-war years by noting that claims and payments in health benefit increased steadily throughout this period – though he qualifies this by stressing that such statistics might, as contemporaries commented, be only claims and that less than half of the population was covered by health schemes in the late 1930s.[33] The thrust of his argument is that it is very difficult to distinguish between those genuinely suffering from ill health and those who were 'malingerers': clearly, unemployment caused ill health, just as ill health caused unemployment. However, there was clear reluctance by the authorities to prevent unemployed people from applying for health relief, for this would have been a political 'hot potato', and a marked tendency for those who were unemployed to remain on health insurance since: 'The rights of the unemployed under the health insurance scheme were safeguarded. The rights of the long-term sick to statutory unemployment benefits were not so.'[34] In addition, with the Anomalies Act and other measures against women who, it was felt, 'abused' the system of unemployment relief, many women preferred to be on health, as opposed to unemployment, insurance. In other words, it is quite likely that some, possibly many, underemployed families used health insurance as an alternative to the standard benefit offered by unemployment insurance, the various types of 'dole', or the Poor Law.

The health insurance which existed and expanded during the inter-war years was based upon part I of the National Insurance Act of 1911 and remained largely unchanged. By 1920 the scheme was paying sickness benefit of 15s. (75p) per week for men and 12s. (60p) per week for women, with basic medical treatment for up to twenty-six weeks a year to all workers earning less than £250 per annum, in return for contributions from the state, employers and employees. After six months those who were still ill could claim disability benefit at half the previous rate. The system operated through approved societies, such as friendly societies, trade unions and insurance companies, whose schemes had to be non-profit-making; there was great duplication in efforts, since the workforce of a factory might be insured by many different approved societies. All such groups had to pay statutory benefits and employ a panel of doctors to care for their members. Yet they often paid discretionary extras. Some societies provided hospital and consultant services, whilst others did not. Dental and opthalmic services were generally provided as extras, whilst convalescent and nursing allowances were less common. Thus the 1911 Act and its amendments provided both insurance against loss of income due to ill health and access to health provision.

Health insurance spread quickly. The numbers involved rose from 11.5 million in 1912 to 13.5 million in 1922, and 20.26 million out of a population of 47.5 million in 1938. A significant number of women were covered by the scheme, the figures rising from 3.68 million to 7.1 million between 1912 and 1938. But once unemployment rose sharply in the 1920s, health insurance, like unemployment insurance, began to cost more than the contributions. Part of the reason for this is that, as with unemployment, temporary solutions were found to allow the payment of benefits to continue to those who could prove unemployment at the labour exchanges. As Whiteside notes, by the time unemployment peaked in the early 1930s the various approved societies were bearing the cost of 6 million members who were wholly or partly in arrears.[35] A Royal Commission on National Health Insurance had been set up by the Labour government of 1924, but its report in 1926, which suggested a system of National Health Insurance to which the government was a significant contributor, was ignored, on its own advice, until the financial situation improved.[36] The Royal Commission also investigated the possibility of generalizing and extending the extra benefits, a necessity if the scheme was to become universal, and suggested that the surplus funds of all societies should be pooled, but this was resisted by the approved societies, who also reacted strongly against the Minority Report suggestion that they be swept away. As Neville Chamberlain advised: 'the political power and influence of the Approved Societies makes it desirable in present circumstances to meet their views'.[37] In such a climate, change was impossible until Attlee's post-war Labour government decided that they would not be part of the National Health Service.

In many respects the health insurance scheme was effective in alleviating the financial suffering due to ill health, or ill health caused by unemployment. But there is no doubt that it lacked administrative uniformity; there were, for instance, more than 7,000 societies and branches operating the system in the early 1920s.[38] The scheme offered medical treatment, sickness benefit and an array of extra benefits, but there was no universal commitment to hospital and specialist treatment.

The chief problem here was that there was no adequately or effectively organized system of hospital or specialist treatment throughout the country. At this time hospital provision was also unevenly distributed throughout the country and between the social classes. For the working class, by far the largest section of the community, there were about 127,000 beds available in the local authority and Poor Law hospitals, the responsibility for the latter being transferred to the local authorities in 1929 and 1930. In addition, there were also voluntary hospitals, with about 83,000 beds, which earned their income from patients' fees, donations and legacies. Although there were also special facilities for such things as infectious diseases, the total provision of hospital beds was low and was not distributed in such a way as to tackle effectively the health problems of the nation as a whole. The only other significant improvement in this situation was the 1936 Public Health Act, which extended the powers of the local authorities to provide hospitals – including, for the first time, the right to set up out-patient departments.[39] It was this inadequate situation, and the problem of financing health insurance in a period of high unemployment, which contributed significantly to the debate which led Nye Bevan to force through his version of the National Health Service after the Second World War, incorporating both the concepts of a free service and the state control of hospitals.

The state was far more organized and effective when it came to old-age pensions. The pension scheme that had been introduced in 1908 was non-contributory and, subject to means, 5s. (25p) per week was paid to all persons reaching the age of 70. This was raised to 10s. (50p) per week in 1919. In 1925 a contributory scheme, the Widows', Orphans' and Old Age Contributory Pensions Act, was passed and provided 10s. (50p) per week (£1 for a married couple) without a means test to those reaching 65 years of age and to the widows and orphans of insured men of any age. A widow received 10s. (50p), with 5s. (25p) for the first child and 3s. (15p) for each subsequent child. Employee, employer and the state contributed to this arrangement.

By 1925, then, there were three types of pensions available. Under the 1908 Act, there were those people over 70 whose pensions were subject to means, nationality and residence tests. Secondly, the same Act also applied to those who, by right of contribution under the 1925 Act, were exempted from the limitations of means, nationality and residence. Thirdly, there were those under the 1925 Act who could draw contributory pensions between the ages of 65 and 70. The 1925 scheme was extended in 1929 and 1937, with the age for widows being reduced to 60 and then to 55.

Yet even the most optimistic of assessments could not conclude that the state adopted a systematic and comprehensive scheme for distributing the wealth of the nation to the poor, the unemployed and the ill. Social security in Britain during these years was clearly an inadequate hotch-potch of ideas with little semblance of organization. In no way were the problems of the unemployed, for instance, tackled in an effective manner. It was this lack of planning which undoubtedly made the housing programme, of central importance to the evolution of social policy, less effective than it might otherwise have been.

The expansion of house building during the inter-war years is often considered to be one of the great achievements of this period, improving the housing stock and accommodation for both middle-class and working-class families. Indeed, there were about 61,000 fewer houses than families in 1918 but a surplus of about 500,000 houses by 1938, despite the removal of slum accommodation. All social classes benefited, but the greatest gains were achieved by the middle classes, who did particularly well out of the house-building boom of the 1930s.

There is no doubt that both the quantity and quality of housing was better in the 1930s than had been the case in the pre-war years. The housing shortage was quickly whittled away as both local councils and private builders tackled the problem – more by the local councils in the 1920s and more by the private builders in the 1930s.

Governments tackled the shortage of houses through a variety of legislation which often betrayed their political bias. The Housing and Town Planning Act of 1919, usually referred to as the Addison Act, committed local authorities to surveying their housing needs and offered government subsidies to encourage them to build houses and then to let them to the working classes at the prevailing level of rents. Any loss of income they incurred as a result of this rent policy would be made up by central government, except for the proceeds of a 1d. (0.4p) rate. About 213,800 houses were built under this legislation before the economy cuts of 1921 eventually brought the efforts of the 'spending minister' to a halt in 1922. Subsequently, the Chamberlain Act of 1923 provided a subsidy of £6 towards the building of both private and local authority housing for a period of twenty years. Chamberlain's main concern was to encourage the building of a large number of private houses which the better-off working classes could purchase. In fact, about 362,700 private houses and 75,300 local authority houses were built with the Chamberlain subsidy between 1923 and 1934. John Wheatley, the Minister of Health in MacDonald's Labour government of 1924, rectified the balance in favour of local authorities. The Wheatley Act of 1924 provided more generous subsidies of £9 and £12 for forty years, though there were more controls applied, which discouraged private builders. As a result, 15,800 private houses were built under this legislation compared with 504,500 local authority houses. Wheatley had rectified the balance and developed the alternative strategy of providing rented accommodation to the working classes. As he said to the House of Commons:

> The real problem is the provision of houses, not to sell but to let, and to let at rents which the working classes can afford to pay. Subsidies to private enterprise for houses to sell are good to the extent that they do get houses, but they do not touch the real problem and even larger subsidies would not get working men's houses built to be let. Let there be no mistake about that; no one will build these houses on any terms ...[40]

The only solution to the working-class housing shortage was the building of partly subsidized local authority housing.

In fact, the inter-war years saw the building of more than four million houses. About 1,100,000 were built by local authorities and 400,000 by private builders, both with subsidies from the state, and another 2,500,000 were built by private builders alone, principally during the mid- and late 1930s. In terms of housing provision, the state had made a significant contribution to the house-building programme in Britain.

This state legislation had also helped to improve the quality of housing by dictating that the houses built would be larger, though the main improvement in the quality of housing came from attempts to remove slums, particularly through the Greenwood Housing Act of 1930, which provided subsidies for slum clearance based upon the number of families rehoused and required local authorities to draw up

five-year plans for slum clearance. The national government developed
its policies along these lines and in 1933 announced that house-building
subsidies would be discontinued and that attention would be focused
upon slum clearance, with one million people being rehoused before the
outbreak of the Second World War. In 1935 it also tackled the problem
of overcrowding, laying down standards and making it a penal offence
for local authorities to permit these minimum standards to be infringed.
In 1936 a census of overcrowding was taken under the 1935 Act and
found that 4 per cent of working-class houses were overcrowded, even
allowing for the wide and generous definition of this (2 persons to 1 room,
7 in 4 rooms and 10 persons to 5 rooms). This census also revealed the
wide regional variations in Britain. Whilst Sunderland experienced 20
per cent overcrowding, other areas were much less, with Bournemouth
experiencing 0.3 per cent. This also had its consequence in terms of
infant mortality and the general health of the communities.

Some of these developments in the 1930s can be seen in Leeds, which
in many ways was backward about housing until the early 1930s. The
Tory-dominated Leeds City Council failed to respond to the Greenwood Act until February 1931, two months after the legislative deadline.
When the survey was finally produced, it was considered to be totally
inadequate, merely advocating 2,000 demolitions and a commensurate
rehousing programme.[41] Labour councillors were dissatisfied with the
small scale of the programme and Councillor Revd C. Jenkinson
(Labour) asked the Tory chairman of the 'Unhealthy Areas Committee'
to speed up his survey of Leeds, adding that there were 72,000 back-to-
back houses in the city, 33,000 of which were concentrated in high
densities of 70 to 80 per acre. He argued that at least 10,000 were in
need of immediate demolition.[42]

Jenkinson's attack forced the city council to take action and to form a
special committee to oversee the slum problem. But the response was
purely cosmetic. The committee was formed in July 1931, met once in
December 1931 and never met again. In January 1932 an improvement
committee took over its functions but did nothing until November 1931.
Slum clearance and rehousing in Leeds was clearly going to be a slow
and painstaking affair. As a result, Councillor O'Donnell (Labour) made
a speech to the council in November 1932 demanding the immediate
clearance of 5,685 houses and outlining the woefully slow progress
of the Tory administration. Feeling that further delay would be politically damaging, the administration announced its intention to clear 400
slum houses and to request tenders, by 30 June 1933, for 1,000 three-
bedroomed houses.

After more than two years of delay, the Tory council had taken
action. But this was not enough to appease the Labour councillors, who
stressed that 54,000 houses had been built in Leeds before 1872, that

37,500 'are very old back-to-back' and that the council's housing scheme would not touch the tip of the problem.[43] They argued that overcrowding and ill health could only be avoided by the demolition of 15,000 or 16,000 houses over a five-year period and the construction of an even greater number of two- and three-bedroomed parlour and non-parlour houses.

The city council's housing policy was one of the key issues in the November 1933 municipal elections, in which Labour's demands for more slum clearance were met by Tory charges of the ruinous threat of 'Red finance'. Nevertheless, the Labour party won a majority on the council and was committed to a more adventurous and challenging housing programme. Slum clearance was to be increased, more houses were to be built, houses were to be built in preference to flats and differential rents were to be charged.[44]

The new Labour administration acted quickly to raise the pace and change the character of the Leeds housing programme. There was a rush of activity. By January 1935 Councillor Revd Jenkinson had announced the slum clearance of more than 2,000 houses and plans to construct a similar number of houses.[45] Indeed, during the two-year period of Labour control about 6,000 houses were demolished and a similar number constructed.[46] All of the demolished houses were subject to a survey by the Leeds Engineers' Department in 1935 and 1936. The City of Leeds Health Exhibition, which ran from 17 to 24 September 1934, also involved the building of two three-bedroomed semis close to Leeds Town Hall and in front of the library in order to show the citizens of Leeds what new housing they could expect. Many of those living in Leeds today would recognize the design in some of the present Leeds estates. There was also a scheme to build council houses at Moortown: according to the needs of the community, 10 per cent of the houses were to be built for the aged, 10 per cent were to be two-bedroomed, 50 per cent three-bedroomed and 10 per cent four- or five-bedroomed houses.[47]

It was at this stage that the national government began to renew its attack upon both slums and overcrowding. At the beginning of 1933, it recognized that:

Overcrowding was characteristically an evil associated with the central areas of large towns. New accommodation in the outskirts was no solution to the problem, involving as it does the uprooting of people from the neighbourhood they looked upon as their home, and moving them far from where they wished to work. What was needed was more rehousing on the overcrowded and slum sites. In order that the rehousing in the central areas concerned might accommodate as large a population as possible, normally redevelopment was necessary, in order to make the best of the land, and more housing in flats.[48]

Shortly afterwards it accepted that Exchequer support would be limited to schemes where:

> the rehousing is effected on or near the central site by means of blocks of flats and should not be given in cases where the rehousing is effected by means of ordinary small houses erected on undeveloped land on the outskirts of the area of the local authority.[49]

Although this policy was later the subject of amendment, it is clear that it was partly responsible for the decision of Leeds Council to move towards the building of flats just before the Second World War.[50]

The Tories had regained control of Leeds City Council in November 1935, claiming to be the initiators of some of the schemes which the Labour party had begun during its period in control. Indeed, the famous Quarry Hill scheme near the centre of Leeds, where 2,000 slum houses were demolished and 938 flats built at a cost of £1,500,000, began life as an idea put forward by Labour party activists and stimulated by the grant policy of the national government. A day nursery for the children of residents was incorporated into this scheme. Nevertheless, the Tories introduced some changes. In particular, the Moortown estate, which would have bordered the houses of the wealthy, was replaced by a scheme to build a council estate at Cookridge.[51]

Conclusion

In their desire to move away from the nineteenth-century policy of dealing only with destitution and to develop a selective strategy of tackling the problems of specific groups, successive inter-war governments had created a confused and complex pattern of social security which barely alleviated the conditions of the vast majority of the unemployed and the poor. If the resultant social security system improved the general conditions of the working classes and offered a greater diversity of relief than had existed in the nineteenth century, it did little for the millions affected by long-term unemployment and acute poverty. This was despite the fact that governments increased their financial commitment to the working classes in the form of unemployment, old-age, health and housing provision. The fact is that there was still a strong streak of hostility to the view that the unemployed and the poor should be treated in a generous manner in case this reduced the incentive to work. The Poor Law, as an institution, disappeared in 1930, but the mentality behind its operation – the view that it must be a final deterrent – lingered on in the Household Means Test, the Anomalies Bill and other legislation. The inter-war years revealed that the nation was not yet ready for the redistribution of income and wealth that was necessary if those in poverty were to be relieved. It was not until the Second

World War that such a change of attitude came about. In the meantime, millions of working-class families, particularly those of the unemployed, failed to benefit fully from the improvements in social provision that had occurred. Their benefits were means tested and their incomes did not necessarily allow them to enjoy the improvement in housing provision which was central to the evolution of social welfare policies affecting the working-class standards of living. In other words: 'Policy had ... evolved pragmatically, was uncoordinated and still far from universal.'[52]

Whilst the majority of the British people had seen a significant improvement in their standard of living – probably up to 30 per cent between 1900 and the mid-1930s – the fact is that a substantial minority were no better off. For many of these, suffering from unemployment and ill health on a large scale, the piecemeal social services and benefits were inadequate to meet their needs. It took the Second World War to develop the concepts necessary for a more co-ordinated, integrated and universal Welfare State.

Notes

1. M. J. Moore, 'Social Work and Social Welfare: The Organisation and Philanthropic Resources in Britain, 1900–1914', *Journal of British Studies* (Spring, 1977), p. 102.
2. F. D'Aeth, 'War Relief Agencies and the Guild of Help Movement', *Progress: Civic, Social, Industrial* 10 (October 1914), pp. 140–7.
3. *Ibid.*, p. 142.
4. *Ibid.*
5. *Ibid.*, p. 143.
6. Borough of Poole Guild of Help, minutes, 5 August 1914.
7. *East Dorset Herald*, 28 October 1915.
8. Middlesbrough Guild of Help, minutes, 7 August 1914, and 26 April 1915; *Croydon Borough Guild of Help Magazine* 40 (January 1915); *The Citizen* (organ of the Reading Guild of Help) 4/2 (November 1916); Wimbledon Guild of Help and Council of Social Welfare, *Eighth Annual Report, 1914–1915* (1915), p. 3; and County Borough of Bolton Guild of Help, *Ninth Annual Report, 1914* (1914), p. 7, and *Fourteenth Annual Report, 1919* (1919).
9. Bolton Guild of Help, *Ninth Annual Report*, p. 7.
10. County Borough of Bolton Guild of Help, *Thirteenth Annual Report, 1918* (1918), p. 8.
11. J. M. Winter, *Socialism and the Challenge of War: Ideas and Politics in Britain, 1912–18* (1974), pp. 202, 222, 259, 268, 272.
12. B. B. Gilbert, *British Social Policy, 1914–1939* (1970), p. 5.
13. Viscountess Rhondda, *et al.*, *D. A. Thomas, Viscount Rhondda* (1921), p. 267, quoted in D. Fraser, *The Evolution of the British Welfare State* 1983), pp. 179–80.

14.   Beveridge to Churchill, 5 February 1930, Beveridge Papers, LII, 218, quoted in Fraser, *Evolution*, p. 191.

15.   A. Deacon, *In Search of the Scrounger* (1976), provides a detailed account of how the system operated.

16.   *The Second Annual Report of the Ministry of Health, 1920–1* (1921).

17.   N. Branson, *George Lansbury and the Councillors' Revolt: Poplarism 1919–1925* (1979).

18.   *The Eighth Annual Report of the Ministry of Health, 1926–7* (1927).

19.   From a variety of sources, including C. L. Mowat, *Britain between the Wars 1918–1940* (1968 edition), pp. 273–5.

20.   K. Laybourn, *Britain on the Breadline: A Social and Political History of Britain between the Wars* (Gloucester, 1990), pp. 17–21.

21.   The details of these policies are outlined in the following: S. Constantine, *Unemployment in Britain between the Wars* (1980); K. J. Hancock, 'The Reduction of Unemployment as a Problem of Public Policy, 1920–1929', *Economic History Review* 15 (1962), and reproduced in S. Pollard (ed.), *The Gold Standard and Employment Policies between the Wars* (1970); K. Laybourn, *Philip Snowden* (Aldershot, 1988); R. Middleton, 'The Constant Employment Budget Balances and British Budgetary Policy, 1929–1939', *Economic History Review* 34/2 (1981); R. Skidelsky, *Politicians and the Slump: The Labour Government 1929–1931* (1967).

22.   Carnegie Trust, *Disinherited Youth* (Edinburgh, 1943); Pilgrim Trust, *Men without Work* (Cambridge, 1938); B. S. Rowntree, *Poverty and Progress: A Second Social Survey of York* (1941); H. Tout, *The Standard of Living in Bristol* (Bristol, 1934); H. Llewellyn Smith (ed.), *The New Survey of London Life and Labour* (1934); E. Wilkinson, *The Town that was Murdered: The Life-Story of Jarrow* (1939).

23.   *Hansard*, 6 December 1934.

24.   *Report of the Unemployment Assistance Board for the Period ended 31 December, 1935* (HMSO, Cmd. 5177, 1936), pp. 7–8.

25.   Violet Markham Papers, particularly 8/14–8/32, in the Special Collections at the British Library of Political and Economic Science, London School of Economics.

26.   *Ibid.*, 8/29, 'Special Enquiry: Report on the Experimental Interviewing of the Women's Register'.

27.   C. Webster, 'Healthy or Hungry Thirties?', *History Workshop* 13 (1982).

28.   M. Mitchell, 'The Effects of Unemployment on the Social Conditions of Women and Children in the 1930s', *History Workshop* 19 (1985), pp. 105–27.

29.   Mowat, *Britain between the Wars*; D. H. Aldcroft, *The Inter-War Economy: Britain 1919–1939* (1970); J. Stevenson and C. Cook, *The Slump* (1977).

30.   A. L. Bowley and M. Hogg, *Has Poverty Diminished?* (1925).

31.   G. C. M. M'Gonigle and J. Kirby, *Poverty and Public Health* (1936).

32.   N. Whiteside, 'Counting the Cost: Sickness and Disability among Working People in an Era of Industrial Recession, 1920–1939', *Economic History Review* 40/2 (1987), pp. 228–46.

33.   *Ibid.*, p. 230, refers to the fact that 20.26 million, out of a total population of 47.5 million, were able to claim sickness and medical benefit.

34.   *Ibid.*, p. 237.

35.   *Ibid.*, p. 231.
36.   *Report of the Royal Commission on National Health Insurance, 1926: Majority Report* (1926), paragraph 151.
37.   Gilbert, *British Social Policy* p. 283.
38.   *Social Insurance and Allied Services* (Beveridge Report) (HMSO, 1942, cmd. 6404), p. 24.
39.   Public Health Act, 1936, paragraph 181, 2 (a).
40.   *Hansard*, 3 June 1924.
41.   *Leeds Citizen*, 11 November 1932.
42.   *Ibid.*, 10 April 1932.
43.   *Ibid.*, 17 November, 2 December 1932; 3 March 1933.
44.   City of Leeds Labour party, minutes, 19 July 1933.
45.   *Ibid.*, 3 January 1935.
46.   *Leeds Citizen*, 6 December 1935.
47.   *Bradford Pioneer*, 7 June 1935.
48.   PRO, Cab. 23, Report of meeting, 31 January 1934.
49.   *Ibid.*, Report of meeting, 21 February 1934.
50.   *Ibid.*, Report of meeting, 31 July 1934.
51.   *Leeds Citizen*, 13 March, 8 May and 18 September 1936.
52.   Fraser, *Evolution*, p. 206.

CHAPTER TEN

THE SECOND WORLD WAR 1939–1945: BEVERIDGE AND THE PAPER CHASE

The social impact of the Second World War upon Britain has been the cause of considerable debate, not least because some historians have reacted strongly to R. M. Titmuss's view that the war created consensus politics and paved the way for the universal ideas outlined in the Beveridge Report of 1942.[1] There have been many critics who have suggested that Titmuss exaggerated his claims and played down earlier influences, which he clearly did. Indeed, it is obviously difficult to establish the precise moment at which changes in social attitudes occurred. Nevertheless, whatever the historical eddies of debate, is it clear that few historians would deny that the Second World War did bring about substantial change, even if those changes were built upon earlier developments. The 'people's war' did help to shape the 'people's peace', even if its impact has to be set within its wider context.

Titmuss's views are obviously at one extreme of the spectrum of opinion in suggesting that the selectivity of the inter-war years gave way to the universalism of the 1940s created by wartime radicalism. He argues that in this 'people's war' the nation as a whole united in sacrifice to achieve victory. The circumstances created an unprecedented sense of social solidarity among the British people, making them responsive to the great increase in egalitarian politics and collectivist state intervention. The bombing and evacuation had exposed social problems which had hitherto remained hidden from public view and generated a sense of commitment among the wartime coalition governments. It was in this social and political environment that the Beveridge Report, related books and White Papers were able to make a clear impact on the public mind.

Titmuss's views have provoked a variety of responses. Several writers have more or less accepted his views with minor qualifications. Gordon Wright feels that, whilst the war speeded up existing trends, it brought about a drastic process of levelling that flattened the social pyramid and paved the way for the social reform and political consensus to which Titmuss referred.[2] Arthur Marwick is also a supporter of the Titmuss line, noting that the Second World War brought disruption and destruction, tested the existing institutions, involved mass participation and created the emotional responses required for social change. Indeed, he argues that by 1941 there was a preoccupation with social reform at all levels in society. It was in that year that the Conservative

'Post War Problems Committee' and the '1941 Committee' of upper-class liberals and socialist intellectuals was formed and by 1942 the problem of reconstruction was becoming the dominant social and political issue.[3] Derek Fraser has also argued much the same line and Paul Addison, despite some reservations, concurs that the war brought about significant changes in the political and social atmosphere of Britain.[4]

Angus Calder and Henry Pelling are the two chief opponents of the Titmuss and quasi-Titmuss view. Calder is rather critical of the suggestion of fundamental wartime change and argues that the conflict did not sweep society on to a new course but, rather, hastened its progress along old grooves. To him, the Second World War simply reinforced the existing trends, developing social reform measures and enhancing the role of women.[5] On the other hand, Pelling notes that there were some improvements in education and social provision during wartime but warns that too much should not be made of this, for it is quite possible that unemployment might have fallen and that other social and political developments might have occurred without the war.[6]

Nonetheless, such criticisms do not appear to be as wounding as they were a quarter of a century ago. The fact is that historians are arguing about a matter of balance and degree. Both Calder and Pelling accept that there was wartime change, but cannot accept that it reduced to insignificance pre-1939 events and current trends. Yet most writers would agree that the Beveridge Report had its origins in the earlier Liberal reforms and that the opportunity to speed up the process of social reform was presented by the Second World War. The emphasis may be different, but most writers have come to accept that, for good or ill, the Second World War did provide major social change, even if that arose partly from pre-war events.[7]

The social problems

The social problems of British society, exposed in particular towns in the 1920s and 1930s, were only a microcosm of what was occurring in all areas of Britain. The outbreak of war and the threat of German bombing did two things, First, it demanded a scale of activity from central and local government that had never been seen before. Secondly, it led to the evacuation of large numbers of children from the threatened towns who were disgorged into safe areas and placed with 'foster' families. Both events caused social consternation and revealed the need for social and administrative change.

The second of these events, the need to evacuate children from those areas threatened by bombing in the early months of the war, created an immediate and major stir. As one newspaper reminded the British people, evacuation 'became the most important subject in the social history of the war because it revealed to the whole people the black spots in its social life'.[8] The poor social and health conditions of many children became apparent to the whole nation and it was recognized that something needed to be done.

This concern was further stimulated by the destruction brought about by the German bombing raids on Britain's great industrial cities. The magnitude of the experience is revealed by Violet Markham, who was a member of the Unemployment Assistance Board (which became the Assistance Board) between 1934 and 1946 and who had acted as its deputy chairman between 1937 and 1946. What she confirmed was that, when faced with massive aerial bombardment, the response of local authorities was not always effective; some did work with government agencies but other did not, partly because of local pride and independence.

During the early years of the war she travelled to the most affected British cities and reported upon the state of local organization. She visited Sheffield in 1941, following heavy raids on 12 and 15 December, and was most critical of Sheffield Corporation. She wrote that:

> The idiosyncrasies of the Sheffield Corporation have long been known to me. They are a self-sufficient, self-satisfied body, dominated by a certain type of Labour politics, and very unreceptive to ideas from outsiders. Their attitude to other official bodies and to representatives of Government Departments in the city is one of exclusiveness amounting at times to hostility. The Town Clerk, Mr Gibson, is the focus of this feeling and it is reflected in Mr Stansfield, the Public Assistance Officer. Mr Stansfield was for a short time an officer of the Board [Unemployment Assistance] and is very hostile to it.[9]

She then related how Councillor Asbury, 'the uncrowned King of Sheffield', and the emergency committee had brought the control of the city almost entirely under the Public Assistance Committee and that there was 'no consultation or co-operation beforehand with the Board or the representatives of any other department'. The result was that they made mistakes. In one air raid, eight of the ten 'food and rest' centres were destroyed, largely because they were too close to each other, and the public assistance office, with all its records, was also destroyed. These problems and mistakes were only rectified by the fact that many different sectors welded together to make good the destroyed local organization. Sheffield's 1,600 schoolteachers came in to help organize 60 new food and rest centres, the city librarian set up an information centre where all city and government agencies were represented, and through this medium 12,000 homeless were dealt with, billeting was arranged and evacuation was organized. Violet Markham could not help but reflect that:

It is difficult to know whether the self-satisfaction of the Sheffield Corporation has been shaken by this recent experience, and how far they are prepared fairly to face their own failures and to learn from them. I was told that Sheffield is under the impression that it is now in a position to provide a model scheme for dealing with air raid for the rest of the country, but more in a sense of a courtesy than as an example to other places.[10]

Markham was more favourably inclined towards the actions of Liverpool, Bootle, Birkenhead and Wallasey, which saw similar devastation to that experienced by Sheffield. Of Mr Molyneaux, the PAC officer for Liverpool, Markham wrote that he was 'a competent and vigorous man' and that relations between the PACs and the UAB were good.[11]

Ultimately, local and government agencies were forced to work together by the sheer magnitude of the social problems they faced. Local and central government activities rose to even greater importance in the lives of the population and it was clear that every sector of the economy would have to be drawn into the war effort. Nothing other than a universal approach to social problems could be adopted. The government worked in line with these needs. In July 1940 Treasury grants were increased to allow twice as many schools and a 50 per cent increase in milk consumption for needy children. By 1945 a third of all children ate at school, ten times the percentage in 1940, 14 per cent of children received their meals free and 10 per cent received free milk. Indeed, the proportion taking milk at school increased from a half in 1940 to three-quarters in 1945.

The UAB, as we have seen, began to diversify its activities and became the Assistance Board. It no longer dealt purely with unemployment but with all social problems. Under the Old Age and Widows' Pension Act, it was allowed to provide pensioners with supplementary pensions based upon proven needs. By 1941 it was dealing with ten times as many pensioners as unemployed people. It also operated a new form of means test from 1941 under the Determination of Needs Act. This replaced the 1931 means test which had created such an outcry and left many claimants without their full benefits. Wartime dislocation meant that it was difficult to operate the old means test and the new arrangement therefore made an assumption about the level of contributions from non-dependent members of the family and immediately improved the circumstances of about a quarter of a million people. The UAB was thus making its transition towards the National Assistance Board (NAB) of 1948 and moving from dispensing unemployment relief to dealing with all social problems.

Hospital provision also required change, given the increased scale of wartime injuries. At the outbreak of the war an emergency medical service had been organized, covering about two-thirds of all hospitals. Services personnel were given free treatment on a national basis and this provision was eventually extended to munitions workers, evacuees, firemen and twenty-six other categories of patients by the end of the war. Very quickly, as Paul Addison has stressed: 'The home front organized for war was becoming a model, and an inspiration, for the reorganization of the peace.'[12] Nevertheless, he believes that the atmosphere of optimistic solidarity was by no means as universal as Titmuss had supposed. Indeed, there was some caution within Conservative ranks about the cost of the hopes and aspirations for the future.

The fact is, however, that the exigent needs of war were fuelling social reform. But most of this was still of a temporary, piecemeal and unco-ordinated nature. What was required was a more comprehensive scheme. This was offered at the end of 1942 by William Beveridge.

The Beveridge Report and its consequences

Arthur Greenwood, the Minister without Portfolio who was in charge of reconstruction, had appointed Beveridge to be chairman of an inter-departmental committee of civil servants to inquire into the whole area of social insurance. When the controversial nature of the report emerged, it was decided that Beveridge should sign it himself and that the civil servants should be regarded as his advisers. For more than a year he drew ideas and papers together to produce his solution to poverty.

The report on *Social Insurance and Allied Services*, to give it its correct title, was published in December 1942, just after the British success at El Alamein and at a time when public confidence and spirit were running high. Indeed, the Beveridge Papers contain numerous letters, from the full range of the political spectrum, supporting all or parts of the Beveridge Report.[13] It was an immediate best seller and established three major guiding principles upon the minds of the British public. First, it claimed to be a break from the past, although in fact it relied very much on the contributory system put forward by the Liberals before the First World War. Beveridge himself wrote that: 'I am sure that it is good Liberal doctrine.'[14] Secondly, social insurance was directed at tackling want, although it assumed that it would be part of an attack upon the five giant problems of want, disease, ignorance, squalor and idleness. Thirdly, it wished to combine state and personal initiative. Beveridge assumed that any government would also wish to establish a family allowance system (as he had suggested while at the London School of Economics), create a comprehensive health service and bring about full employment. With these in place, he argued that his attack upon want would work.

The Beveridge scheme itself was not particularly revolutionary or extreme. It simply suggested that, in return for a single and uniform weekly contribution, an individual would have the right to the standard benefits of sickness, medical, unemployment, widows', orphans', old-age, maternity, industrial injuries and funeral benefits. The system would be universal and would provide subsistence benefits for all on the six principles of flat-rate subsistence benefits, flat-rate contributions, the unification of administrative responsibilities, the adequacy of bene-fits, comprehensiveness and classification (i.e. adjustment to the needs of differing circumstances).[15]

It was a vitally important document, for it built up a scheme based upon proven past experience and applied it to the whole nation. What was distinctive about it was that it was to be universal rather than selective and that dependents would also be covered by the new arrange-ments. Even more significant was the fact that this attempt to tackle want was linked to the other four giants of need in order to tackle poverty from all its angles. As Derek Fraser suggests: 'Here, in the totality of vision, was the revolutionary element in the Beveridge Report.'[16] It would work, too, if unemployment was no more than 3.5 per cent and if governments maintained a commitment to full employment, by which he meant a level of about 3 per cent.

Rodney Lowe is not so convinced of the revolutionary nature or effectiveness of the Beveridge Report. He regards it as being a flawed and illogical document. Its universalism led to vast and unnecessary expenditure, it did not eliminate the means test, which still survived for pensioners who might be expected to contribute to their rents, and it failed to consider the need to merge the tax and benefits system.[17] Above all, it did not eliminate poverty. These criticisms are, with hindsight, justified. Yet these are clearly issues that have not been resolved to this day. The recent, more selective, approach to benefits has not eliminated poverty and the major political parties are still examining, with little progress, how to merge the tax and benefit system (as we shall see in Chapter 12).

Whatever the current criticisms, it is clear that, within the context of the Second World War and in the euphoria of a recent military victory, the Beveridge Report was seen as utopia by many contemporaries. However, this was not a view held by Churchill and some of his colleagues. He was suspicious about the ultimate direction of such demands and was already on record as having noted that: 'Recon-struction was in the air' and that there was 'a dangerous optimism ... growing about post-war conditions'.[18] The Beveridge Report confirmed his suspicions. Indeed, his government refused to implement the policy straight away and this hesitancy was compounded by War Office orders to withdraw the survey produced by the Army Bureau of Current Affairs on the Beveridge Report two days after its publication. Such actions provoked the only major anti-government revolt by the Parliamentary Labour party during the Second World War.

Attlee had already given interviews to the effect that social security was effectively socialism: 'Socialism does not admit to an alternative, Social Security to us can only mean Socialism.'[19] To him and his supporters it was seen as vital that the Beveridge Report should be accepted quickly as an essential commitment by the government. But it was quite clear that Churchill intended to delay its publication and Attlee even felt that it might be saved until the end of the war to form part of the Tory programme. He was also hostile to the memorandum that Churchill sent round government circles in which it was suggested that the economics of life might be such as to force a choice between 'social insurance and other urgent claims on limited resources'. Attlee sent a counter-memorandum to the government urging that 'decisions must be taken and implemented in the field of post-war reconstruction *before* the end of the war.'[20] Churchill relented; the government accepted most of the report but gave the impression that it was committed to nothing. A Labour resolution that the government should both support and implement the Beveridge Report was defeated by 335 votes to 119, but 97 Labour MPs had voted against the government – 22 of them government ministers.

Churchill's reluctance partly stemmed from the Treasury belief that the post-war economic revival could be delayed if industry was burdened with high costs. A secret report to the Conservative party had also advised him that the Beveridge scheme was unsustainable and there were other criticisms that the children's allowance would depress wages and that fairness could not be achieved by flat-rate benefits.[21]

It is clear that the Beveridge Report had become a sensitive issue, especially after the Gallup poll in the summer of 1943, which registered a Labour lead of 11 per cent over the Conservatives, and after James Griffiths, a prominent Labour politician, had reflected that the parliamentary vote on the Beveridge Report made Labour's return at the next general election almost inevitable.[22] In the end the government was forced to set up a reconstruction committee towards the close of 1943. This saw the publication of a White Paper, *A National Health Service*, which advocated the creation of a comprehensive health service. The committee also inherited R. A. Butler's 1943 White Paper on *Educational Reconstruction*, which anticipated the 1944 Education Act and its commitment to raising the school-leaving age to 15, its creation of primary, secondary and further education and the reorganization of secondary education along Hadow and Spens lines (see the chapter on education).[23] In 1944 the reconstruction committee also put forward the White Paper on *Employment Policy* which accepted Keynes's proposals about using public expenditure to manage the economy if unemployment rose to high levels. However, this was rather modest in comparison to Beveridge's *Full Employment in a Free Society*, which offered much the same approach, although, as Beveridge noted, the government paper was essentially a 'policy of public works planned five years at a time and kept on tap to mitigate fluctuations', whilst his scheme was a 'Policy for Full Employment, defined as meaning always more vacant jobs than idle men', and was to be part of the wider scheme that he had envisaged in his 1942 Beveridge Report. It would include policies on housing, health, children's allowances, the extension of government control of industry, the organization of the mobility of labour and the creation of a battery of policies, including the vital elements of multilateral trade – full employment, balancing international accounts, and stability of economic policy.[24] In other words, the White Paper was an 'anti-cycle policy, not a policy for full employment', whilst Beveridge offered a policy for full employment.[25]

Beveridge's private publication did not appear until November 1944, by which time Parliament had already adopted the White Paper. Ernest Bevin had moved its adoption by Parliament in June 1944, but found himself opposed from within his own party by Aneurin Bevan, who felt that it was simply a device for propping up capitalism and that socialism alone was the cure for unemployment.[26]

The 'paper chase' was completed by the publication of the White Paper on *Social Insurance* in September 1944 which accepted many aspects of the 1942 Beveridge Report. The major difference was that it did not advocate subsistence benefits and it became the model of the Labour government's 1946 Insurance Act.

Despite Attlee's support for the Beveridge Report, the Labour party and the left were by no means unified in their support of Beveridge and the policies that emanated from his work. Hugh Dalton, a leading light in the Labour party, was very critical, constantly referring to the vanity of Beveridge and the 'Beveridge muddle' in his diary.[27] Whilst accepting the bulk of the Beveridge Report, acknowledging that it was a 'fine stimulating document', he warned a group of delegates from the Bishop Auckland Labour party that:

I knew Beveridge better than most people having served under and over him; that he is not 'one of us' and has no first-hand knowledge of industrial conditions; that there are a number of things in his Report to which we could not subscribe, e.g. the penalizing of miners and railway workers because their jobs are inherently more risky than a carpenter's, and the proposal to take twenty years to reach the appropriate rate of old-age pension.[28]

Others were similarly critical. Henry R. Aldridge, of the War Emergency Social Legislation Committee, wrote to Beveridge thanking him for some of his ideas contained in the 1942 report, but adding that:

> I sincerely believe that only the direct threat of the basic wage will succeed in lifting folk, whose name is legion, out of the relative helplessness in which they live in normal times. Having said this, I am sure you will understand that I shall follow this light as I see it in continuing to advocate the basic wage as a fundamental reform.[29]

If contemporary politicians expressed doubts about the Beveridge Report and the 'Welfare State' which it anticipated, their concerns are nothing as compared with the reactions of such recent right-wing writers as Max Beloff and Correlli Barnett.[30] Just as Mrs Thatcher's early traumas in office focused upon the war years and the restrictions of the 1940s, so they have criticized the social policies forced upon Britain by the Beveridge Report and wartime radicalism. To Barnett it was the 'Beveridge Report that provided the battlefield on which the decisive struggle to win a national commitment to New Jerusalem was waged and won'.[31] It was Beveridge who was the main architect of the report and the post-war Welfare State:

> As appropriate for a prophet and a brilliant Oxford intellect, Beveridge thought a lot of himself, so that righteousness went hand in hand with authoritarian arrogance and skill at manipulating the press to make him the Field Marshal Montgomery of social welfare.[32]

According to Barnett, the War Cabinet was misguided by its advisers, most notably Beveridge, into building a comprehensive Welfare State system, the 'New Jerusalem', which Britain's industrial economy has been unable to support.

Conclusion

Social reform in the Second World War has been identified with the work of Beveridge, although it was clearly much more broadly based. It is obvious that the Beveridge scheme derived its ideas from the advanced Liberal policies which he had inherited and influenced in the early part of the twentieth century. Nevertheless, there is no doubt that wartime conditions gave rise to opportunities for social reform that might possibly, in the fullness of time, have emerged in any case. But they speeded up the process and provided an element of universalism that was not apparent in social legislation and Liberal policies before

1939. In addition, the wartime situation necessitated state intervention in order to make the hospital system and other social provisions work more flexibly than ever before. Undoubtedly, then, the Second World War speeded up the process of social reform and demanded universalism. The Beveridge approach might have had its flaws, but it was the best scheme on offer at the time and many of its so-called flaws have not been tackled to this day. In any case, political parties and their governments have used the Beveridge scheme as they wished. The Attlee Labour government, returned in 1945, drew widely on Beveridge's ideas but also offered its own distinctive contribution to the modern Welfare State that it forged.

Notes

1. R. M. Titmuss, *Problems of Social Policy* (1951), p. 508.
2. Gordon Wright, *The Ordeal of Total War* (1968).
3. A. Marwick, *Britain in the Century of Total War* (1965).
4. D. Fraser, *The Evolution of the British Welfare State* (Second edition, 1983), chapter 9; P. Addison, *The Road to 1945: British Politics and the Second World War* (1975), p. 15. See also H. L. Smith (ed.), *War and Social Change in British Society and the Second World War* (Manchester, 1986).
5. A. Calder, *The People's War* (1965).
6. H. Pelling, *Britain and the Second World War* (1970).
7. C. Barnett, *The Audit of War: The Illusion and Reality of Britain as a Great Nation* (1986), agrees with this line whilst condemning Beveridge's action in forcing the Welfare State upon a reluctant wartime government.
8. *Economist*, 1 May 1943, quoted in Titmuss, *Problems of Social Policy*, p. 516.
9. Violet Markham Papers, 8/36, deposited at the British Library of Political and Economic Science.
10. *Ibid.*
11. *Ibid.*
12. Addison, *The Road to 1945*, p. 118.
13. Beveridge Papers, IIb, 42, in alphabetical order throughout 1943 and early 1944.
14. *Ibid.*, letter dated 14 January 1943.
15. *Report on Social Insurance and Allied Services*, Cmd 6404 (1942), pp. 120–2.
16. Fraser, *Evolution*, p. 216.
17. R. Lowe, *The Welfare System in Britain since 1945* (1993), pp. 129–31.
18. Quoted in Pelling, *Britain and the Second World War*, p. 170.
19. J. Harris, *Attlee* (1982), p. 220.
20. *Ibid.*
21. Fraser, *Evolution*, p. 294, quoting Clive Saxton, *Beveridge Report Criticised* (1943), p. 31.
22. Harris, *Attlee*, p. 223.
23. *Ibid.*, pp. 227–30.
24. Sir William Beveridge, *Full Employment in a Free Society* (1944), pp. 272–3.

25. *Ibid.*, p. 272.
26. Harris, *Attlee*, p. 231.
27. H. Dalton, The *Second World War Diary of Hugh Dalton 1940–45*, ed.
     B. Pimlott (1986), pp. 455, 538, 564.
28. *Ibid.*, p. 564.
29. Beveridge Papers, IIb, 42, a letter sent sometime in January 1943.
30. Barnett, *Audit of War*; M. Beloff, *Wars and Welfare* (1982).
31. *Ibid.*, p. 26.
32. *Ibid.*

CHAPTER ELEVEN

THE ATTLEE YEARS AND THE MODERN WELFARE STATE
1945–1951

Until recently, politicians of all parties have treated the Attlee years with respect, viewing them variously as evidence of the success of planned socialism, of the shift to the left, of the emergence of the modern Welfare State, of the working-out of Liberal policies forged in the 1930s and the Second World War, and even of a period of Conservative social reform – 'Butskellism'. It is only in recent years, with the emergence of 'new right', feminist and other critics, that the fundamental philosophy and achievements of the period have been seriously challenged and the Welfare State has come under attack. Yet if the Attlee years were seen until recently as the apotheosis of Labour's planned socialist economy and Welfare State by many politicians, this is not a view held by many historians. They have been less sympathetic, willing to challenge the mythology which has been built around the events of 1945–51, though not without the type of partiality shown by practising politicians.

In respect of the emergence of the Welfare State, there are two dominating questions for these years. First, to what extent was the legislation of the Labour governments a product of the social blueprint laid down during the Second World War and before? Secondly, why did the modern Welfare State emerge as it did? Why was Labour's Welfare State a form of 'social security' or 'welfare capitalism'? Was this due to the pluralism of British society or a natural product of the incremental approach that had occurred throughout the history of British social policy?

It will be argued that, whilst the modern Welfare State drew upon past experiences, particularly the far from revolutionary Beveridge Report, there was a distinctive Labour contribution in the form of the National Health Service (NHS) which diverged from the application of Beveridge's evolutionary Liberal policies. In addition, it is clear that, apart from the NHS, the majority of the social policies were built upon earlier policies and influenced by the aspirations of Labour leaders just as much as employers, doctors and civil servants.

The Welfare State: a legacy of the war?

Labour won a landslide victory in the general election of July 1945, securing 393 seats to the Conservative party's 213 and the 34 won by other political parties. Labour won 47.8 per cent of the vote compared to the 39.8 per cent of the Conservatives, thus confirming the indications of wartime polls whilst confounding those who believed that Churchill would win the election as he had won the war.

The electorate had placed their faith in Labour as the party of social reform. Apart from nationalizing various industries and services, such as coal and the railways, the Labour government focused upon the need to tackle unemployment and its attendant problems of poverty, housing, health and old age. The social problems outlined by Beveridge had to be addressed. The problem was: how was this to be done? Should Labour rely upon the past or pave out a socialist package for the future?

Despite the horrific and frightening economic problems that it faced, the new Labour government was able greatly to extend the responsibilities of the state during its early years in office. Its particular claim to fame is that it created the modern Welfare State. The Labour manifesto proclaimed that 'Labour had honoured the pledge it made in 1945 to make social security the birthright of every citizen. Today destitution has been banished. The best medical care is available to everybody in the land.'[1] Allowing for the natural exuberance of a party manifesto, the claims were largely true.

There is little doubt that Labour's social programme would not have been possible without the American loan that provided the financial flexibility essential to the expansion of social provision. If this is accepted, the main issue for many historians is the originality of the programme: was it a product of the war, the result of Labour party policies or an extension of the Liberal policies of Beveridge and Keynes? These questions have divided historians. Whilst Kenneth Morgan has emphasized the distinctive contribution of Labour after 1945, it is clear that Michael Hill believes that the battle for the Welfare State was largely won by the time Labour came to power in 1945.[2] Yet perhaps the reality is that it was a combination of both suggestions and neither is totally incompatible with the other.

Social welfare measures have never been the prerogative of any one party, but it is clear that the Labour party had laid claim to some detailed welfare planning before the Second World War. It had built up its policies during the mid-1930s and in 1937 issued *Labour's Immediate Programme*, written by Hugh Dalton, which advanced schemes of welfare and the creation of full employment. In essence, it was this programme that was offered to the electorate in the Labour party's *Let Us Face the Future*, presented in 1945. Both documents made vague reference to the need for a National Health Service, national insurance and house-building. Although specific detailed programmes were thin, it was widely assumed by the public that the Labour party would be the one likely to introduce comprehensive welfare measures.

In a sense, the distinction between the wartime coalition and Labour's contribution is artificial, for the Labour party was part of the coalition government and played its full part in the development of the blueprints of social welfare. It was Arthur Greenwood, Labour MP for Wakefield, who, as the minister concerned with reconstruction, was responsible for setting up the Inter-Departmental Committee on Social Insurance and Allied Services, out of which sprang the Beveridge Report. There were many common features between pre-war Labour policies and the Beveridge recommendations on social insurance, national health and full employment, though the Beveridge Report was far more detailed.

In as far as they shared a common objective, Labour's welfare proposals and the wartime blueprints complemented each other. In some areas the Beveridge Report did provide the basis of Labour's social welfare provisions, but in other areas it, and other wartime reports, was far removed from what the Labour government actually introduced. In fact, the Labour government's welfare programme was a rich mosaic of wartime collectivism, Labour policies and practical necessity.

In the widest sense, the Beveridge Report provided the context in which the Labour party was able to press a reluctant Churchill to accept some form of commitment to post-war reconstruction and social welfare. The wartime conditions also ensured that the 1944 Education Act, the R. A. Butler measure which recognized the need for secondary education for all in either secondary modern, central or grammar schools, would be accepted. It was this Act which Ellen Wilkinson, Minister of Education, began to apply in 1945.

Yet the strongest evidence of the influence of the Beveridge Report is the National Insurance Act of August 1946, introduced in July 1948. James Griffiths, the Minister for National Insurance, was intent upon implementing the Beveridge Report and introduced a scheme along similar lines in 1946, committed to the principle of providing a 'National Minimum Standard'.[3] It established that, in return for a single payment, an employed man would receive entitlement to seven types of benefit – sickness, unemployment, retirement pension, maternity and widows' benefits, a guardians' allowances for orphans and a death grant – all at a flat-rate level, as Beveridge had suggested. Sickness benefit was raised to 26s. per week, the standard rate also applied to retirement pensions and unemployment (with allowances of 15s. for a wife and 7s. 6d. for a child) and the time period for receiving unemployment benefit was extended. There were some differences between Labour's scheme and the Beveridge Report and the White Paper. The National Insurance Act of 1946 was less complex than the Beveridge Report and the earlier guidelines, rather more generous and demanded higher contributions. It gave unemployment benefit for six months – and up to a year for those with good contribution records – and pensions were given straight away instead of after twenty years of contributions, as Beveridge had suggested. Nevertheless, it should also be remembered that the Ministry of National Insurance had been created in 1944 to take over a whole range of health insurance, contributory, non-contributory, and supplementary pensions from the Ministry of Health and unemployment insurance. The Labour government inherited this new mechanism and the wartime assumptions that underlay it.

The Beveridge Report and the wartime blueprints had also paved the way for the introduction of the 1945 Family Allowance Act. Beveridge had been convinced of the need for family allowances and, in the inter-war years, as director of the London School of Economics had actually built a family allowance into the salaries of his staff. He had argued for a similar development and the Labour government, influenced by some within the Labour ranks, introduced the Act, though not at the level Beveridge had suggested. It established a universal 5s. (25p) child allowance, financed by the Exchequer, for second and subsequent children. An official report explained: 'The State now accepted the responsibility of making a financial contribution to the cost of bringing up every family of two or more children, regardless of the parents' means.'[4] This new allowance was paid from August 1946 and by 1949 about 4,700,000 million family allowances were being paid to 3,000,000 families, at a cost of £59 million per year.

Labour's first insurance measure, the National Insurance (Industrial Injuries) Act of August 1945, implemented in July 1946, was also broadly in line with the coalition proposals of 1944 and Beveridge's own ideas. The Beveridge Report had originally argued that all interruptions in work should be treated the same, but Beveridge came to accept that such a comprehensive arrangement was unlikely to emerge and reluctantly accepted the need for a separate industrial injuries scheme. Labour's scheme, which was separate from the National Insurance Act, paid four types of benefit: injury benefit, payable for six months; disablement benefit, payable thereafter upon the degree of disability; supplementary benefits, such as hardship allowances; and death benefits for dependents. It was established as a principle that the latter should be higher than the normal insurance benefit and it was set at 45s. (£2.25p) per week, with 16s. (80p) for a wife and 7s. 6d. (37.5p) for the first or only child.

The fourth major piece of social security legislation, the National Assistance Act, introduced in 1948, also bore the mark of Beveridge's universal approach. It emerged to deal with those either without insurance benefit entitlement or whose entitlement had run out and it set up a National Assistance Board (NAB) to act as a residual relief agency. Effectively, it took over the duties of the Unemployment Assistance Board established in 1934 and the Assistance Board established during the war. NAB's creation was seen as representing the end of the old Poor Law system and it acted as a safety net for the whole security system. As with the old PACs, the benefits were means tested, moving from the household to the personal means test in the process. Yet with allowances for rents and dependents on top of the standard £2 benefit, many married couples found themselves better off on national assistance than they would have been on insurance benefits paid out of contributions. The anomaly arose from the fact that the cost of living had gone up between 1946, when the standard insurance benefit was laid down, and 1948, when the National Assistance Act came into being. Griffiths decided that the difference would be subject to a means test. Nevertheless, the anomaly tended to imply that insurance was not at a subsistence level. Indeed, the anomaly seems to have been made worse by the fact that there were two upward adjustments of national assistance rates in 1950 and 1951, which left the standard assistance rate at £2.10s., pensions at £2.10s. and other short-term benefit rates at £2.2s. in September 1951.[5]

Housing policy also owed rather less to wartime measures than it did to pre-war Labour policies and post-war practicalities. The inter-war Labour governments had established the commitment to local authority mass housing programmes and slum clearance and the post-war Labour government undertook to build about four million houses in a decade to compensate for the shortage of 750,000 houses. Bevan followed directly in the wake of Labour's inter-war housing policy by ensuring that four out of every five houses were built by local authorities. But even this commitment to planning and local authority involvement could not ensure that there was a speedy return to the late 1930s situation, when house-building reached 350,000 per year, mainly through private building. Nonetheless, given the financial and resources difficulties, the Labour government did remarkably well to increase house-building and Bevan, with varied success, was able to push up the size of the standard house from 750 square feet to 900 square feet.

Table 11.1   House completions, 1945–1951 (000s)[6]

Year	Local authorities	Private builders	Others	Total
1945	1	0	0	1
1946	21	30	0	51
1947	87	40	1	128
1948	171	31	5	207
1949	142	25	5	172
1950	139	27	7	173
1951	142	21	9	172

Labour's policy towards personal social services also owes more to accident and necessity than to any wartime blueprint or Labour commitment. This area was not dealt with by Beveridge, nor was it specifically identified in the Labour manifesto of 1945. The fact is that local authorities began, rather slowly at first, to acquire health and caring responsibilities as a result of two actions. The first was the killing of Denis O'Neill by his foster-father in 1945, which eventually led to the Children's Act of 1948. The Monckton Inquiry suggested that existing legislation did not define clear responsibilities for children and argued that a children's committee, with its own chief officer and staff, should be set up in each local authority. The committees had to investigate cases of child neglect and establish protection. The 1948 Children's Act did this. Also, with the dismantling of the Poor Law approach and the creation of the National Assistance Act in 1948, local authorities were given the responsibility of dealing with old people. From these two starting-points, a confused package of community health provision gradually emerged. There appears to have been little ideological input from any quarter; rather, the responsibilities for the old and the poor arose out of necessity.

Obviously, it is far too simple to suggest that Labour's Welfare State was solely a legacy of the Second World War. The fact is that it drew upon some aspects of the Beveridge scheme and the work of the reconstruction committee, but it also included some of the distinctive qualities of Labour policy. Aneurin Bevan, whose proposals owed distinctly less to liberal thinkers than to the ideas of some of his colleagues, was the chief architect of the modern Welfare State.[7] To all intents and purposes, the Labour government proved to be a faithful advocate of Beveridge's scheme in the area of social security. This should cause no major surprise, given that the Labour party was part-instigator of some of the schemes envisaged. Nevertheless, there was no straight line of argument flowing from the Beveridge Report and the work of the reconstruction committee to the post-war Labour government's Welfare State and James Hinton is wrong to suggest that 'the 1946 legislation on National Insurance and on the National Health Service gave concrete form to the reconstruction promises of the wartime coalition.'[8] This was generally true of the National Insurance Act; it was most certainly not the case for the National Health Service, which was largely a product of Aneurin Bevan's initiative, as the Cabinet and government records which have recently become available have confirmed.

The National Health Service

The Beveridge Report deliberated on the need for a comprehensive health and rehabilitation service and emphasized the need for a universal contributory scheme of health provision which would make medical and dental treatment immediately available, whether in private or public hospitals. There was an assumption, however, that contemporary private and public health provision might be better organized.[9] Because there was a Beveridge-type blueprint on health, though no coalition commitment towards creating a National Health Service, the Labour party's *A National Service for Health* (1943) more or less accepted Beveridge's broad ideas, though it envisaged the creation of a 'national, full-time, salaried and pensionable service' for general practitioners.[10] Henry Willink, Churchill's Minister of Health, also offered a scheme which contemplated some state control over doctors, with patients receiving free care from family practitioners under bodies modelled upon the existing National Health Insurance committees. He even proposed that the hospital system would be under local authority control but with voluntary hospitals remaining independent and working under contract (shades, possibly, of the recent development of NHS Trusts). Yet none of these reports or schemes ever envisaged the nationalization of the hospitals which Bevan's National Health Service scheme intended nor the extent to which Bevan's scheme contemplated GPs being drawn into the NHS on a quasi-salaried basis. The fact is that the National Health Service Bill, put forward by Bevan in 1946, went much further than the wartime blueprints and it is just not good enough for James Hinton to suggest that 'the scheme did not go significantly beyond what had been accepted in principle by all during the war.'[11] This is simply not the case. Bevan's scheme was innovative, focused upon the supply rather than the demand for health, and was, in contrast to the Beveridge scheme, non-contributory. The National Insurance Act might have provided a contributory sickness benefits scheme but it did not pay for the National Health Service, only for loss of earnings. The NHS was paid for out of taxation, apart from a small contribution from national insurance, and Bevan was rightly peeved when he wrote that:

> Its revenues are provided by the Exchequer in the same way as other forms of public expenditure. I am afraid this is not yet fully understood. Many people still think they pay for the National Health Service by way of their contribution to the National Insurance Scheme. This confusion arose because the new service sounded so much like the old National Health Insurance, and it was launched on the same day as the National Insurance Scheme.[12]

The passing of the National Health Service Bill in 1946 and its introduction in 1948 were events that were accompanied by a tremendous outburst of opposition from the British Medical Association, which held plebiscites of its members to reveal their opposition to what they saw as a loss of professional independence. The National Health

Act of 1946 was, indeed, far more revolutionary than anything that had gone before. It envisaged a complete overhaul of the three areas of health provided by the individual practitioners (doctors, dentists and opticians), hospitals and the local authorities. It recognized, as suggested earlier, that the individual practitioners often felt demoralized at the low pay and high costs of their service, that hospitals were a chaotic mixture of local authority (inherited from the Poor Law) and voluntary hospitals, that they were often strapped for cash, and that local authorities assumed responsibilities for school medical services (1907), sanatoriums (1911) and welfare clinics. Cutting against many of the interested parties and buffeted about by their opposition, it emerged to offer a more centralized and efficient administrative system than ever before.

Under the Act, local authorities lost their responsibility for hospitals and 14 regional hospital boards (RHBs) were set up in their place, composed solely of persons appointed by the Minister of Health. They had the job of supervising 380 hospital management committees (HMCs), also appointed by the Minister of Health. They ran a hospital or a group of hospitals but could not fully co-ordinate hospital policy, since they were designed to include at least one major teaching hospital, which would remain independent under their own boards of governors. Their policy-making powers were even more circumscribed due to the fact that family doctors, dentists and opticians remained independent under their own executive councils, which were an updated version of the insurance committees introduced under the National Insurance Act of 1911. Given that the local authority health and welfare services were separate, this means that there were still three sets of health organizations working in their own separate spheres. In other words, there were still problems, even if the chaos was less than before. Invariably, the implementation of the new structure did create serious problems. The general practitioners were unhappy, the local authorities felt aggrieved and the leading figures in the Labour government became concerned at the escalating costs of the NHS within months of it being introduced in February1948.

It was the GPs who posed the most serious problem for Bevan and the NHS. The details of their opposition have frequently been recorded. Within weeks of the passing of the Act, a poll of GPs indicated that almost two-thirds were opposed to participating in the new service. In December 1946 a special meeting of the British Medical Association voted by 252 to 17 to call off all discussions with Bevan. He decided to break down the BMA to capture the support of the GPs. Consultants were offered 'merit awards', allowed to work part-time in hospitals for high salaries and permitted to continue in private practice and have their own pay-beds in hospitals for private patients. Lord Moran of the Royal College of Surgeons helped to force the BMA, led by Dr Guy Dain (president) and Dr Charles Hill (secretary), to re-open negotiations with Bevan but to little avail. The doctors were concerned that they would become salaried civil servants, wished to continue to be able to sell their private practices, which had often cost them £2,000–£3,000 before the Second World War, were concerned about the fairness of the dismissal procedures and also about the possibility that they could be directed towards working in 'undoctored' areas. It was these issues which were still dominating thinking in March 1947, when another referendum ended with a 9 to 1 vote against the new health service. Tact was never Bevan's strong point and it was at this juncture that he referred to the doctors' leaders as a 'small body of politically poisoned people' engaged in 'a squalid political conspiracy'.

The sticking points for the doctors were the sale of the goodwill of practices – which the 1946 Act had expressly forbidden and on which Bevan would not budge – and the creation of a salaried profession. In order to compensate doctors for their inability to sell goodwill, Bevan set aside £66 million from which they could draw their share upon retirement. On the second issue, although the 1946 Act gave Bevan the right to create a fully salaried profession, he had no intention of doing so. However, Bevan's famous quip that: 'There is all the difference in the world between plucking fruit when it is ripe and when it is green' upset the doctors, who saw Bevan progressing towards a salaried profession.[13] Yet opposition to this melted away quickly once Bevan announced, in April 1948, that a salaried service would not be introduced without a further Act of Parliament and that most doctors would be paid solely by capitation fees. This led Lord Moran to plead for the acceptance of the new system in the House of Lords and in another ballot the number of doctors opposed to the health service fell from 17,000 to 10,000. By that time a quarter of the doctors in England and about one-third in Scotland and Wales had already signed up for the health service and the BMA decided, on 28 May 1948, to join the NHS. More than 18,000 had done so by the end of 1948. The creation of the National Health Service was, by any terms, a success. Bevan could rightly stress, with a certain amount of pride, that the 'National Health Service and the Welfare State have come to be used as interchangeable terms ...'[14]

The removal of local authority control of hospitals and of some of the other sectors of the health service was less controversial, but it did create short-term problems. During the war it had seemed that the creation of a local authority based system would have been logical, except that the doctors feared becoming municipal employees more than they were later to fear becoming civil servants. It was also evident that the larger councils would have had to incorporate the borough councils, which, since the former were largely Conservative-dominated and the latter Labour-controlled, was unlikely to occur.

After Labour's victory in 1945 it appeared that the local authorities would still have a major part to play in running hospitals. The Labour manifesto of 1945 had said nothing about the need to build up a centrally controlled NHS and Herbert Morrison was quick to remind Bevan of this in Cabinet on 18 October 1945:

> It would be unwise to underrate the pride which local people took in their hospitals, whether voluntary or municipal, and he feared that the Minister's scheme, for which there was no authority in the Party programme ... would arouse such a stir of opposition as to jeopardize the passage of the National Health Service Bill in the current Session.[15]

Bevan retorted by suggesting that the only way to make hospital services efficient was to centralize responsibility and he won support for his schemes from Ellen Wilkinson and other Cabinet colleagues.

Despite this victory, Bevan found Morrison, who had been appointed Lord President of the Privy Council in 1945, remained his major political opponent within the Labour government. The formal duties of Morrison's post were hardly demanding, for he was responsible for the work of the Privy Council Office and presented the business to the King and the Council when it met, which was infrequently. But the post brought with it the position of deputy premier and the leadership of the House of Commons. Between 1945 and 1947 the Privy Council Office gained additional responsibilities – most notably, that of co-ordinating the principal measures of nationalization and planning Labour's legislative programme over five years. In effect, Morrison was to act as a sort of overlord on the home front.[16] He was the fulcrum around which the Labour policy revolved and was seen, especially by his critics, as the personification of the domestic policy of the Labour government. But the Labour left also saw Morrison as the stumbling block to the rapid transition to socialism which it sought, though it was his battles with Bevan which produced most animus. Just at the moment that Morrison was pronouncing the need for 'consolidation', Bevan was presiding over the formation of the NHS, which was to prove an increasing financial burden to the Labour administration, faced with the need to implement the Chancellor of the Exchequer, Stafford Cripps's, programme of austerity. The widely divergent policies being advocated by Morrison and Bevan were to make the provision of the NHS one of the most contentious issues faced by the Labour government – ultimately leading to Bevan's highly emotional resignation from government in 1951.

The NHS came into existence in July 1948, at a time when Sir Stafford Cripps was attempting to control public expenditure in the wake of the Dalton years of expansion. When the decision to form the NHS had been taken in 1946, it was estimated that it would cost £126 million. During its first year, 1948–9 (nine months), expenditure exceeded £278 million and by 1951–2 it was in the region of £400 million.[17] By December 1948 about 21 million people had signed acceptance forms for medical treatment and there were about 19 million insured workers on doctors' lists. Prescriptions, which were 7 million per month under the old scheme, rose to 13.5 million in September 1948 and to almost 19 million a month in early 1951. Dental services, planned for a level of 4 million per year, rose to about 8 million per year. Similar growth was to be found in the provision of spectacles.

As Cabinet and government records now reveal, the conflict over finance and expenditure first emerged in the autumn of 1949, at a time when the Labour government had decided to devalue the pound. Cabinet and committee discussions were quite clearly heading towards an attack upon the finances of the health service and Bevan pre-empted serious debate by announcing at a Labour rally in Staffordshire on 25 September that:

I have made up my mind that the National Health Service is not going to be touched, and there is no disposition by the government to touch it. The government had made up their mind to solve the problem without ruining the social services, and the health service is sacrosanct.[18]

On 6 October, holding his first press conference for three years, he said that the government had 'set their face against a Health Tax, if what was meant was a payment made by a patient at the moment he needed treatment'.[19]

Bevan's statements clearly reflected the debate which had been going on within government circles for some time, a debate which continued well beyond the Cabinet meeting on 20 October 1949, when Morrison raised the possibility of charges on teeth and spectacles and which Morgan suggests saw the end of the preliminary attempts to reduce health costs.[20] In fact, the debate raged within government circles well into the spring of 1950.

The whole episode stemmed from the attempt by Cripps to reduce and control public expenditure. He and Morrison were already discussing such matters by September 1949; hence Bevan's attempt to pre-empt decisions. The matter was raised in Cabinet on 20 October and Cripps sent a letter to Bevan on 28 November suggesting a variety of ways of reducing NHS costs, including the removal of merit awards for doctors and the introduction of prescription charges.[21] Morrison and his advisers, E. M. Nicholson and Miss Jane Lidderdale, continued to press for further cuts and orchestrated the increasing isolation of

Bevan from the rest of the Cabinet by demanding that he should present a paper to Cabinet explaining how he intended to reduce the costs of the NHS.[22] It was Nicholson who, in his memorandums, paved the way for the final showdown. He informed Morrison of his fears and remedies:

> It ought, however, to be emphasized that however much the Minister of Health can say on the virtue and merits of vast expenditure on the sick he is leading the government straight for another 1931 crisis in the very near future, and unless the government can show that it knows how to adopt a pace of development of the Health Service which the National economy can bear something will have to go before long.
>
> Probably the best approach would be for the Cabinet to set a ceiling figure on the National Health Service as on the Defence Services ... £300 millions. This would give the Health Service well over double the figure (£126 millions) on the basis of which the government decided to go forward with the Service in 1946.[23]

The emotive threat of a repeat of 1931 carried much weight with a minister who had lived through those events.

Bevan's response to these pressures was to suggest that Labour's supporters would not understand any withdrawal from a completely free health service. He also urged delay due to the impending general election. Replying to Cripps on 9 December 1949, he wrote that: 'I think that a proposal to charge two or three shillings for some 40 per cent of "prescriptions" would give rise to a lot of surprise, resentment, and, in many cases, hardship.'[24] He was determined to protect the NHS and concluded his letter with an emotive flourish:

> I think we must see the problem clearly and make up our minds; either we must stand to the health service as a whole, sticking to all principles on which we founded it, or else we should clearly admit that – much as we still believe that it was, and is, the right service to aim at – our economic position renders it impossible to have it for some years to come; in the latter event, we leave it to the statute books for the future but in the meantime substitute a revised, interim and austerity service being worked out on different principles and after an intensive review of the whole field. I personally should reject the latter, as you know. But I should infinitely prefer to tackle it that way, if financially it proved essential, than to go on with a whittling away which brings small savings coupled with large discredit in many people's eyes.

In fact, he was being less than fair in his assessment, for he was drawing too sharp a contrast between the universal and free provision of health care and the rejection of that principle which some relatively minor changes would bring. The principle of free provision would have been destroyed, though what remained would have been immeasurably better than the situation before the war. In any case, Bevan had no intention of drawing up any scheme of cuts, even when specifically asked to do so. The timing of the 1950 general election had put paid to the immediate debate and Bevan indicated to Attlee his reluctance to take action:

> You have, no doubt, noted that at the last meeting of the Lord President's Committee, it was decided in my absence (unfortunately I had a slight cold and could not attend) that should at once proceed with discussions with chemists and doctors about the arrangements for charging a shilling [5p] for prescriptions, despite the fact that because of exemptions the savings will now be no more than £5 millions.
>
> I have submitted a paper to the Cabinet but it was not possible to discuss it on Tuesday. As you no doubt know, I am now leaving London on a long speaking tour for the Party and then must visit my own constituency.
>
> I am, therefore, instructing my office not to proceed with the discussions until after the Election. This will not prejudice a final decision on the question of making a charge, but I am sure that you will appreciate that to start discussions with the British Medical Association, including Charles Hill, who is a Conservative candidate ... would be the height of folly, for our proposals would be certain to become known and would lend themselves to grotesque misrepresentation by the Opposition.[25]

Bevan had his way and the issue of health charges subsided for the time being, as the Labour government fought the 'demure' general election of February 1950.[26] Bevan was kept away from the limelight, played down its radicalism and was returned with 315 seats, compared to 298 for the Conservatives and 9 for the Liberals. With its narrow majority, the new Labour government seemed reluctant to become involved in controversial and expensive policies, especially at a time when the Korean war threatened to bring about huge increases in the defence budget. In an atmosphere of political hesitancy and economic retrenchment, the rapidly rising costs of the NHS were bound to throw Bevan into conflict with his Cabinet colleagues.

Yet the new assault on the NHS finances was conducted with rather more stealth than previously. Although Bevan and Cripps had clashed over the proposed NHS charges in March and April 1950, what had initially appeared to be a victory for Bevan proved to be a triumph for Morrison and Cripps. Having reversed his immediate views, he had 'forced the Chancellor then to drop the charges in favour of a ceiling on Health expenditure' – though this was the fall-back position that Nicholson had suggested to Morrison.[27] This was followed by Bevan's switch from the Ministry of Health and his appointment to the Ministry of Labour in mid-January 1951 and the removal of his former post from the Cabinet. Bevan was no longer in a position to fight off the attacks upon the NHS. Marginalized, his only recourse was to resign from the Cabinet in one of the most celebrated episodes in British political history.

Hugh Gaitskell, who had become Chancellor of the Exchequer after Cripps in October 1950, announced his intention to levy NHS charges on dentures and optical services to the Cabinet Committee on Health in March and April 1951, following intensive discussions with the new health minister and various committees of government. The precise proposal was that half the cost of dentures, £1 for each pair of spectacles (other than for children) and a 1s. prescription charge should be raised from patients. Bevan made it clear that 'he had always been opposed to the introduction of charges for dentures and spectacles'.[28]

In the next few days Bevan threatened resignation and informed Dalton that he was 'opposed to rootless men like Gaitskell ... who are dismantling the welfare state'.[29] After some vacillation, he resigned on 22 April 1951, to be followed into political exile by Harold Wilson, president of the Board of Trade, and John Freeman, a junior minister of supply. Bevan left, ranting about the threat which Gaitskell, 'the second Snowden', posed to his NHS. The formal comment of the Cabinet was more sober: 'It had not been found possible to find a form of words which would satisfy the Minister of Labour, and he had now resigned from the government.'[30] The Cabinet had clearly found in favour of Gaitskell, who had also threatened resignation if the charges were not announced.

Conclusion

It is generally accepted that the 'classic' Welfare State emerged in Britain during the 1940s. What is not so clear is whether or not it was new. Derek Fraser has argued that: 'The British Welfare State was not born – it had evolved.'[31] As regards the essential social security aspects of the Welfare State, this was correct, but for the NHS, housing and some other welfare provisions, it is clear that there was a distinctive element that owed much to the ideas of socialists in the 1930s and 1940s. The Beveridge Report had its limits. But it is not at all clear what had emerged. There was no sign of the more state-based, less contributory and more generous provisions of welfare to be found in Scandinavia. Instead there was a cautious, conservative and more subsistence-based, if universal, system, which might be more accurately described as welfare capitalism. As will be stressed in the next chapter, it was this system which, until the Thatcher years, proved perfectly acceptable to the Conservative party as well as the Labour party. Even the Civil Service appears to have been happy with the arrangement, since the Labour governments had always made a determined attempt to work with them. Only the NHS, the coping-stone of Labour's Welfare State, stood out against the incremental build-up of the insurance principle throughout the twentieth century. Yet even this was accepted quickly as an essential item in what the British public saw to be their Welfare State. By 1951, then, no political party was showing any inclination to dismantle the British Welfare State. That propensity did not occur until the mid-1970s, when economic conditions worsened and when critics began to emerge on both the left and the right.

Notes

1.   The Labour Party, *Labour Believes in Britain* (1949).
2.   K. O. Morgan, *Labour in Power 1945–51* (Oxford, 1984), and M. Hill, *The Welfare State in Britain* (Aldershot, 1993), chapter 2, pp. 11–24.
3.   Morgan, *Labour in Power*, pp. 170–3.
4.   *Report of the Ministry of National Insurance, 1944–1949* (Cmd 7955, 1950), p. 5. Also quoted in D. Fraser, *The Evolution of the British Welfare State* (Second edition, 1983), p. 227.
5.   Hill, *The Welfare State in Britain*, p. 31.
6.   *Ibid.*, p. 37.
7.   J. Campbell, *Nye Bevan and the Mirage of British Socialism* (1987); J. Campbell, 'Demythologising Nye Bevan', *History Today* 37 (1987), pp. 13–18.
8.   J. Hinton, *Labour and Socialism: A History of the British Labour Movement* (Brighton, 1983), pp. 169–70.
9.   *Social Insurance and Allied Services*, report by William Beveridge (1942), pp. 158–9.
10. H. Pelling, *The Labour Governments 1945–1951* (1984), p. 103.
11. Hinton, *Labour and Socialism*, p. 170.
12. A. Bevan, *In Place of Fear* (1952), p. 80.
13. Fraser, *Evolution*, p. 236; B. Watkin, *The National Health Service* (1987), p. 21; R. Lowe, *The Welfare State in Britain since 1945* (1993), p. 173.
14. Lowe, *Welfare State since 1945*, p. 173.
15. Cab. 128, Cab. 43 (45), 18 October 1945; K. Laybourn (ed.), *The Labour Party 1881–1951: A Reader in History* (Gloucester, 1988), p. 132.
16. B. Donoghue and G. W. Jones, *Herbert Morrison* (1973), pp. 348–51.
17. Cab. 124, file 1187, memorandum of Miss J. H. Lidderdale to Herbert Morrison, Lord President of the Council, 4 October 1949, suggests that expenditure would rise to £356 million between 1950–1. C. Webster, *The Health Service since the War* (1988), p. 136, provides the parliamentary estimates for health and examined gross totals, appropriation in aid and

net totals. He suggests that net expenditure was £208.3 million in 1948–9, an excess of £58.6 million, £358.5 million in 1949–50, an excess of £98.8 million, £392.9 million in 1950–1, and £399.5 million in 1951–2, about £1.4 million above the original estimate. This is net, not gross, expenditure.

18.   *The Times*, 26 September 1949; cutting in Cab. 124, file 1187, memorandum of Lidderdale to Morrison.
19.   *The Telegraph*, 7 October 1949, cutting in Cab. 124, file 1187.
20.   Morgan, *Labour in Power*, pp. 400–1.
21.   Letter from Cripps to Bevan, 28 November 1949, Cab. 124, file 1187.
22.   Cab. 124, file 1187. Also quoted in letter of E. M. Nicholson to Lord President (Morrison), 18 January 1950.
23.   Cab. 124, file 1188, letter dated 11 March 1950.
24.   Cab. 124, file 1187, letter from Bevan to Cripps, 9 December 1949.
25.   *Ibid.*, letter from Bevan to Attlee, 2 February 1950.
26.   Morgan, *Labour in Power*, p. 403.
27.   *Ibid.*, p. 444.
28.   Cab. 128/1, Cab. 25, 9 April 1951.
29.   Morgan, *Labour in Power*, p. 450; Dalton's diary, 9 April 1951.
30.   Cab. 128/1, Cab. 30 (51), 23 April 1951.
31.   Fraser, *Evolution*, p. 239.

CHAPTER TWELVE

THE WELFARE STATE: CONSENSUS AND CHALLENGE
1951–1993

By 1951 the British Welfare State had become an almost untouchable institution, the 'sacred cow' of British politics. This situation continued almost unchallenged for more than twenty years as successive governments, Conservative as well as Labour, maintained and developed the Welfare State as the central plank of the so-called post-war political consensus. But the survival and development of the Welfare State was based upon continued economic growth. In the mid-1950s this link raised few concerns and Anthony Crosland, amongst others, argued that unleashed economic growth made a radical welfare programme viable.[1] Yet the relative economic decline of Britain, particularly since the mid-1960s, and the rising challenge of the monetarist policies that have become associated with 'Thatcherism' have done much to undermine confidence in the continuance of even a welfare capitalist Welfare State. The Labour government's move to monetarism in 1975 saw the abandonment of full employment as a central plank of welfare policy. By 1979 the last vestiges of a dying Keynesian economic approach were being laid to rest and, with the return of a Conservative party under the leadership of Margaret Thatcher, to whom consensus politics was anathema, it became clear that the whole relationship between the Welfare State and Britain's economic performance would be re-examined. The introduction of a supply-led, rather than demand-led, approach to competition and output meant that the 'Beveridge revolution', the initiatives of the post-war Attlee government and the 'post-war consensus' would be scrutinized and brought into line with current economic monetarist directives.

Nevertheless, whilst there may have been something of a post-war consensus operating on welfare matters up to 1979, one must be aware of the emerging tensions within the Welfare State before that watershed date and that, since that time, widespread, if not universal criticism, has placed its future on the political agenda. Indeed, the 1981 OECD pamphlet, *The Welfare State in Crisis*, seems to have highlighted the problem of the structure of welfare states throughout the world which has dominated political thinking ever since.[2] The British Welfare State is changing to meet the challenge, but it will be political decisions, not economic issues alone, that will determine whether or not the Welfare State becomes more individualistic or collectivist over time.

Post-war consensus, 1951–1979?

The British Welfare State was, and still is, an interconnected network of support agencies, each one under the financial and directional control of government. Prior to 1945, social welfare had been a rather haphazard arrangement of social benefits that attempted to alleviate the worst symptoms of poverty. During the Second World War British social policy became more direct and positive. The Beveridge Report laid out the future lines of social policy, the Attlee Labour governments built upon this by adding the coping-stone of the National Health Service and Keynesian interventionist economics paved the way for what became a minimalist Welfare State, but with an easily sustainable system of benefits and provisions. These were designed to tackle Beveridge's five giant evils of want, disease, ignorance, squalor and idleness.

The social and economic evils of the pre-1945 decades were to be attacked by introducing 'welfare capitalism' in the form of social and economic protection, as we have already seen in the previous chapter. The National Insurance Act of 1946 provided the sick, widowed and unemployed with protection based upon a tripartite arrangement of financial participation from the employer, worker and the state. The 1948 National Assistance Act provided a safety net for those who fell through, or were not eligible for, the benefits of the National Insurance Act, and the National Health Act of 1946 provided free and universal medical care and services from 1948. Education was to be provided for all up to the age of 15, through the 1944 Education Act, and unemployment was to be tackled using Keynes's demand-driven and planned economics which rejuvenated British industry via the nationalization of some key industries and governmental industrial initiatives. In a sense, the whole concept of the Welfare State was that it was to be seen as both an economic and a social package. This intent should be noted, since it has figured prominently in recent debates.

There have been many explanations for the creation of the British Welfare State. The mainstream argument, both in the past and the present, has been that the side effects of capitalism have necessitated government intervention. Voluntary agencies had failed, the Second World War had produced popular participation in social conditions, and Labour's welfare provision was the first stage in the implementation of socialism. The end product was a type of welfare, or reform, capitalism. Socialist and feminist critics have suggested that the current weakness of the Welfare State is that it does not go far enough, it is too bureaucratic and not sufficiently sensitive to the specific needs of women, whose dependency upon husbands is reflected in a welfare system which condemns them to being second-class citizens. Nevertheless, it can be developed in order to rectify the situation.

In contrast, the classic Marxist argument has been that the Welfare State is a defence mechanism for capitalism, offering minimal protection from poverty and instilling social control. All governments under capitalism are there to protect the interests of capital. Yet in order to do this, it is necessary for them to placate the working class and to deflect the criticisms that might arise from the unequal and class-based conditions of the system. In other words, the British Welfare State is an end in itself; it was never meant to go further, for it was a dupe to the working class. Not surprisingly, Marxism has played a very small role in the discussions on social welfare provision in Britain.[3]

After the defeat of Attlee's Labour government in 1951, the country entered a period often referred to as the 'post-war consensus'. There are some writers on the subject, such as Ben Pimlott, who maintain that this consensus never emerged, but the majority appear to recognize that, in most areas of social policy, there was little real difference between Conservative and Labour governments. The leftward stance and popularity of the Attlee governments ensured that mainstream politics would adopt a centre-left approach. Yet a few on the hard-line left did seriously believe that a Tory government would undo the reforms achieved between 1945 and 1951. Alice Bacon, addressing the TUC in 1951, explained:

> All in Britain that suffered unemployment between the wars look to us with hope. They dread, and they are right to dread, the return of a Tory Government. They dread the re-emergence of unemployment, reductions in social services and the catastrophic price increases that would surely follow a Tory victory.[4]

Indeed, there were reasons for such concern, since Enoch Powell and other leading Tories had, as early as 1948, begun to question the rising level of expenditure on the Welfare State. Subsequently, in 1957–8, Peter Thorneycroft, the Conservative Chancellor of the Exchequer, had raised the prospect of cutting welfare provision and raising interest rates from 2 per cent to 7 per cent, although Harold Macmillan acted quickly to remove 'Mr Seven Per Cent' from his government.

Nothing could have been further removed from reality, however. The Conservative government of 1951 – and all successive governments up to 1975, when Dennis Healey introduced monetarism – accepted the need for a universalistic Welfare State. Social cohesion was the order of the day; the Welfare State and Keynesian economics ensured continuity. The primacy of these two factors became the motivating force of British politics; Butskellist collectivism had been created without disturbing the fundamental premise of capitalist relations.

On the one hand, then, Britain was entering a period of unparalleled social and economic change epitomized by consensus and the continuation of existing policy. On the other hand, it was possible that Britain was storing up problems, since social cohesion depended upon economic performance.

The British Welfare State is a social package whose survival depends upon several factors. The successful performance of the economy is the most important. The 'new society' was forged upon the principles of economic participation and popular consultation between the government, the employers and the trade unions. When the economy was strong, as it was in the 1950s and early 1960s, the government was able to intervene directly in subsidies without necessarily affecting the overall economy. This can be seen in the fact that full employment increased and stimulated growth in the welfare sector. Such a situation was regarded as beneficial to all elements of society. Participation, social welfare, and social cohesion were policies that, in theory, would enhance the economic and social infrastructure of the country.

Anthony Crosland's book, *The Future of Socialism*, reflected these new sentiments in its attempt to deflect the Labour party from its nationalization programme. Angry that British society was class-ridden and faced with social inequality and class consciousness, Crosland demanded a social revolution to follow up the Labour party's victorious campaign of 1945. A Labour government needed to extend egalitarian changes in the distribution of wealth, to bring about the extension of educational opportunity and the scope of social services. Crosland argued that, taken together, these policies were far more relevant to the future of socialism than planning or nationalization. The issue of planning, he regarded as settled: the objective should not be to draft an overall plan but simply to ensure adequate industrial investment and necessary social expenditure. Nationalization was not needed and the focus of Crosland's book was to extend liberty and justice within an expanding industrial economy. The Welfare State was to be at the centre of an appeal for socialism in an attempt to level the population upwards. The dominating themes were thus economic growth, the redistribution of wealth through the Welfare State and equity.[5]

The famous statement of Harold Macmillan in 1957 that 'most of our people have never had it so good' endorsed this optimistic picture of existing conditions and opportunities.[6] In such boom conditions the new policies that had emerged with the Welfare State were not under attack. It was only when matters began to go wrong that the theory behind the Welfare State was to be called into question.

Governments that spend, we have been told by both the Labour government of 1974–9 and the new right from the 1960s to the present day, must – first and foremost – have access to financial resources. *The Future of Socialism* recognized this. The problem is that economic growth began to lag in the late 1960s and the 1970s – and, indeed, has done so ever since. Crosland reflected upon this problem in his famous speech to local government in 1975,[7] and the information coming from the Institute of Economic Affairs (the think-tank of the new right) expressed concerns about the burden that the Welfare State placed upon a failing economy.[8] An expanding and effective Welfare State could be achieved by increasing either taxation or public borrowing or both, and by ensuring that the industrial base of the country is healthy and profitable. The problem was that governments between 1945 and 1979 increased spending, taxation and public borrowing but were unable to maintain a healthy industrial economy. Despite rising government expenditure, unemployment was on the increase and fiscal crises were epitomized by the stop–go policies of deflation and reinflation and Britain's decline in world trade.

The development of social policy, 1951–1979

Notwithstanding the fact that the Welfare State was coming under strain by the late 1960s and 1970s, it is clear that there were major extensions in the 'Attlee' pattern of social policy until the Labour government's withdrawal from its financial commitment to full employment in 1975, although this was to be partly offset by the moves towards relating benefits to earnings and means testing.

Full employment was one of the basic assumptions of the Beveridge Report, for it was felt that this would help to generate growth and permit the expansion of welfare provision. In fact, employment was maintained at very high levels between 1945 and 1975, until Callaghan admitted in 1976 that the expenditure level required for full employment was no longer viable. The 1944 White Paper on employment policy was thus being abandoned. This was despite the fact that, under the Industry Act of 1972 and other legislation, the government had expanded its ability to intervene in British industry. The fact is that the economic stop–go policies had led to some doubts as to whether Keynesian demand-management or the private economy should take care of employment.

The provision of universal social security was also central to the Beveridge Report. The provision had to be comprehensive and adequate. The result, of course, was that there was vast expenditure on social security provision, a situation made worse by the fact that rising inflation and other factors increased costs. Despite this, it was noted that the number of people living in poverty had increased substantially (based on 140 per cent of national assistance plus rent), from 600,000 in 1964 to 4 million in 1974 and 7.5 million in 1984.[9] Something had to be done.

Faced with rising costs and increasing levels of poverty, governments gradually drifted away from the Beveridge principles, although such moves were often offset by the need to implement some political commitment. In 1957 the Conservative government initiated the savings process by reducing the Treasury contribution to the national insurance fund. As a result, the Treasury contribution fell from 33 per cent in 1957 to 14 per cent in 1973–4. Insurance was to be paid increasingly out of employer and employee contributions. In the 1960s Labour governments found it difficult to keep their promise to upgrade national insurance benefits in line with earnings – despite some increases in 1966, 1967 and 1969. The growth of means testing in many other areas of social security in the 1960s and 1970s also served further to undermine the Beveridge principle of a flat-rate benefit. Indeed, in 1966 the Labour government, faced with financial difficulties, applied the earnings-related rule to unemployment, sickness, industrial injury and widows' benefit. By 1975 there were 45 major means-tested benefits being operated under the 1975 Social Security Act. By the late 1970s, then, the targeting of beneficiaries had replaced the universalism offered by Beveridge. This was evident in many, if not all, of the reforms that followed.

In 1966 the National Assistance Act was abolished and was replaced by a Supplementary Benefit Commission, under which the payment of supplementary benefit was no longer to be discretionary. This commission led a chequered career before being subjected, in the late 1970s, to a review by David Donnison which suggested that benefits would have to be means tested.

In 1971 the Conservative government's family income supplement was introduced, guaranteeing to pay the low paid half the difference between their gross pay and the appropriate level of supplementary benefit. It was a means-tested benefit for which low-income families with children could apply and lasted until 1986, when it was replaced by family credit, which operated on very much the same principles.

Up to the late 1970s, however, the biggest change was the action initiated by Barbara Castle, Secretary of State for the Department of Health and Social Security between the spring of 1974 and the spring of 1976. With her Social Security Act of 1975, all insurance contributions were made earnings-related; the Beveridge class 4 contributions (made by those of working age not gainfully employed) and women were allowed to opt out of paying full insurance contributions. There were some advantages derived from this, but it was the other legislation that she offered which proved to be more contentious and long-lasting. The Child Benefit Act of 1975, passed in May and introduced in August, replaced the family allowance and the child tax allowance with a child benefit paid by the state for each child, including the first. Nonetheless, interim measures had to be taken until the Chancellor of the Exchequer

announced that it would be instituted officially in April 1977; under the
Conservative administrations since 1970 the allowance has not always
been uprated.

More controversial was the decision to introduce earnings-related
pensions. The 1959 National Insurance Act established a graduated pension scheme which gave some growth in benefits for extra contributions,
although it was not inflation-proofed. Richard Crossman campaigned,
unsuccessfully, for inflation-proofed pensions in 1969 and Sir Keith
Joseph suggested a far less generous state scheme, designed to encourage
contributors to opt out of the initial scheme and not inflation-proofed.
Barbara Castle's proposal was far more ambitious, for she outlined a state
scheme that would be better than most private schemes (which would
also have to reach the same standard to be approved). The Social
Security Pensions Act of 1975 guaranteed everyone an inflation-proof,
flat-rate and earnings-related pension and allowed women to take the
best twenty years of their working life as the basis for their pension
rights. This state earnings-related pensions scheme, SERPS for short,
was subject to some delays, largely because Barbara Castle left office with
Harold Wilson in 1976 and James Callaghan, the new Prime Minister,
was rather hesitant about the costs involved. It was eventually introduced
in 1978, although in 1984 Norman Fowler and the Conservative government began to query the expenditure involved. Nevertheless, the passing
of the Pensions Bill was a remarkable achievement, recognized by the
'great Pensions Bill party' of 27 July 1975, presided over by an ebullient
Barbara Castle celebrating her success.[10]

Effectively, then, despite some progressive movement, the thrust of
developments in social security was towards challenging the Beveridge
principles. By the mid-1970s the welfare system was no longer comprehensive or universal. Targeting and attempting to reduce the costs of this
ever-expanding service had become the key strategies of government.

Even the National Health Service was not entirely impervious to
such changes. Faced with an enormous burden of ill health which had
been stored up before its creation, its costs increased rapidly. Nonetheless, its universalism ensured its popularity, despite the fact that, up to
the mid-1970s, it was incapable of working efficiently and of providing
an effective health care arrangement. There was some consolidation to
counter this problem but improvements were slow, partly due to the fact
that the Guillebaud Report of the early 1950s suggested that the NHS
was working well and required no fundamental changes. Indeed, change
was slow to come, even though there were some moves towards
community care.

Educational changes were rather more dramatic. The 1944 Butler
Act provided the basis for secondary education for all within a tripartite
system, but the Labour party was never happy with a division which

essentially confined the working-class child to secondary schools whilst permitting the middle-class child to attend grammar schools, with a few working-class children slipping into the hybrid institutions. Educational equality became a major issue on the political agenda. Despite the large number of reports produced in the late 1950s and early 1960s on primary and secondary education, the most important development was the ending of this tripartite system and the introduction of comprehensive schooling. Circular 10/65 was the means by which Anthony Crosland, the Secretary of State for Education, requested local education authorities to submit plans for the reorganization of secondary education along comprehensive lines. Even though Margaret Thatcher withdrew the circular in the Heath Conservative government of the early 1970s, it is clear that the momentum towards comprehensivization continued.

There was almost equal contention in housing, where the Labour government pressed for more local authority housing whilst the Conservatives have moved increasingly towards the idea of a property-owning democracy. Consequently, the Labour party/government introduced the Town and Country Planning Act in 1947, the 1967 Land Commission Act and the 1975 Community Land Act to enable the state and local authorities to buy land, with the 1975 Act allowing local authorities to buy land below its full 'developmental' value. The Conservative party took the opposite view and, feeling that the wartime housing shortage was over, abolished the two land commissions in 1953 and 1971, respectively. The issue of betterment taxes and a variety of associated issues also emerged to divide the two major political parties

Ignoring the politics involved, house-building was remarkably successful in overcoming the housing shortage of the immediate post-war period. The local authorities continued to build houses at a pace, although they never again reached the 1948 peak of 217,000 houses, fluctuating up and down, and reaching 176,000 in 1951, 181,000 in 1956 and 176,000 in 1976. In contrast, of course, private building increased from 25,000 in 1951 to 209,000 in 1966, although it fell away to 155,000 in 1976.[11] State housing became less dominant as time progressed, and the 1980s saw the rising importance of private housing.

The personal social services, mainly the residual services provided by, or through, local government, became a growing, if rather neglected, section of the Welfare State, providing care, social work and homes for children and the aged. From 1948 onwards each local authority had to have a children's committee, but other welfare functions were divided between health and welfare committees. There was clearly a sense of unity in dealing with children, but they did not have the right to deal with prevention and neglect until after the committee of 1960 (Cmnd 1191) and the subsequent Children and Young Persons Act of 1963.

The Seebohm Committee of the late 1960s did, however, see the need for greater unity within local authority provision for children, the aged and others, and saw its policies partly implemented in the 1970 Local Authority Social Services Act, which demanded that each local authority establish a social services department, that these should be headed by a director approved by the Secretary of State for Health and Social Security, and that research and training should be encouraged. This Act and its proposals were criticized, and there were problems with the probation services and many others. Nevertheless, the overall impact was to see the growth of a statutory personal social service which grew rapidly after the Seebohm Report into a more comprehensive and professionalized service. Thus, local authority growth was massive and overwhelmed the care provided by organized voluntary bodies.

The end product of all these developments in social provision was that the British Welfare State grew rapidly in cost and range. There is no doubt that it raised standards and improved the quality of life for many. Although it has been criticized for inefficiency, and there is evidence of this in some sectors, Rodney Lowe concludes that 'the classic welfare state represented a general gain in efficiency in relation to both expenditure and the distribution of resources.'[12]

Nevertheless, such argument and evidence have not impressed the critics of the Welfare State, who feel both that its enormous cost is unsustainable and that its redistribution of wealth and income is undesirable. The demand-led management approach of Beveridge and Keynesian economic interventionism came under attack and were effectively being abandoned by the mid-1970s. The Labour government's refusal to buy Britain out of depression and unemployment in the mid-1970s certainly encouraged the critics of the Welfare State, especially those on the right.

The challenge to the Welfare State since 1979

What is to be done? Why is the Welfare State ailing? These two questions have challenged politicians of all parties, both socialist and capitalist alike. All interested parties have emerged with their rival interpretations of what is wrong and what has to be done. There have been many explanations, ranging from those presented by the new right, Marxists, socialists, Fabians and feminists. The most critically destructive have been those of the new right.

A. The new right's criticism

The new right owe their ideas (philosophy, not ideology) to the work of Friedrich von Hayek and Milton Friedman. To Hayek, liberty and individualism are in direct opposition to equality gained through collective measures. This runs deep throughout his philosophy, which suggests that all governments which support equality and attempt to redress the 'natural' social balance of inequality only create imbalance and oppression. He maintains that all beings are competitive individuals and, as such, must live within the boundaries of 'natural' market forces. For him and his supporters, this situation enhances wealth creation and safeguards liberty. He wanted liberty but not equality and fraternity. The sole nexus of social relationship is thus based on the needs of individuals and the individual contract. Collective ideas and state bureaucracies cause severe economic problems for the individual and the state.[13] Hayek argued that socialism was the political twin of fascism and the pathway to totalitarianism, for it offered an economic and social security which held hidden dangers: 'when security is understood in too absolute a sense, the general striving for it, far from increasing the chances of freedom, becomes the gravest threat to it.'[14]

Not surprisingly, from its early beginnings the Welfare State was seen by some Conservative politicians such as Enoch Powell and Ian Macleod as a burden and an institution of unfairness. Those that put the least in were those who took the most out. Powell had been associated with Peter Thorneycroft, the Conservative Chancellor of the Exchequer who resigned in January 1958, and Nigel Birch, a junior minister, in their determination to keep public expenditure under control by reducing it by £50 million and raising interest rates from 2 to 7 per cent. Powell took up the issue of controlling public expenditure in the 1960s. He suggested that selective benefits might be the way forward, a solution to the conundrum of how to reduce the burden of welfare in a state that was facing economic decline.

Powell's views were endorsed by the Institute of Economic Affairs, the right-wing think-tank, which produced a pamphlet entitled *Towards a Welfare State* (1967) which argued that:

> If poverty in the absolute sense is to be abolished by state aid, it must be measured in terms of individual needs and means, and the individual aid must be varied accordingly. The matching of aid to individual needs and means requires a measure of test of means and needs. Reluctance to match aid to individual circumstances, based largely on recollection of the household means test in the 1930s, is a barrier to more generous and more humane aid to the remaining needs.
>
> Generous and humane aid is hindered by the continuance of equal social benefits irrespective of individual circumstances, as in the provision of free or subsidised education, health services, housing, pension and other state services.

The new right emphasis was thus to be placed firmly upon the selective provision of benefits for the poor.

Margaret Thatcher soon took up a similar stance. On 10 October 1968 she gave a lecture at the Conservative party conference at Blackpool and announced that:

> We have now put so much emphasis on the control of incomes that we have too little regard for the essential role of government which is to control the money supply and the management of demand. Greater attention to this role and less to the outward detailed control would have achieved more for the economy. It would mean, of course, that the government had to exercise itself some of the disciplines on expenditure it is so keen to impose on others. It would mean that expenditure in the vast public sector would not have to be greater than the amount which could be financed out of taxation plus genuine savings. For a number of years some expenditure has been financed by what amounts to printing money.

These views were developed and applied to the Welfare State by Rhodes Boyson in a collection of essays which he edited entitled *Down with the Poor* (1971) and were given some support by the actions of the Heath Conservative government of 1970, which aimed to restrict the powers of trade unions (through the Industrial Relations Act of 1971) and to encourage private enterprise by freeing it from state restrictions.[15] Boyson referred to the end of paternalism and clearly stated that: 'Not only is the present welfare state inefficient and destructive of personal liberty, individual responsibility and moral growth, but it saps the collective moral fibre of our people as a nation.'[16]

Not surprisingly, given the economic tribulations of the Labour government in the mid-1970s, James Callaghan came to hold similar views about the economic efficacy of the combination of Keynesian and Beveridgian ideas. At the 1976 Labour party conference he noted that:

> We used to think that you could just spend your way out of a recession and increase employment by cutting taxes and boosting government spending. I tell you in all honesty that option no longer exists and that, insofar as it ever did exist, it worked by injecting inflation into the economy. And each time that happened, the average level of unemployment has risen. High inflation followed by higher unemployment. That is the history of the last twenty years.[17]

Callaghan's comments came relatively late in the debate and called into question the type of commitment that the Labour party was prepared to make to the future Welfare State. Indeed, it moved quickly towards corporatism, the 'social contract' and similar policies. In contrast, the new right had been working on Thatcher and other Conservatives to cultivate a new attitude since the mid-1960s.

Sir Keith Joseph became the chief standard-bearer of the new philosophy of monetarism. Having been persuaded that Keynesianism was dead, he felt the need for a rethink on policy. The rise of Thatcher and her band of evangelicals transformed this new philosophy into action. The sheer force of authority makes the idea legitimate under Thatcher. 'There is no alternative' became the theme song as she set a new agenda and attacked the false trails of social democratic delusions.

There were other powerful advocates of this type of approach. The main reason why the Welfare State had been created, according to T. H. Marshall, was the removal of poverty from society. The Welfare State was thus seen as a temporary measure to fill the gap between pre-war poverty and a future affluence. By 1960 the affluent society had arrived and embourgeoisement had meant the 'death of ideology'. Poverty was seen to be in retreat and, to T. H. Marshall, the war against poverty had been won:

> ... the time had come to give the Austerity Society a decent burial, and to welcome the Affluent Society in its place ... an Affluent Society should not need to maintain a complicated and expensive apparatus for waging war on poverty.[18]

The Welfare State was thus a defunct institution.

This approach contrasted with the views of Peter Townsend, Sir Douglas Black, Joanna Mack, Stewart Lansley and others who have maintained that the Welfare State had not eradicated poverty. Townsend's late 1960s survey, which appeared as *Poverty in the United Kingdom*, suggested that Britain still experienced relative poverty of about 25 to 30 per cent. His relative poverty was based upon a survey of 2,000 families and used sixty items of family life in Britain, such as diet, fuel and light, clothing, housing, family support and other features. From this he produced a 'deprivation index' based upon twelve major items. Townsend's findings were supported by the Black Report, which was researched in 1980. Although strongly criticized at the time for the techniques that it adopted, Sir Douglas Black's enquiry into the health of the nation suggested that, at all stages of life, those households where the head was an unskilled manual worker were disadvantaged compared with others. Indeed, men and women in unskilled households were two and a half times more likely to die before reaching retirement age than their professional counterparts. Also, the mortality rates for those born into unskilled families were over three and a half times higher than those born to professional families. Being poor in Britain in 1980 was still very much a matter of life and death. In effect, the gap between the death rates of the poor and the rest of the nation had not changed since 1900.

The government severely restricted the circulation of this embarrassing report, attacked the notion of relative inequality and suggested that the benefits system ensured that no one lived in poverty in Britain. These criticisms were partly answered by Joanna Mack and Stewart Lansley, however, whose book *Poor Britain* was produced (by George Allen & Unwin in 1985) in conjunction with the London Weekend Television series 'Breadline Britain', which appeared in the summer of 1983. They examined poverty from the point of view of the 'general social perception of need'. In other words, they moved to an objective assessment of poverty based upon the subjective view of a cross-section of society. They found that the 'poor today are too poor', that there were about 4 million adults and 2.5 million children living in poverty, and that another 4.5 million were living on the margins of poverty. In other words, something between 14 and 22 per cent of the nation were living in poverty in Britain during the early 1980s. The implications were clear; welfare capitalism had failed because it had not solved poverty. Something more dramatic was required.

The new right rejected this evidence and came to their view that the Welfare State was failing from an entirely different direction. They believed that the economic growth of the country was inextricably inter-linked with the growth of the Welfare State. Economic growth had been held back by welfare, which had imposed an impossible burden. This had to be rolled back. In a version of the classical wage-fund theory, they argued that governments fixed the rate of inflation through the control of the money supply, whilst trade unions fixed the corresponding rate of unemployment through the medium of their wage-bargaining. Therefore, if trade-union wage demands were pitched too high, this would then result in the loss of their members' jobs. Conversely, the rate of unemployment could be lowered by labour market reforms – that is, by pricing oneself back into work. Once government relinquished responsibility for unemployment, then the *raison d'être* for budget deficits would disappear and the public sector borrowing requirement, seen as an important contributory factor in the excessive growth of the money supply, could be cut back. Traditionally, Conservatives have always disliked the public sector; such cut-backs, it was argued, would not only control inflation but also enable direct taxation to be reduced. This in turn would improve the supply side of the economy through work incentives and the opportunity for higher personal savings – what Gladstone saw as allowing money to fructify in the pockets of the people. Finally, and of vital importance, a retreat from the Welfare State would remove the threat to liberty which liberal Conservatives have always associated with the continuous expansion of the state. Once this 'rolling back of the frontiers of the state' had been accomplished, then there would be, it was hoped, a return to the classical political and moral virtues of individual responsibility and prudent housekeeping.

The ideas of the new right are, of course, enveloped within the philosophy of individualism. The Welfare State was, and still is, viewed with distrust by the new right for several reasons. First, the Welfare State denies people a choice of service; it exemplifies the coercion inherent in a system that dictates universal ideals of equality – or, in other words, it sets maximum standards.[19] Indeed, 'The British welfare state has logically and ineluctably become the main instrument for the creation of equality by coercion.'[20] Secondly, they feel that the Welfare State has diverted resources away from 'wealth creating' sectors of the economy.[21] Thirdly, it has resulted in high taxation and government borrowing, which led to a spiral of inflation. This is due to people's expectations, their reliance on a 'dependency culture', and government's unwillingness to put unpopular but necessary policies into action. Fourthly, they argue that welfare undermines the work ethic and culture; the unemployed have no incentive to work.[22] Fifthly, that 'the [national] insurance principle is fraudulent, as a mechanism used to introduce back door socialism ... [and] imposing higher taxation ... In practice ... contributions are a tax on employment.'[23] For these reasons, the new right in general, and Sir Keith Joseph in particular, saw a situation in Britain that was described as 'dysfunctional democracy'. Out of this situation, the 'overload thesis' was developed.

This thesis is crucial in understanding the new right perspective on the Welfare State in the 1970s. David Held's concise interpretation of its main tenets is useful.[24] It develops thus. The post-war boom created consumer confidence and general prosperity. Expectations were high that standards of living would increase, as would social welfare systems and benefits. However, there was a general decline in deference and respect for authority, due in part to new affluence, 'free welfare, health and education'.[25] This in turn weakened individual work and incentives, but aspirations for state egalitarian principles become more pronounced. The plurality of groups in welfare social democracies pressed the government to intervene to protect their interests by offering higher wages, employment security, and contrasting high and low interest rates and prices. To secure power, the political parties promised to fulfil the desires of the competing interest groups. In the 1960s and 1970s, it is argued, the contradictions in policy were all too apparent. To placate the trade unions and to alleviate social disturbances, the governments of the day attempted to juggle with the economy. Price freezes, wage freezes, reflation, deflation and similar actions became the order of the day. The Labour government of Harold Wilson in 1968 attempted to introduce legislation on incomes policy, as did the Heath Conservative government of the early 1970s and the Labour government of 1974–9. Nonetheless, aspirations continued to rise and were reinforced by each successive government. 'Appeasement strategies', according to the new right, 'lead to even more state agencies.'[26] These included health and welfare service increases which led to an ever-increasing circle of public spending and spiralling costs. The expansion of the state's welfare mechanism not only destroyed individual motivation through the development of dependency and higher taxation, but it also, if Bacon and Eltis are to be believed, left the system with too few producers to pay for the services of the Welfare State.[27] Only by rolling back the state's involvement can prosperity be assured.

Such an interpretation has, of course, been rejected by socialists. However, one of its main critics is Alan Sked, a Conservative Eurosceptic, who suggests that the creation of a Welfare State does not necessarily mean the economic ruination of a country. Britain's expenditure on welfare services has been comparable with that of other economies, some of which were expanding. Income tax was also less of a burden than has been described and tax rates were favourable compared with those in Europe. Taxation does not necessarily discourage hard work; rather, according to the OECD, it makes people work harder.[28] Also, a government working party concluded in 1967 that 'high taxes do not discourage savings'; this can be seen by increases in domestic savings during a period in the 1970s when taxation actually rose.[29]

New right critics expressed the view that the Welfare State leads to an enforced and coercive equality. By this they mean universal equality. Nothing could be further from the truth. Equality using a socialist framework means more than universal welfare initiatives. It means a totality of relationships – some economic, some social and some personal. It is essentially about power, not about welfare. Hayek, Joseph and other members of the new right have failed to appreciate the very nature of the welfare capitalism which they are attacking. The Welfare State was introduced to remove the most obvious social disadvantages of capitalism without necessarily changing the relationships that are part and parcel of the construction of capitalism.

Sked writes that welfare benefits are complementary to growth and efficiency. A healthy workforce is a productive one. Welfare benefits such as the 'dole' or supplementary benefit do not necessarily create a dependency culture or work-shyness. Sked points to the reviews by the National Assistance Board in 1951, 1956, 1958, 1961 and 1964 and to the reports by the Supplementary Benefits Commission in 1978 to provide evidence for his arguments. Both of these authorities showed clearly that only a small minority of claimants benefited from the welfare system, and most of these were disabled, ill, or unable to work due to personal problems.[30] This being the case, the Welfare State has been cleared of some of the charges levelled against it by its new right critics, most obviously that it has produced a breed of 'scroungers' or 'beggars' who take advantage of the system.

The fact is that the new right and the anti-collectivists need to explain why Britain is no longer a leading industrial nation. The past is seen as the yardstick for the future. What the nation did in the nineteenth century can, for those who believe in the new right analysis, be reproduced in the latter stages of the twentieth century. The *laissez-faire* economic approach can be reborn. Many of those on the left in the 1970s felt that the right were deflecting criticism away from the overall system. Before we explore the left's attitude to the Welfare State and the crises of the late 1960s and 1970s, it is perhaps useful to indicate other possible reasons for Britain's decline.

Bacon and Eltis view the industrial decline of Britain in terms of low industrial output, high taxation, low spending and consumer caution, and a negative economic policy which stimulated the growth of the service sector and the welfare sector but ignored the industrial base. The burdened state therefore has too much control and stifles initiative. Britain's economic failings are thus due to the 'structure of the economy and not the level of demand or the exchange rate'.[31] Of course, this approach has wider implications. The Welfare State, for example – and the public sector at large, in theory – would need to be privatized or at least slimmed down. Such a stance has been severely criticized by Sidney Pollard, whose astute analysis of the British economy reveals that the single most important factor is defence spending, not the Welfare State.[32]

This argument is a poignant one and follows the work that Mancer carried out in 1971.[33] Both look at the balance of payments and then deduct defence spending. If defence spending is not included in the overall balance, Britain was in line with her European and Japanese competitors. Furthermore, if they had defence budgets, then they too would be seen to have economic problems. Moreover, the technical and scientific expertise available to other nations to use on non-military industries was not available to Britain because of her military spending. The new right have misinterpreted the problem of Britain's economic misgivings. The criticisms that they level at the Welfare State are unfounded and inaccurate.

B. Socialist and Marxist criticism

If the new right have been critical of the Welfare State, so have the left and Marxists. By the 1970s they were most critical of the failings of the Welfare State. They reflected, in a more intense form, some of the concerns that were being echoed by even the supporters of the Welfare State on the Labour left and right.

Richard Titmuss had seen the Welfare State as a way of alleviating the worst conditions of poverty and recognized the contradictions inherent in welfare capitalism. However, his main concern was the eradication of poverty and the universality of the welfare system. Social policy and the Welfare State were avenues that were divorced in a sense from the economic sphere of labour relationships. The Welfare State was a tool that would help to redistribute resource; the universality of benefits would break down class distinctions which discriminated against under-privileged groups. By the late 1960s and the early 1970s, however, Titmuss's attitude towards its development had begun to change. The Welfare State had not abolished poverty and had not managed to reach and target the groups who most needed assistance. The wealthiest groups had benefited the most, the poorest the least. The Welfare State, for Titmuss, Crosland and other socialists, had become hierarchical, too centralized and bureaucratic. Moreover, the redistribution that they had wanted so much had not taken place. From their vantage point in the 1970s their criticism appeared accurate, but they failed to see the exact nature of the Welfare State and were wrong in parts.

Poverty is a necessary component of capitalism. To 'have' must necessarily mean that others 'have not'. In relative terms, the 'haves' and the 'have nots' had remained fairly constant. Nonetheless, poverty had been attacked and challenged. The bureaucracies and the hierarchical nature of the welfare services were in direct opposition to socialist beliefs. Of course, the Welfare State does not operate within a socialist state. The Welfare State and the benefits deriving from it, even from Beveridge's initial conception, were never meant to challenge the fundamental nature of the state. Welfare benefits take the sting out of capitalism; they do not remove inequality. Titmuss and Crosland's arguments therefore seem to be misplaced in the context of a capitalist society. To a certain degree, their criticisms are similar to those put forward by Marxists.

Marxists have always been sceptical about the Welfare State. To them, it is seen as a necessary, if contradictory, institution to the survival of capitalism. If capitalism is concerned with accumulation which is contrary to the benefits of the working class, it must also attempt to legitimize its practice. Gough writes that: 'The welfare state is a product of the contradictory development of capitalist society and in turn has generated new contradictions which every day become more apparent.'[34] The contradiction is explicitly clear; the capitalist state cannot function effectively with the Welfare State but, in a democracy, it cannot function without it. These arguments are relevant and apt.

All people make demands upon the state and so, ultimately, it must be neutral. All post-war governments up to 1979 attempted to be neutral, frequently juggling policy to placate either the employers or the workers. The legitimacy of the state is obtained by parading equality of service in an otherwise unequal society. The welfare services and the social services are thus seen as accessible and accumulating forms of social control. Social harmony is maintained by alleviating the detrimental effects of capitalism.

In 'boom' years the Welfare State and social services can expand; workers can make demands that are easily accommodated. Demands on government in the 1960s and 1970s increased as living standards and welfare services were threatened. Financial difficulties, the devaluation of the pound, and similar events undermined these developments. Faced with relative economic decline and growing expectations, the Heath government of 1970–4 and the Labour government of 1974–9 looked to either incomes policies or new national strategies to increase private investment and control the money supply. An impossible scenario ensued; the premise of the nation now lay with the welfare services. Expansion of these services was expensive, both politically and economically. To cut the Welfare State was political suicide to a Labour government which was supposedly working in the interests of the people – at least, not in the interests of capital. The background to all this was Britain's balance of payments deficit, the oil crisis of the early 1970s, the fact that the government had to 'beg' the International Monetary Fund for a loan to support the economy and the demands made upon it by the various groups and sections of society. Indeed, the left, the Marxists and the new right saw that Britain was becoming ungovernable. The Welfare State was in crisis and had to be changed in some way or other.

C. Feminist criticisms

Feminist criticisms are not concerned with the economics of the situation and the unsupportable nature of present welfare provisions, but focus upon the need to make women into first-class citizens in their own society. The feminist criticism of the British Welfare State starts from the basic assumption that women experience social inequality due to their dependent position within the marriage and the household. Since men have traditionally been the breadwinners, women have, and still are, expected to assume household duties and low-paid, often part-time, jobs if they go out to work. Their career prospects are thus blighted. From this inequality stems the denial of full citizenship to women. The British Welfare State, based as it is upon the minimal provision of benefits, care, and the redistribution of resources within a competitive capitalist system which regards such provision as compensating for the failures of the system, denies first-class citizenship to women.

The Beveridge Welfare State, based upon contributions from lifetime employment, reduced the benefits and provision for those who do not meet this ideal; women often do not meet this standard because of their family and biological circumstances. The British Welfare State has therefore done a lot to legitimize traditional discriminatory values and attitudes towards women. The Beveridge Report is thus seen as 'one of the most crudely ideological documents of its kind ever written'.[35] The feminist is, by and large, critical of the existing British Welfare State, with its emphasis upon reform capitalism, and looks towards the Scandinavian social democratic model, which is far more generous and redistributive in its provision for women. To feminists, then, the reorganization of the British Welfare State in such a way as to recognize the need to place women's needs at the centre of its evolution – and to recognize that women's demands are often different from those of men – is essential. Such a change requires women to have a greater say in the formulation of public policy and presupposes that the British Welfare State will go some way towards providing benefits that will undermine the concept of the traditional nuclear family. It would also assume that capitalism, which is fundamentally in contradiction with welfare provision but cannot do without it in a democratic state, is prepared to see such changes.[36] Feminist views, therefore, are not within the mainstream of current developments. The British Welfare State has failed because it has not become more social democratic in form.

Whether these views are justified or not is open to much discussion. Rodney Lowe certainly feels that the Welfare State has provided the 'psychological and material advantages of a guaranteed income and free access to health care, as well as the foremost demand of interwar feminists – family allowances'.[37] Yet he acknowledges that the social services and the NHS still disadvantage women and place them in a subordinate role. This impression of how women have fared in the British Welfare State has been examined in a wide-ranging article on international welfare states by Professor Jane Lewis. She argues that in the early twentieth century, when municipal authorities and voluntary organizations were given extra responsibilities by the state, women did quite well as a result of operating in materialist politics. But as the 'paternalist' British Welfare State emerged, their opportunities to influence its core legislation was reduced, as was their right to benefits when compared with men. Nevertheless, she argues that the more institutional welfare states, like that of Sweden, seem to become more 'women-friendly'.[38]

D. Analysis

Where do all these viewpoints leave the Welfare State? The criticisms of it have not always been fair and accurate. The Marxists, for example, saw it as a necessary component of capitalism's social control mechanism. This is true to a certain degree; it is essential for modern capitalist societies to have some form of benefit system, for this gives them legitimacy and principle. On recognizing this, one must also acknowledge that the Welfare State is essentially an institution that came about because the workforce demanded it and that the politicians in power recognized such a demand. Whether it is useful to capital is beside the point. Its defence in the 1960 and 1970s was a matter of principle.

The new right picked up some nineteenth-century ideas concerning the individual, the deserving and undeserving, and a limited role for government. The Welfare State was targeted on purely ideological grounds. If the post-war governments 'tinkered' with the economy, as Bacon and Eltis have suggested, they did so not because of welfare demands, but because of other factors that ultimately got in the way of Britain's economic and social progress. To feminists, the concern has been that the Welfare State has not been collectivist enough in conferring benefits – and thus full citizenship – to women. Even the Labour party and the left recognized that the high industrial output which Crosland presumed was no longer achievable by the mid-1970s and demanded a scaling-down of welfare expectations and increased targeting of deprived social groups.

The Welfare State in crisis?

If most sections of British society are demanding changes in the Welfare State, does that mean that it is facing a crisis? Certainly, the OECD perceived there to be a crisis in welfare provision in Britain and throughout the world at its 1980 conference. The welfare states of the world are still with us, in some form or other, and perhaps the crisis was exaggerated.

Exaggerated or not, there is a crisis relating to the increasing burden of the Welfare State and the economic inability of nations to deliver the provisions and benefits in the face of poor economic conditions. It is certainly the case that rising unemployment, the ageing of society, the problem of immigration and social control, and the rising number of one-parent families through divorce and other issues are imposing burdens upon all welfare systems. The Swedish social democratic model, with its goal of equalization, faced the biggest financial strains. It has helped the Scandinavian countries to avoid social disorder, but at the price of enormous debt, inflation and low work morale.[39] The highly selective Liberal model developed by the United States, committed to low spending, has failed to control social disorder; therefore, whilst expenditure has been relatively low, the social policy cannot deal with the situation of high poverty.[40] The Bismarckian system was introduced into Germany in February 1881 through the *Kaiserliche Botschaft* (Emperor's message); it offers a market income in its benefits and the maintenance of status, rather than help according to needs. It is also very selective and conservative in its approach. Until the reunification of Germany in 1990, it was generous enough to reduce poverty considerably but not selective enough to reduce aggregate spending. But since 1990 reunification has stretched its resources.[41]

Whilst the Scandinavian and German welfare systems are facing the strain of their systems, the British Welfare State, like the welfare provisions of the United States, is not feeling the same level of crisis. The universally based Beveridge/Labour party model provides a national minimum for every citizen. The underlying principle is help according to need at a basic level. Its success against poverty has therefore been somewhat limited and, despite Conservative views to the contrary, expenditure levels are relatively low; for this reason, British social policy can operate in a poor economic environment.

Despite, or perhaps because of, the British Welfare State, poverty has continued to be a major problem in British society in the last forty years. Indeed, David Piachaud makes the point that poverty rose in Britain over the years 1953–83, despite the attempts of the social policy to provide relief.[42] His detailed study also reveals the most vulnerable groups to poverty in British society: 'One-parent families and unemployed families were, in 1983, far the most likely to be poor with 53.2 per cent and 79.9 per cent below the constant relative poverty level respectively.'[43]

Old age also accounts for most poverty. Indeed, a recent article by Alan Walker makes the point that:

despite the significant political commitment given to pensions in the 1970s – culminating in the State Earnings Related Pension Scheme (SERPS) in 1975 and a series of pledges to uprate pensions in line with earnings or prices, whichever was the greater – which resulted in some improvements in the relative position of elderly people in the income distribution ... poverty is still the principal financial problem faced by elderly people.[44]

Poverty is also, for many, an enduring experience. With respect to the Welfare State, Walker's argument is that it is an important factor in shaping the conditions which make the old poor. He argues that it is the insurance principle, relating the benefits to earnings in employment and the number of dependents (claimants get benefits only when they give up employment), which creates poverty. This has to be seen against the background of rising numbers of elderly people in society and the debate about whether present levels of old-age benefits can continue to be paid in a country which already has one of the highest rates of old-age poverty.[45]

National figures are not broken down sufficiently to allow ethnic minorities to be examined, but the general evidence tends to suggest that poverty is more prevalent among some of the ethnic minorities and particularly amongst the New Commonwealth immigrants.[46] The British Welfare State has done little to rectify this situation.

There are clearly serious financial problems facing the British Welfare State and decisions will have to be made. Currently, they are being made on political grounds rather than economic and social ones. The mentality which promotes individualism, monetarism and a return to basic, if not Victorian, values is one which justifies inequality, attacks the scrounger and ignores the fact that family relationships are changing and that the nuclear family is becoming less common. The perpetrators of such views achieved political power in 1979 and have retained it ever since.

Developments in the Welfare State since 1979

In 1979 Thatcherism signalled a very radical break in the pattern of post-war British political economy. What it set out to achieve was nothing less than a total restructuring of capital, labour, the state and relations between them and an attempt to undermine the old pluralism which had dominated the Welfare State. The assumption was that Britain declined because of the financial and social burdens of the Welfare State. Thatcherite policies consisted of strict monetary curbs, inroads into public spending, privatization and legal constraints on what was construed as the privileged position of trade unions under the law – or, rather, outside the law.

The government's medium-term financial strategy was vital to all this, for it announced the growth of the money supply. By making credit more difficult to obtain, it would control inflation and bring about deflation. The tighter the policy, the greater would be the liquidity problems and the higher the unemployment. In total, what it amounted to was a reversal of Keynesianism, in which competitiveness rather than demand was the operating criterion. Driving the less competitive to the wall would release resources in competitive areas.

This strategy appeared almost immediately in Sir Geoffrey Howe's budget speech of 12 June 1979, when he set the public sector borrowing requirement at £8.25 billion, £3 billion less than it was, increased interest rates and pledged to slash public expenditure by £1.5 billion. The whole strategy was to have big implications for the Welfare State.

The growth rate for social expenditure was around 5 per cent per annum between 1964 and 1975 and declined marginally in the Thatcher years, although Michael Hill stresses that, if Dennis Healey's cuts of 1975 and 1976 are taken separately, then Healey was probably a more effective 'butcher' of public expenditure than Margaret Thatcher's Chancellors.[47] Between 1973/4 and 1977/89 all expenditure rose by 1.8 per cent in real terms, compared with 1.1 per cent between 1978/9 and 1990/1.[48] There were clear areas of cuts. For the same periods, social security spending rose only 3 per cent in the Thatcher years compared with 5.4 per cent in the earlier period and housing fell from 4.8 per cent to 3 per cent growth per annum in the Thatcher years, although this fall has something to do with the new accounting procedures which were adopted. This contrasts with the real increases in levels of expenditure for health and personal social service, rising from 2 per cent to 3.4 per cent, and education from 0 per cent to 1.3 per cent. The overall picture is of a decline in the growth rate of real public expenditure, but some variability in terms of where the reductions in growth have been applied.

Housing has been the area most obviously affected by cuts, as the Conservative governments implemented their decision to sell council houses to occupiers through the Housing Act of 1980 – at the market price, less a discount based upon the number of years of occupancy. In addition, Conservative governments have reduced the freedom of the local authorities to build council houses and have threatened them with the 1988 Housing Act, which permitted landlords to purchase blocks of flats from the local authorities and allowed local authorities to consider the need to seek housing associations to whom they could transfer housing stock. Yet one should not be too pessimistic. It is clear that there have been some improvements in the housing stock, from 74,000 in 1976 to 234,000 in 1988, and the shortage of houses fell from 1,500,000 in 1971 to about 500,000 in 1986.

Social security has also come under close scrutiny. Here the Beveridge principles were eroded, although the Conservatives were never able to go as far as they would have liked. They introduced many measures, including a review of supplementary benefits, changes in housing benefit arrangements, and reductions in the value of contributory benefits by altering the procedure for inflation-related increases and by extending the taxation of benefits. But this tinkering was considered to be limited.

In 1983 Norman Fowler, the Secretary of State, decided that a more radical reform of social security was necessary. He set up a number of ministerially dominated committees to explore the options and the outcome was a report published in 1985 (Secretary of State for Social Service, Cmnd. 9517, 1985) which declared that the social security system had 'lost its way'. Benefits needed to be better targeted and simpler. It suggested the need for a less complicated means-tested benefit arrangement and expressed the view that the SERPS, the state pension scheme, would impose excessive burdens upon future generations. He was unable to remove this scheme, however, simply reducing the benefit arrangements and introducing changes which means that shorter-term contributors, such as women, lose out. The 1986 Social Security Act therefore modified SERPS, replaced supplementary benefit with income support, and the family income supplement with family credit. Maternity and death grants were also abolished and replaced by means-test-related benefits for the very poor. The biggest change was that the supplementary fund was replaced by a social fund, 70 per cent of the expenditure of which was be in the form of loans.

Despite this pruning and simplifying, Conservative governments have found it difficult to reduce social security expenditure as they would have liked, largely because of rising unemployment. In the end they have tinkered with unemployment benefit and changed the conditions on which it can be gained. Nevertheless, figures of more than 2.5–3 million unemployed have made that component of social security expenditure extremely high. This has motivated the government to employ other measures to reduce expenditure. The most recent and politically contentious one has been the creation of the Child Support Agency, designed to reduce the £8 billion social security bill for single parents. When the new agency was created in 1993, it was given the task of reducing benefits by £530 million. In the event, the agency saved about £400 million in its first year (rather more than was saved by the Child Support Unit in 1992–3 and by the Benefits Agency in 1991–2). The government has, in the course of trying to reduce the benefit costs to the state, transferred the cost to the separated fathers and created a controversy which has led them to ease up on the targets they are setting.[49]

The issue has also brought into the open the debate within government about the sanctity of the family and the position of lone parents. Whilst Virginia Bottomley, Health Secretary and the minister responsible for family issues, has adopted something of a benign stance towards lone parents, suggesting that there has never been a golden age of the family, Peter Lilley feels that the growth of family disruption is 'deeply disturbing' and leads to divorce, violence and social breakdown on a vast scale.[50] Whilst Lilley feels that part of the reason for this may be, regrettably, the fact that wage levels for the unskilled are barely more than benefits, Michael Portillo, the Treasury Chief Secretary, has waded in with the suggestion that 'over-generous benefits' were undermining the family.[51] Clearly, the problem is that government ministers and officials want to reduce the costs of the social security bill but are faced with the reality that their own policies and social trends are operating against them. It is the growth rate of social security that has gone down in real terms, not the actual overall levels of monetary expenditure.

Elsewhere, annual expenditure levels have risen in real terms. In education this has largely been due to the fact that the promised wage settlements to teachers were honoured once the Conservatives came to power in May 1979 and that the numerous educational experiments of the government have cost money. The most important of these changes has been the 1988 Education Act, which effectively replaced the 1944 Education Act, set up the national curriculum with its core and foundation subjects, required a religious education reflecting the dominance of Christianity and allowed the more widely empowered governors of county and voluntary maintained schools, if they had the support of the parents, to apply to the Secretary of State for maintenance by a grant from the government rather than from the local education authority. The 'opting-out' arrangement theoretically gave the parents more choice, whilst in fact strengthening the hand of the state over education. Like many other areas of recent welfare policy, there was comparatively little prior discussion of the changes and the legislation could be considered to be a little too previous. As one commentator noted of the 1988 Act, it was 'action before words, decision before debate, the presumption of guilt exceeding all possibility of innocence in the previous way of doing things'.[52]

The only other major area of extension has been the provision of health, health care and personal services. In 1979 the Royal Commission on the National Health Service endorsed the existing service whilst criticizing its excessive bureaucracy. As a result, the government took away one of the bureaucratic layers, the area health authorities, in 1982, leaving the planning to the regional and district health authorities alone. To enable them to do this, they had to appoint general managers to balance the medical and administrative requirements of the service. However, it was another eight years before a really fundamental piece of health legislation emerged. This allowed for the setting-up of National Health Trusts. These are semi-autonomous bodies which answer to the Secretary of State, which are able to manage their own finances, appoint their own staff and offer a package of services that they can sell to the district health authorities. The latter bodies purchase services on behalf of the patients. These new trusts may also offer private work. In addition, GPs may also apply to become 'fund-holders', able to make independent arrangements with hospitals. In the early 1990s – and especially before the 1992 general election – the Conservative government claimed that the new trusts were operating effectively and efficiently and were reducing the waiting-lists, one of the main objectives of John Major's 'Citizen's Charter'. Extra resources were found and the lists were reduced, but since then a large number of hospital trusts seem to have been facing serious financial difficulties and waiting-lists actually grew by 7.1 per cent in the third year of operation of the hospital trusts, between March 1993 and March 1994, to a figure of 1.07 million.[53]

It is one of the ironies of the current situation that the doctors, once the great critics of the NHS, have become one of the defenders of the pre-trust period. Dr Sandy Macara, chairman of the British Medical

Association, suggested at its annual meeting in Birmingham on 4 July 1994 that doctors were in despair at the business culture of the new NHS. He stated that:

> Co-operation has been supplanted by commercial competition. There is an uncontrolled, ill-managed internal market pitting purchaser against provider, fund-holding GP against non-fund-holding GP, GP against consultant, junior against senior, hospital against hospital and all to serve a perverse philosophy of winners and losers.
>
> Business plans override clinical priority. Money does not follow the patient: the patient has no choice but to follow the money. Treatment, except in emergencies and one begins to see it even in emergencies, has become a national and local lottery. Slow tracking, not fast tracking is the reality for too many patients.[54]

The clear concern today is that there is inequality of access, that treatment depends upon the area and practice, and that inequality of access has been worsened by purchasing consortia and provider units fighting for survival. In this climate the NHS is likely to prove a bitter battleground, especially in the light of its enduring love affair with the British public.

In other areas, state resources have also been diverted into dealing with the increasing number of old people in the community. Throughout the 1980s there was an increase in the numbers entering private residential care, especially as the Department of Social Security met part of the charges in full, even though relatives were often called upon to 'top them up'. In addition, individuals in private residential care have been able to apply for supplementary benefit (income support after the 1986 Act). The potential cost of care was also increased by the fact that the Griffiths Report of 1988, which the government accepted and included in the new health structure in 1990, suggested that the local authority social services department should use social, rather than financial, grounds to determine whether care was necessary and then had the responsibility to ensure that care, from either the public or the private sector. If individuals could not pay for it from their own income or from standard social security benefits, then the local authority had to provide the subsidy. The local authorities could buy packages of care from private homes. The government obviously had to transfer resources from the social security budget to the local authority budget and the new system became effective from April 1993, although there is evidence that the government is not transferring sufficient resources.

Like many other aspects of social policy, little in the way of new money is being provided. Effectively, there is more privatization and consumers and their families are often faced with picking up some of the costs of the change in structure.

One might also reflect that many aspects of social policy are moving out of the hands of publicly elected bodies. An almost invisible army of quangos, run by over 70,000 quangocrats, administers a considerable amount of British public expenditure. The government insists that there are only 1,389 quangos, or non-department public bodies, even though there are 5,521 such bodies administering £46 billion of the taxpayers' money. For instance, one estimate suggests that 55 per cent of the money spent on schools and colleges is channelled through unaccountable quangos. This means that taxpayers can no longer exercise their vote in local elections in order to influence spending. Indeed, in 1994 the Funding Agency for Schools, currently responsible for grant-maintained schools, is expected to take over responsibility for all school funding. As Barry Hugill noted: 'Local councillors can be voted out of office – only the Secretary of State for Education can remove, or appoint, members of the FAS.' [55]

The future: a conclusion

It is now clear that the Welfare State is going to change, whatever political party is in power. The problem remains one of how to balance the needs of the poor against the limited resources of a state whose economic growth has lagged behind most other industrialized nations. If the new right continues to influence events, then there is a possibility that it will became more privatized, more targeted in the provision of social security and a much reduced version of the Beveridge welfare capitalist system that has emerged since the 1940s. Even if the Labour party gains power, change is inevitable. The new discussion paper from the Labour party's National Commission on Social Justice outlined a number of possibilities. [56] It accepts that an integration of the tax and social security systems could offer the solution to tackling poverty, but also that this negative income tax technique, whereby income tax returns are used to calculate the right to means-tested benefits, may not work. The problem with this suggestion is that it is not sensitive to changes and may have to be calculated on the basis of a family unit. Alternatively, there is the idea of providing each person with a basic minimum income according to age, with less for children and more for those in retirement, as a replacement for child benefit, the state retirement pension, income support and family credit. The trouble is that this would be very costly to implement and would involve an income tax of 70 per cent. Even a partial, rather than a full, basic income of £33–5 per week would add 10p in the pound to the basic rate of income tax. Others have suggested that the link between income and benefits is as 'elusive as the Holy Grail' and that more mundane solutions might have to be sought.

As it is, the last forty years or so have revealed no easy solutions to changing the balance of the Welfare State. Despite the 'Thatcher Revolution', expenditure levels remain high and the Welfare State has not been 'rolled back', although it has changed. The new right have a commitment to the free market and have introduced measures within the NHS and other areas of welfare to achieve that goal, but they have found that their policies have been less successful than they might have supposed and that public opinion has sometimes forced them to trim their political sails. Nevertheless, the classic Beveridge-type Welfare State, with its universalism, fixed benefits and so on, has gone in the last twenty years. What seems clear at the present is that future welfare policies will either reduce the level of provision so that it is essentially targeted upon the 20 or 25 per cent of the British population who live their life in relative or consensual poverty, or, alternatively, there will be a slightly less generous system on much the same lines. There seems little chance that the feminist vision of a social democratic welfare state is likely to emerge, given the enormous costs of dealing with such current problems as an ageing population. It is even less likely that Britain will develop welfare provisions along the all-embracing Marxist lines. In future, the rate of Britain's economic growth will determine what the British Welfare State can offer the British public. For the present, the prospects look bleak and we may be heading back to 1834 rather than forward. At least, Anthony Crosland's mid-1970s statement that 'The party is over' seems a fair assessment for the classic Beveridge-styled British Welfare State.

Notes

1. C. A. R. Crosland, *The Future of Socialism* (1956).
2. OECD, *The Welfare State in Crisis. An Account of the Conference on Social Policies in the 1980s*, Paris, 20–3 October 1980 (Paris, 1981).
3. Robert Lowe, *The Welfare State in Britain since 1945* (1993), pp. 29–33.
4. T. Cliff and D. Gluckstein, *The Labour Party – A Marxist History* (1988), p. 256.
5. Charles Anthony Raven Crosland papers, British Library of Political and Economic Science, 13/10, which deals with Crosland's book and reviews by Asa Briggs, Philip Elliott and others.
6. D. Kavanagh and P. Morris, *Consensus Politics* (Oxford, 1989), p. 40.
7. Rodney Lowe, *The Welfare State in Britain since 1945* (1993), p. 301.
8. *Ibid.*, p. 46.
9. *Ibid.*, p. 138.
10. Barbara Castle, *The Castle Diaries 1974–76* (1980), p. 476.
11. Lowe, *Welfare State*, p. 246.
12. *Ibid.*, p. 295.
13. D. Held, *Models of Democracy* (Oxford, 1991), chapters six and seven.

14. Quoted in J. Clarke, A. Cochrane and C. Smart, *Ideologies of Welfare: From Dreams to Disillusions* (1987), p. 119.

15. *Ibid.*, pp. 130–4.

16. *Ibid.*, p. 133.

17. Labour Party, *Report of the 75th Annual Conference* (1976), p. 188, this is also quoted in Lowe, *Welfare State*, p. 1.

18. D. Jones, J. Brown, J. Bradshaw, *Issues in Social Policy* (1985), p. 37.

19. V. George and P. Wilding, *Ideology and Social Welfare* (1985), p. 37.

20. *Ibid.*, pp. 37–8.

21. A. Sked, *Britain's Decline* (1988), p. 77.

22. *Ibid.*

23. George and Wilding, *Ideology and Social Welfare*, p. 41.

24. Held, *Models of Democracy*.

25. *Ibid.*, p. 232.

26. *Ibid.*

27. R. Bacon and W. Eltis, *Britain's Economic Problem: Too Few Producers* (1978).

28. Sked, *Britain's Decline*, p. 77.

29. *Ibid.*, p. 78.

30. *Ibid.*, pp. 76–80.

31. Bacon and Eltis, *Britain's Economic Problems*, p. 62.

32. Sked, *Britain's Decline*, p. 23.

33. George and Wilding, *Ideology and Social Welfare*, p. 114.

34. *Ibid.*

35. E. Wilson, *Women and the Welfare State* (1977), p. 148, quoted in Lowe, *Welfare State*, p. 33.

36. I owe some of the ideas offered here to an unpublished paper by Valerie Bryson entitled 'Women, Citizenship and Social Policy', a small section of which deals with feminists and the Welfare State. In addition there are numerous books and articles which deal with feminists and the Welfare State and with housing, benefits, child care, and other aspects of its development. The more accessible ones include Jennifer Dale and Peggy Foster, *Feminists and State Welfare* (1986); M. Maclean and D. Groves (eds.), *Women's Issues in Social Policy* (1991); Gillian Pascall, *Social Policy: A Feminist Analysis* (1986); Fiona Wallace, *Social Policy: A Critical Introduction* (Cambridge, 1989); and Elizabeth Wilson, *Women and the Welfare State* (1977). There have also been two recent additions to this list which argue much the same line. Gisela Bock and Pat Thane (eds.), *Maternity and Gender Policies: Women and the Rise of the European Welfare States 1880s–1950s* (1994), and, less directly relevant, Susan Pederson, *Family Dependence and the Origins of the Welfare State in Britain and France 1914–1945* (Cambridge, 1993).

37. Lowe, *Welfare State*, p. 34.

38. Jane Lewis, 'Gender, the Family and Women's Agency in the Building of "Welfare States": The British Case', *Social History* 19/1 (1994), pp. 37–55; Jane Lewis, *The Politics of Motherhood: Child and Maternal Welfare in England, 1900–1939* (1980).

39. *Economist*, 23 October 1993, 'Farewell, welfare: After almost 60 years of

triumph, the Nordic welfare states have found there must be limits to taxing and spending'; *Economist*, 9 October 1993, 'Worse and worse: Sweden's gathering political crisis'.

40. Robert D. Plotnick, 'Changes in Poverty, Income Inequality, and the Standard of Living in the United States during the Regan Years', *International Journal of Health Services* 23/2, pp. 347–58; T. Daniel Slesnick, 'Gaining Ground: Poverty in the Postwar United States', *Journal of Political Economy* 101/1, pp. 1–38.

41. Michael Wilson, 'The German Welfare State: A Conservative Regime in Crisis', in *Comparing Welfare States: Britain in International Context*, edited by Allan Cochrane and John Clarke (1993), pp. 141–72.

42. David Piachaud, 'Poverty in Britain 1899–1983', *Journal of Social Policy* 17/3 (1988), pp. 335–49; Frances Fox Piven and Richard A. Cloward, *Regulating the Poor: The Functions of Public Welfare* (1974).

43. *Ibid.*, pp. 344–5; *Economist*, 26 December 1992, 'Family values the bargain breaks – Marriage is a bargain between men and women. That bargain is increasingly broken through divorce. The sufferers are men, women and children'; *Economist*, 20 March 1993, 'Unhappy families: Governments are increasingly unable to ignore the costs of divorce'.

44. Alan Walker, 'The Persistence of Poverty among Older People', in *Research Highlights of Social Work, 22: Poverty Deprivation and Social Work*, edited by Ralph Davidson and Angus Erskine (1992), pp. 86–7.

45. Peter Hedstrom and Stein Ringen, 'Age and Income in Contemporary Society: A Research Note', *Journal of Social Policy* 16/2 (1887), pp. 227–39, suggests (p. 235) that Britain has one of the highest poverty rates of the advanced nations and that this situation probably worsened due to the de-indexation of pensions from earnings; Walker, 'Persistence of Poverty', p. 92.

46. Kaushika Amin with Carey Oppenheim, *Poverty in Black and White: Deprivation and Ethnic Minorities* (1992).

47. Michael Hill, *The Welfare State in Britain: A Political History since 1945* (Aldershot, 1993), p. 124.

48. *Ibid.*, p. 125, quoting from the Central Statistics Office, *Social Trends* and *National Income and Expenditure*, annual publications. These form the basis of the other statistics given in this section.

49. *The Observer*, 2 July 1993.

50. *The Guardian*, 21 June 1994.

51. *The Times*, 29 June 1994.

52. Lowe, *Welfare State*, p. 325, quoting Hugo Young, *One of Us* (1990), p. 521.

53. *The Guardian*, 7 May 1994.

54. *Ibid.*, 5 July 1994.

55. *The Observer*, 3 July 1994.

56. William Goodhart, 'Rebuilding the Welfare State', *The Guardian*, 4 May 1994.

CONCLUSION

The last two centuries have seen the enormous extension of social policy in Britain. The basis of much of it has been the attempt to tackle poverty. In other words, the failures of the Poor Law – or, more particularly, the 1834 New Poor Law – have provided the impetus for the evolution of social policy from the 1830s to the late 1940s, shaping attitudes towards health, unemployment and old age. Of course, the irony is that, in relative terms, and allowing for the changing nature of society, poverty today remains broadly at the same 25 and 30 per cent level that it was at the end of the nineteenth century. Indeed, there is evidence that, after having fallen in the 1950s, the levels of poverty rose rapidly in the 1980s.

The New Poor Law attempted to distinguish between the pauper (the destitute) and the poor, although it failed to achieve this objective until the 1870s. The COS, the Guild of Help and other voluntary bodies sought to deal with the poor rather than with the destitute or 'hopeless' cases, in a rescue bid to encourage self-help, respect for authority and other Victorian and Edwardian values. In the end, however, neither voluntary help nor the Poor Law, which came under intense scrutiny in the Edwardian years, was able to tackle the problem of the poor in any effective manner. Indeed, the Liberal reforms of 1906–14 were partly a pragmatic response to these failures and an attempt to lighten the burden of responsibilities on the Poor Law in a more politically sensitive and enlightened society by attempting to relieve it of some of those driven to poor relief by illness, unemployment and old age. The Labour reforms of 1945–8 took matters further and replaced the selective social policies of the Liberal reforms with a universal provision of benefits which created a safety net to prevent individuals and families falling into destitution and poverty.

The British Welfare State had developed largely in order to protect its citizens from the exigencies of life. There were many ways in which this could be achieved. The major question, then, is why did the state intervene and extend its responsibilities in the way that it did? Why did the British social security system emerge as it did in 1948?

Several possible explanations were outlined in the introduction and most of these have appeared as partial explanations in various areas of social policy and at particular times. Bentham's ideas certainly found some influence in such areas as the New Poor Law, health and policing, since his disciples were to be found in these areas but were often absent in others. Even where Benthamism carried influence, the domination of central control was never easily accomplished. The New Poor Law was not uniform but subject to immense local variation and compromise. Many areas were not directly controlled by the General Board of Health and there were three types of local policing arrangement – the metropolitan, municipal and county – which were often subject to local diversity as cultural factors shaped their local experiences. Marxists such as R. D. Storch might have believed in the central power of the police state, but there is little evidence to suggest that it was ever put in place for England and Wales as a whole. Localism was obviously a major factor inhibiting centralization and influencing the evolution of Victorian social policy, although it appears to have become rather less so from the First World War onwards, even though Poplarism and the Public Assistance Committees indicated some semblance of continued local variation. Ideology often hit a brick wall when it came to local application.

Social policy has also failed to progress as the Whig tradition of history would expect and the bureaucratic explanation has not been free from the challenges posed by local resistance. The Whig approach has tended to focus upon the 'enlightened' legislation passed rather than upon what actually happened. The New Poor Law could barely be recognized in many localities in the 1850s and 1860s because of the compromises that had been made to the application of 'less eligibility' and the workhouse test. The bureaucratic tradition fails to offer sufficient explanation, for it quite clearly did not work in health, the Poor Law and education in the 1840s and 1850s, when there was something of an administrative hiatus. Nevertheless, the bureaucratic tradition can claim some influence from the 1860s onwards in education, with the 1862 Revised Code, and in health and the Poor Law with the formation of the Local Government Board in 1871.

The conspiratorial Marxist approach and the capitalistic perspective have their deficiencies as well, even though it is obvious that the British Welfare State has always operated within a capitalist framework, particularly in the last two decades. Even at its height, in the late 1940s, the modern Welfare State commanded influence over less than one-fifth of the British economy. Indeed, one must accept that nationalization and the extension of the Welfare State lay dormant after the summer of 1948 and that it is the employers and their capitalism that have written the social agenda over the last twenty years or so.

The evolution of social policy may owe much more to democratic control, pragmatism and pluralism. The extension of both parliamentary and local voting powers in the nineteenth century certainly provoked reforms in local government and education. Much of social policy was clearly pragmatic, as were the financial reforms of the Poor Law in the

1860s which related Poor Law rates to the ability to pay and ensured that more money was available for relief. Pluralism has always been evident, with the state having to balance the various interests in the social legislation that emerged. This was particularly evident in the history of national insurance in the twentieth century and the evolution and development of the National Health Service between 1946 and 1948, with insurance companies, employers, doctors and other groups vying with political parties, governments and their leaders to shape the precise contours of social policy. Nye Bevan was very well aware of the pluralistic influences shaping his NHS in the late 1940s. However, pluralism was less evident in the Thatcher years, when many interest groups, particularly the trade unions, were simply not listened to.

Notwithstanding the assertion that pragmatism, pluralism and democratic influences have greatly shaped the evolution of social policy, it is obviously the case that British social policy has followed no straight line. Developments in one direction have often been offset by moves in the other. In other words, there is no particular trajectory or integrated explanation on offer, but many different policies developing at any one time and often for different reasons.

The political attitudes of parties that form government are clearly vital in the evolution of the Welfare State. Today, as the last chapter made clear, the Thatcherite commitment or ideology, based upon the rolling back of the state, has assumed rather more importance that anyone could have envisaged in 1979 – even though Dennis Healey's monetarism eased the return to the so-called 'Victorian values' espoused by Thatcherite Conservatism. Yet selectivity and the curbing of the enormous social expenditure budgets would have had to have been considered by any British government, regardless of its political complexion, by the 1970s. The fact is that the relative economic decline of Britain has forced politicians to think the unthinkable and to challenge the notion that the Welfare State should be universal. The British Welfare State, based upon the principle of universality, would appear to be unsustainable and, as a result, the Beveridge-style Welfare State is already effectively dead – killed more by the monetarism of Healey in 1976 than the monetarism of Thatcher in the 1980s. By the same token, there is a level of expectation about pensions, unemployment benefit and so on which makes it difficult for even the most Draconian of governments to reduce social expenditure. Even under Thatcher and Major, the Tories have failed to make substantial cuts in social expenditure, even if universalism has been replaced by selectivity and targeting.

Perhaps British social policy has come full circle, although this is not to suggest that the return of a Labour government, the emergence of some pressing political issue or the influence of some great thinker may not change its line of development once again. The only thing that seems certain is that the Beveridge commitment to universalism is almost certainly dead, victim of the enormous costs involved and the limited resources available to a declining industrial economy with a rapidly ageing population. Even now, as indicated in Chapter Twelve, the alternatives are being discussed.

DOCUMENTS

The Poor Law, c. 1780–1870s

Document 1 *Report of the Poor Law Commissioners*, xxvii (1834), pp. 227–8, 261–2.

The principle of 'less eligibility'

The most pressing of the evils which we have described are those connected with the relief of the Able-bodied. They are the evils, therefore, for which we shall first propose remedies ... If we believed the evils stated ... to be necessarily incidental to the compulsory relief of the able-bodied, we should not hesitate in recommending its entire abolition. But we do not believe that, under strict regulations, adequately enforced, such relief may be afforded safely and even beneficially ...

It may be assumed, that in the administration of relief the public is warranted in imposing such conditions on the individual relieved, as one conducive to the benefit either of the individual himself, or the country at large, at whose expense he is to be relieved.

The first and most essential of all conditions, a principle which we find universally admitted, even by those whose practice is at variance with it, is, that his situation on the whole shall not be made really or apparently so eligible as the situation of the independent labourers, the condition of the independent class is depressed; their industry is impaired, their employment becomes unsteady, and its remuneration in wages is diminished. Such persons, therefore, are under the strongest inducements to quit the less eligible class of labourers and enter the more eligible class of paupers. The converse is the effect when the pauper class is placed in its proper position, below the condition of the independent labourer. Every penny bestowed, that tends to render the condition of the pauper more eligible than that of the independent labourer, is a bounty on indolence and vice. We have found, that as the poor-rates are at present administered they operate as bounties of this description, to the amount of several millions annually.

The Workhouse Test
We have seen that in every instance in which the able-bodied labourers have been rendered independent of partial relief, or of relief otherwise than in a well-regulated workhouse –

1. Their industry has been restored and improved.
2. Frugal habits have been created and strengthened.
3. The permanent demand for their labour has increased.
4. And the increase has been such, that their wages, so far from being depressed by the increased amount of labour in the market, have in general advanced.
5. The number of improvident and wretched marriages has diminished.
6. Their discontent has been abated and their moral and social conditions in every way improved ...

The chief specific measures that we recommend ... are –

First, that except as to medical attendance ... all relief whatever to able-bodied persons or to their families, otherwise than in well-regulated workhouses (i.e. places where they may be set to work according to the spirit and intention of the 43rd Elizabeth) shall be declared unlawful and shall cease ...

A well regulated workhouse meets all cases, and appears to be the only means by which the intention of the statute of Elizabeth, that all the able-bodied men shall be set to work, can be carried into execution. ... And although we admit that able-bodied persons in the receipt of out-door allowances and partial relief, may be and in some cases are, placed in a condition less eligible than that of an independent labourer of the lowest class; yet to persons so situated relief in a workhouse would not be a hardship ... The express or implied ground of his application is, that he is in danger of perishing from want.

Document 2 Halifax Union, from a bundle of letters on settlement and other matters, Calderdale Branch of the West Yorkshire Archives Service, Central Library, Halifax, Has/B 34/4/, dealing with a loan to build a workhouse.

Halifax 1 December 1838

My dear Sir,

In the course of a short conversation which Mr. E Waterhouse and myself had today [with the clerk?] it appeared that he had received a letter from the Poor Law Commission in answer to our application from this Union for a loan of £8,000 with reference to which Mr. Pollard's absence from home I have undertaken to communicate with you. ... when the propriety of introducing the question as to building an Union workhouse was discussed and you gave us to understand that the requisite funds would be furnished from the Exchequer Loan office which was afterwards confirmed by a private letter to Mr. Brear. It now appears that the Poor Law Commission wish us now to endeavour to raise the loan from private sources. A plan having been proposed to the board on the strength of what has passed for borrowing the money at

4% and repaying the money by installments extending over twenty years and that plan having been approved by the board it would be very unpolitic under the existing circumstances to disturb that arrangements particularly as it is pretty certain that the money could not be otherwise raised. It would be very much better not again to raise the question if it can possibly be avoided.

My object therefore is under the peculiar circumstances of the case to suggest that you should give to the Commission such explanation as may induce them to procure for us the necessary loan without further mentioning the question at our local board. In fact I hesitate not to say that if our procuring depends on local loans we shall raise nothing whilst the very mention of a doubt as to the funds will tend greatly to embarrass us. I hope therefore that you will be able to arrange this matter and maintain the answer of the forward to our application for a loan with be withheld for the final Board of Guardians summonsed.

WB
A. Power Esq. Copy

Policing in the Early and Mid-Nineteenth Century

Document 3 Extract from the 1853 Select Committee Report to Consider the Expediency of adopting a more Uniform System of Police in England and Wales, and in Scotland, evidence of Charles Harris (Chief Constable of Hampshire 1842–1856), presented 26 May 1853.

Question:
30. (Chairman) Do you think the expense of the constabulary in the county and borough together, would be materially increased by the union of the boroughs with the county? – No, if the whole were consolidated into one new force the expense of each would be lessened …
34. (Mr. Rich) You have stated that you think it would be conducive to an efficient police, if the police of the boroughs were incorporated in the police of the country; will you state the inconveniences which now result from those boroughs not being incorporated? – The want of co-operation between the boroughs and the counties is a great evil; if the forces were not consolidated fewer men would be needed. The boroughs are generally the central points from whence criminals issue into the surrounding districts to commit offences, and to which they return with their plunder; the town forces having no interest in the prevention or direction of the offences committed in the county, parties are allowed to pass unquestioned.

35. (Mr. Fitzroy) Can you tell the Committee in which of the boroughs in Hampshire there is a police force separate from the county? – Portsmouth, Winchester, Newport and Basingstoke.

36. (Mr. Rich) You say you find there is a want of co-operation in the police force? – Yes, there is a want of co-operation, there is no denying that a jealousy exists between the two forces, but not in my opinion to such an extent on the part of the county as the boroughs, the county constabulary being the larger force of the two....

38. In the event of the occurrence of a crime, do your superintendents immediately communicate the fact that crime having been committed to the superintendents of the various boroughs? – Certainly they do, if it is a matter of importance; they would perhaps not mention the petty depredation.

39. Inversely, do the superintendents of the boroughs communicate with your superintendents? – Very rarely ...

The Factory Question, c. 1802–1870s

Document 4   Extract from the famous letter on 'Yorkshire Slavery' written by Richard Oastler and published in the *Leeds Mercury*, 16 October 1830.

Let truth speak out, appalling as the statement may appear. The fact is true. Thousands of our fellow-creatures and fellow subjects, both male and female, the miserable inhabitants of a Yorkshire town (Yorkshire now represented in Parliament by the giant of anti-slavery principles) are this very moment existing in a state of slavery, more horrid than are the victims of that hellish system 'colonial slavery'. These innocent creatures drawl out, unpitied, their short but miserable existence, in a place famed for its profession of religious zeal, whose inhabitants are ever foremost in professing 'temperance' and 'reformation', and are striving to outrun their neighbours in missionary exertions, and would fain send the Bible to the farthest corner of the globe – aye, in the very place where the anti-slavery fever rages most furiously, her apparent charity is not more admired on earth, than her real cruelty is abhorred in Heaven. The very streets which receive the droppings of an Anti-Slavery Society are every morning wet by the tears of innocent victims at the accursed shrine of avarice, who are compelled (not by the cart-whip of the negro slave driver) but by the dread of the equally appalling thong or strap of the overlooker, to hasten, half-dressed, but not half-fed to those magazines of British infantile slavery – the worsted mills in the town and neighbourhood of Bradford!!! ...

Thousands of little children, both male and female, but principally female, from seven to fourteen years of age, are daily compelled to labour from six o'clock in the morning to seven in the evening, with only – Britons, blush while you read it! – with only thirty minutes allowed for eating and recreation. Poor infants! ye are indeed sacrificed at the shrine of avarice, without even the solace of the negro slave; ye are no more than he is, free agents; ye are compelled to work as long as the necessity of your needy parents may require, or the cold-blooded avarice of your worse than barbarian masters demand! ...

Document 5   A poster printed by H. Wardman, printer, of 6, Chapel-Lane, Bradford, supporting Richard Oastler and the ten hours movement and reporting upon their treatment of the factory commissioners. This is deposited in the Bradford branch of West Yorkshire Archives.

GET AWAY!!

Get Away!!!

Said 'King Richard'

THE COMMISSIONERS

have obeyed the *Royal* Word!!! Having *seen* in Leeds, and *felt* in Bradford, and everywhere, that they had disgusted all honest Men, and having been sickened by the Songs and terrified by the Groans, and haunted by the withered Forms of the Factory slaves, they are off to London to get their £200, for this *bad* Job, and to seek a better *if they can find it*. They set off from Bradford at Half-past Seven on Thursday Evening, the Road Ticket was made out for Keighley, but after they had ordered the Carriage, the Ticket was altered for Wakefield and the London Road. The Secretary of the Bradford Short Time Committee who had taken good Care of them in Bradford, kindly followed them out 34 Miles to Doncaster, and joined then, and warmed himself along with them at the Kitchen Fire of the Inn, at Two in the Morning!!

After such Rest as they could get, and a Saunter in Doncaster, and after trying to 'commissioner' the Bradford Secretary in vain, their Worships went of to London at One o'clock on Friday Afternoon as cross as old patch, when the Representative of the Short Time Committee of Yorkshire bade them a Long, Long Farewell!!!

'Confound their Politics, Frustrate their Knavish Tricks'

Live 'King Richard' and the Ten Hour Bill!!!

Document 6   Extract from L. Horner (1785–1864), a leading factory inspector, who in 1840 wrote a report *On the Employment of Children, in Factories and Other Works in the United Kingdom, and in some foreign countries*.

The Act of 1833 has been productive of much good: it has put an end to a large proportion of the evils which made the interference of the legislature then necessary. But it has not done nearly all the good that was intended: it has not by any means accomplished all the purposes for which it was passed. The failures have mainly arisen from the defects in the law itself; not in the principles it lays down, but in the machinery which was constructed for the purpose of carrying the principles into operation ... it was in some degree legislating in the dark ...

The defects of the existing law have been repeatedly pointed out by the inspectors in their reports; and the Bill that was brought in by Government last year, but withdrawn on account of the then advanced period of the session, remedied nearly the whole of the defects; although, in my opinion, not all of them, nor in the best way. The evidence given before the Committee, now sitting, has made the imperfections still more apparent; and there is, therefore, every reason to expect that a much better act will be obtained than would have passed before this late enquiry took place ...

Judging from the Government Bill of last year, it is not very probable that any material extension of the principles of the present Act will be made, except in the case of silk mills ... There never was any sound reason for these exemptions in favour if silk mill-owners, and there is none now.... And Parliament must tell the masters, that they must accommodate themselves the best way they can to the conditions upon which alone the State will allow them to purchase infant labour; and those conditions must be such as will effectually protect the health of the children, and secure some education for them, as to all other mill-owners, and to the workers of all ages employed in the factories ...

Document 7   Circular of the Keighley Short Time Committee to Members of Parliament, 1844.

AT A MEETING
Of the Short Time Committee of Keighley, in the West Riding of the County of York, held on Friday Evening, March 8th, 1844, the following resolution was unanimously adopted to which we beg respect-fully to draw your attention, in the hope that you may be pleased to give Lord Ashley your cordial support in the effort he is about to make to obtain a Law to protect Young Persons employed in Factories, from being worked in them more than Ten Hours per day for Five Days of the Week, and EIGHT on Saturday.

JOSEPH VICKERS, Secretary

Resolved – That this Meeting is deeply convinced that the just claims of the Factory Population require that the Hours of Labour for all Young Persons under 21 Years of Age, employed in Factories, should be limited to Ten per day, for Five days of the Week, and EIGHT on Saturday.

Health, Towns and the State, c. 1800–c. 1914

Document 8   Edwin Chadwick, *Report on the Sanitary Condition of the Labouring Population of Great Britain* (1842, 1965 edn.), pp. 422–4.

First, as to the extent and operation of the evils which are the subject of enquiry:

That the various forms of epidemic, endemic, and other diseases caused, or aggravated, or propagated chiefly amongst the labouring classes by atmospheric impurities produced by decomposing animal and vegetable substances, by damp and filthy, and close and overcrowded dwelling prevail amongst the population in every part of the kingdom, whether dwelling in separate houses, in rural villages, in small towns, in the larger towns – as they have been found to prevail in the lowest districts of the metropolis.

That such disease, wherever its attacks are frequent, is always found in connexion with the physical circumstances above specified, and that where those circumstances are removed by drainage, proper cleansing, better ventilation, and other means of diminishing atmospheric impurity, the frequency and intensity of such disease is abated; and where the removal of the noxious agencies appears to be complete, such disease almost entirely disappears. ...

That high prosperity in respect of employment and wages, and various abundant food, have afforded to the labouring classes no exemptions from attacks of epidemic disease, which have been frequent and as fatal in periods of commercial and manufacturing prosperity as in any others.

That the formation of all habits of cleanliness in obstructed by defective supplies of water.

That the annual loss of life from filth and bad ventilation are greater than the loss from death or wounds in any wars in which the country has been engaged in modern times.

Secondly, as to the means by which the present sanitary condition of the labouring classes may be improved:

The primary and most important measures, and at the same time the most practicable, and within the recognized province of public administration, are drainage, the removal of all refuse of habitations, streets, and roads, and the improvement of the supplies of water.

That the chief obstacles to the immediate removal of decomposing refuse of towns and habitations have been the expense and annoyance of the hand labour and cartage requisite for the purpose.

That this expense may be reduced by one-twentieth or to one-thirteenth, or rendered inconsiderable, by the use of water and self-acting means of removal by improved and cheaper sewers and drains.

That refuse when thus held in suspension in water may be most cheaply and innoxiously conveyed to any distance out of towns, and also in the best form for productive use, and that the loss and injury by the pollution of natural streams may be avoided.

That for all these purposes, as well as for domestic use, better supplies of water are absolutely necessary.

Education, c. 1800–1944

Document 9   Extract from the Report of the Parliamentary Committee (Select Committee inquiring into the Education of the Lower Orders), 20 June 1816.

The Select Committee appointed to inquire into the Education of the Lower Orders in the Metropolis, and to report their Observations thereupon ... have found reason to conclude, that a very large number of the poor Children are wholly without the means of Instruction, although their parents appear to be generally very desirous of obtaining that advantage for them.

Your Committee have also observed with much satisfaction, the highly beneficial effects produced upon all parts of the Population which, assisted in whole or in part by various Charitable Institutions have enjoyed the benefits of Education.

Your Committee have not had time this Session fully to report their Opinion upon the different branches of their enquiry, but they feel persuaded that the greatest advantage would result in this Country from Parliament taking proper measures, in concurrence with the prevailing disposition of the Community, for supplying the deficiency of the means of Instruction which exist at present, and for extending the blessing to the Poor of all descriptions.

Document 10   An extract from a letter from Lord John Russell to Lord Lansdowne, Lord President of the Privy Council, 4 February 1839.

After a lengthy discussion on the defects of English and Welsh education, the letter continues in the following manner, referring mainly to 'normal school' or teacher training establishments.

Some of these defects appear to admit of an immediate remedy, and I am directed by Her Majesty to desire in the first place, that your Lordship, with four other of the Queen's Servants should form a board or Committee, for the consideration of all matters affecting the Education of the People.

For the present it is thought advisable that this Board should consist of:

> the Lord President of the Council
> the Lord Privy Seal
> the Chancellor of the Exchequer
> the Secretary of State for the Home Department
> the Master of the Mint.

It is proposed that the Board should be entrusted with the application of any sums which may be voted by Parliament for the purpose of Education in England and Wales.

Among the first objects to which any grant may be applied will be the establishment of a Normal School.

In such a school a body of schoolmasters may be formed, competent to assume the management of similar institutions in all parts of the country. In such a school likewise the best modes of teaching may be introduced, and those who wish to improve the schools of their neighbourhood may have an opportunity of observing their results.

The Board will consider whether it may not be advisable for some years to apply a sum of money annually in aid of the Normal Schools of the National and of the British and Foreign School Societies.

They will likewise determine whether their measures will allow them to afford gratuities to deserving schoolmasters ...

In any Normal or Model School to be established by the Board, four principal objects should be kept in view, viz.

1. Religious Instruction
2. General Instruction
3. Moral Training
4. Habits of Industry

Of these four I need only allude to the first; with respect to Religious Instruction there is, as your Lordship is aware, a wide or apparently wide difference of opinion among those who have been most forward in promoting education.

The National Society, supported by the Established Church, contend that the schoolmaster should be invariably a Churchman; that the Church catechism should be taught in a school to all scholars, that all should be required to attend Church on Sundays, and that the schools should be in every case under the superintendance of the clergyman of the parish.

The British and Foreign School Society, on the other hand, admit Churchmen and Dissenters equally as schoolmasters, require that the Bible should be taught in their schools, but insist that no Catechism should be admitted.

Document 11   *The Report of the Commissioners appointed to Inquire into the State of Popular Education in England and Wales* (Newcastle Report), xxi (1861), I, chapter six, pp. 294–5.

Majority View

The greater portion of the members of the Commission are of opinion that the course pursued by the Government in 1839, in recommending a grant of public money for the assistance of education, was worse than the methods adopted to carry out the object have proved successful; and that while it is expedient to make considerable alterations in the form in which this public assistance is given, it would not be desirable either to withdraw it or largely to diminish its amount. Without entering into general considerations of duty of a State with regard to the education of the poorer classes of the community, they think it sufficient to refer to the fact that all the principal nations of Europe, and the United States of America, as well as British North America, have felt it necessary to provide for the education of the people by public taxation; and to express their own belief that when the grant of education was first begun, the education of the greater portion of the labouring classes had long been in a neglected state, that the parents were insensible to its advantage, and were (and still continue to be) in most cases incapable from poverty of providing it for their children, and that religious and charitable persons, interested in the conditions of the poor, had not the power to supply the main cost of an education which, to be good, must always be expensive.

The Role of the State, Philanthropy and the Treatment of Poverty in the Second Half of the Nineteenth Century

Document 12   Extract from the *Eighth Annual Report of the Charity Organisation Society* (1876), appendix iv, pp. 24–5.

The principle is, that it is good for the poor that they should meet all the ordinary contingencies of life, relying not upon public and private charity but upon their own industry and thrift, and upon the powers of self-help that are to be developed by individual and collective effort. Ample room will still be left for the exercise of an abundant charity in dealing with exceptional misfortune ... But it is hurtful misuse of money to spend on assisting the labouring classes to meet emergencies which they should have anticipated and provided for.

Document 13 Extracts from the Chamberlain Circular (1886), *Pauperism and Distress: Circular Letter to Boards of Guardians*.

Local Government Board, Whitehall, SW   15 March 1886

Sir,

The enquiries which have been recently undertaken by the Local Government Board unfortunately confirm the prevailing impression as to the existence of exceptional distress amongst the working classes. This distress is partial as to its locality, and is no doubt due in some measure to the long continued severity of the weather.

... They [the Local Government Board] are convinced that in the ranks of those who do not ordinarily seek poor law relief there is evidence of much and increasing privation, and if the depression in trade continues it is to be feared that large numbers of persons usually in regular employment will be reduced to the greater straits.

Any relaxation of the general rule at present obtaining, which requires as a condition of relief to able-bodied male persons on the ground of their being out of employment, the acceptance of an order for admission to the workhouse, or the performance of an adequate task of work as a labour test, would be most disastrous, as tending directly to restore the condition of things which, before the reform of the poor always destroyed the independence of the labouring classes and increased the poor rate until it became an almost unsupportable burden.

It is not desirable that the working classes should be familiarised with poor relief ...

What is required in the endeavour to relieve artisans and others who have hitherto avoided poor law assistance, and who are temporarily deprived of employment is:

1. Work which will not involve the stigma of pauperism;
2. Work which all can perform, whatever may have been their previous avocations;
3. Work which does not compete with that of other labourers at present in employment;

And, lastly, work which is not likely to interfere with the resumption of regular employment in their own trade by those who seek it.

The Board have no power to enforce the adoption of any particular proposals, and the object of this circular is to bring the subject generally under the notice of the boards of guardians and local authorities.

In districts in which exceptional distress prevails, the Board recommend that the guardians should confer with the local authorities, and endeavour to arrange with the latter for the execution of work on which unskilled labour may be immediately employed.

These works may be of the following kind among others:

(a) Spade husbandry on sewage farm;
(b) Laying out of open spaces, recreation grounds, new cemeteries, or disused burial grounds;
(c) Cleansing of streets not usually undertaken by local authorities;
(d) Laying out and paving of new streets, etc.
(e) Paving of unpaved streets and making of footpaths in country roads;
(f) Providing or extending sewerage works and works of water supply.

… When the works are of such a character that the expenses may properly be defrayed out of borrowed money, the local authorities may rely that there will be every desire on the part of the Board to deal promptly with the application for their sanction to a loan. …

(Signed) J. Chamberlain

Document 14 Extracts from B. S. Rowntree, *Poverty: A Study of Town Life* (1901; 2nd edn., 1906), pp. 297–300.

In chapter four it was shown that for a family of father, mother, and three children, the minimum weekly expenditure upon which physical efficiency can be maintained in York is 21s. 8d. made up as follows:

	s.	d.
Food	12.	9
Rent (say)	4.	0
Clothing, light, fuel, etc.	4.	11
	21.	8

The necessary expenditure for families larger or smaller than the above will be correspondingly greater or less. This estimate was based upon the assumptions that the diet is selected with a careful regard to the nutritive values of various foods stuffs, and that these are all purchased at the lowest current prices. It only allows for a diet less generous as regards variety than that supplied to able-bodied paupers in workhouses. It further assumes that no clothing is purchased which is not absolutely necessary for health, and assumed too that it is of the plainest and most economical description.

The number of persons whose earnings are so low that they cannot meet the expenditure necessary for the above standard of living, stringent to severity though it is, and bare of all creature comforts, was shown to be no less than 7,230, or almost exactly 10 per cent of the total population of the city. These persons, then, represent those who are in 'primary' poverty.

The number of those in 'secondary' poverty was arrived at by ascertaining the total number living in poverty, and subtracting those living in 'primary' poverty. The investigators, in the course of their house-to-house visitation, noted those families who were obviously living in a state of poverty, i.e. in obvious want and squalor. Sometimes they obtained definite information that the bulk of the earnings was spent on drink or otherwise squandered, sometimes the external evidence of poverty in the home was so clear as to make verbal evidence superfluous.

In this way 20,302 persons, or 27.84 per cent of the total population, were returned as living in poverty. Subtracting those whose poverty is 'primary', we arrive at the number living in 'secondary' poverty, viz. 13,072, or 17.93 per cent of the total population.

Voluntary help and the state, 1900–1914

Document 15   *Report on the Guilds of Help in England* by G. R. Snowden, an assistant general inspector of the Local Government Board (Cd 56664, 1911).

Origin and Development of the Movement
1.   The first Guild of Help was inaugurated chiefly by the efforts of Mr. Bentham and Mrs. Moser, in Bradford, in 1904. In 1905 Guilds were founded at Bolton, Eccles, Halifax, Heckmondwike, Salford and Swinton (near Manchester) ... Among the number of Guilds of Help are not reckoned the Charity Organisation Societies, or such bodies as the Central Relief Committee at Liverpool or the Council of Social Services at Hampstead, which pursue the same objects by not dissimilar methods.
2.   The idea of the Guild of Help movement no doubt came partly from the Elberfeld poor law system ...

General Objects
4.   The general objects of the Guilds of Help may be summarised as follows from their published statements:–
(1) To deepen the sense of civic responsibility for the care of the poor, and to promote, through personal services, a neighbourly feeling among all classes of the community.
(2) To provide a friend for all those in need of help and advice, and to encourage them in efforts towards self-help.
(3) To discourage indiscriminate almsgiving by private persons, and to organise methods whereby the generosity of such persons may be wisely directed and enabled to secure results of permanent benefit.

(4) To co-operate with all existing charitable agencies in order to prevent overlapping.

(5) To arrest the inroads of poverty in its initial stages in order to prevent the poor from sinking into destitution and to ensure, so far as possible, that no home shall be broken up which can be saved by friendly advice and assistance.

(6) To consider the causes of poverty in the town and to bring influence to bear through public bodies or by private efforts to lessen or remove them.

5. Attention should be directed to two general characteristics common to all Guilds. First, the work is carried on by voluntary assistance and unpaid personal service; and, as in Elberfeld, the person who visits and investigates a case has a voice in deciding what assistance is to be given. Second, a prominent position is given to the idea of a man's civic responsibilities, his special duties to the place in which he lives and to his fellow-citizens as such. It is sought to foster local patriotism and to create an interest in all matters of local importance. The field of the Guild's work coincides usually, with the borough and other areas of municipal government; the Mayor, or the Chairman of the District Council, is its President ... In order to emphasize this point of view, some such words as 'The City' or 'Citizens', or 'Civic' are frequently prefixed to the title Guild of Help. It should be added that all Guilds profess absolute independence of all parties in politics and religion.

Organisation and Methods

10. The town is divided into a number of units named 'districts' ... The helpers in each district form the 'district committee'.

11. The helpers are drawn from all classes of society; in a few Guilds half or more than half are men and women of the working classes. ...

Promotion of Co-operation among Charities

25. The promotion of co-operation among charities is one of the foremost aims of the Guild of Help movement; and perhaps the most practical step in this direction, as a means to the prevention of overlapping in the distribution of relief, is the establishment of a general register of all persons receiving aid from charitable sources. ...

Co-operation with Public Authorities

34. The civic ideal of a Guild of Help ... comprehends essentially the closest possible co-operation with the public authorities. This ideal, unfortunately, seems at present to be far from attainment, but some advances have been made towards it.

Document 16   A small selection of extracts from a casebook of the Bradford Guild of Help, amongst 5,682 casebooks deposited in West Yorkshire Archives, Bradford.

Mrs 32   Mr .... 35 woolcomber, 23s. per week full time, works at Clough's Canal Road.

Harold	12	School	St. Patrick's
Herbert	9		
Joseph	6		
Leonard	3		a home
Eilene	6 months		Died 7 November 1907

First Visit 20.6.07

... children very clean and tidy. Mrs .... would like two days work and then could manage. Husband gives wife 18/- a week out of 23/-. He repairs the children's boots himself and keeps himself in clothes, smokes but does not drink. Recommended them to the COS for holiday which they have done ... Mrs .... is not a good manager. [Comment of Director of District Committee] The moral influence in teaching how to cook & to make clothes. If gifts are made, let it be a demonstration of economical cookery or in the making of clothes. JM 18/7/07.

21.11.07 [Youngest child taken to the infirmary.] Dr. Martin examined her & found she was suffering from pneumonia. Mrs .... left her in the infirmary but went to see her frequently but the little thing got gradually worse & died on the third day. Mrs .... said the child was insured & after the funeral was paid for there still remained sufficient money to pay off what she owed the Insurance people. Now the baby is not there to be looked after she is anxious to get a little work to help her over the winter ... I have given her clothes so that she would look quite tidy if work could be got for her. ...

16.12. 07 ... Went to see Mrs .... I told her that I had found she was not telling me the truth as to the amount of the wages ... had. She said she had told me what her husband had given her, and she was sure he would not keep her short of fire and food if he had it. I told her to tell Mr .... what I had said, and she will tell me what he said next time I called. I am afraid to say too much to her for fear of causing trouble between them. They seem so comfortably together. The man seems to be a good husband and father. I gave her a Xmas dinner and Toys for the children ...

Document 17   Extract from a letter from Beatrice Webb to W. H. Beveridge, 4 May 1907, asking for assistance in connection with the Poor Law Inquiry, taken from the Beveridge Collection, Letters, IIb, 6, in the British Library of Political and Economic Science.

Dear Mr. Beveridge,

I want your help in respect to the Poor Law Enquiry into the working of the Unemployed Act. We begin this Enquiry next Autumn. But from past experience of the work of the Commission I see that we shall get little else but 'opinion' and those mostly in a negative direction. Messrs Pringle and Jackson's investigation did little else but discredit Relief work and suggested no alternative ways of dealing with the Unemployed. Moreover their investigation was limited by their Reference to the working of the Unemployment Acts and they were not asked to Enquire or Report into the working of the Poor Law alternative to the Workhouse test, the Labour Yard. These alternatives have also been ruled out of our Enquiry next Autumn, as it is assumed that we have dealt with it in our general Enquiry into Poor Law Administration which is now practically concluded. That is not the case, and these alternatives therefore hold the field if we arrive at our unfavourable verdict on Relief Work. What I wanted (but was over-ruled) was an Enquiry into all ways of dealing with the Able-bodied or persons assumed to be able-bodied, including the Casual Ward, and therefore vagrancy. Only in that way shall we get a statesmanlike grasp on the question. The Charity Organisation Society, on the other hand, is to break the subject up into little bits and get a negative conclusion on each division so as to fall back in the 'non Possumous'.

Now what I should like would be some help both in suggestions as to possible reform and actual investigations into fact. Would it be possible to form a little Committee to take each way of dealing with the Able-bodied into consideration, getting all the evidence together on each part, and looking at each by the light of the other. If then we could get a secretary (for a small salary to do the clerk's work and possibly some additional investigation) we might draw up a report of our own which the Progressive members of the Commission might circulate as Memorandum. ...

Beatrice Webb

Document 18   Extract from the evidence given by Sir William Beveridge on employment exchanges (1906), drawing upon the 'Criticism of the Existing Methods of Relief to Able-Bodied' (1906). Beveridge Collection, III, 32.

We have now shown that municipal relief-works have not been assisted but rather prejudiced the better classes of workmen they were intended to help. On the other hand they have encouraged the casual labourers, by giving them a further supply of that casual work which is so dear to their hearts and so demanding to their character. They have encouraged and not helped the incapables. Moreover, the provision of artificial work for the unskilled labourers in particular localities can only tend to fix in such localities there agglomerations of unskilled labour, to digress, which is one of the solutions of local employment. We regard, therefore, that we must preserve the system of relief-works suggested by the Local Government Board Circular of 1886 a failure, and we support our condemnation of this by the following extract for the Report of our Special Investigators:-

The Municipal Relief Works, encouraged by Mr. Chamberlain's circular in 1886 have been in operation for twenty years, and must, we think, be pronounced a complete failure – a failure accentuated by the attempt to organise them by the Unemployed Workmen's Act of 1905. The evidence we have collected seems conclusive that relief works are economically useless. Either ordinary work is taken, in which case it is merely forestalled, and later, throws out of employment the men who are in the more or less regular employ of the council, or else it is sham work which we believe to be even more deteriorating than direct relief. If the 'right to work' is to be construed as the right to easy work, we are directly encouraging the lazy and incompetent and discouraging the trade unionists and the thrifty. The evidence seems very strong that most men on relief work do not do their best, and to pay them less than ordinary wages only encourages the belief that they are not expected to do so. Competence to do the work required should be the basis for selection, not destitution and a large family. These are very good reasons for giving relief but not for giving work.

Document 19 Winston Churchill speaking to the House of Commons, 19 May 1909, from *Hansard*, 19 May 1909, on the issue of unemployment insurance.

So I come to unemployment insurance. It is not practicable at the present time to establish a universal system of unemployment insurance. … We have therefore to choose at the very outset of this subject between insuring some workmen in all trades and insuring all workmen in some trades. That is the first parting of the ways upon unemployment insurance. In the first case we can have a voluntary system and in the second a compulsory system. If you adopt a voluntary system of unemployment insurance, you are always exposed to this difficulty. The risk of unemployment varies so much between man and man, according to their qualities … and the risk varies so much between man and man that a voluntary system of unemployment insurance which the State subsidises always attracts those workers who are most likely to be unemployed. That is why all voluntary systems have broken down when they have been tried, because they accumulate a preponderance of bad risks against the insurance office, which is fatal to financial stability. On the other hand, a compulsory system of insurance, which does not add a contribution from outside, has always broken down, because of the refusal of the higher class of worker to assume unsupported a share of the burden of the weaker members of the community. We have decided to avoid these main difficulties. Our insurance scheme will present four main features. It will involve contributions from the workpeople and from the employers; those contributions will be aided by a substantial subvention from the State: it will be insurance by trade, following the suggestion of the Royal Commission; and it will be compulsory within those trades upon all unionists and non-unionists, skilled and unskilled, workmen and employers alike.

Document 20   Extract from the *Minority Report*, p. 684, of the Royal Commission on the Poor Laws and Relief of Distress (1905–9).

'UTOPIAN'

[Our] elaborate scheme for national organisation for dealing with the grave social evils of Unemployment, with its resultant Able-bodied Destitution, and the deterioration of hundreds of thousands of working class families, will seem to many persons Utopian. Experience proves, however, that this may mean no more than that it will take a little time to accustom people to the proposals, and to get them carried into operation. The first step is to make the whole community realise that the evil exists. At present, it is not too much to say that the average citizen of the middle or upper class takes for granted the constantly recurring destitution among wage-earning families due to Unemployment as part of the natural order of things ...

We have to report that, in our judgement, it is now administratively possible, if it is sincerely wished to do so, to remedy most of the evils of Unemployment ...

Document 21 Extract from the speech of David Lloyd George, Chancellor of the Exchequer, in the House of Commons debate, *Hansard*, 4 May 1911, referring to the health and unemployment aspects of the National Insurance Act of 1911.

In this country ... 30 per cent of pauperism is attributable to sickness. A considerable percentage would probably have to be added to that for unemployment. The administration of the Old Age Pensions Act has revealed the fact that there is mass poverty and destitution in this country which is too proud to wear the badge of pauperism, and which declines to pin that badge to its children. They would rather deprivation than do so …

The efforts made by the working classes to insure against the troubles of life indicate they are fully alive to the need of some provision being made. There are three contingencies against which they insure – death, sickness and unemployment There are 42,000,000 industrial policies against death in this country. … There is hardly a household in this country where there is not a policy of insurance against death. It is no part of our scheme at all, partly because the general ground has been covered …

Sickness comes next in order of urgency in the working-class mind. Between 6,000,000 and 7,000,000 people in this country have made provision against sickness, not all adequate and a good deal of it defective. Then come the third class, the insurance against unemployment. Here not a tenth of the working classes have made any provision against unemployment. …

What is the explanation that only a portion of the working-classes have made provision against sickness and unemployment? Is it that they consider it not necessary. Quite the reverse, as I shall prove by figures. In fact, those who stand in need of it make up the bulk of the uninsured. Why? Because very few can afford to pay the premiums, and pay them continually, which enable a man to provide against those three contingencies. As a matter of fact, you could not provide against all those three contingencies anything which would be worth a workman's while, without paying at any rate 1s. 6d. and 2s. per week at the very lowest. There are a multitude of working classes who cannot spare that, and ought not to be asked to spare it, because it involves the deprivation of children of the necessaries of life. Therefore, they are compelled to select, and the vast majority choose to insure against death alone. Those who can afford to take up all three insure against death, sickness and unemployment in that order. What are the explanations why they do not insure against all three? The first is that their wages are too low. The second difficulty, and it is the greatest of all, is that during the period of sickness and unemployment, when they are earning nothing, they cannot keep up premiums. … I do not think there is any better method, or one more practicable at the present moment, than a system of national which would invoke the aid of the State and the aid of the employer to enable the workmen to get over all these difficulties and make provision for himself for sickness and, as far as most precarious trades are concerned, against unemployment …

I now come to the machinery of the Bill we have got to work. Collection is the first thing. We shall collect out funds by means of stamps. That is purely the German system … Then comes the question, who is to dispense the benefits? In this country we have fortunately a number of very well-organised, well-managed, well-conducted benefit societies who have a great tradition behind them, and an accumulation of experience which is very valuable when you come to deal with questions like malingering.

I will now briefly outline the unemployment insurance. ... The scheme only applies to one-sixth of the industrial population. We propose to apply it only to the precarious trades, which are liable to very comfortable fluctuations. The benefit will be of a very simple character; it is purely a weekly allowance ... The machinery will be the Labour Exchanges and the existing unions which deal with unemployment ...

We have started, first of all, by taking two groups of trades, and we propose to organise them individually – the engineering group and the building group. They include building, construction of works, shipbuilding, mechanical engineering and the construction of vehicles. These are in trades in which you have the most serious fluctuations ... I ought to say here that you have not the same basis of actuarial calculation that you can in sicknesses that a certain fund will produce such and such benefits. In the case of sickness you have nearly 100 years' experience behind you, and you have the facts with regard to unemployment ...

I have explained as best I could the details of our scheme – the system of contributions and benefits and the machinery whereby something like 15,000,000 of people will be insured at any rate against the acute distress which now darkens the homes of the workmen, wherever there is sickness and unemployment.

The First World War and the Inter-War Years, 1914–1939

Document 22 Extract from the Increase of Rent and Mortgage Interest (War Restrictions) Act, 1915.

1. (1) Where the rent of a dwelling-house to which this Act applies, or the rate of interest on a mortgage to which this Act applies, has been, since the continuance of this Act, increased above the standard rent or the standard rate of interest as hereinafter defined, the amount by which the rent or interest payable exceeds the amount which would have been payable had the increase not been made, shall, notwithstanding any agreement to the contrary, be irrecoverable ...

    (3) No order for the recovery of possession of a dwelling-house to which this Act applies or for the ejectment of a tenant therefrom shall be made so long as the tenant continues to pay rent at the agreed rate ... and performs the other conditions of the tenancy ...

Document 23   Extract from a report on the conference on War Relief and Personal Service and council meeting of the National Association of the Guilds of Help, June 1915, quoted in *The Citizen* (organ of the Reading Guild of Help) 3/2 (September 1915).

There were 300 representatives from Local Representative Committees, branches of Soldiers' and Sailors' Family Association, C.O.S., the Guild of Help and a few others.
Miss Marsland, Secretary.
There were papers on the following subjects

1. The work of the Soldiers' and Sailors' Families Associations ...
2. Problems of finding employment for discharged and disabled soldiers and sailors and for widows after the war.
3. Features of the Local Representative Committee were described by Mr. D'Aeth of Liverpool and others. The general opinion was (except possibly in country districts) the Committees would not continue in their present form, and it was most desirable that the splendid output of voluntary effort and co-operation that they had shown should be preserved either as an extension of the existing bodies dealing with case work, or, where such did not exist, by others being transferred into such bodies after the war. ...

Document 24 Extract from the *Report of the Unemployment Insurance Committee*, 1927 (Blanesburgh Committee).

67. Rates of Benefit. – We have accepted the principle advocated on all sides that extended benefit as such shall disappear. Under our proposals there will be only one kind of benefit. To that benefit the contributor, if he complies with the conditions, shall be entitled according to these conditions.
Many suggestions have been made to us as to the rates of benefit ... This, it must never be forgotten, is a matter in which only a very limited range of choice is permissible. Ideal benefits must not be more generous than is consistent with the necessary conditions of a good scheme; on the other hand, they should certainly be so substantial that the insured contributor can feel that, if he has the misfortune to need them, then, taken in conjunction with such resources as may reasonably in the generality of cases, be expected to have been built up, they will be sufficient to prevent him from being haunted while at work by the fear of what must happen to him if he is unemployed. Subject to these considerations, the amount of benefit must depend upon the contributions that can be fairly called for ...

83. In its true conception an Unemployment Insurance Scheme should provide for the great bulk of genuine in a manner honourable to those whom it benefits. We understand that the Poor Law Acts ... prohibit ... the unconditional out-door relief of able-bodied persons, and ... we think both from the point of view of the parties to the Unemployment Insurance Scheme, and on general grounds, that, in so far as it deals with the able-bodied unemployed, Poor Law Relief should retain the deterrent effect which now attaches thereto ...

178. The really desirable thing is to get rid of unemployment itself ... The risk of genuine unemployment should be insured. An unemployment insurance scheme, compulsory, and covering at least the persons at present covered by the State scheme, should be a permanent feature of our Code of Social Legislation ...

Document 25 Extract from the *First Report of the Unemployment Assistance Board*, 1935.

Under the Act unemployment allowances are based on the 'household', that is, by reference to the needs of the applicant and the members of this household dependent on him; they are essentially different from unemployment benefit which is an individual and contractual right to a fixed sum ...

In considering the 'needs' of a household, it is also necessary to consider what 'means' are available towards those needs. The Act recognises that the members of a household who have resources, particularly wages ... are entitled to some part of their earnings for the purpose of living their own lives ... Thus it does not require a destitution test to be applied to the household.

The Act, however, contains no definition of 'members of the household'. The household does not necessarily correspond with family relationship ... The Board instructed its officers that the facts of a particular case might be examined along two broad lines. These are, first, that a person who was a member of a household during childhood should be regarded as a member of the household; and second, that a person who came into the household after reaching the age of employment on terms that made it clear that he was paying a reasonable rate for his board and lodgings should be regarded as a 'lodger' ... Thus, an adult son in the house of his unemployed father is a member of his father's household; but a girl going to live with her married sister and agreeing to pay a reasonable sum to her married sister for her board and lodging is not generally regarded as a member of her brother-in-law's household.

Document 26 Extracts from Violet Markham's Papers dealing with the interviews with long-term unemployed women conducted by the Unemployment Assistance Board, located in the British Library of Political and Economic Science, 8/29.

Special Enquiry: Report on the Experimental Interviewing of the Women's Register, Liverpool.

... The Problem

Numerically the problem of female applicants in Liverpool District is formidable, the number of women in receipt of the Unemployment Assistance allowance in the Liverpool areas being approximately 3,700. In relation to the total number of applicants in receipt of allowances for the District, this figure represents only 8.02% of the wholly unemployed Live Register of Women in the Merseyside Local Offices, the remaining 64 per cent being in receipt of Unemployment Insurance Benefit.

From this it may be inferred that there is a considerable amount of casual employment and seasonal work available for women, which serves to keep many in benefit who cannot obtain permanent employment throughout the year. ... 58% of the women on the Unemployment Assistance Board Live Register are over the age of 35. It will therefore be appreciated how obscure is the solution of the problem of finding alternative employment for such persons faced by the improbability of re-entering into factory work.

A large percentage of the younger long-term unemployed women are unskilled factory workers and others who are unsuitable for factory work by reason of lower mental and physical calibre. ...

2. Aim

The aim of the interviewing procedures as set forth in Mr. Owen's letter of the 6th September 1937 was 'to find women able to take advantage of existing training facilities, to discuss whether such facilities are adequate, and to suggest methods of extending them if that was not the case.

Interviews were arranged along with dependents and women members of the applicants' households not in receipt of U.I. Benefit or an allowance from the Board, in order to find the reason for their retention in their household, and to encourage and direct them to take advantage of the facilities provided for training, or obtaining suitable employment.

Additionally, 27 boys and 28 girls were specially interviewed with a parent or parents in an endeavour to assist in their welfare and to indicate the various provisions made through the Education Committee for their training and employment.

3. Training Courses ...
   (ii) Resident District Training Centre, Waldernheath, Harrogate
        12 Weeks – Domestic Subjects
        Women and girls 15 + 2/6 Pocket Money per week for Trainees
   (iii) Greycourt, nr. Lancaster.
        For older women of 40 years of age plus offered by the Central
        Committee for Women's Training and Employment
   2 Courses one commencing 25 October 1937 for 8 weeks and the
other 3 January 1938 for 11 weeks. Introduction to cooking ... dress-
making, upholstery ...

Part II
   (i) Younger applicants
   (ii) Age Group 25–40 Years
   The large amount of female casual employment available in Liverpool is obtained by women of this groups.
   The opportunities are good for work for periods ranging from a few
weeks to several months, and the expectations of these women prevent
them from taking serious attention to domestic work, whether
permanent or otherwise.
   (iii) Older women
   With the older women sympathy is the paramount feeling around.
Many of them have a substantial record of employment in the distant
past, but work was lost usually between the ages of 35 and 40 years.
Efforts to get back into wage earning employment have been genuine as
is evidenced by the number of short periods of work obtained during the
more recent years. These older women have deteriorated in health and
general stamina, or have genuine ailments which lower their vitality and
gradually they have to all appearances become practically unemployable.
   The number of shawl type, rough cleaner and bag and salvage
workers for whom nothing is likely to be offered in the way of wage
earning employment makes any generalisation of palliative measures
abortive for this group. ...

The Second World War, 1939–1945:
Beveridge and the Paper Chase

Document 27   Extract from the Beveridge Report (*Report on Social
Insurance and Allied Services*, 20 November 1942, Cmd 6404), para 17.

   A scheme of social insurance against interruption and destruction of
earning power and for special expenditure arising at birth, marriage
or death. The scheme embodies six fundamental principles: flat rate of

subsistence benefit; flat rate of contribution; unification of administrative responsibility; adequacy of benefit; comprehensives and classification ... Based on them, and in combination with national assistance and voluntary insurance as subsidiary methods, the aim of the Plan for Social Security is to make want under any circumstances unnecessary.

Document 28   Extract from *Tribune*, 4 December 1942.

Sir William Beveridge is a social evangelist of the old Liberal school. He is an honoured member of the Reform Club, and the horizon of his political aspirations is, therefore, not boundless. He specifically disavows many of the tenets of revolutionary Socialism, but he has a good heart and a clear, well-stocked head, and he has discharged his task with Liberal fervour and even a trace of Liberal innocence.

What kind of world would the honest Liberal like to establish? He would like to make a truce between private enterprise and State ownership. He would like the two to work in harness together, but above all, he would like, by resolute action, to appease the most obvious pains and succour the most grievous casualties which capitalism produced. From this dangerous angle Sir William has approached his task. He would like to establish a tolerable minimum standard of security for every citizen, for the injured worker, for the widow, for the aged, for the unemployed, for the sick and for the growing child.

This is a commendable ambition, and the desire to achieve it is certainly not confined to those who have dabbled or delved into Socialism. But the merit and novelty of Sir William is that he has set down with the authority of a statistician and on Government note paper the conditions which must be satisfied if this modest ambition is to be achieved. Here it is in black and white – a plain description of men's necessities, how much (or how little) he must have in his pocket if fear and want and hunger are to be lifted from his cares ... In short, Sir William has described the conditions in which the tears might be taken out of capitalism.

Document 29   *Employment Policy*, 1944 White Paper, Cmd 6527, paragraphs 41 and 66.

The Government accepts as one of their primary aims and responsibilities the maintenance of a high and stable level of employment after the war ... A country will not suffer from mass unemployment so long as the total demand for its goods and services is maintained at a high level.

The Attlee Years and the Modern Welfare State, 1945–1951

Document 30   Extracts from D. Houghton, *The Family Circle*, pp. 11, 13, 23.

The Family Allowance Act was passed by the Coalition Government and brought into operation by the Labour Government in August 1946.

The family Allowance is 5s. a week for each child *after the first*. This is paid out of taxation and not out of contributions we pay under the insurance scheme ...

The Labour Government's National Insurance Scheme is a better-than-Beveridge plan – and better than the Coalition Government's plan.

We received a big instalment of the new scheme when in October 1946, the Labour Government increased existing pensions from 20s. to 42s. for a married couple, and from 10s. to 26s. for a single person. Over three million old-age and widowed pensioners benefited from that increase. The higher standard of pension *reduced by a million* the number of folk who had previously sought extra help from the Assistance Board ...

The scheme provides for each insurance class, benefits suited to their way of life.

Class 1, the *employed*, no matter what their position or pay, are entitled to *all* benefits.

Class 2, *the man (or woman) in business on his own*, is *not* insured for *unemployment benefit* or for *industrial injuries benefits*; the risk of unemployment to a man (or woman) working on his own account, and the risk of injury at his work, were not considered to be risks against which the State need insure him; but he *is* insured for *sickness*.

Class 3, *the man (or woman) who is not in any kind of paid employment*; it follows that people in this class are entitled to any of the worker's benefits. Therefore a man or woman doing no paid work is *not* able to claim (a) *unemployment*, (b) *sickness* or (c) *industrial injuries benefits*. A woman doing no paid work has *no claim* to maternity allowances. This is paid only to women in jobs or in business, to make up for loss of *earnings* ...

For more than three centuries the Poor Law has imposed on local ratepayers the duty of relieving the 'needy poor', old and young, who look in vain for help from other sources.

The National Assistance Act makes this a *nation-wide* instead of a local charge, and transfers that work to the new National Assistance Board, a central board working to a single co-ordinated plan through its own local officers.

The National Assistance replaces existing schemes for the assistance of the aged and inform, the sick, and the unemployed, who are unable to get help, or enough help from elsewhere. ...

Document 31   Extract from Aneurin Bevan, *In Place of Fear* (1952), pp. 75–6, dealing with the 'Free Health Service'.

When I was engaged in formulating the main principles of the British Health Service, I had to give careful study to various proposals for financing it, and as this aspect of the scheme is a matter of anxious discussion in many parts of the world, it may be useful if I set down the main considerations that guided my choice. In the first place, what was to be its financial relationship with National Insurance; should the Health Service be on an insurance basis? I decided against this. It had always seemed to me that a personal contributory basis was peculiarly inappropriate to a National Health Service. There is, for example, the question of the qualifying period. That is to say, so many contributions for this benefit, and so many more for additional benefits until enough contributions are eventually paid to qualify the contributor for the full range of benefits.

In the case of health treatment this would give rise to endless anomalies, quite apart from the administrative jungle which would be created. This is already the case in countries where people insure privately for operations as distinct from hospital or vice versa. Whatever may be said for it in private insurance, it would be out of place in a national scheme. Imagine a patient lying in hospital after an operation and ruefully reflecting that if the operation had been delayed another month he would have qualified for the operation benefit. Limited benefits for limited contributions ignore the overriding consideration that the full range of health machinery must be there in any case, independent of the patient's right of access to it. ...

The Welfare State: Consensus and Challenge, 1951–1993

Document 32   Extract from Labour Manifesto of 1964

Labour will get rid of the segregation of children into separate schools caused by 11 plus selection: secondary education will be reorganised on comprehensive lines. Within the new system, grammar school education will be extended: in future no child will be denied the opportunity of benefiting from it through arbitrary selection at the age of eleven.

Document 33   Extract from P. Townsend, *Poverty in the United Kingdom* (1979), p. 31.

Individuals, families and groups in the population can be said to be in poverty when they lack the resources to obtain the type of diet, participate in the activities or have the living standards and amenities which are customary, or at least widely encouraged or approved, in the societies to which they belong. Their resources are so seriously below those commanded by the average individual or family that they are, in effect, excluded from ordinary living, customs and activities.

Document 34   Extract from T. Raison, *Tories and the Welfare State* (1990), pp. 73–4, paraphrasing Sir Keith Joseph's views on poverty.

First ... family allowances gave no help for families with only one child – yet to bring in first children would take time and also add greatly to the cost of the scheme. Second, an increase in family allowance, whether or not taxed, could not be at a level which would give significant help to the ... poorest of wage-earning households. And thirdly, the lowering of the standard rate income tax threshold by Labour meant that certain people who should be seen as in the category of family poverty were actually paying income tax and would therefore derive no benefit from family allowance after tax had been clawed back.

BIBLIOGRAPHY

The listing below indicates only the main sources consulted in the process of producing this book, in alphabetical order. The location of publication is London, unless otherwise stated.

P. Addison, *The Road to 1945: British Politics and the Second World War* (1975)

D. H. Aldcroft, *The Inter-War Economy: Britain 1919–1939* (1970)

K. Amin and C. Oppenheim, *Poverty in Black and White: Deprivation and Ethnic Minorities* (1992)

Annual Reports of the Halifax Workhouse, 1804–1811

D. Ashforth, 'The Urban Poor Law', in D. Fraser, *The New Poor Law in the Nineteenth Century* (1976)

D. Ashforth, 'The Treatment of Poverty', in D. G. Wright and J. A. Jowitt (eds.), *Victorian Bradford* (Bradford, 1982)

C. Attlee, *The Social Worker* (1920)

R. Bacon and W. Eltis, *Britain's Economic Problem: Too Few Producers* (1978)

R. S. Barker, *Education and Politics 1900–1951: A Study of the Labour Party* (Oxford, 1972)

C. Barnett, *The Audit of War: The Illusion and Reality of Britain as a Great Nation* (1986)

S. Barnett, 'A Friendly Criticism of the Charity Organisation Society', *Charity Organisation Review* 10 (1895)

P. W. J. Bartrip and P. T. Fenn, 'The Administration of Safety: The Enforcement Policy of the Early Factory Inspectorate 1844–1864', *Public Administration* 57 (1980)

D. A. Baugh, 'The Cost of Poor Relief in South-East England', *Economic History Review*, 2nd ser., 28 (1975)

J. Bentham, *Pauper Management Improved: Particularly by Means of an Application of the Panopticon Principle of Construction*, ed. E. Chadwick (1812)

G. F. A. Best, *Lord Shaftsbury* (1965)

A. Bevan, *In Place of Fear* (1952)

W. H. Beveridge, *Unemployment: A Problem of Industry* (1912)

Sir William Beveridge, *Full Employment in a Free Society* (1944)

William Henry Beveridge Papers, British Library of Political and Economic Science

M. Blaug, 'The Myth of the Old Poor Law and the Making of the New', *Journal of Economic History* 23 (1963)

M. Blaug, 'The Poor Law Report Re-examined', *Journal of Economic History* 24 (1964)

G. Bock and P. Thane (eds.), *Maternity and Gender Policies: Women and the Rise of European Welfare States 1880s–1950s* (1994)

Borough of Poole League of Help, minutes

A. L. Bowley and M. Hogg, *Has Poverty Diminished?* (1925)

G. R. Boyer, *An Economic History of the English Poor Law 1750–1850* (Cambridge, 1990)

Bradford City Guild of Help, *Annual Reports, casebooks and minute-book*, 1903–6

Bradford Daily Telegraph

Bradford Independent Labour Party Commission on Education, *Draft of the Interim Report on Nursery Schools* (1927)

Bradford Observer

Bradford Trades and Labour Council, Report of Evidence of the Enquiry conducted … into the Conditions of the Woolcombing Industry, 1897–8

Bradford Trades and Labour Council, *Yearbooks*

P. Bramham, 'Parish Constables or Police Officers? The Development of a County Force in the West Riding', *The Journal of Regional and Local Studies* 7/2 (1987)

N. Branson, *George Lansbury and the Councillors' Revolt: Poplarism 1919–1925* (1979)

M. Brasnett, *Voluntary Social Action: A History of the National Council of Social Services 1919–1969* (1969)

F. Brockway, *Socialism over Sixty Years: The Life of Jowett of Bradford* (1946)

J. R. Brooks, 'Labour and Educational Reconstruction 1916–26: A Case Study in the Evolution of Policy', *History and Education* 20/3 (1991)

A. Brundage, 'The Landed Interest in the New Poor Law: A Reappraisal of the Evolution in Government', *English Historical Review* 87 (1972)

A. Brundage, 'The English Poor Law and the Cohesion of Agricultural Society', *Agricultural History* 48 (1974)

A. Brundage, *The Making of the New Poor Law: The Politics of Inquiry, Enactment and Implementation, 1832–1839* (1978)

Sir Henry B. Bunbury (ed.), *Lloyd George's Ambulance Wagon: The Memoirs of William J. Braithwaite 1911–1912* (1957)

Cabinet minutes, files and records, in the Public Record Office

M. Cahill and T. Jowitt, 'The New Philanthropy: The Emergence of the Bradford City Guild of Help', *Journal of Social Policy* 9/3 (1990)

A. Calder, *The People's War* (Cape, 1965)

J. Campbell, *Nye Bevan and the Mirage of British Socialism* (1987)

J. Campbell, 'Demythologising Nye Bevan', *History Today* 37 (1987)

S. C. Cannon, 'The Influence of Religion on Education Policy 1902–1944', *British Journal of Educational Studies* 12/2 (1964)

Carnegie Trust, *Disinherited Youth* (Edinburgh, 1943)

B. Castle, *The Castle Diaries 1974–76* (1980)

E. Chadwick, *Report on the Sanitary Condition of the Labouring Population of Great Britain* (1842, 1965 edn.)

Charity Organisation Review

S. G. and E. O. Checkland (eds.), *The Poor Law Report of 1834* (1974)

C. Chinn, *They Worked All Their Lives: Women of the Urban Poor in England 1880–1939* (Manchester, 1988)

City Guild of Help, *Journal of Social Policy* 9/3 (1980)

City of Leeds Labour Party, minutes

P. F. Clarke, *Lancashire and the New Liberalism* (Cambridge,1971)

S. Constantine, *Unemployment in Britain between the Wars 1918–1940* (1980)

Contemporary Review

County Borough of Bolton Guild of Help, *Annual Reports*

County Borough of Bolton Guild of Help, *The Helper*

County Borough of Bolton Guild of Help Magazine

T. A. Critchley, *A History of Police in England and Wales* (1978)

V. Cromwell, 'Interpretations in Nineteenth-Century Administration: An Analysis', *Victorian Studies* 31 (1966)

C. A. R. Crosland, *The Future of Socialism* (1956)

M. Crowther, *The Workhouse System 1834–1929: The History of an English Social Institution* (Cambridge, 1983)

Croydon Guild of Help Magazine

M. Cruikshank, 'The Denominational Schools' Issue in the Twentieth Century', *History of Education* 18/2 (1972)

F. D'Aeth, 'War Relief Agencies and the Guild of Help Movement', *Progress: Civic, Social and Industrial* 10 (1915)

J. Dale and P. Foster, *Feminists and State Welfare* (1986)

H. Dalton, *The Second World War Diary of Hugh Dalton 1940–45*, ed. B. Pimlott (1986)

A. Deacon, *In Search of the Scrounger* (1976)

A. Digby, 'The Rural Poor Law', in D. Fraser (ed.), *The New Poor Law in the Nineteenth Century* (1976)

A. Digby, *Pauper Palaces* (1978)

A. Digby, *The Poor Law in Nineteenth–Century England and Wales* (1982)

K. J. Dodds, '"Much ado about nothing": Cholera, Local Politics and Public Health in Nineteenth-Century Reading', *Local Historian* 21/4 (1991)

A. Donajgrodski, *Social Control in Nineteenth Century Britain* (1977)

B. Donoghue and G. W. Jones, *Herbert Morrison* (1973)

C. Driver, *The Life of Richard Oastler* (1946)

F. Driver, *Power and Pauperism: The Workhouse System 1834–1884* (Cambridge, 1993)

East Dorset Herald

Economist

N. C. Edsall, *The Anti-Poor Law Movement 1834–1844* (Manchester, 1971)

A. Elliott, 'The Establishment of Municipal Government in Bradford 1837–57', unpublished PhD dissertation, University of Bradford, 1976

E. A. Elton, 'A Victorian City Mission: The Unitarian Contribution to Social Progress in Holbeck and New Wortley, 1844–78', *Publications of the Thoresby Society Miscellany* 16/4 (1977)

C. Emsley, *The English Police: A Political and Social History* (Hemel Hempstead, 1991)

S. E. Finer, *The Life and Times of Sir Edwin Chadwick* (1952)

S. E. Finer, 'The Transmission of Benthamite Ideas 1820–1850', in G. Sutherland (ed.), *Studies in the Growth of Nineteenth-Century Government* (Totowa, New Jersey, 1972)

Forward

D. Foster, 'Police Reform and Public Opinion in Rural Yorkshire', *The Journal of Local Studies* 2/1 (1982)

D. Foster, 'The East Riding Constabulary in the Nineteenth Century', *Northern History* (1985)

J. Foster, *Class Struggle and the Industrial Revolution: Early Industrial Capitalism in Three English Towns* (1974)

D. Fraser (ed.), *The New Poor Law in the Nineteenth Century* (1976)

D. Fraser, *The Evolution of the British Welfare State* (1983)

V. A. C. Gattrell and T. B. Hadden, 'Criminal Statistics and their Interpretation', in E. A. Wrigley (ed.), *Nineteenth Century Society* (Cambridge, 1972)

V. George and P. Wilding, *Ideology and Social Welfare* (1985)

B. B. Gilbert, *British Social Policy, 1914–1939* (1970)

J. M. Goldstrom, *Education: Elementary Education 1780–1900* (Newton Abbot, 1972)

B. Kirkman Gray, *Philanthropy and the State, or Social Politics* (1908)

R. Gray, 'The Language of Factory Reform', in P. Joyce (ed.), *The Historical Meaning of Work* (Cambridge, 1987)

R. Gray, 'Medical Men, Industrial Labour and the State in Britain, 1830–50', *Social History* 16 (1991)

C. Griggs, *The Trades Union Congress and the Struggle for Education, 1868–1925* (Lewes, 1983)

R. M. Gutchen, 'Local Improvements and Centralisation in Nineteenth-Century England', *Historical Journal* 4 (1961)

Halifax Citizens' Guild of Help, *Annual Reports*

Halifax Guardian

C. Hamlin, 'Muddling in Bumbledom: On the Enormity of Large Sanitary Improvements in Four British Towns, 1855–1885', *Victorian Studies* 32 (1988)

K. J. Hancock, 'The Reduction of Unemployment as a Problem of Public Policy, 1920–1929', *Economic History Review* (1962)

J. Harris, *Attlee* (1982)

José Harris, 'Society and State in Twentieth-Century Britain', in F. M. L. Thompson (ed.), *The Cambridge Social History of Britain 1750–1950*, iii. *Social Agencies and Institutions* (Cambridge, 1990)

J. Harris, 'Political Thought and the Welfare State 1870–1914: An Intellectual Framework for British Social Policy', *Past and Present* 135 (May 1992)

J. Harris, *Private Lives, Public Spirit: A Social History of Britain 1870–1914* (Oxford, 1993)

J. Hart, 'Reform of the Borough Police 1835–1856', *English Historical Review* 70 (1955)

J. Hart, 'Nineteenth-Century Social Reform: A Tory Interpretation of History', *Past and Present* 31 (1965)

P. Hastings, *More Essays in North Riding History* (Northallerton, 1984)

R. Hay, 'Employers and Social Policy in Britain: The Evolution of Welfare Legislation, 1905–14', *Social History* 2 (1977)

R. Hay, 'Employers' Attitudes to Social Policy and the Concept of "Social Control", 1900–1920', in P. Thane (ed.), *The Origins of British Social Policy* (1978)

P. Hedstrom and S. Ringen, 'Age and Income in Contemporary Society: A Research Note', *Journal of Social Policy* 16/2 (1987)

Help (journal of the Bradford City Guild of Help)

E. P. Hennock, 'The Measurement of Poverty; from the Metropolis to the Nation, 1880–1920', *Economic History Review* (1987)

U. Henriques, 'How Cruel was the Victorian Poor Law?', *Historical Journal* (1968)

U. R. Q. Henriques, *The Early Factory Acts and their Enforcement* (Historical Association 12, 1970)

M. Hill, *The Welfare State in Britain* (Aldershot, 1993)

Home Office Papers

R. Humphreys, *Scientific Charity in Victorian London: Claims and Achievements of the Charity Organisation Society, 1869–1890*, London School of Economics and Political Science, Working Papers in Economic History (1993)

B. L. Hutchins and A. Harrison, *A History of Factory Legislation* (1966)

J. P. Huzel, 'The Demographic Impact of the Old Poor Law', *Economic History Review*, 2nd ser., 33 (1980)

Independent Labour Party, various *Annual Reports* and Reports, 1917 and 1918

H. Jennings, 'Voluntary Social Service in Urban Areas', in H. E. Mess (ed.), *Voluntary Social Services since 1918* (Bristol, 1947)

P. Joyce, *Work, Society and Politics* (Brighton, 1980)

B. Keith-Lucas, 'Some Influences Affecting the Development of Sanitary Legislation in England', *Economic History Review* (1953–4)

A. J. Kidd, 'Charity Organisation and the Unemployed in Manchester c. 1870–1914', *Social History* 9 (1984)

Labour Party, *Labour Believes in Britain* (1949)

Labour Party, *Report of the Annual Conference of the Labour Party held in Albert*

Hall, Peter Street, Manchester on Tuesday, January 23rd, and three following days, 1917 (1917)

Labour Party, *Secondary Education for All: A Policy for Labour* (1988)

R. Lambert, 'Central and Local Relations in Mid-Victorian England: The Local Government Act Office, 1853–1971', *Victorian Studies* 6 (1962)

R. Lambert, *Sir John Simon, 1816–1904, and English Social Administration* (1963)

K. Laybourn, '"The Defence of Bottom Dog": The Independent Labour Party in Local Politics', in D. G. Wright and T. Jowitt (eds.), *Victorian Bradford* (Bradford, 1981)

K. Laybourn, 'The Issue of School Feeding in Bradford, 1904–7', *Journal of Educational Administration and History* 14/2 (1982)

K. Laybourn and J. Reynolds, *Liberalism the Rise of Labour* (1984)

K. Laybourn, *Philip Snowden* (Aldershot, 1988)

K. Laybourn (ed.), *The Labour Party 1881–1951: A Reader in History* (Gloucester, 1988)

K. Laybourn, *Britain on the Breadline: A Social and Political History of Britain between the Wars* (Gloucester, 1990)

K. Laybourn, 'The Guild of Help and the Changing Face of Edwardian Philanthropy', *Urban History* 20/1 (1993)

K. Laybourn, *The Guild of Help and the Changing Face of Edwardian Philanthropy: The Guild of Help, Voluntary Work and the State, 1904–1919* (Lampeter, 1994)

Leeds Citizen

Leeds Intelligencer

Leeds Mercury

J. Lewis, *The Politics of Motherhood: Child and Maternity Welfare in England, 1900–1939* (1980)

J. Lewis, *Women and Social Action in Victorian and Edwardian England* (Stanford, 1991)

J. Lewis, 'Gender, the Family and Women's Agency in the Building of "Welfare States": The British Case', *Social History* 19/1 (1994)

R. A. Lewis, *Edwin Chadwick and the Public Health Movement 1832–1854* (1952)

J. Lindsay, 'The Problems of the Caernarfon Union Workhouse from 1846 to 1930', *Caernarvonshire Historical Transactions* (1991–2)

R. Lowe, *The Welfare System in Britain since 1945* (1993)

W. J. Lowe, 'The Lancashire Constabulary 1845–1870: The Social and Occupational Function of a Victorian Police Force', *Criminal Justice History* 4 (1984)

G. A. N. Lowndes, *The Silent Social Revolution: An Account of the Expansion of Public Education in England and Wales 1895–1965* (1979)

W. C. Lubenow, *The Politics of Government Growth: Early Victorian Attitudes towards State Intervention 1833–1848* (Newton Abbot, 1971)

E. Macadam, *The New Philanthropy* (1934)

D. McCloskey, 'New Perspectives on the Old Poor Law', *Exploration in Economic History* 10 (1973)

O. MacDonagh, 'The Nineteenth-Century Revolution in Government: A Reappraisal', *Historical Journal* 1 (1958)

O. MacDonagh, *The Passenger Acts: A Pattern of Government Growth* (1961)

O. MacDonagh, 'The Nineteenth-Century Social Reform: A Tory Interpretation of History', *Past and Present* 31 (1965)

O. MacDonagh, *Early Victorian Government* (1977)

M. Maclean and D. Groves (eds.), *Women's Issues in Social Policy* (1991)

G. C. M. M'Gonigle and J. Kirby, *Poverty and Public Health* (1936)

Manchester Guardian

P. Mandler, 'The Making of the New Poor Law *Redidivus*', *Past and Present* 117 (1987)

P. Mandler, with A. Brundage and D. Eastwood, 'Debate: The Making of the New Poor Law *Redidivus*', *Past and Present* (1990)

Manifesto of the Bradford Unemployed Emergency Committee, 1894 (Bradford, 1894)

Violet Markham Papers in the British Library of Political and Economic Science

J. D. Marshall, *The Old Poor Law, 1795–1834* (1968)

B. Martin, 'Leonard Horner: A Portrait of an Inspector of Factories', *International Review of Social History* 14 (1969)

H. P. Marvel, 'Factory Regulation; A Reinterpretation of Early English Experience', *Journal of Law and Economics* 20 (1971)

A. Marwick, *Britain in the Century of Total War* (1965)

J. Melling, ' Welfare Capitalism and the Origins of Welfare States: British Industry, Workplace, Welfare and Social Reform 1870–1914', *Social History* 17/3 (1992)

E. C. Midwinter, *Social Administration in Lancashire 1830–1860: Poor Law, Public Health and Police* (Manchester, Press, 1969)

E. C. Midwinter, *Law and Order in Early Victorian Lancashire* (York, 1971)

M. Mitchell, 'The Effects of Unemployment on the Social Conditions of Women and Children in the 1930s', *History Workshop* (1985)

M. J. Moore, 'Social Work and Social Welfare: The Organisation of Philanthropic Resources in Britain, 1900–1914', *The Journal of British Studies* (1977)

K. O. Morgan, *Labour in Power 1945–51* (Oxford, 1984)

C. L. Mowat, *The Charity Organisation Society 1869–1913: Its Ideas and Work* (1961)

C. L. Mowat, *Britain between the Wars, 1918–1940* (1968)

C. Nardinelli, 'The Successful Prosecution of the Factory Acts: A Suggested Explanation', *Economic History Review*, 2nd ser., 38/3 (1985)

OECD, *The Welfare State in Crisis. An Account of the Conference on Social Policies in the 1980s*, Paris, 20–3 October 1980 (Paris, 1981)

D. Paichaud, 'Poverty in Britain 1889–1983', *Journal of Social Policy* 17/3 (1988)

R. Paley, '"An Imperfect, Inadequate and Wretched System"? Policing in London before Peel', *Criminal Justice History* 19 (1989)

J. H. Palin, *Bradford and its Children: How they are Fed* (1908)

S. H. Palmer, *Police and Protest in England and Ireland 1789–1850* (Cambridge, 1988)

Parliamentary Papers, 1852–3 (715), xxxvi, *Second Report of the Select Committee on Police*s

H. Parris, 'The Nineteenth-Century Revolution in Government: A Reappraisal Reappraised', *Historical Journal* (1958)

G. Pascall, *Social Policy: A Feminist Analysis* (1986)

A. E. Peacock, 'The Justices of the Peace and the Prosecution of the Factory Acts, 1833–55', *Economic History Review*, 2nd ser., 37/2 (1984)

S. Pederson, *Family, Dependence and the Origins of the Welfare State in Britain and France 1914–1945* (Cambridge, 1993)

H. Pelling, 'The Working Class and the Welfare State', in H. Pelling, *Popular Politics and Society in Late Victorian Britain* (1968)

H. Pelling, *Britain and the Second World War* (1970)

H. Pelling, *The Labour Governments 1945–51* (1984)

J. Pellow, *The Home Office 1848–1914* (1982)

D. Philips, *Crime and Authority in Victorian England: The Black Country, 1835–1860* (1977)

Pilgrim Trust, *Men without Work* (Cambridge, 1938)

F. F. Piven and R. A. Cloward, *Regulating the Poor: The Functions of Public Welfare* (Tavistock, 1974)

Plymouth Civic Guild of Help, *Annual Reports*

S. Pollard (ed.), *The Gold Standard and Employment Policies between the Wars* (1970)

D. Powell, 'The New Liberalism: The Rise of Labour, 1886–1906', *Historical Journal* 19/2 (1986)

J. R. Poynter, *Society and Pauperism: English Ideas on Poor Relief 1795–1834* (1969)

F. K. Prochaska, *Women and Philanthropy in Nineteenth-Century England* (Oxford, 1980)

F. K. Prochaska, 'Philanthropy', in F. M. L. Thompson (ed.), *The Cambridge Social History of Britain 1750–1950*, iii. *Social Agencies and Institutions* (Cambridge, 1990)

F. K. Prochaska, *Philanthropy and the Hospitals of London: The King's Fund, 1897–1990* (Oxford, 1992)

L. A. Radzinowicz, *A History of English Criminal Law and its Administration from 1750*, 4 vols. (1948–68)

J. Redlich and F. W. Hirst, *The History of Local Government in England*, 2nd edn., ed. B. Keith-Lucas (1970)

J. W. Reilly, *Policing Birmingham* (Birmingham, 1989)

C. Reith, *A New Study of Police in History* (1956)

Report of the Committee of Council on Education (1867–8, 1868–9)

Report of the Consultative Committee of the Board of Education: The Education of the Adolescent 1926 (Hadow Report)

Report of the Commission for Inquiry into the Employment and Conditions of Children in Mines and Manufactories (1843)

Report of Minutes of Evidence Respecting the State of Health and Morals of Children Employed in Manufactories (1816)

Report of the Ministry of National Insurance, 1944–1949 (Cmd 7955, 1950)

Report of the Royal Commission on National Health Insurance, 1926, Majority Report, paragraph 151

Report of the Unemployment Assistance Board for the Period Ended 31 December, 1935 (Cmd. 5177, 1936)

D. Roberts, *Victorian Origins of the British Welfare State* (1960)

D. Roberts, 'How Cruel was the Victorian Poor Law', *Historical Journal* (1963)

M. E. Rose, 'The Allowance System under the New Poor Law', *Economic History Review* 34 (1966)

M. E. Rose, 'The Anti-Poor Law Movement in the North of England', *Northern History* 1 (1966)

M. E. Rose, 'The Anti-Poor Law Agitation', in J. T. Ward (ed.), *Popular Movements (1830–1850)* (1970)

M. E. Rose, *The English Poor Law 1780–1914* (1972)

M. E. Rose, 'Settlement, Removal and the New Poor Law', in D. Fraser (ed.), *The New Poor Law in the Nineteenth Century* (1976)

M. E. Rose, 'The Crisis in the Poor Relief in England', in W. J. Mommsen (ed.), *The Emergence of the Welfare State in Britain and Germany* (1981)

B. S. Rowntree, *Poverty and Progress: A Second Social Survey of York* (1941)

Royal Commission on the Aged Poor (1895)

J. Saville, 'The Welfare State: An Historical Approach', *New Reasoner* (1957)

Second Report of the Commissioners for Inquiries into the State of Large Towns and Populous Districts (1845)

G. R. Searle, 'The Edwardian Liberal Party and Business', *English Historical Review* 98 (1983)

N. Senior, *Letters on the Factory Act, as it Affects the Cotton Manufacturer Addressed to the Right Honourable the President of the Board of Trade* (1837)

M. B. Simey, *Charitable Effort in Liverpool* (Liverpool, 1951), since republished as *Charity Rediscovered: A Study of Philanthropic Effort in Nineteenth-Century Liverpool* (Liverpool, 1992)

B. Simon, *The Politics of Educational Reform 1920–1940* (1974)

B. Simon, *Education and the Labour Movement 1870–1920* (1965)

A. Sked, *Britain's Decline* (1988)

H. Llewellyn Smith (ed.), *The New Survey of London Life* (1934)

H. L. Smith (ed.), *War and Social Change in British Society and the Second World War* (Manchester, 1986)

P. Smith, *Disraelian Conservatism and Social Reform* (1967)

G. R. Snowden, *Report of the Local Government Board on the Guilds of Help in England*, Cd. 56664 (1911)

Social Insurance and Allied Services (Beveridge Report), Cmd. 6404 (1942)

C. Steedman, *Policing the Victorian Community: The Formation of the English Provincial Police from 1856–1880* (1984)

C. Steedman, 'The ILP and Education: The Bradford Charter', in D. James, Tony Jowitt and K. Laybourn (eds.), *The Centennial History of the Independent Labour Party* (Halifax, 1992)

R. D. Storch, '"The plague of blue locusts": Police Reform and Popular Resistance in Northern England 1840–1857', *International Review of Social History* 20 (1975)

R. D. Storch, 'The Policeman as Domestic Missionary: Urban Discipline and Popular Culture in Northern England, 1850–1880', *Journal of Social Policy* 9 (1976)

M. Sturt, *The Education of the People* (1967)

J. Sutter, *Britain's Next Campaign* (1903)

R. Swift, *Police Reform in Early Victorian York, 1838–1856* (York, 1988)

R. Swift, 'Urban Policing in Early Victorian England, 1835–56: A Reappraisal, *History* 73 (1988)

D. W. Sylvester, *Robert Lowe and Education* (1974)

D. Taylor, 'Crime and Policing in Early Victorian Middlesbrough, 1835–55', *The Journal of Regional and Local Studies* 11/1 (1991)

P. Thane, 'Contributory *versus* Non-Contributory Old Age Pensions', in P. Thane (ed.), *The Origins of British Social Policy* (1978)

P. Thane, 'The Working Class and State "Welfare" in Britain 1880–1914', *Historical Journal* 27/4 (1984)

P. Thane, 'Government and Society in England and Wales, 1750–1914', in F. M. L. Thompson (ed.), *The Cambridge Social History of Britain 1750–1950*, iii. *Social Agencies and Institutions* (Cambridge, 1990)

P. Thane, *The Foundations of the Welfare State* (1982)

B. Thompson, 'Public Provision and Private Neglect: Public Health', in D. G. Wright and T. Jowitt (eds.), *Victorian Bradford* (Bradford, 1981)

F. M. L. Thompson (ed.), *The Cambridge Social History of Britain 1750–1950*, iii. *Social Agencies and Institutions* (Cambridge, 1990)

M. W. Thomas, *The Early Factory Legislation* (1948)

R. M. Titmuss, *Problems of Social Policy* (1951)

H. Tout, *The Standard of Survey of London Life and Labour* (Bristol, 1934)

J. H. Veit-Wilson, 'Paradigms of Poverty: Rehabilitation of B. S. Rowntree', *Journal of Social Policy* 15/1 (1986)

D. Vincent, *Poor Citizens: The State and the Poor in Twentieth Century Britain* (1992)

E. W. Wakefield, 'The Growth of Charity Organisation in the North of England', *Charity Organisation Review* 34 (1908)

F. Wallace, *Social Policy: A Critical Introduction* (Cambridge, 1989)

J. T. Ward, *The Factory System*, i. *The Factory System and Society* (Newton Abbot, 1970)

J. T. Ward (ed.), *Popular Movements, 1830–1850* (1970)

B. Watkin, *The National Health Service* (1987)

S. and B. Webb, *English Poor Law History, 1: The Old Poor Law* (1927) and *English Poor Law History, 2: The Last Hundred Years*, 2 vols. (1929)

C. Webster, 'Healthy or Hungry Thirties?', *History Workshop* (1982)

C. Webster, *The Health Service since the War* (1988)

N. Whiteside, 'Counting the Cost: Sickness and Disability among Working People in an Era of Industrial Recession, 1920–1939', *Economic History Review* 40/2 (1987)

E. Wilkinson, *The Town that was Murdered: The Life Story of Jarrow* (1939)

K. Williams, *From Pauperism to Poverty* (1981)

E. Wilson, *Women and the Welfare State* (1977)

A. S. Wohl, *Endangered Lives: Public Health in Victorian Britain* (1983)

P. Wood, 'Finance and the Urban Poor Law: Sunderland Union, 1836–1914', in M. E. Rose (ed.), *The Poor and the City: The English Poor Law in its Urban Context* (Leicester, 1985)

P. Wood, *Poverty and the Workhouse in Victorian Britain* (Stroud, 1991)

K. Woodroffe, *Scientific Charity to Social Work* (1968)

R. Woods, 'Mortality Patterns in the Nineteenth Century', in R. Woods and J. Woodward (eds.), *Urban Mortality in Nineteenth Century England* (1984)

G. Wright, *The Ordeal of Total War* (1968)

S. Yeo, *Religion and Voluntary Organisations* (1976)

Yorkshire Daily Observer

INDEX

DATE DUE

GAYLORD			PRINTED IN U.S.A.